American Hotel

American Hotel

*The Waldorf-Astoria and
the Making of a Century*

DAVID FREELAND

RUTGERS UNIVERSITY PRESS
NEW BRUNSWICK, CAMDEN, AND NEWARK,
NEW JERSEY, AND LONDON

Library of Congress Cataloging-in-Publication Data
Names: Freeland, David, author.
Title: American hotel: the Waldorf-Astoria and the making of a century /
    David Freeland.
Description: New Brunswick, NJ: Rutgers University, [2021] |
    Includes bibliographical references and index.
Identifiers: LCCN 2020036049 | ISBN 9780813594392 (hardcover) |
    ISBN 9780813594408 (epub) | ISBN 9780813594415 (mobi) | ISBN 9780813594422 (pdf)
Subjects: LCSH: Waldorf-Astoria Hotel (New York, N.Y.)
Classification: LCC TX941.W33 F74 2021 | DDC 647.9409747/1—dc23
LC record available at https://lccn.loc.gov/2020036049

A British Cataloging-in-Publication record for this book is available from the British
Library.

www.rutgersuniversitypress.org

Manufactured in the United States of America

I am manager of a hotel—a community center where men, women, and children from every station in society congregate for food, shelter, and entertainment.

—"A HOTEL MAN'S CREED," ANONYMOUS

Contents

Contents

Prologue

It's the last week of the Waldorf-Astoria. The legendary hotel, part of New York's landscape since 1931 (or, if we're counting the first Waldorf, built where the Empire State Building now stands, 1893), is set to close on the first of March. News articles and television reports have informed us that Anbang Insurance Group, the Chinese investment company that purchased the Waldorf in 2014—for $1.95 billion, the largest hotel sale in American history—plans to convert most of the property's 1,400-plus rooms into luxury condos. The remainder, somewhere between 300 and 500 rooms, will become a boutique hotel run by the Hilton corporation—which, prior to Anbang, owned the Waldorf but now just manages it. New Yorkers, still shaken over the loss of their beloved Plaza Hotel (which closed under similar circumstances in 2005 and, to many, "hasn't been the same" since its 2008 reopening), are now lining up to take one final look at the Waldorf before renovations begin. They know that only the facade and outer shell—a gray limestone slab with twin Art Deco peaks that resemble, from a distance, giant baby-bottle nipples—are officially landmarked by the city and thus protected from insensitive alteration or worse. All the rest—the soaring Park Avenue lobby, mauve in the light that streams from expansive windows; the Basildon Room, transplanted, according to legend, from an eighteenth-century English manor house; the Starlight Roof, where wartime sailors and their dates with

"Victory Roll" hairstyles once hoofed it to the big-band sounds of Benny Goodman and Xavier Cugat—is at the mercy, it would seem, of Anbang.

I ask, upon checking in at the mahogany-paneled front desk, if there have been other New Yorkers like myself, not content with a mere stroll and who are opting instead for a full night to spend inside one of the guest suites—boasting, as architecture critic Paul Goldberger once put it, "some of the greatest 1930s bathrooms in all New York"—to be followed, perhaps, by breakfast in bed, served under auspices of the hotel credited (in one of the Waldorf's many intriguing, if unsubstantiated, "firsts") with inventing the concept of room service.[1]

"Yes," responds the clerk, "*too* many." This is a flash of rudeness that, as I will discover through research to come, would have horrified the hotel's long-departed founders. Lucius Boomer, who shepherded the Waldorf's move from its old location on a then-commercializing stretch of Fifth Avenue to the present site and who once, the story goes, dismissed an employee he caught leaning against a wall, would likely have fired the man on the spot. But then, in a sudden shift that banishes the earlier tone of asperity, the clerk adds, "Welcome to the Waldorf-Astoria . . . enjoy your stay," and hands me two room cards along with a coupon for free drinks at the Peacock Alley bar—intimating in the process that, like a retailer who posts final mark-downs before going out of business, the hotel has an excess supply of which it needs to divest itself. Still, the point of his earlier remark is clear: Why are all of you coming to the Waldorf *now*? And I have to wonder: Is it silly to show support exactly at the moment it means, so far as the hotel's fortunes are concerned, the least? Indeed, as much as we love the Waldorf, there is also the feeling that, especially since the Anbang takeover and President Obama's subsequent decision not to stay here out of purported security concerns, its glory days have passed. This perception is, if anything, reinforced by the state of the guest room into which I subsequently bring my overnight bag. Few "run of house" rooms in New York would contain this much space. Still, I notice that one of the lights in the mock-candlestick sconce above the mantelpiece is broken; the vinyl pull-down shades over the windows are uneven and don't quite fit.

Downstairs, though, in the public spaces, the Waldorf's age becomes less evident. A fresh rosewater scent, emanating from some unknown source, permeates the main inner lobby (distinct from the "outer" lobby, off Park Avenue), whose vastness is minimized by a sequence of black marble pillars, wisps of white vein crossing their shiny surfaces. And then, standing at the center of the lobby, in both acknowledgment and defiance of passing time, is the Waldorf's prized souvenir from olden days: a nine-foot bronze clock, decorated with bas-reliefs of American presidents, that came from the original hotel (and, before that, the 1893 Chicago World's Fair). It marks every quarter hour with euphonious chimes that waft above the hum of people moving in the direction of Lexington Avenue or talking in velvety armchairs. Were it not for the presence of a woman playing "I'll Be Seeing You" on the lobby piano—it once belonged to composer Cole Porter, a longtime resident of the adjacent Waldorf Towers—it would be hard to know that anything about this night is different from the many thousands that have preceded it. Quickly the music changes to something cozier and less elegiac, "Embraceable You."

Later, over a dinner of Berkshire pork glazed in honey made by the Waldorf's own rooftop bees, I begin a conversation with the man sitting next to me. It turns out that he is a longtime Waldorf employee who made plans to dine with his friend here at La Chine restaurant, where chef Kong Khai Meng's inventive take on Chinese food has earned critical plaudits. He admits to having been dismayed by Hilton's decision to sell to Anbang Insurance Group: "The hotel was making money." Still, the vastness of this money, as represented by Anbang, cannot be compared to anything the Waldorf has known previously—even during its palmiest days in the wartime 1940s, when occupancy neared 100 percent and reservation requests often had to be declined. The man, who worked at the Waldorf as a waiter, mentions a party where Anbang—in an attempt to woo a potential tenant, a Chinese bank—spent more than $170,000 just on wine. To prove it, he pulls out his iPhone and shows me a photo of the bill, which has, evidently, made the rounds of Waldorf workers as an indication of how high the marker of what constitutes big spending has risen. We're in another world now, the receipt announces.

Last night at the Waldorf-Astoria, February 28, 2017, main lobby
(Drew Angerer, Getty Images).

Next morning, with only five days of the Waldorf left, the air of sadness becomes palpable. Through the hotel's head concierge, Michael Romei, I arrange for a private tour with guide Karen Stockbridge, a warm, gregarious woman who tells me she's been "waking up every morning with tears" in her eyes. Karen has a New York story of her own: as Karen Weiler, in 1950, she fell from a tenth-floor window in her family's apartment at Stuyvesant Town, a residential complex on First Avenue. Four years old at the time, she had somehow squeezed through a seven-inch opening from which the screen had been temporarily removed (to allow for exterior painting) and landed on a patch of grass that gave her a springy cushion. After ten days spent in Bellevue—during which time her distraught father, an office manager at the Hotel Lexington, was forced into a hospital himself—she emerged without injury and became, for a few weeks that September, a child celebrity. Exploring the Park Avenue lobby, this survivor looks down at the *Wheel of Life*, a giant floor mosaic by the French artist Louis Rigal. Each figure in the artwork—composed of some 148,000 marble tiles hand-cut by craftspeople from around the world and assembled at the Waldorf over the course of eight years (from 1931 to 1938)—represents a different stage in the human journey, starting with birth.

"You know, a hotel has a cycle, too," Karen observes as we fixate on the death figure: muscular, with heaps of ridges and contours, but slumped, resignedly, into the arms of a waiting angel. *Wheel of Life* is a fitting metaphor for the Waldorf, made of variegated parts that somehow, to those approaching it from a distance, merge into a seamless whole. Indeed, one of the Waldorf's core qualities has been its solidity in the face of innumerable comings and goings—hotels, after all, are transient by definition—as the doors revolve, day after day. On the surface it appears little different today than it would have in 1931, but a closer examination reveals, if anything, the opposite: the Waldorf has maintained its relevance and vitality through linking itself with the forces of change. For much of its history, it shaped—and, in turn, was shaped by—political and social life in New York, the United States, and even, during its fertile postwar years, the world. This is how the Waldorf surpassed its identity as a mere hotel to become an *institution*, what former owner Conrad Hilton called "the greatest of them all." And, like the stages in Rigal's mosaic, it experienced youthful excitement, love, struggle, and, beyond it all, the wisdom and security of old age.[2]

Many have cited humorist and playwright Oliver Herford (1863–1935) as originator of the observation, repeated at different times with slight changes in wording, that the Waldorf cultivated "exclusiveness among the masses." Although the quip, dating from around 1900, has never been irrefutably documented as Herford's, its substance is accurate. With perhaps its earliest years (the 1890s) as an exception, the Waldorf was elitist in reputation only. The hotel democratized elegance, making of it a product that could be consumed and enjoyed by middle-class buyers. It was they who, by and large, populated the Waldorf's restaurants, lobbies, and corridors and transformed them into grand settings for the viewing of humanity. Resultingly, and inevitably, the Waldorf became a mirror of larger societal changes. At first, for example, African Americans were tolerated only under special circumstances; people of color themselves generally thought of the Waldorf as a

Park Avenue lobby, February 28, 2017, with Cole Porter's piano moved to the center of Louis Rigal's *Wheel of Life* mosaic (Drew Angerer, Getty Images).

"white" hotel. By the 1950s, however, as the civil rights movement pushed for the breaking down, however incompletely, of discriminatory practices in American life, the hotel had become a place where leaders such as Martin Luther King not only resided during their stays in New York but lectured, spoke, and—for those who gathered to listen to them—taught. During the 1980s, in turn, the gay community became publicly visible at the hotel in ways it seldom had before. How the Waldorf got to these points—markers in the evolution of American norms during the twentieth century—forms the narrative of this book.[3]

My own acquaintanceship with the Waldorf began one night during my early years in New York, around 1994, when a friend and I decided to enter the hotel from Park Avenue and begin exploring. For the better part of an hour, we ambled through the lobbies and the ground-floor banquet spaces; rode the walnut-paneled elevators up and down; peeked into the Grand Ballroom; and, finally, terminated our expedition at the Starlight Roof, where the flutter of curtains provided the only movement in a long, tall space that, aside from the air-conditioning's billowy purr, remained silent. The spell of eerie, almost sepulchral, calm—unexpected in a room that, we knew, was usually given over to dancing and other bouts of conviviality—was never broken. No one at the Waldorf approached or questioned us. It was as if we had the hotel to ourselves. Longtime staff member Jim Blauvelt, who often served, during the 1990s and early 2000s, as the hotel's semiofficial spokesperson, would later confirm that we weren't just lucky that evening: the Waldorf "never discouraged people from walking around." Of course, even in the less stringent days prior to the attacks of September 11, 2001, hotels used cameras to monitor activity in their public areas. But it was precisely because the Waldorf had faith in its own security system—and, by extension, itself, its position in the life of the city—that it never felt the need, figuratively speaking, to install a "Keep Out" sign. Ejecting us that night would have been a sign of weakness, not strength.[4]

American Hotel treats the Waldorf-Astoria as public space. Throughout the chapters that follow, I'll give an occasional mention to the adjacent Waldorf Towers, which, as onetime home to Frank Sinatra, the Duke and Duchess of Windsor, Herbert Hoover, and many others, truly *were* elite. The residential Towers remained, however, separate from the rest of the hotel. Those who lived there had the option of going down, if they chose, into one of the Waldorf's restaurants, bars, or cafés. But they weren't required to as a normal part of getting around: apartments in the Towers were reachable through a separate entrance, located on Fiftieth Street. Though residents shared kitchen facilities with the rest of the hotel, they otherwise inhabited a distinct and discrete sphere—luxury apartment quarters that were kept from public view. My story, generally, emphasizes those aspects of the Waldorf that were most visible, that emerged as components of the hotel's formative role within the life of New York. In terms of both space and function, the Waldorf—structured so that pedestrians could enter on Park Avenue, pass the outer and then the main lobby and keep walking all the way through, until they reached the shops and escalators near Lexington— became an extension of the streets. Writing in 1981, critic Goldberger expressed this quality with perceptiveness and accuracy: "The Waldorf was not where you went to escape from the hectic pace of the city, but to feel it throbbing through your veins."[5]

Ask New Yorkers of a certain age why the Waldorf is special, and they are likely to answer, "Because it's the *Waldorf*." So many of them went there for sweet sixteen parties, jobs, or shopping (for years, the Waldorf housed, among other establishments, a bookstore, florist, and clothing boutique); to have a drink in Sir Harry's Bar, get their hair done, sit in the lobby, celebrate birthdays, or have a love affair, that they think of the hotel as a community possession. There is the sense in its closure of something that is being taken from them. Shifting forward to the hotel's final night, February 28, 2017, it's clear that employees feel the same way. The mood alternates between ebullience and gloom. Workers dressed in evening clothes march out of the ballroom holding little boxes that contain, someone tells me, an original doorknob from the 1931 hotel. They pose for photographs in the lobby and take turns at Cole Porter's piano, reminiscing about giddy times (so many wild things happened here that staff members once dubbed it the Waldorf-*Hysteria*). But the most emblematic figure, for me, is a muscular middle-aged man in bellhop uniform, walking the entirety of the ground floor with his iPhone, capturing it all in sequence and narrating to himself as he films, holding back tears that, in the subdued lobby lighting, only barely reveal themselves at the corners of his eyes: "I worked here for 32 years and every time I came to work, it was like a party."

American Hotel

Introduction

Hotel manager Eugene Scanlan once observed, "There's only one type of person staying at the Waldorf—a Waldorf guest." Though speaking in the late 1970s, when social mores within the United States had loosened—no longer, for instance, did hotels try to prevent unmarried couples from sharing a room—Scanlan was encapsulating a philosophy that had always been followed at the Waldorf, however imperfectly its implied goals may have been realized. At its most basic level, the Waldorf-Astoria was a *hotel*, defined (in the words of executive Lucius Boomer, citing the common law) as "a place where all who conduct themselves properly, and who, being able and ready to pay for their entertainment, are received" and, further, are supplied "with their meals, lodging, and such services and attention as are necessarily incident to the use of the [hotel] as a temporary home." Hotel guests, aside from paying for their room, are no different from those who are housed without charge in private quarters; they are entitled to all the manifestations of a homeowner's hospitality, and, in turn, a degree of socially acceptable behavior is expected of them. The concept of hospitality, one that has been part of human civilization for millennia, thus informs the hotelkeeper's mission. In opening their doors to outsiders, hotels provide, in a phrase whose origin was once credited to Boomer, a "home away from home."[1]

Many components went into making the Waldorf *the Waldorf*. The Waldorf helped introduce Americans, separated from their rural backgrounds by a generation or less, to fine dining as practiced in the capitals of Europe; its entertainment spaces, in particular, the long-running Empire Room, advanced the careers of numerous performers and, in the process, cultivated a distinctly Manhattanite brand of chic midcentury nightlife. The Waldorf hosted kings, princesses, prime ministers, and diplomats—so many that it became known, in the words of one self-financed book, as "The Unofficial Palace of New York." At various times it formed a backdrop for hit motion pictures; appeared in the titles of top-selling record albums (such as 1957's *Lena Horne at the Waldorf Astoria*); became a setting for radio programs in which "Jinx" Falkenburg, 1940s fashion model and tennis player, chatted with famous guests in a tone of hushed intimacy; and even found its way into literature—novels by Theodore Dreiser, poems by Wallace Stevens and Langston Hughes. But, in the end, what most emblematized the Waldorf—what made it more than the equivalent, say, of the St. Regis plus extra floor space—was its fulfillment of the hotelkeeper's obligation to provide food, lodging, and entertainment in ways that honored the anonymous "Hotel Man's Creed," also cited by Lucius Boomer, in his influential 1925 book, *Hotel Management*: "I am manager of a hotel—a community center where men, women and children from every station in society congregate."[2]

The creed, particularly its reference to "every station in society," is essential to an understanding of the Waldorf. As historian A. K. Sandoval-Strausz has explained, hotels, as we think of them today, are relatively modern inventions. The idea of a hotel as a distinct building type coalesced only in the late eighteenth century and began to flourish early in the nineteenth. Indeed, prior to the post-Revolutionary years in the United States, hotels were known simply as inns or taverns, places of lodging that—aside from being fitted with beds for overnight travelers—did not differ greatly in appearance from private homes. During the 1760s in England, Sandoval-Strausz writes, "hotel" came to denote an inn "of particularly high quality"; by the 1790s, the term had migrated to the United States, where the cornerstone of the first American hotel, the Union Public, in the new, mostly unbuilt capital of Washington, DC, was laid on the Fourth of July, 1793. Early American hotels, often poorly financed and vulnerable to fires—one, Boston's Exchange Coffee House and Hotel, burned after it was discovered the city did not possess a ladder tall enough to reach the attic, where the conflagration began—were designed for the patronage of a wealthy merchant class. But, as the nature of America's economy changed, after the 1825 completion of the Erie Canal and, later, the expansion of railways in the 1840s, so, too, did the nature and makeup of its hotels. By the middle of the nineteenth century, therefore, hotels in the United States had taken on a markedly demotic character, one that reflected the variety of urban life.[3]

What this meant for the Waldorf, through most of its history, was that management generally made room for all who were "able and ready to pay" and who further displayed willingness to "conduct themselves properly." Of course, the idea of what constituted proper behavior shifted over the decades: thus, in the years just after 1900, the restaurants at the Waldorf admitted women dining alone—even when other establishments refused them—but still didn't allow them to smoke. Hotels, like the centrist figure in politics, are always inclined toward mainstream forces in society. But, within this framework—one that acknowledged the primacy of societal rules—the Waldorf frequently pushed boundaries in ways that allowed its own reputation, so durably proven after years of fame and success, to stay intact. It was not a place to be undone by a single untoward incident, such as the uproar it faced in 1974, after Palestinian leader Yasser Arafat along with ten members of the PLO (in town for the United Nations General Assembly) let it be known they were not interested in staying at quarters the U.S. government had secured for them on Randall's Island. They wanted to stay at the Waldorf, just like the other UN delegates. So, amid death threats issued by the Jewish Defense League and the cries of protesters outside the hotel on Park Avenue—"Hell, no, PLO"—stay at the Waldorf they did.[4]

"No hotel should ever take sides in the political arena," stated Joe Rantisi, who began working at the Waldorf the year prior to Arafat's visit and eventually became manager. After "word got out that the Waldorf took Arafat in," Rantisi recalled, "a lot of Jewish organizations started cutting cords with us and they canceled events." At first, Rantisi tried explaining to the groups that, technically, the U.S. Department of State, not the PLO, was the client (the State Department would often reserve rooms at the Waldorf for visiting UN delegates). When that approach proved unsuccessful, he spoke with the Waldorf's then senior VP, hotel veteran Frank Wangeman, whose perspective, Rantisi said, gave him "respect for the old-fashioned management style": "[Wangeman] said, 'We're in the hotel business; we're not in politics. We rent rooms; we feed the people. We're not in the business to be politically affiliated with any organization, nor support any organization. If they're willing to pay and they're not harming anything in the hotel, we have to accept the business. We can't discriminate.'"[5]

Indeed, one month after the flap with Arafat, Golda Meir, having recently resigned as prime minister of Israel, also appeared at the Waldorf, addressing a group of American Jewish leaders at a dinner given in her honor. At various times, the hotel played host to Soviet prime minister Nikita Khrushchev and FBI chief J. Edgar Hoover, civil rights leaders and segregationists, Republicans and Democrats, members of the far left and the extreme right, debutantes and young revolutionaries, ex-communists, Trotskyites, socialists, infamous murderers such as Ruth Snyder (whose 1927 killing of her husband inspired the book and film *Double Indemnity*), teams of Olympians, twine manufacturers, American Legionnaires, Polish folk dancers, and contestants in the Pillsbury Bake-Off contest. In the hotel business, Rantisi further observed, "you can't declare allegiance to a specific group," because that would be "your death warrant."[6]

Still, the Waldorf did not initially conceive of itself as a human panorama. The original 1893 entrance at the hotel's first location, set between elaborately carved pilasters, was built on Thirty-Third Street, in an attempt to distance it from more populous Fifth Avenue. George Boldt, who managed the Waldorf for the Astor family and who later (with his wife, Louise) leased the building, conceived of his establishment as a preserve for wealthy families, one that would guard their privacy and secrets. In retrospect, this would seem like the final stirring of a hoary Victorian ideal: eventually, even the snobbish Boldt had to accept that such a degree of elitism was not economically feasible. In 1897, the Waldorf grew dramatically in size with the opening of the adjacent Astoria. Now containing 1,200 rooms, the new Waldorf-Astoria lowered the threshold in a tacit way, one that maintained Boldt's earlier standards of what he characterized as "luxury" and "ease of living." In the public's mind, the Waldorf-Astoria symbolized fineness and elegance, and, through assiduous training of staff and emphasis on service, the hotel's directors ensured it always would.[7]

For three decades the original Waldorf's size and relative closeness to Manhattan's two train stations—Penn and Grand Central—kept it busy as a site for large gatherings, dinners, and political conventions. The hotel's fortunes began to wane somewhat in the 1910s, as the last vestige of theatrical and entertainment life around Thirty-Fourth Street moved northward, to Times Square. Prohibition further dented business, to the point that the Waldorf's new manager, dynamic and aggressive Lucius Boomer, led a public battle against what he saw as its unequal enforcement. The authorities, he claimed, regularly turned a blind eye to the proliferation of speakeasies that, through illegal dispensation of liquor, were taking away a sizable chunk of the hotel industry's profit. What good was the Waldorf's famed cuisine if you had to drink grape soda with it? But even as it declined, the Waldorf-Astoria remained in the spotlight, thanks largely to Boomer's forward-thinking promotional techniques. Earlier, during the Boldt years, the Waldorf had refused to advertise. Solicitation through papers and magazines, Boldt felt, was vulgar. Not only did Boomer advertise, willingly and frequently, but he hired, starting in 1921, a young public relations specialist, Edward Bernays. The Austrian-born Bernays, whose books, namely, *Crystallizing Public Opinion* (1923) and *Propaganda* (1928), would revolutionize the field of PR, encouraged Boomer to make of the Waldorf's advancing years an asset. The old-fashioned glamour of the Boldt era was now promoted, through media outlets, as a *brand*.

"Every channel to the public was used to project the hotel," Bernays later wrote. Under his guidance, the Waldorf took active steps in the shaping of its own narrative, one that de-emphasized the hotel's now-unfortunate location in favor of a rich, venerable past. At an elaborate thirtieth-anniversary party in 1923, Oscar Tschirky, an all-around host who had been working at the hotel since it opened, regaled newspapermen with stories of gluttonous dinners served in the 1890s. In another instance, as part of an effort to squelch rumors that the Waldorf would be replaced by a department store, Boomer made a public ceremony of the re-signing of Oscar's contract as, in Bernays's recollection, the "flash powder" from news cameras "sparkled and exploded." Such publicity was extended by means of Edward Hungerford's *Story of the Waldorf-Astoria* (1925), the first of several biographies that appeared in the 1920s and 1930s. In the kind of language that permeated the book (and hinted, in its frothy enthusiasm, at the presence of Boomer's orchestrating hand), the author looked sanguinely ahead: "For a decade—two decades—three decades—to come, the future of the Waldorf seems assured."[8]

In reality the hotel, unprofitably wide and boxy in an era of skyscraper construction, was doomed to join the list of Manhattan Gilded Age structures—Rector's restaurant, the Casino and Knickerbocker theaters, architect Stanford White's Madison Square Garden—that wouldn't live to see the 1930s. In December 1928, Boomer announced to employees that their showplace would be "done away with" the following May. The sad news, which prompted scores of New Yorkers to call Boomer in an attempt to bid on their favorite Waldorf chairs, lamps, and paintings, barely had time to sink in before it was overtaken by another announcement, made in March 1929 (as the old hotel continued to operate): there would soon be a new Waldorf-Astoria, as glamorous as the first. Furthermore, it was revealed that Boomer and Oscar, along with various managers, clerks, heads of staff, waiters, and other familiar faces, would be returning. Plans by Schultze & Weaver, noted hotel architects, unveiled a forty-story skyscraper with more than 2,000 guest rooms and a grand ballroom the *New York Times* would describe as "larger and more beautiful than the one in the old Waldorf-Astoria." Although the future Waldorf would be operated by a different corporation, the promise of many returning employees, various pieces of original decoration, and, above all, Boomer's organizational system (one that emphasized, to a degree previously unknown in the hotel industry, department "standardization") ensured that it would represent more than a case of a famous name being slapped onto a new building to confer legitimacy.[9]

In what has become an oft-repeated bit of Waldorf lore, financing for the new structure was ready just in time for the 1929 stock market crash.

Nineteenth-century relics: Oscar and the Chicago World's Fair clock in 1945 (Alfred Eisenstaedt/The LIFE Picture Collection via Getty Images).

Suddenly, New York found itself with a glut of hotels, completed during the speculative 1920s and now sitting nearly empty, prepared to go into receivership. So unusual had it been for plans to move forward at the Waldorf that the hotel's grand opening in October 1931 took on the dimensions of a political event. President Herbert Hoover, whose putative responsibility for the Great Depression would eventually make him a figure of scorn, addressed the first-night celebrants with a radio broadcast on NBC. Reporters, eager for some bit of news that did not involve devastation, extolled the Waldorf as a pinnacle of modernity, reveling in its underground platform that could welcome private railroad cars directly from Grand Central, the rooms that were already wired—in anticipation of technological advances to come—for television. The Waldorf thus became a symbol not only of progress but of faith in the future, of the ideals of entrepreneurship that seemed, in their persistence at this most challenging of times, to reaffirm the American Dream itself.[10]

After its glorious opening, the Waldorf spent the remainder of the 1930s in financial struggle. If there was any consolation it lay in knowing that nearly every other American hotel was in the same situation. Boomer was able to keep the Waldorf afloat by instituting a corporate reorganization plan, but the hotel didn't start turning a profit until the onset of the United States' involvement in the Second World War. Overnight, the surge in activity that would bring thousands of people to New York—servicemen and their families, manufacturing representatives, military and government personnel— meant that hotel rooms could not be had, and managers frequently resigned themselves to sleeping on their office sofas. After such a long drought, it would have been picayune, they felt, to complain over having to give up their in-house living quarters. Most of them also knew that, once the war ended, patronage would likely dip back to its pre-1941 levels: best to take advantage of the extra business while they could. The Waldorf, though, not only survived the inevitable postwar slump but ascended to new heights of financial success. Though a number of factors informed this development—the Waldorf, for example, was one of the few Manhattan hotels with a ballroom large enough to hold corporate and political conventions—the biggest contributor was the United Nations.

New York's selection, in 1946, as temporary and then permanent head-quarters for the UN, created an acute spatial challenge. International delegates were set to begin arriving that October for the General Assembly; the question of where to house them led to numerous logistical and (given American prejudice and its potentially disastrous implications for multiracial visitors) social dilemmas. Not only was the Waldorf one of the closest large hotels to UN temporary headquarters in Flushing Meadows, Queens; it already possessed a long-standing reputation for hosting prime ministers, diplomats, and other international guests—one the UN no doubt had in mind when it first approached Lucius Boomer, in April 1946, about holding meetings there. Further, at a time when some New York hotels still practiced a de facto form of segregation, the Waldorf-Astoria agreed to admit all delegates regardless of race. It thus saved the U.S. government from the embarrassment that occasionally resulted from situations in which America's practices were unmasked as not living up to its ideals (in 1957, for example, the finance minister of Ghana, staying at the Waldorf, decided to take a road trip and was refused service at a Howard Johnson's restaurant in Delaware). In time the Waldorf's diplomatic identity became so cemented that suite 42-A of the Towers, home to the U.S. representative at the United Nations, was known, due to its status as an ambassador's residence, as the only U.S. embassy located in the United States. In 1968, a *Times* report described the embassy's function: "Full-dress debates and open clashes take place in the United Nations. But, when there is need for private talks between the United States and the Soviet Union, which can make agreement possible on delicate matters of major importance, they usually take place over dinners held alternately in the Soviet mission and 42-A."[11]

Given the Waldorf's prominence, and that of the city it inhabited, it's not surprising that many of the hotel's most publicly dramatic events were connected, in varying ways, to larger turns in the social, political, and artistic life of the nation. Ideological battles over twentieth-century questions—those related to gender equality, Prohibition, organized labor, communism, racial segregation, welfare and public relief, rights for the LGBT community—played out within the hotel's walls. In an age of radio and, later, television, the

Waldorf offered a show the entire country, through press reports and their dissemination, could witness. The relationship between the Waldorf and those who operated within the nation's cultural and political spheres became reciprocal: if the hotel gained its reputation, in part, from the significant events that had taken place there, then numerous officials, activists, and social and religious leaders in turn drew upon its renown to make statements that were guaranteed publicity. This, perhaps, was the most significant factor in making the Waldorf, the *Waldorf*. Other luxury hotels such as the Plaza preserved a reputation that was, if anything, more elite, but none acquired the Waldorf's stature in reflecting—and even, in some cases, shaping—developments in American life. Whenever public figures wanted to make a statement and have it promoted, they went to the Waldorf—along with anyone who sought to counter that statement through demonstration or protest.

Waldorf managers and staff perfected equanimity. Protesters on Park Avenue might get obstreperous; some, occasionally, would try to break police barricades and get inside the hotel, hoping to derail planned events with a stentorian address or an act of civil disobedience. Popes, presidents, rajahs, movie stars—even gangsters such as Lucky Luciano—regularly appeared at the hotel's doors, along with others whose degree of public visibility was more muted: board presidents, community leaders, statisticians, academics. Outwardly, at times, it might have seemed the Waldorf was a passive vessel, the recipient of whoever might be coming through—a place that was everything to everybody. In reality the hotel, even when its function was consigned to providing space for a routine speech, was working in active fulfillment of the innkeeper's core mission: to *host* ("The Waldorf-Astoria lives by serving," Lucius Boomer wrote in the foreword to his 1935 employee handbook. "It succeeds as it serves well"). In every case, though, whether events were unusual or quotidian, the attitude on the part of employees remained one of "What can I do for you?" This was a testament to the philosophy behind their training, as further outlined by Boomer in the handbook:

> Unless our work is done with a real desire to serve, we would merely be selling refreshment and lodging. We must try to make every Waldorf-

Astoria patron feel that his comfort and satisfaction are what matters most to us. That's the spirit which has made The Waldorf-Astoria the premier hotel of America. Law, social custom and the comfort of other patrons are the only limitations to what we shall try to do to please. We are in the business of *catering* to people. It is for them to decide what they wish; our part is to accomplish their wishes as *they prefer.*[12]

Much of the hotel's success—what longtime employee James Locker described as the way it "maintained a culture"—lay in presenting a smoothly calibrated image to the public. Boomer, along with later managers and executives, worked to ensure that, from outside, visitors would see little of the hotel's inner workings and instead perceive the Waldorf as an entity, operating as if through hidden force. The hard work was concealed beneath piles of figures and statistics fired off by Waldorf publicity representatives with the mechanical inevitability of ticker tape. In a 1951 *Town & Country* piece, journalist Horace Sutton reported that the hotel had a telephone system that "could service a city the size of Miami Beach." It used "enough steam every year to have kept an average-sized house warm from the time of the Crusades to the present." If all the trips made by the Waldorf's elevators in a single year were "strung end to end," they would extend "from Fiftieth Street and Park Avenue to the moon and part way back." Such figures, intended to present the Waldorf as a high-functioning machine, offer a window into how the hotel promoted itself and, as such, represented its personality. But, assessing those unwonted moments where things *didn't* go smoothly (in many of the chapters that follow, the machine is temporarily forced out of whack) reveals, in the way the Waldorf responded to problems, its character.[13]

Hotels offer an ideal lens through which to view urban society and its changes. They are privately owned (in most cases) but designed for the public; indeed, without the public's use and involvement they couldn't exist. Further, their neutrality—what, looking back to Joe Rantisi's observations, might be paraphrased as "open to all, exclusive to none"—moves them into a realm different from that inhabited by other privately owned, publicly patronized establishments, such as museums, banks, churches, or even restaurants.

Unlike a church, a restaurant does not presume religious belief (or the potential for it) as a qualification of entry, and thus opens its doors, in theory, to a wider range of people. Still, vegetarians would not choose to visit a steakhouse. More to the point when discussing the economic underpinnings of American life, even an inexpensive restaurant presupposes a certain level of financial freedom on the part of the guest. The freedom to pass time inside a hotel, meanwhile, has historically not been contingent on spending money. Many people have enjoyed sitting in a hotel lobby simply to watch the groups come and go, or else to pause for a rest inside what is effectively middle ground—neither fully public nor fully (in the sense that a guest room would be) private. The mainstream orientation of hotels thus becomes a distinguishing asset, particularly in the study of history: few other American institutions have the potential to embrace such a wide swath of the populace.

Scholar Annabel Jane Wharton observes how the "innovative character of the American hotel [as it developed in the nineteenth century] was related to its distinct social function," adding that, unlike their European counterparts (built largely "for the rich and powerful"), hotels in the United States "functioned as public space for the private individual." Wharton quotes an observation by English essayist Gilbert K. Chesterton, writing in 1922, that American hotels "are used almost as public streets, or rather as public squares." Describing a visit to one hotel lobby, Chesterton registered amazement at how visitors "did nothing whatever except drift into it and out again." Further, he pointed out how "most of them" appeared to have had "no more to do with the hotel than I have with Buckingham Palace." The multivalent nature of American hotels—journalist Sutton once observed how, at the Waldorf, it was possible to "send a cable to Bombay; buy a steamship ticket on the Queen Mary; undergo minor surgery" and "eat a plover's egg or a ham sandwich"—meant that only a portion of those inhabiting their spaces were overnight guests who had rented rooms. In 1903, St. Louis–based newspaper editor William Marion Reedy compared the Waldorf to "Port Said as Kipling described it": "You meet the 'magnets' from everywhere in the provinces. You bump into adventurers, pikers, *chevaliers d'industrie*. . . . Senators from the far West are in evidence with wives who still wear big diamond earrings. . . . Everywhere the pathetic hanger-on, who lingers near the big broker or the great railroad manager in the hope of picking up some hint or tip on which he can make a quick and profitable turn in the market. . . . There are the *roués* who hope to find a new face in the four-o'clock crush."[14]

As Reedy implied, there was little way, on the surface, to distinguish the Waldorf's legitimate elements from those that might be fraudulent: a well-dressed man in the lobby could be magnate or con artist, senator or gigolo. For many, the appeal of hotels was that they offered both the comfort associated with private homes and the anonymity of the street. Once-comfortable, now-struggling George Hurstwood, a central character in Theodore Dreiser's novel *Sister Carrie*, faces the "trouble of deluding" when he sets out to find work dressed in clothes that don't yet reveal the degradation of his poverty. Searching for a place to warm up as he walks the city, pondering options, he steps inside the real-life Broadway Central. Hurstwood, as former manager of a successful bar, is familiar enough with hotels "to know that any decent looking individual" would be "welcome to a chair in the lobby." Still, "taking a chair here," Dreiser writes, is like "a painful thing to him": "To think he should come to this. He had heard loungers about hotels called chair-warmers. He had called them that himself in his day. But here he was, despite the possibility of meeting someone who knew him, shielding himself from the cold, and the weariness of the streets, in a hotel lobby."[15]

In *Born with the Blues*, a memoir of jazz and the early twentieth-century metropolis, African American songwriter Perry Bradford recalled how musicians used to say that "nobody goes hungry in New York." Bradford was referring to the so-called free lunch of pre-Prohibition days, when saloons often provided complimentary food as an assurance that patrons wouldn't be drinking on empty stomachs. Hotel bars, in particular, were known for the generosity of their spreads: in the 1890s, for example, the Fifth Avenue Hotel would position an entire ham, along with crackers and mustard, at one end of the bar, while the Waldorf served sandwiches and other light items intended to accompany cocktails. Between the lobby sofas and free lunches, it was possible for those who might be low on cash to spend hours within the domain of a hotel without making significant expenditure. Not all "chair-warmers," however, were driven by budgetary concerns. Some passed time in hotels merely because they enjoyed the environment. Indeed, for certain people, especially those who were older and no longer tied to a work schedule, lobby-sitting was just a thing to do, tolerated by hotel managers as long as the participants comported themselves respectably. Among New York hotels, the Waldorf was considered, in the words of Jacob Wolff (once described as "King" of the "Seat Warmers"), a first-class "sit joint." Along with the Astor and Knickerbocker, it became one of the "great congregating places."[16]

In the 1890s and just after the turn of century, "Jake" Wolff had been proprietor of several of Broadway's most illustrious saloons, among them the bar in the Casino Theater's basement, where walls glistened with images of stage stars (most of whom Wolff knew by first name) and the "free lunch" specialty was fried oyster served on a fork. The coming of Prohibition in 1919 ended Wolff's saloon career: financially stable, with a wife but no children, he took to spending much of his time in hotel lobbies. In a 1932 profile for the *Herald Tribune*, Wolff recalled how the Hotel Astor had lobby-sitters so ubiquitous that they "might as well have been ornaments, statues or something." There were cases, remembered Wolff (who still wore sideburns and a tight Edwardian collar), of people remaining in a lobby from eight in the morning until eleven at night. But the Depression marked the onset of hard times for chair-warmers. With so many now filling lobbies out of the need for shelter rather than a love of people-watching, the Astor took to pulling up cushions, and other establishments began asking for room keys. One man, Wolff observed sadly, had been accustomed to keeping regular "lobby hours" in the evening from five to eleven but, in the discouraging climate of the 1930s, was too often finding himself shown the door: "It got so the poor guy couldn't sit anywhere for more than a few minutes at a time. It broke up his day. Now he's through with Broadway sitting for good, I think."[17]

Still, the Depression witnessed one great moment in the field of lobby-sitting—namely, the new Waldorf-Astoria's public opening on October 1, 1931, which, given that no large New York hotels would be built again until the early 1960s, turned out to be the last event of its kind for the next three decades. "There never was anything quite like it in any other hotel," claimed one reporter, who added, "The great American habit of going into hotel lobbies merely to loaf and to look around reached its highest development." Hundreds of people not registered as guests transformed the Waldorf into a giant living room; for New Yorkers, it became an extension of their apartments. Some sat "for a few minutes," others "for hours." Many left the lobby to explore, leading themselves from the ground floor Sert Room, with its murals depicting scenes from the second part of *Don Quixote*, to the mirrored foyers surrounding the Grand Ballroom (whose entrance was on the third floor) and on up to the eighteenth-floor entertainment space that would later be known as the Starlight Roof.[18] Some, in their determination to see everything, went so far as to ask to be shown the lavish Waldorf Towers, though they had no intention of staying there. The curious visitors rubbernecking their way past colonial desks and French card tables pretended to consider then left, as the *Herald Tribune* put it, with a "smile of content upon their faces," telling their guides they would "'let them know.'"[19]

Eighty-five years later, the same Towers apartments, initially created to house long-term residents, had become available for rental. For as little as $4,000, guests could spend a night in the Presidential Suite, 35A, where a rocking chair donated by JFK sat alongside General Douglas MacArthur's writing desk and various decorative items formerly owned by the Reagans and Nixons (a bronze plaque told visitors that the three-bedroom suite had housed "EVERY PRESIDENT OF THE UNITED STATES *SINCE 1931*," along with Queen Elizabeth, Emperor Hirohito, and Nikita Khrushchev). At times the Waldorf's reputation as an American palace fostered concern, on the part of administration, that people might think it was more expensive than it really was. One ad campaign, designed for newspapers in the 1930s, sought to remind prospective guests that rates at the Waldorf-Astoria began at $6 per night—around $102 in contemporary dollars. Even in the late 1940s, when occupancy was at a peak, rooms could be had for $12—the equivalent of $139 in 2020. A suite housing five to six people cost $36, or $480 today. While the Waldorf never shed its luxurious image (one built up, in large part, through the hotel's own efforts), the truth was that rooms were always offered at what could be described, in modern parlance, as a range of price points.[20]

At the time of its closing in 2017, the Waldorf-Astoria was among the last of the great personality hotels in the United States. With some exceptions—the Seelbach in Louisville, Memphis's Peabody with its parade of fountain-bathing ducks, the Morris Lapidus–designed Fontainebleau in Miami Beach—the majority of today's American hotels vary little in appearance, especially from an indoor perspective. Stand in the average Marriott, for instance, and one would be hard-pressed to tell whether the surrounding town is Savannah or Kansas City: there will be the same high lobby or atrium with potted plants, a prevalence of stucco, dropped ceilings, a Starbucks with a long line and one register, black vinyl chairs in the restaurant that doubles as a breakfast buffet, and the same cafeteria smell of half-washed plates. The indistinguishability of many hotels feeds into their utilitarian character. Few people stay at hotels anymore for their reputation alone; instead, they base their choices on which place can offer them the best online deal. When journalist Ward Morehouse III checked into the Waldorf Towers sometime around 1990, hoping to experience what it felt like to live in "limitless luxury," a butler offered to dry-clean his underwear. Today most guests are content with a fast internet connection. But it's worth remembering that when we check into even the smallest "boutique" hotel, we're connecting with a great tradition of American hotelkeeping, one whose role within the life of the expanding country was paramount.[21]

A midsize city may now contain close to a dozen major hotels, but there was a time when it only had one, and that lone establishment would have been a source of pride for the community. Town boosters would have pointed to it as a symbol of progress, an indication that Lima, Amarillo, or Coeur d'Alene was now on the map as a modern place. The Lions Club and local Jaycees would have held meetings in its ballroom, where an annual party or cotillion would be thought of by generations of residents as signifying a special event. The Waldorf-Astoria was all of this on a grander scale. Its story is that of America in the twentieth century, and, if it would be difficult to imagine any hotel bearing the same degree of influence again, that's because the forces propelling the Waldorf's rise and dominance have shifted themselves. America in the twenty-first century finds itself in the position of defending what often appears, to observers around the world, as the abandonment of its ideals—or else of struggling to agree on just what those ideals were. There is much talk of recapturing them, but little consensus on how. In any case, a negative political climate is antithetical to the goals of an institution—the American hotel—that was built on optimism. It is for this reason, more than any other, that the Waldorf represents a point in time that may never be repeated. But, through examining Conrad Hilton's "greatest of them all" in light of its social contributions to the city and nation, we can better understand the unique role taken up by hotels throughout much of their history: that of bearer of hospitality, of the American practice of opening doors.

CHAPTER 1

A Haven for the Well-to-Do

As far as Oscar could remember, William Waldorf Astor only made one visit to the hotel that bore a portion of his name. The taciturn real estate heir, generally thought to be the richest man in America, walked the carpeted hallways, "head down" and "slightly bent." Oscar, acting in his capacity as escort and chief greeter, was dismayed. The Hotel Waldorf had been lauded for its magnificence. Reporters published encomiums of the Turkish Salon with its bulging pillows and silk curtains; the delicate Marie Antoinette Room, mirrored and enameled like a powder box; and the verdant Palm Garden, where patrons lunched under a dome of tessellated glass. The upper facade of the building, inspired by Germany's Heidelberg castle, was an enchantment of gables and spires. How could Mr. Astor "pay no heed" to all the "frescoes, murals and luxurious furnishings"—everything that his own "vast wealth" had financed?[1]

Melancholic by nature, Astor had grown increasingly gloomy with the recent death of his wife, who had succumbed, lonely and depressed, to intestinal sickness at Cliveden, the couple's palatial English estate. When he met Oscar in January 1895, Astor had returned to the United States for a single week, to bury the former Mary Dahlgren Paul on her native soil. Otherwise, William, or "Willy," as he was known to family, would have preferred to stay in England. Much had been made, in the papers, of Willy's purported statement that America wasn't a fit place for gentlemen to live. This child of privilege, inheritor of a fortune that, only three generations before, had grown

18

at the hands of a former butcher's assistant, appeared to think himself too good for his countrymen. A range of pursuits—boxing, law, politics, history—had failed to soothe Willy's dissatisfaction with popular sentiment, which cast his family in an unflattering and, to his view, unfairly critical light. Wealth, in the United States, was both admired and resented. As hard-nosed landlords, the Astors had often found themselves made into symbols of greed. One editorialist linked the Astor fortune to "the agency of exhorbitant [sic] rents"; another grouped Willy with "gilded cads and snobs" and pronounced his removal to England as "'a good riddance of bad rubbish.'"[2]

No surprise, then, that William Waldorf Astor would express little interest as Oscar led him through what many were calling a "palace." He was a man who, through luck of birth, had benefited from American entrepreneurship but for whom all personal optimism, at least as it related to his home country, had evaporated. The Hotel Waldorf was chiefly a way to make the most of his family's holdings. Even before Willy's father, John Jacob III, died in 1890, there had been plans for an eventual commercial structure on the site of the family house at Thirty-Third Street and Fifth Avenue in Manhattan. There, Willy had grown up next door to his cousin, John Jacob IV, son of Caroline Schermerhorn Astor (known, through her own determinedness, as "the" Mrs. Astor), in an environment of great luxury counterbalanced by a rigid attention to cost-saving and economy. One visitor recalled walking in on John Jacob III and his brother, Willy's uncle (also named William), on the hottest day of the year. As sweat rolled from their faces the men, who easily could have hired an assistant, engaged in the methodical act of cutting the quarterly interest coupons off of bond certificates.[3]

By the time the Hotel Waldorf opened in 1893, much gossip would be made of "feuding" between the Astor clan's two divisions, one headed by Willy, the other by cousin John Jacob IV and his mother. Caroline Astor remained in her Fifth Avenue house, separated from the Waldorf site by nothing more than a garden, throughout the hotel's construction during 1891 and 1892, in what must have been a state of extreme noise and annoyance. No doubt she was upset with her nephew: rifts that had started some years prior, through a tussle over naming rights with Mary, Willy's wife (who, through marriage, had a right to "Mrs. Astor" too), now widened. Eventually, Caroline would move northward, higher up Fifth Avenue, clearing the way for a sister hotel adjacent to the Waldorf, the Astoria, which opened in 1897.[4]

Still, the idea of two cousins at battle in a Hatfield and McCoy–type showdown gives a distorted picture of Willy and John Jacob's day-to-day relationship, which appeared, from the outside, to be formed of a coolness bordering on indifference. Wary of the populace, they maintained an almost impenetrable guard and, like the bulk of their money, kept any mutual rivalry to themselves. An observer recalled how the two cousins once entered the same café for lunch, some minutes apart. William Waldorf read a book and drank tea while John Jacob ate in a different corner; it appeared that neither was aware of the other. When William Waldorf left, however, he came across his father on the street. This encounter was accompanied, on the older man's part, by nothing more than a nodding of the head, in recognition. No one ever accused the Astors of being overly demonstrative.[5]

Stories of William's plans to use the Waldorf as his New York residence proved inaccurate. Regardless, the Astor connection benefited the hotel in remunerative ways, lending it built-in publicity. It would take years for Willy to establish himself socially in England. Despite hiring genealogists to support his dubious claims of nobility, overseas acceptance proved more difficult than he had imagined. But in New York, Astor money was old enough: when the first John Jacob Astor (Willy's great-grandfather) died back in 1848, Manhattan scarcely existed, in the developed sense, beyond the lush confines of Union Square and genteel Chelsea to its northwest. Growth of the Astor fortune had accompanied that of the city, and New Yorkers habitually paid attention to anything bearing the family's name. Old Mr. Astor's hotel, known as Astor House, was heralded for its luxury ("the number of . . . splendid mirrors, sofas, Brussels carpets . . . almost bewilders one") when it opened at Broadway and Vesey Street, near City Hall, in May 1836. That of his great-grandson, which, during the onset of construction, had been referred to not as the Waldorf but as the "new" Astor House, was expected to carry the same standards into a new era of American prosperity.[6]

The Waldorf, named after John Jacob Astor's native village in Germany, arrived as part of a larger wave of hotel development that overtook Manhattan between 1890 and 1893. There were several factors behind this. Plans for the 1893 Chicago World's Fair, also known as the World's Columbian Exposition, inspired property owners to build hotels in hopes of attracting European patrons stopping in New York, on the way to and from the Midwest. Simultaneously, the 1890 opening of Madison Square Garden, which could accommodate 15,000 people, bode well for the future influx of visitors associated with industrial and political conventions. For years people had complained of New York's being outpaced by other American cities in the construction of modern, comfortable lodging. There was also concern that its current hotels—many of which had been built in the years after the Civil War—did not meet late nineteenth-century standards of safety. The 1887 Richmond Hotel fire, in Buffalo, which killed fifteen and burned many others, only sharpened the public's anxiety. For this reason, ads for Holland House, at Thirtieth Street and Fifth Avenue, touted a "fire proof" construction of "stone, brick and iron," with "no wood except doors and trim."[7]

Holland House, though small by comparison, could be thought of as a predecessor to the Waldorf in its reputation for exclusiveness, one that implied the presence of a wealthy clientele. It opened at the end of 1891, a time when the surrounding neighborhood was in transition. To the immediate south lay Madison Square, once a quiet outpost of brownstone houses and private clubs but now Manhattan's leading entertainment district. Theaters, hotels, and restaurants, including the epicurean pacesetter Delmonico's, dotted Broadway and Fifth Avenue near the cross streets of the East Twenties. At the same time, much of the area to the north remained stolidly residential: notwithstanding its role as a fashionable promenade, Fifth Avenue, according to the memory of publicist and newspaper writer Albert Crockett, "looked rather dead." True, the Hotel Buckingham had opened at Fiftieth and Fifth in the 1870s, but this was often described as having "the quiet elegance of a refined home." Unveiled in March 1893, the Waldorf, extending a full third of a block along Thirty-Third Street, was part of something new: a generation of what the *New York Tribune* described, not unapprovingly, as Fifth Avenue "monsters."[8]

Henry Janeway Hardenbergh, already known in artistic circles for his Dakota (1884), an imposing apartment edifice on Seventy-Second Street and Central Park West, received the plum commission as architect for the Waldorf. Thirteen stories tall, his new building overshadowed the earlier Dakota in both size and intricacy of detail. A large turret dominated the southeast corner at Thirty-Third Street and Fifth Avenue, where it rose eight floors before tapering in a pointed cap. Loggia with columns and projecting balconies decorated each of the building's sides, while a sequence of arches, pediments, and iron railings punctuated the facade. Like many late nineteenth-century structures in Manhattan, the Waldorf featured a sloping mansard roof, which Hardenbergh used, in this case, as a backdrop for his most striking decorative touches. The roof, extending vertically across three stories, moved inward as it went higher, creating a diagonal line that Hardenbergh filled with chimneys, tiny windows, and stone ornamentation. Like the froth at the tip of a wave, Hardenbergh's roof alleviated the impact of the hulking lower floors. Taken as a whole, then, the Waldorf, in its combination of force and whimsy, German Renaissance with Second Empire and Chateauesque design, represented a distinctly American ideal: one that looked to the Old World for inspiration but found a modern verve through the blending of diverse architectural styles.

Entering the main doors, set to the side on Thirty-Third Street, a visitor would first notice the Palm Garden, shimmering with light from Mrs. Astor's yard. To the immediate left was a reception area filled with damask sofas, alabaster statuary, ferns, and polished escritoires. Rightward lay a sequence of parlors: the Turkish Salon, dripping with tassels, led to the Marie Antoinette Room, dominated by a ceiling of Nereids, cherubim, birds, and lyres. Offering multiple positions for sitting, talking, and watching the parade of activity, the Waldorf emerged, during its earliest years, as a place to show off and be seen. By 1900, one hallway had become such a popular marching ground that newspaper reporters would give it a facetious nickname, unacknowledged by the hotel (in either its public statements or internal correspondence) for decades: "Peacock Alley."[9]

The Hotel Waldorf in 1893, shortly after completion, with the canopied main entrance to the left on Thirty-Third Street and a glimpse of Mrs. Astor's garden on the right (Pictorial Press Ltd/Alamy Stock Photo).

Beyond its architecture and design, the Waldorf was distinguished by a range of human characters, "built in" to the fabric of the institution. Chief among them was Oscar. No other hotel figure, in the nineteenth century or much of the twentieth, would hold quite the degree of visibility and popular recognition as Oscar Tschirky. Indeed, "Oscar of the Waldorf" (few could pronounce his last name, and most gave up trying) was one of the famous New Yorkers of his day, an 1890s celebrity chef who, though he never actually cooked a meal, captured the public's imagination with appearances in periodicals, newspaper articles, and product endorsements. There was Oscar's own sauce, bottled and sold nationwide with a label that bore his handsome visage, set impassively above a pair of lapels. And then there was his 1896 cookbook, made up of sundry recipes he had gathered from associates and patrons. Through numerous editions it became a primer for Americans wanting to replicate the experience of Waldorf dining, and the atmosphere of easeful prosperity that went with it, inside their homes.

So legendary did Oscar become that it would be difficult, at times, to separate fact from embellishment. Was he really the first to assemble a seemingly random collection of foodstuffs—apples, celery, walnuts, mayonnaise—into the concoction known, then and after, as "Waldorf salad," as he always claimed? And what about his similar role in the creation of Thousand Island dressing? The detailed nature of his recollection, as presented in *Oscar of the Waldorf*, a 1943 biography, suggests that he did, in all likelihood, watch millionaire gambler John Gates as the latter ventured a bet on which of two raindrops running down a windowpane would hit bottom first. But the assertion, repeated in a number of sources, that Oscar was the inventor of the velvet rope—drawn to keep out the unprivileged or uninvited—is more dubious, as a similar device had been used in locales as diverse as the White House and Paris Opera during the nineteenth century. The paradox was that Oscar (who did, at times, give evidence of subscribing to his own myth) was far from an outwardly boastful or grandiose person. While he possessed no small amount of political cunning, his essential drive grew out of the principles of hard work and loyalty he once expressed in a letter to a former employee: "Faithful performance of duty will always find its reward."[10]

Ad for Oscar Tschirky's cookbook, 1896 (Miriam and Ira D. Wallach Division of Art, Prints and Photographs: Print Collection, New York Public Library).

Oscar Tschirky came from the small Swiss city of La Chaux-de-Fonds, an early example of a single "industry town," devoted, in this case, to the watchmaking trade. After a destructive fire, streets were remapped in the early nineteenth century using a grid-like pattern unique, at the time, in Europe. The organizational scheme of La Chaux-de-Fonds, with living quarters and work spaces side by side in an integrated environment, made it a symbol of industrialized modernity (no surprise, perhaps, that one of its most renowned natives would be the modernist architect Le Corbusier). For Oscar, the experience of living in a rigidly structured townscape devoted to the actual business of timekeeping, with houses, offices, and factories laid along straight lines, no doubt prepared him for his later success at the Waldorf, where his restaurant service ran, he often stated, with the "smoothness of clockwork." Oscar spoke of using "military discipline" in the handling of his waiters, who tended to view him as a martinet. Staff complained of heavy fines for lateness, for omitting a small portion of a diner's order, for serving food with china that was imperceptibly chipped. Voicing dissatisfaction to a reporter in 1899, one man told of having to work from twelve noon to four o'clock the next morning, of contracting pneumonia as a result of working conditions (because a courtyard doubled as storage, waiters had to run into the cold every time a spot or stain necessitated the changing of aprons). "My intention is to follow my own methods," Oscar once asserted in a letter to Thomas Hilliard, formerly the hotel's chief manager, "and it will be a hard battle for anyone who opposes me."[11]

Oscar was around seventeen when he immigrated to New York, following the path of an older brother, in May 1883. Even allowing for a touch of exaggeration, Oscar's account of his first day in Manhattan, arriving by ship at six o'clock in the morning, applying for citizenship papers and finding a job by two that afternoon, was a tribute to his own ethic of industry. Hoffman House, located on Madison Square at Twenty-Fifth Street, was then one of the noted hostelries of New York, a rendezvous for politicians, railroad magnates, and theatrical personalities. Oscar's brother, working at a different hotel nearby, took him to meet the Hoffman restaurant manager, who hired him as a busboy. Impressing superiors with his high personal and hygienic standards—"I was always scrupulously clean," he recalled around 1943, "a quality much rarer in the Eighties and Nineties than it is today"— Oscar was promoted to waiter. From the beginning, he made "an emphatic point of serving sincerely," so that none of his guests would "have the feeling" that his "hand was stuck out for a tip."[12]

Still, the tips materialized. It became evident that, despite the strenuous labor, working for an establishment patronized by the well-to-do had advantages. Proprietor of the Hoffman House was Edward "Ned" Stokes, a man of chiseled looks who had scandalized New York some years earlier by shooting and killing Jim Fisk, notorious financier and "robber baron," after a failed extortion attempt—one in which Stokes and his lover, Josie Mansfield, had threatened to expose Fisk's underhanded business practices. By the time Oscar worked at Hoffman House, Stokes's notoriety had dimmed, but the "gallows bird" (as one newspaper put it) retained a fondness for illicit pastimes. His Sunday parties, held for wealthy male friends on a private yacht, were lavish affairs noted for poker games and, in some cases, the presence of women who were either hired or invited as company for bachelor guests. As Stokes's favorite waiter, Oscar was brought on to steward these events, where the gamblers adhered to their host's one condition: Oscar was to receive, as tip, a share of the final jackpot. At the end of the first night he discovered, sitting on the poker table, forty-nine dollars plus change— enough, around 1885, to pay one month's rent for a family apartment in Manhattan's respectable Murray Hill district. Perhaps imagining a test, Oscar, with characteristic cleverness, went to Stokes instead of pocketing the money outright.[13]

"That's all right, Oscar," his employer laughed. "They know the rule. Whatever you find on the table is yours." In later years there would be much conjecture in the press about Oscar's true financial intake: by 1905 he was rumored to earn as much, through tips, as the yearly salary of a railroad company president. While circumspect when questioned by reporters, in private he could be more forthright. Writing a prospective head waiter, in 1906, he offered to pay, "to a man such as you," $175 a month—"and you know what there is to be made over and above this." Other letters speak to hefty bonus checks from institutions such as the Chamber of Commerce, a frequent host of banquets at the Waldorf. Eventually Oscar's savings would be large enough for him to purchase a dairy farm in New Paltz, eighty miles north of Manhattan, where guests were amused to observe his punctilious ideas transplanted to a rural setting: each tool on the wall of his shed had been precisely outlined in red, so that anyone taking down a hammer would know just where it needed to be put back. Cumbrous farm equipment, a giant tractor, was disassembled and stored each winter, then greased and put back on the field. In the recollection of one visitor, "All of it looked like it just came out of the dealers."[14]

After leaving Hoffman House, in 1887, Oscar landed at Delmonico's, the restaurant that, along with its chief competitor, Sherry's, most fully exemplified ideals of high dining in the 1880s and 1890s. During this period of speculation and corporate trusts, increasing numbers of Americans, flush with newly acquired wealth, discovered in the pursuit of gastronomy a fittingly ostentatious way to spend money. Meals could be lengthy and elaborate, stretching out over as many as nine courses that included oysters, green turtle soup, lobster, a chicken dish, roast mountain sheep accompanied by sautéed brussels sprouts or other vegetables, sherbet as a palate cleanser, terrapin (a small turtle, once a staple of expensive meals), duck salad, and ice cream or vanilla mousse with raspberries—all accompanied, course by course, with sherry, champagne, burgundy wine, port, liqueurs, and coffee.

For some, meals such as these represented the apex of luxury, a sign of healthful prosperity. For others, Delmonico's and Sherry's were temples to indulgence. In his landmark novel *Sister Carrie* (1900), Theodore Dreiser, in one pungent scene of a night at Sherry's, took a gimlet-eyed view of the "exhibition of showy, wasteful and unwholesome gastronomy as practiced by wealthy Americans which is the wonder and astonishment of true culture and dignity the world over." For Dreiser, who drew extensively for the novel on his own experiences with his pleasure-loving older brother, Paul (who had been a successful, if undisciplined, Tin Pan Alley songwriter), the waiters and their "little genuflections and attentions" were key accessories in the creation of an "air of exclusiveness" he found mercenary and specious: "Oysters—certainly—half-dozen—yes. Asparagus! Olives—yes."[15]

It was as a waiter at Delmonico's, first in the main restaurant and, later, in the more select and (from his point of view) remunerative private rooms, that Oscar acquired his personal connections with leaders of politics, finance, and industry. This was a madcap six-year period in which he catered small parties, banquets, and rowdy stag dinners, moving at the whim of high-living and tireless characters such as financier "Diamond Jim" Brady, famed for his appetite and collection of egg-sized garnet pendants. Oscar recalled one poker game, hosted by a millionaire, that went on for a record three days and three nights. Switching off with each other in shifts of twelve hours, he and his fellow waiters lost all sense of time, as "meals grew more and more confused." By the final day they were serving "breakfast at midnight, luncheon at five in the morning, and dinner at ten in the forenoon."[16]

Soon, Oscar explained, he "began to make friends," not by addressing guests directly—"because a good waiter knows better than to speak unless he is spoken to, or to remember anything he overhears"—but instead through "giving them service and attention." In fact, it was these same contacts who would help secure for him the position most associated with his life and career. On Easter Sunday, 1890, he and his father, who by now had also come to live in New York, were walking up Fifth Avenue to St. Patrick's Cathedral. At Thirty-Third Street they paused to remark upon a wooden construction fence that surrounded a giant hole. This was when Oscar first heard, from his father, of the "new Astor House," whose planning had already been announced in newspapers. The next morning, Oscar went to the Astor business office, where he saw Abner Bartlett, chief representative of William Waldorf's estate. Bartlett, who already knew "Oscar of Delmonico's" and was familiar with his personality and skill, promised to see what he could do. A year later, while serving Bartlett at lunch, the older man gave him a name that Oscar wrote on the back of a menu: "George C. Boldt." Once Boldt asked for references, not long after, Oscar acquired signatures from so many of his famous acquaintances that the list "looked like a *Who's Who* of

New York." By the time he attached a letter, on Delmonico's stationery, and mailed it to Mr. Boldt, Oscar had ten pages' worth of supporters. The Waldorf job was his.[17]

Thirty-Third Street was a congestion of horses, humans, and rain-slicked capes, as wind snapped at an awning in front of the Waldorf's main entrance. Below, a carpet laid for the official opening that night—March 14, 1893—was soft and soggy. Once inside, guests were rewarded for enduring what all agreed was the season's most miserable weather, when a range of gilt furnishings, shimmering with light from candelabras, met their eyes. Marble pillars, pilasters, ferns planted in brass urns, giant bowls fed by streams of water from lion's head mouths—all these melded in an atmosphere of warm, cultured placidity. The scent of American Beauty roses, drawn together in bundles on side tables, encircled visitors in a wafting cloud. Dark carpet on the stairway leading to "state apartments"—hung with tapestries and reserved for dignitaries—felt cushiony underfoot. Later, strains from Bizet's "Danse Bohème," performed by the New York Symphony Orchestra, filled the halls with darting surges of oboes, horns, and strings. Those who couldn't fit inside the wood-paneled dining room, where the concert was held, were content to wander and admire the scores of fauteuil chairs, the hand-painted ceilings and pressed copper chandeliers.

The Symphony Orchestra, led by Walter Damrosch, had been donated through the goodwill of Mrs. Alva Vanderbilt, who canceled a dinner at her own home so she could oversee the night's entertainment. Guests who paid the then-sizable price of five dollars a ticket could feel content in knowing they had supported the laudable work of the St. Mary's Free Hospital, cited by Albert Crockett as "perhaps the pet benevolence of the greatest number of New York's fashionable folk." Founded in 1870, the hospital provided free medical treatment and convalescent care to children under the age of thirteen. It occupied an august Queen Anne–style edifice on the western end of Thirty-Fourth Street, fringing Hell's Kitchen—then an economically troubled district of wooden houses and 1860s "dumbbell-style" tenements, in which apartments wrapped around a central stairwell with minimal access to light or air. Many children in Hell's Kitchen and other poor neighborhoods were suffering from life-threatening diseases such as tuberculosis: the *New York Times* reported in 1875 that, out of ninety-four patients admitted to the hospital during the previous year, "46 were cured" and "13 died." At a time in which the city was still very much divided, geographically, along ethnic lines, the hospital took a notably nonprejudicial stance, administering to all races and religions.[18]

"[St. Mary's] numbered among its patronesses women about whom revolved the most exclusive social circles of the day," Crockett wrote. Tellingly, the nuns who administered the hospital were members of an Episcopalian Protestant order: it would have been unusual for New York's Anglo-Saxon elite to give such vigorous support, in the late nineteenth century, to a Roman Catholic–run charity. In deciding to launch with a benefit, the Waldorf had chosen St. Mary's carefully, with the specific goal of modeling itself into a locus of fashionable life: "It was necessary only to place all the facilities of the gorgeous new [Waldorf] at the disposal of a committee of active social leaders representing the hospital—and they did the rest."[19]

From the beginning, then, the Waldorf attracted the support and involvement of venerable families, all present on opening night: Vanderbilt, Carnegie, Frick, Choate, Depew. It also contained extensive space for the hosting of parties and dinners: while the year's other Astor-financed hotel, the New Netherland, had a large ground-floor restaurant and multiple private dinner spaces, it was built without a ballroom, so that functions with dancing would have been impossible. The Waldorf also had political advantages that set it apart from competitors: later in March 1893, the Entertainment Committee of the State of New York began using the hotel as its headquarters, with the goal of planning official events for the hosting of European notables on their way to and from the Columbian Exposition in Chicago. The first such Waldorf visitor was the Spanish Duke of Veragua, reputedly a descendant of Christopher Columbus. He was set to be followed by the Infanta (Princess) Eulalia, known for her progressive views on divorce and women's rights, but she capriciously switched to the Hotel Savoy at the last minute. Nevertheless, the Waldorf's reputation as a host for royalty and international personages was cemented.

Most important of the Waldorf's resources was undoubtedly its manager, George C. Boldt, who became, along with Oscar, the defining figure of the early years of the hotel. Though prominent in New York social life, an investor in banks and real estate who is best remembered as builder of the gargantuan, long-unfinished Boldt Castle in the Thousand Islands upstate, Boldt never aspired to Oscar's degree of public visibility. The latter, possessing an admiration for his boss that bordered on hero worship, was the enforcer— one who implemented Boldt's policies in a way often described as "Napoleonic." Once, during a financial dispute, Oscar (whose relations with his staff were, as might be expected, not always peaceable) told each waiter to *take off his apron* (i.e., resign) if he wasn't satisfied with the pay. To a newspaper reporter Oscar observed how some waiters "never know when they are well off." Men, like soldiers in a regiment, were replaceable: "I do not know how many have gone. It is really of very little significance. Everything moves on wheels here, as you see."[20]

Boldt, by contrast, was genial and mild-mannered: with his pince-nez and Vandyke beard, prematurely white, he looked the part of an avuncular professor. Known for his willingness to extend credit to patrons and cash their checks, he often assured employees that "men are not going to the penitentiary" for the sake of twenty-five or fifty dollars. House detective Joe Smith once cautioned Boldt that "a man was looking for him to ask him to O.K. a check" that Smith "knew was no good." Boldt either forgot about the warning or else, because he possessed "such a kind heart," felt it would be "impossible to refuse the request." When the check was returned by the bank, unpaid, Boldt "simply smiled" then "made it good out of his own pocket." Such losses, Boldt believed, were small compared with the goodwill engendered by policies designed to make visitors feel their needs were being met. "The guest," Boldt stated in an oft-repeated maxim (not yet, in the 1890s, as much of a cliché as it was to become), "is always right."[21]

One letter from 1906, while of minor significance (in terms of the situation it addressed), nonetheless points to Boldt's diplomatic skill and his understanding of human psychology. Catharine Cameron, daughter of one of the country's top horse breeders, requested use of the Waldorf's roof for a competitive dog show. In his response Boldt referenced an earlier canine exhibition, adroitly declining Miss Cameron in a way that also showed empathy:

> I am under the impression that the [hotel] management as a whole has finally reached the conclusion that it is not advisable to have any animal shows in this house in the future. This conclusion has been reached after mature deliberation, and is not because they had any fault to find with the way they have been conducted heretofore. On the contrary everything has been most pleasant, but there have been a number of complaints made by valuable patrons, which could not be well overlooked.
>
> I regret extremely that this conclusion has been reached; being so fond of animals as I am, it rather affects me personally.[22]

Boldt had his eccentricities. One of them was a belief in his ability as a vocalist—an "impression" that was not, in an observer's view, "universal." One evening George invited a group of friends to his family apartments in the Waldorf for a recital. Midway through the performance, "when Mr. Boldt was doing his prettiest," one of his beloved pet dogs initiated a howl that wouldn't let up: "It was only with a strong effort that the guests could keep straight faces." Later, when one guest remarked to a young woman who had also been present, "'Wasn't it amusing, that dog howling . . . ?'" she responded, with "an archness in tone and manner. . . . 'Hobart, could you blame the dog?'" As for the question of Boldt's personality as an employer and his relationship with staff, it could best "be summed up," in the words of a writer for the *New York Sun*, by describing an interchange that occurred near the end of his life: "'Son,' he said to a little bell hop who was passing as he stopped the boy and placed his hand on the boy's head, 'if you have time would you mind running up to my room and getting my hat for me?'"[23]

George Boldt came from Rugen, an island in the Baltic Sea in what was then the kingdom of Prussia. Part of modern Germany, Rugen is only thirty-two miles from north to south, but it contains a remarkably diverse array of

George Boldt in 1915, one year before his death (Bain News Service/
Library of Congress).

plants and geologic formations, including the majestic chalk cliffs that make
the island a scenic destination. By the time George was born, in 1851, Rugen
had enjoyed long success as a mercantile center: the nearby town, Stral-
sund, bore evidence of its history as part of the late-medieval Hanseatic
League, through florid Gothic structures of multihued brick. George's parents, it was said, belonged to the middle class as government administra-

tors, relatively well-off financially but far removed from the wealthy circles within which their son would travel later in his life. When George immigrated to the United States in 1868, at the age of seventeen, he hoped to find work for a trading concern but soon realized his lack of English would be a handicap. So, instead of remaining in New York, he went to Texas and built a farm. Later George would look upon this time as the hardest of his life: after years spent fighting the cotton bollworm, he lost all his crops to a hurricane and subsequent flood. Climbing a tree to escape the waters, he found rescue in a passing skiff and thereby initiated the journey that, after a few detours, took him back north.

Returning to New York, George found a job assisting the vegetable cook in the kitchen at Parker's Restaurant, a popular oyster house at Thirty-Third Street and Sixth Avenue, in the upper fringes of the Tenderloin (then, in the 1870s, building its identity as the city's most expensive vice district). One guest in particular intrigued him: an elderly man who came two to three times a week from upstate New York and took his lunches at the restaurant. George, whose English had now improved, felt sorry for the man (who, as a poor tipper, was generally ignored by the wait staff) and made efforts to engage him in conversation. Impressed with George's kindness and observing the care with which he performed his duties, which by now included handling receipts and making coffee, the man one day surprised Boldt with a question that, in its tone of insistence, came off more as a declaration: "Wouldn't you like to run a hotel of your own?"[24]

The Cornwall Mountain House, at Cornwall-on-Hudson some sixty-five miles north of the city, was not, as certain accounts of Boldt would later claim, a small country inn. Surrounded by hills, it encompassed at least five distinct buildings: a Victorian guest house with wraparound porch and an entrance for carriages, another hotel structure of three stories, a central farmhouse and adjacent building, along with a large gazebo and performance space. Once a remote village, Cornwall had blossomed during the 1850s as a health retreat for the wealthy, popularized through the efforts of writer and editor Nathaniel Parker Willis (his *Home Journal* would eventually become the magazine *Town & Country*). When Boldt arrived to manage Mountain

House around 1874, having accepted his stingy but benevolent patron's offer, Cornwall had passed its peak of popularity. Still, it held on to a core of wealthy visitors seeking to escape the congestion of New York and other cities in summer. It was here, according to one account, that Boldt first had contact with Abner Bartlett and members of the Astor family. It was also at the Mountain House, which succeeded through his oversight, that George met the representatives of high Philadelphia society who led him to William Kehrer.

Since 1856, Kehrer had managed the Philadelphia Club, a bastion of that city's social life. When Boldt started as Kehrer's assistant about 1875, the male-only club could claim some of the most prominent figures in Philadelphia, among them former mayor Richard Vaux; the banker Anthony Joseph Drexel; poet and diplomat George Henry Boker; and John Johnson, a lawyer and art collector. While distinguished, members were valued more for their interests in fields outside of professional life; in this way, the club inculcated an atmosphere of eclecticism and discernment. Boldt, who early had developed an interest in collecting fine chinaware, fit into the general ambience, which featured an extensive library, backgammon tables, and easy chairs placed in front of the "cheerful blaze" (as a *Philadelphia Times* account put it) of well-tended fires. Here also Boldt found the air of quiet civility, as described in the *Times*, that would later be his personal trademark at the Waldorf: "The distinguishing qualities of the Philadelphia Club are its domesticity and good fellowship. . . . When a member gets objectionable all the others give him the cold shoulder, so that he does not find the atmosphere of the place pleasant."[25]

In 1877, twenty-six-year-old Boldt married Louise Kehrer, William's daughter, not quite seventeen at the time. Despite her youth, Louise would participate actively in her husband's business affairs, through an arrangement that was unusual for nineteenth-century American marriages. Mr. Kehrer, as club steward, had not been a member himself. All the same, his daughter grew up in an atmosphere colored by the artistic interests of people she encountered. With funding from members of the Philadelphia Club, George became proprietor, in 1881, of his own hotel, the Bellevue, housed in a converted mansion next to the aristocratic Union Club. By all accounts, Louise was his bona fide partner, running the Bellevue and catering to patrons with the gentility for which her father had been known. Louise encouraged George to shape operational policy from a woman's point of view, believing that husbands were inclined to accede to their wives' desires in the style and arrangement of lodging. So visible was she that at least one newspaper cited her as the Bellevue's actual proprietor; years later, when the Astoria was added to the Waldorf, George himself would mention that his wife's name was on the lease.[26]

The Bellevue was small—thirty-six rooms—but its reputation for service and cuisine spread until it became known as "the nearest approach in Philadelphia to 'a Delmonico's.'" In fact, its guest register could have been a condensed edition of that of the later Waldorf: names included Princess Eulalia, poet and essayist Matthew Arnold, and the Crown Prince of Siam. As hotel and restaurant, the Bellevue was also a favored spot for the Astors and those connected with their estate—especially Abner Bartlett, who, according to the newspaper writer Albert Crockett, had a "weakness" for "strong spirits." Crockett recalled how Boldt once confessed, "in a rare moment of revelation," that it was Bartlett who had thought of the idea of George's running the new Hotel Waldorf, and that the reason was partly rooted in gratitude. In the discreet George Boldt, Bartlett always had a valuable cover: "[Boldt] became early aware of the identity of his frequent patron and made it a point to see that he was well taken care of and that any little aberration never became public property."[27]

A more polite story of how Boldt came to run the Waldorf was related by Cincinnati political boss George B. Cox. William Waldorf Astor, in Philadelphia for John Jacob's wedding in 1891, stopped at the Bellevue and was told by a desk clerk that no rooms were available: "Mr. Astor was much put out and made that plain." George, standing nearby and "listening to the conversation," offered, "'Mr. Astor, if you and your party go in to dinner I will arrange an apartment for you.'" After dinner, William Waldorf, "much taken by [the apartment's] elegance," was informed by a maid that it belonged, in fact, to Boldt himself. The next morning an appreciative Astor took George's hand: "'You are too big a man in your business for a slow-going place like Philadelphia.'" Astor's telegram arrived a week later. Whichever story more closely approximated the truth, by the spring of 1892 George was making weekly trips from Philadelphia to New York, where he watched the "skyward course" of the building that would contain, among its other amenities, something characterized as novel by observers of the day: a men's lounge also open to women, who could take coffee while their husbands smoked.[28]

Despite its being touted in the press as a "Home for Millionaires," the Waldorf got off to a slow start financially. The Columbian Exposition brought fewer travelers to New York than expected, and, in an example of what would befall the later edition of the hotel on Park Avenue (financed in 1929), there was a sudden drop in the nation's economic confidence. What became known as the Panic of 1893, in which stock prices fell to their lowest in two decades, hit just as the Waldorf was opening. Even in best of times the months of June, July, and August were typically quiet for hotels; the standard summer tourist trade, so marked a feature of later decades in New York, had yet to develop in the 1890s. Further, many of those who could afford to pay the Waldorf's rates, which averaged around six dollars per night (considered expensive at a time when comfortable rooms, in less elegant establishments, could be had for two dollars), were passing the season at Newport and other resorts. Boldt, who by now had been in business for twelve years and had even opened a second Philadelphia hotel, the Stratford, looked upon all this with a veteran's equanimity.

"Things will straighten out in the fall," Oscar remembered him saying. "If only we can get through this first summer everything will be all right." The hotel, he believed, should "pad on the luxury and the ease of living." From the outset, he and Oscar wrested business away from Delmonico's, establishing the Waldorf as one of the few places where fashionable New Yorkers considered it socially acceptable to host dinners outside their homes. One early dinner was that given in December 1893 by the Society of Colonial Wars, whose members included John Jacob Astor and others with venerable names preserved through their appearance in New York streets: Howland Pell and J. William Beekman. Associations such as Philadelphia's esteemed

Clover Club, inventor of the cocktail affiliated with its name, also began scheduling their New York dinners at the Waldorf. Boldt, who had supervised many a Clover Club dinner in Philadelphia, already knew of the group's reputation for joking and tomfoolery when he tried to make a speech during its first Waldorf gathering, on April 20, 1893: "I was thinking of that day when I first opened the Bellevue—." One member interrupted, in a characteristic riposte, "What did you do with the jimmy?"[29]

Augmenting trade from dinners and banquets was that associated with the Monday "Morning Musicales" of Arthur Morris Bagby, a pianist, conductor, and former student of Franz Liszt. Bagby had already built up a following of society women when Boldt approached him, in the fall of 1893, about transferring his popular series of lectures and concerts to the Waldorf. Described, perhaps euphemistically, as a lifelong "bachelor," Bagby embodied George Boldt's ideals for the Waldorf: he was refined and continental, played bridge skillfully, and knew many leading performers of the Metropolitan Opera. It was a time of "fewer contractual obligations" for operatic stars, as Bagby later wrote: many of them, starting with Nellie Melba and continuing through Enrico Caruso (who appeared at the Waldorf eighteen times), proved willing to get up at seven in advance of an eleven o'clock morning concert. Singer Frieda Hempel recalled how the artists, who were "handsomely paid," enjoyed performing for the ladies who "clapped gloved hands with great gentility." Though, she added, they "often left me wondering if they had really enjoyed my singing!"[30]

Bagby "really deserved the highest praise and admiration for his achievement," wrote Hempel. He would "select his own artists" and "supervise the choice of selections" as well as the "gowns the prima donnas had chosen to wear." He was, Hempel attested, "politeness and tact personified," and his concerts generated additional business for the Waldorf, as the women in attendance generally stayed afterward for lunch. Bagby's Morning Musicales quickly became sold-out society events; members of the "unfortunate general public," recalled Hempel, "could not obtain tickets." The concerts would remain at the Waldorf for close to fifty years, continuing at the new hotel on Park Avenue into the early 1940s, when Bagby, now over eighty, would approach the ballroom's center stage with waxed moustache and immaculately groomed white hair—a natty relic from the fabled "mauve decade" of the 1890s.[31]

By the end of 1893, Boldt's and Oscar's efforts—bringing in the musicales, hosting dinners of out-of-town organizations whose members would stay the night—had made a difference. All the guest rooms, according to one account, were full on New Year's Eve. Still, with success came a degree of sacrifice. The final name signed to the hotel's guest register, on New Year's Day, 1894, pointed to the future in ways Boldt, though unaware of it at the time, would not completely have liked: John W. Gates.

———

If Albert Morris Bagby personified the fusty sense of taste and decorum affiliated with Boldt's conception of the monied class in New York, John "Bet-a-Million" Gates was a brashly different ideal, even more nouveau riche than the parvenu families whose wealth had supported New York's economic growth a generation or two earlier. In person, he was coarse and loud without possessing much of the likable ebullience that would have made him a fun "character." Corpulent and cigar-chomping, afflicted with bouts of colitis, Gates brought with him a crudeness that would eventually turn an older brand of "nice" patron away from the Waldorf. But, vulgar as he may have been, Gates helped steer the Waldorf toward a more demotic identity in the latter part of the 1890s. Indeed, the years around 1900 could be portrayed, with respect to the Waldorf, as a move from Society, in its highest and most rarefied sense, toward society as a broader concept that included a diverse range of backgrounds and values. In this way, Gates prepared the Waldorf for the twentieth century.

Raised by deeply religious parents on an Illinois farm, Gates barely finished grade school. By the time he was fifteen, in 1870, both of his older brothers had died violently: one in the Civil War and the other at the hands of a marauding predator. Marrying at eighteen, Gates opened a small hardware store in Turner Junction, Illinois (today's West Chicago), and set the pattern for what would become a successful but undisciplined life: he made money, then gambled away much of it. Impressed with tales from a traveling sales-man, who recounted in detail the concupiscence of life on the road, Gates was encouraged to move to Texas, alone, in order to peddle barbed metal wire—an invention that promised to revolutionize cattle farming by elimi-nating the need for professional cowhands. Little happened at first: farmers were hesitant to invest in a product they were certain would not contain their livestock and might even injure escaping cattle. Displaying the Barnumesque flair that characterized his ideas and business approach (if not always his per-sonality), Gates conceived of a giant rodeo in the middle of San Antonio's plaza. He "received a permit," according to his biographers, "bought mes-quite posts where he could find them, ordered rolls of barbed wire [and] hired Mexicans to string it across the Plaza," then "bet against any comer that not a cow would break through."[32]

Fourteen years later, John W. Gates was the undisputed leader of the American wire industry. By the time he arrived at the Waldorf, Gates was known as a wild speculator who delighted in risk-taking—on the racing turf, in the stock market, and in his son Charlie's suite, where all-night poker games, catered by Oscar, were not uncommon. Though he always hated the moniker, "Bet a Million" suited Gates's temperament and personal style: he was tightfisted with his businesses but personally cavalier. According to one story, an aspiring politician without money (unnamed but likely the future governor, Al Smith) joined one of Gates's games, terrified of a potential loss but desiring social acceptance into the gambler's inner circle. The young man relaxed somewhat after Gates informed him, gruffly, that play was for "one a point," which, presumably, meant one dollar. Things got even better when the newcomer won by 330 points: at the time, $330 was much needed in his household. Relief turned to shock the following day when a check arrived from Gates's secretary for $33,000. "One" had stood for $100. Gates demurred when the man, guilty that he had won the money under a false understand-ing, tried to return it: "You won, didn't you? Well, let's forget about it."[33]

Fond of horse racing, Gates eventually traveled to Europe with his wife, who bedecked herself in wide-brimmed hats topped by mounds of fur. In England he became known as part of the "American invasion" of overnight millionaires who disconcerted the British with their vulgarianism. Albert Crockett quipped how Gates's mouth "seldom proved as large as the load his knife—or occasionally his fork—elevated to its general location." Once, Crockett alleged, managers of London's Carlton restaurant went to elaborate ends to prevent Gates from sitting in his usual spot, on an evening when the Prince of Wales was expected for dinner at an adjacent table. Knowing that Gates would be susceptible to flattery, they created a mock table, set for service as if the prince were going to sit at it, so that Gates, as their "most distinguished American visitor," who certainly would want the honor of the table "next to that which is reserved for His Royal Highness," would be fooled into moving. Crockett repeated a joke popular in London around the turn of the century:

"What are you going to do for dinner, this evening . . ." one Britisher would ask another at a tea, or perhaps in a club.

"Oh, deah chap," the reply would be, "I have absolutely nothing on. I rawther think I shall drop in at the Carlton and listen to the Americans eating soup."[34]

Clearly, these were not the kinds of Americans George Boldt had in mind when he envisioned the Waldorf as a "haven for the well-to-do." He remained, by some accounts, a "snob," once heard to remark of an outsize Gates-type character, in private: "I would rather see Mrs. Astor sitting in my Palm Garden and drinking a cup of hot water, than view Soandso in there eating the costliest dinner I could serve him!"

These views, Crockett observed, were never shared with Boldt's patrons, "fortunately for him." Social bars could not be so high, especially after 1897, when the opening of the Astoria more than doubled the size of the original Waldorf (which had already, in late 1895, been extended along West Thirty-Third Street by ninety feet). Architect Hardenbergh was brought back to design the Astoria, which conjoined its predecessor through a series of doorways that allowed visitors to walk between the two structures. The new hotel, named in honor of the city John Jacob Astor (the first) had established as a trading center in Washington State, shifted its main entrance to Thirty-Fourth

The Waldorf and the life of the city: Fifth Avenue, ca. 1895, with flower
sellers to the left and right and an African American man strolling in front
of the hotel, center (Museum of the City of New York).

Street and occupied the site of the "other" Astor mansion, that of Caroline
Astor and her son. George Boldt, who had been concerned from the start
about what might eventually replace Mrs. Astor's house, brokered the deal,
which, according to legend, contained a clause that would allow for all connecting doors to be sealed up in case of future disagreement between the
malcontent cousins, John Jacob and William Waldorf. Barring that
unlikely possibility, and irrespective of the fact that each building retained
separate power facilities, the combined hotel would be known thereafter as
the Waldorf-Astoria.[35]

"It has never proved possible, in New York or any foreign city," Crockett
wrote, "to keep a big hotel 'exclusive.'" With 1,200 rooms, the new Waldorf-
Astoria would need to open its doors, literally and figuratively, to a wider spectrum. Concomitant with the hotel's growth in size and popularity at the turn

of the century—indeed, what supported that growth—was a national economy bolstered, in part, by the United States' involvement in the Spanish-
American War. For the first time, America was flexing its muscles on the
international stage, and the boisterous national spirit—however false or
trumped-up its initial source, the explosion of the USS *Maine*—found expression in New York. The ten-year period after 1898 was one of wide development in urban society, as manifested through greater opportunities for
women, the stirring of dialogues around racial justice, and the growth of
what would become known as popular culture. Still, reminders surfaced,
here and there, that the ways of New York did not always reflect those of the
larger United States. In 1907, when a Waldorf-Astoria manager wrote the
Marlborough-Blenheim Hotel in Atlantic City, requesting a room for a frequent Waldorf guest named J. P. Rosenberg, he received the following
reply: "We beg to take this opportunity of stating that for strictly business
reasons, we cater to Gentile patronage only."[36]

Nothing symbolized the new Waldorf-Astoria, in terms of difference from
the genteel establishment that preceded it, more fully than the men's bar. The
original hotel had been constructed without a barroom; patrons sat at café
tables, where drinks were carried to them by waiters. The new bar in the
Astoria portion of the hotel was a mahogany, four-sided affair that sat, with
imposing bulk, in one corner of the floor. It became one of the sights of New
York, home to a dramatis personae of stockbrokers, politicians, actors, Tin
Pan Alley songwriters, gamblers, winemakers' representatives, con men, and
hangers-on of all kinds. The bar's liquid output—mixed drinks—took form
and changed with the headlines of William Randolph Hearst's tabloid papers,
as house bartenders like the storied Johnnie Solon invented cocktails named
after technological developments (the "Marconi Wireless"), police procedures of uncertain ethicality (the "Third Degree"), hit Broadway shows
("Peg O' My Heart"), battles in the Spanish-American War (the "Victory
Swizzle"), and famous places or schools (the "Harvard")—the latter a combination of brandy and vermouth that often, joked Crockett, made alumni
who drank it lose their eponymous accent.

With the bar's success came new dangers from outside. So many patrons were reputed to be wealthy men of the western provinces, naive when it came to the minatory ways of New York, that George Boldt's in-house detectives found themselves tasked with an additional job: that of bodyguard or chaperone for those who wanted to make the rounds of nearby gambling houses and pleasure resorts, late at night. The Tenderloin, extending to the west of the high-class Fifth Avenue and Broadway hotels, catered to these kinds of men: upright citizens of Dubuque or St. Paul, unencumbered by wife, children, or thoughts of disapproving eyes at home. If the pleasure-seeker was a valued regular guest of the hotel, it was important that he make it back next morning in possession of his wallet and most of what had been in it. At the same time, house detectives had to be vigilant against the wiles of confidence men and pickpockets who viewed the bar, restaurants, and lobbies as a hunting ground. What went out had to come back; what threatened to damage the hotel's reputation must not be allowed in.

Inevitably this dictum pointed to areas beyond thievery; at stake were larger questions related to public behavior and morality. The Waldorf-Astoria, in the new years of the twentieth century, was determined to hold on to its cherished respectability, even at the occasional expense of a guest's personal liberty. But, in a seeming paradox, the same efforts that made the hotel repressive also, at times, gave it the security to push for advances as a social leader, in ways that could be seen as forward-thinking and, coming at a time of great change for the city and country, influential. Nowhere was the Waldorf's dual understanding of itself, as pacesetter and guardian of morals, more evident than in its treatment of female guests.

CHAPTER 2

Woman Spelled with a Big "W"

On October 6, 1902, Dr. Julius H. Woodward, noted physician and ophthalmologist, checked into the Waldorf-Astoria and was assigned room 1468. His close friend, Mrs. Mary Phelps Loomis, reached the hotel separately and was also given a room. They had known one another since at least 1890, when Woodward, along with Mrs. Loomis's husband, Horatio, were on staff together at the University of Vermont. Indeed, starting around 1897, when he moved to New York, Woodward boarded at the Loomis residence across from Bryant Park (then recently divested of the adjacent reservoir that would, after a nine-year period of construction, give way to the Forty-Second Street branch of the New York Public Library). Establishing a private practice in the city, Dr. Woodward lectured widely and even, in 1898, published a small book on the diagnosis and treatment of cataracts. He was a respected member of the Fencers' Club and the New York Athletic Club, proficient in combat and a frequent judge of sword competitions.

To outward appearances he and Mrs. Loomis were model Waldorf guests, the kind George Boldt would have been proud to emphasize over a rich philistine like John Gates. Mary Phelps Loomis was the daughter of Edward J. Phelps, onetime minister to Great Britain and the Kent Professor of Law at Yale. Her husband, Horatio Loomis—Dr. Woodward's colleague at the University of Vermont—was a chemist and mineralogist whose father helped found the Chicago Board of Trade in 1848. Two streets, one in Chicago and the other in Burlington, Vermont, were named after the Loomises. Meanwhile, the family of which Woodward was scion had roots in the War of 1812; his grandfather Theodore was surgeon at the Battle of Plattsburgh on Lake Champlain. All three friends—Woodward, Horatio Loomis, and his wife, Mary—were listed on the New York Social Register, established in 1880 to self-identify members of the city's Anglo-Saxon elite. During its peak of influence in the late nineteenth and early twentieth centuries, the Social Register sought to codify who was accepted and who was not. Once added, members could be removed for what would have been considered, in less rarefied circles, rather mild breaches: marrying an actor, marrying a Roman Catholic, and so forth.[1]

All the strength and association of their pedigree could not save Dr. Woodward and Mrs. Loomis on Sunday, October 12, when they were interrupted by a knocking at the latter's room door. The knocking served as their notice; legal precedence had established it as sufficient. In a moment Mr. Barse, one of George Boldt's managers, was inside, along with smooth-faced Joe Smith, chief house detective for the Waldorf-Astoria. Smith reported the encounter in the hotel's secret "black book," a log detailing criminal or suspected immoral activity (along with more prosaic items such as misplaced overcoats), kept hidden from all but the most senior Waldorf staff. Both Mrs. Loomis and Dr. Woodward were found, in the words of Smith, "undressed." Whether judging from its rumpled appearance or else from more specific evidence, Smith added that the couple "had used the bed." As adulterers, violating the hotel's policies against unmarried couples sharing a room, they were ordered to "pay their bill and get out."[2]

Downstairs, meanwhile, in Peacock Alley, guests idled in leather chairs studded with brass, as wisps of a sonata drifted past. Talcum-scented women from Akron, Ames, and Peoria affected nonchalance as they hoped for glimpses of an Astor or Vanderbilt—or could that be one of the Stuyvesant Fishes? Moving to the Palm Garden, they were directed to little round tables, draped in creamy linen and set for lunchtime service. Napkins lay across plates horizontally, leaving space for the Waldorf-Astoria insignia—two letters encircled by garlands—to appear in the twelve o'clock position, gold against the shiny porcelain. Glasses sat upturned, ready to be flipped and filled by waiters moving silently across terrazzo floors. A few women, if they were known to the house, received the service of Oscar himself, who handled them with his mixture of deference and solicitude: "We have particularly fine terrapin today. Shall I order a little for madam and her friend, with a very good little Sauterne, and then we shall see after, or—shall I just order the whole luncheon and not trouble madam?"[3]

At other tables, women might take charge "like four generals," as an observer described it, with one ordering "crab meat a la Newberg" and another "the salad," until the party of four made "a very comfortable luncheon" out of what normally would have been just two orders. Either way it was fine with the Waldorf, a place where women were given freedom to exert an active hand. They polished cues in a billiard room constructed for their use, took classes and became proficient in the deft technique of pocketing the eight ball; they sipped dense Turkish coffee while their husbands smoked, in violation of long-established custom (proper women, it had formerly been assumed, retired for the evening once men pulled out cigars); they organized banquets and dinners, consulting with Oscar on the social rivalries that threatened to turn a simple seating map into a battle plan. Cater to the desires of women, Boldt often stated, and men will follow. This dictum reflected his sympathies and was also good business.[4]

But what about Mrs. Loomis? As a woman she had lost stature, forfeited her rights. Getting out of the hotel would have been a devastating prospect: knowing that Sunday afternoon was when her peers would be lunching, she faced a gauntlet of shame and recrimination. If seen emerging from an elevator, headed for the checkout desk in the company of Dr. Woodward and Mr. Barse, the hotel official, her ostracization would have been sealed (Detective Smith admitted this when referring to a "stigma" put on ejected couples that "may follow them for years"). But to the Waldorf, Mrs. Loomis was a necessary sacrifice. In this it was no different from any other top New York hotel. For Boldt and his colleagues, welcoming women meant protecting them from unwholesome presences, including, as it happened, those of other women who, through their actions, had revealed themselves as loose, disreputable, or immoral. The Waldorf's policy toward women was therefore both restricted and open, rigid and permissive, rooted in Victorian mores but anticipating feminist currents. How to make sense of the contradiction?[5]

Detective Joe Smith once defended the Waldorf-Astoria's anticohabitation policy: "When it comes to a question of morality we don't play favorites and have no friends." This certainly was the case in his treatment of the lovers. Woodward was widowed, and although Mrs. Loomis was still married, her husband, Horatio, suffered from weak health. The length of time Dr. Woodward and Mrs. Loomis had known one another, combined with evidence of their caring relationship (when she was sick with what turned out to be a final illness, nine years later, Woodward traveled to Vermont to be with her), indicates that this was not a onetime dalliance or momentary slip. Clearly these were people in love; going to a comfortable hotel gave them a freedom they would not have felt under Horatio's roof, six blocks away. A hotel near the Bowery, where the proprietors may have been less concerned about the preservation of morality, would not have suited them. The Waldorf, they probably thought, offered protective cover. Ironically, its vaunted care and treatment of guests did Mrs. Loomis and Dr. Woodward in: with a system of clerks posted on every floor to cater to patron needs, the Waldorf could easily keep track of who was coming and going. Infractions were reported quickly; Joe Smith or one of the other house detectives could be on the scene within minutes.[6]

Unmarried men and women were expected to socialize in parlors on each floor, set aside for that purpose; otherwise, a woman could only go so far as the threshold of a man's door. These rules, because they touched upon indecorous matters, were never posted publicly—with the result that certain people, whether lovers or no, felt more secure than they really were. Paradoxically, the hotel's most "private" areas—the guest rooms—were exactly those in which privacy was most vulnerable to invasion. Two days after the Woodward and Loomis incident, a detective reminded a guest that "it was against the rules of Hotel to entertain Lady in appartment [sic]." The man "left room at once," explaining that the woman "was his stenographer." The potential for humiliation was great: on another occasion a woman, broken in upon while she and her lover were "undressed," ran into the bathroom, "locking door behind her," to avoid being seen by the male detectives. Any situation involving the threat of a lawsuit was documented: An assistant manager once wrote a report about a man who claimed the woman in his room was his aunt. The man announced he would "go where there were no such dammed [*sic*] rules," then "handed [the detective on duty] his card, and said that he would make the hotel pay for this." Most, though, were afraid to protest and risk a hint of scandal becoming public. All they could do was pay their bill, leave as unobtrusively as possible, and try to put the experience behind them.[7]

Adultery was not a crime in New York until 1907, when it became a misdemeanor, through legislation intended to curb the rate of divorces (couples, the thinking went, would be less inclined to separate if they knew the primary grounds for divorce were illegal). The state did not require couples to have a government-issued marriage license until 1908. Before then, it was possible to live as husband and wife under common law. Most couples possessed a certificate signed by a minister or town official, but its existence was not the product of a regulated system. Enforcing moral standards, then, was a way for the Waldorf-Astoria to take control over areas the state had neglected. The irony was that actual illegal activity, in the form of poker (viewed by the district attorney as a type of gambling), was given a pass. Joe Smith himself, in a biography published shortly before his death, was quoted as speaking of the "old days," when John W. Gates and others engaged in "some famous games nearly every night," but clarified how "they were always played in private apartments and there was no disturbance so they were nobody's affair." Julius Woodward and Mary Loomis were not bothering other guests, and their romance was carried out within the same private setting, but they threatened the hotel and its reputation in ways a male gathering of gamblers did not.[8]

The legality of ejecting guests on moral grounds was hard to pin down, but generally hotelkeepers could point to the courts for support. According to a compendium, *Law of Hotels, Boarding Houses and Lodging Houses* (1890), hotels were obligated to "receive all fit persons who make proper application for accommodations as guests," but those who were "filthy, . . . drunk, disorderly, notoriously dishonest, immoral, or affected with any contagious or infectious diseases" could be "put out . . . as nuisances." The *Annotated Consolidated Laws of the State of New York* (1909) classed any innkeeper who might refuse a guest, "without just cause or excuse," as guilty of a misdemeanor. The Waldorf and other hotels relied on this exemption of "just cause." In one case, a judge affirmed that every hotel owner possessed "the right to make and enforce proper rules to prevent immorality, or any other form of misconduct tending to injure the reputation of his house." The emphasis on reputation as something to be preserved and fought for, if necessary, spoke to anxieties about the nature of hotelkeeping itself.[9]

Though few proprietors would have acknowledged it, hotels had long been connected in the public imagination with undesirable people, especially prostitutes. One 1905 court case, involving common-law marriage, referenced a woman who spent nights with a man in "hotels and various houses of ill repute." Brothels, by implication, were the wicked siblings of hotels. The writers of *The Social Evil* (1902), a book designed in part to expose vice in the Tenderloin and other areas of New York, could have been recalling passages from Cervantes when they observed how "the transient has always been of notoriously loose habits, and it is only natural that vicious women should congregate wherever he is entertained." In the case of the Waldorf-Astoria, located on the Tenderloin's edge, there was an acute need to protect good women from the wiles and depredations of the bad; the more the hotel welcomed women into its ambit, the more careful it needed to be. In *Doing the Town: The Rise of Urban Tourism in the United States*, Catherine Cocks suggests how the fear of prostitution led to what could have been described, at times, as excessive caution on the part of hotel proprietors and their detectives:

> To maintain its first-class business in domestic accommodations, hotel keepers had to assure their potential patrons that all their female guests were entirely respectable. If they were not, the establishment degenerated into an assignation house.[10]

By the time of Detective Joe Smith's visit to Dr. Woodward and Mrs. Loomis in 1902, "respectable" New York hotels were under additional threat. The Raines law of 1896, drafted as a means of controlling liquor trade through taxation, featured a clause that permitted what had formerly been illegal—the sale of alcohol on Sunday—but only for guests in hotels. Of course, the law proved beneficial for the Waldorf-Astoria and, especially, Sunday beverage sales. But it also had an unfortunate result, when working-class saloon owners, eager to reap profits on a day most men had free, quickly applied for hotel licenses after adding the requisite number of beds. The "Raines law hotel" became a target of moral reformers, who viewed it as an incubator of prostitution and vice. Police raids ensued, as saloon owners faced charges from violations of the "disorderly house" clause of the New York State Penal Code, the 1902 version of which read, in part, "a person who keeps a house of ill-fame or assignation of any description" for "lewd, obscene, or indecent purpose . . . is guilty of a misdemeanor."

Of course, no one would have mistaken the luxury Waldorf-Astoria for a Raines law hotel or, even worse, a disorderly house. But the existence of such "low" establishments, functioning as brothels yet classed officially as hotels, tainted the industry and gave proprietors new impetus to bear down on immorality. The Raines law had been beneficial; the "Raines law hotel" was an embarrassment. As head of the New York State Hotel Association, George Boldt lobbied successfully for amendments: in 1910, it became illegal for proprietors to rent the same room more than once between nine in the evening and six o'clock the next morning. Guests faced misdemeanor charges if they attempted to register under false names. Finally, to apply for a license, a hotel, if located in a large city, needed fifty rooms; for smaller New York localities such as Beacon or Poughkeepsie, the requirement was twenty-five. During a meeting of the Hotel Association in December 1910, Boldt asserted that the amendments' goal had been to "bring about a separation from the so-called Raines law hotel, now so disgraceful and distasteful to us."[11]

Detectives and hotel staff felt the need to guard against pernicious influences that were forever waiting outside. Joe Smith related stories of "Chicago May," whom he described as "the most notorious woman thief in the world."

Using the Tenderloin streets as her base, Chicago May (born Mary Anne Duignan) targeted guests of the Waldorf and other hotels, luring them into alleys with an accomplice known as "Little Cleo." With characteristic equivocation, Smith explained that while the male victim was "embracing one of the pair," either May or Cleo "was busily engaged in relieving him of everything of value he had on him." Although May was "too smart" to enter the hotel, it's clear from the detective logbooks that other men and women of dubious character made it in. Once, a "semi-intoxicated" man was written up for desiring to have a woman "go to his room under . . . pretense to massage him." Another time Smith approached two women whose "appearance and actions were very loose" and informed them they could not sit in the lobby, while a "disreputable woman" was removed for "covertly soliciting" in the "Waldorf corridor." Men or women thought to be "flirting" with guests in the Turkish Salon would be asked to leave, along with those using "indecent language." Occasionally detectives employed physical force to remove such people; this was believed necessary for the protection of guests—in particular, women.[12]

"I was the first man in New York," George Boldt once claimed, "to make it possible for a woman to come into a New York hotel alone." Boldt meant that women could enter the Waldorf-Astoria through the main doors (early, there had been a separate "ladies' entrance," but its use was phased out), rest in the lobby, and partake of the atmosphere without having to worry about mashers, pickpockets, con men, fake barons on the prowl for heiresses, and what were known generally as "hotel pests." Boldt's assurance—the Waldorf-Astoria was a hotel that took special care of its female guests—had a practical root. Certain hotels, including the 630-room Grand Central, on Broadway near Bleecker Street downtown, relied heavily on the patronage of traveling businessmen. The Waldorf, nearly twice as large, could not afford to limit itself as a "man's hotel." Further, predominantly male-oriented establishments tended to be those most associated with women of "doubtful character." One late nineteenth-century American traveler recalled certain businessmen's hotels where the desk clerks routinely asked, upon check-in, "a room with, or without?"—a question taken by him to refer to the services of a prostitute.[13]

Peacock Alley, ca. 1900, with a hint of indecorousness suggested at left
(Bettman).

At the Waldorf-Astoria, therefore, welcoming the right kind of women
meant excluding others. Maintaining its identity as a "hotel for the women,"
the Waldorf worked aggressively to stanch the threat of prostitution and
illicit sexual relations. But this initiative is what allowed the hotel to be liberal
when it came to the advances of women in a broader cultural sense. Boldt's
conception of himself was that of a community leader whose openness to
change brought with it a degree of responsibility. Like most prominent
social figures of the time, he emphasized standards of morality as being con-
sonant with progress. In the end, though, Boldt's desire to please "good"
women bore an influence more lasting than that of his need to punish the
bad. If, as he insisted, "the guest is always right," then women—provided they
were respectable—would have to be listened to. None of this would have been
possible, however, if George had not been specially attuned to the concerns
of women in the first place.

Oscar's biographer once paraphrased a rule George Boldt gave his employees shortly before the Hotel Waldorf opened: "Never speak abruptly to a
woman guest nor be indifferent to her complaints. Woman's attitude in a
hotel is based on two assumptions: That she is there to have things done for
her without any trouble to herself, and that she can leave when she wants to,
on five minutes notice." Another early chronicler of the Waldorf, Edward
Hungerford, pointed to George's wife as an influence, noting how "'I'll ask
Louise,' was the most frequent response that he gave when important matters were first put to him for decision." While Hungerford's portrayal veers
toward cliché when he observes how "the greatest of [Boldt's] successes were
due to the quick wit and unfailing good sense of his wife," there is no question that Louise inhabited a power extending beyond what was customary
for the day. Boldt appears not to have had a lease during the first years of
the Waldorf. Instead, according to one account, the Astor estate paid him a
guaranteed yearly income of $25,000 plus an agreed-upon percentage of the
profits. This arrangement was short-lived. In 1904, a columnist for *Broadway Weekly* recalled a conversation he had had around the time of the
Astoria's opening in 1897. Boldt, attempting to squelch rumors of a possible
corporation, referenced himself in the third person to reveal that "the lessees
of the hotel" were, without question, "George C. Boldt and his wife."[14]

Women, of course, were known during the late 1800s as operators of
boardinghouses, often their residences converted for purposes of offering
guests temporary or semipermanent lodging. But a female leaseholder of a
hotel of the Waldorf-Astoria's size and preeminence would have been
extremely rare. Boldt's statement suggests that the relationship he and Louise forged during their early married years, operating the Bellevue jointly,
continued through the successes of the Waldorf and Waldorf-Astoria. Certainly, Mr. Boldt was the more visible partner; societal norms would have
mandated that Louise remain, to a large extent, behind the scenes, unless
ushered to the front through supervision of balls or charity events. At the
same time, there is little question that Louise remained her own person. Few

were aware that the property housing Boldt Castle in the Thousand Islands belonged, in fact, to Louise. George was naturally upset over his wife's early death, but the reason he stopped work on the castle probably had less to do with heartbreak (as a well-known legend propounds) than with legal complications surrounding Louise's having died intestate at the age of forty-three.[15]

It would be simplistic to argue that Boldt was open to the needs and concerns of women solely because of his wife's status as leaseholder. All the same, evidence suggests that Louise helped inspire the policy George once cited as "Always spell woman with a great big capital W." Because of his natural inclination to lead with thoughtfulness and restraint, Boldt proved more open-minded than many of his contemporaries—especially when it came to the presence of women in the hotel's main restaurant and other dining spaces. This was not customary in New York during the years just before and after the twentieth century's debut. A story once told about Charles C. Delmonico, owner of the fabled restaurant that bore his name, had to do with a "certain society woman" who entered with her daughter, asking to be served. Delmonico refused the pair, explaining how "he could not serve them because of the fixed rule not to serve women unaccompanied by men."[16]

"What do you mean?" the woman demanded. "You know perfectly well who I am." Delmonico replied how that fact "made it all the harder for him to carry out a rule that he could not break." Later, the woman was reported as understanding "the justice of his position" and would recount the experience "as a proof of [Delmonico's] knowledge of how a restaurant ought to be run." For many early advocates of women's rights, this part would have been the most obnoxious, as it offered implicit praise for the woman who acceded to a man's demands—a woman who knew her place.[17]

Decades later, it would seem unthinkable that a time existed when women could not enter a restaurant, alone or with a group of friends, and be given service. But for many women attempting to dine in late nineteenth-century and early twentieth-century Manhattan, the Delmonico's experience was all too common. First to be credited with fighting the ban against women dining alone in restaurants at lunchtime was Susan A. King, once described as "one of the oddest people in Gotham." King, who came to the city from Maine with twenty-five cents, went on to amass a fortune (said in the 1870s to be half a million dollars) through real estate. With a portion of this savings she traveled to China, going beyond port cities for voyages deep within the country's interior—despite fearsome warnings from others of European descent. Declaring herself an admirer of Confucius, King (then well into her fifties) visited numerous joss houses, explaining later that she "always made friends" with the Chinese because she "respected their religion." She returned to New York with batches of "pure, sun-dried tea" she had purchased directly from Chinese farmers. In 1872, with the hope of countering "the monopoly" enjoyed by men in "most every variety of business," she set up the Woman's Tea Company, managed and staffed entirely by women, at 838 Broadway, south of Union Square.[18]

It was perhaps in this locality that King, according to the *New York Journal*, suffered "mortification" and "humiliation" in the struggle for proprietors to "respect her right to enter a downtown restaurant for a midday meal." Thanks to her efforts and those of women who lobbied in her wake, lunchtime dining no longer presented a challenge by the 1890s. In fact, it became popular for groups of female friends or coworkers to gather for an enjoyable hour of food and conversation. The sensationalist and conservative *New York Press* ridiculed these women, in 1904, for succumbing to the "false Bohemianism" of an "odd belief that to be a real New Yorker one must eat often in public places." In years past, bemoaned the writer, "restaurants, hotels and cafes were for the poor unfortunates who had no homes . . . but not for the woman who had her establishment, her retinue of servants and the true spirit of hospitality!" Now, in places ranging from high ("the palm room of the Waldorf") to low ("the basement of the shop"), one discovers how "New York women are the restaurant fiends of the world." Blame for this unfortunate development could be placed, in the writer's view, on the "progressive—or, more properly speaking—aggressive spirit of the modern business woman."[19]

Implied in plaints such as these was the belief that women belonged at home—not, as a rule, on city streets, and certainly not within the male province of business. But by the early 1900s, such views had become outdated.

More than serving as a genial place for women to socialize, the lunchtime restaurant was a necessity, set up to cater to an expanding female workforce. According to historian Nancy Dye, 132,535 women were employed in manufacturing jobs in New York City in 1900; an "additional tens of thousands labored as retail clerks, waitresses, and laundresses." Playwright Eleanor Gates, in a January 1907 article for *Cosmopolitan*, depicted the "girl who is earning alone in the business world" as an "inspiring study." As wage earners, women were not looking for "drawing-room treatment"; at the same time, they defied a sentiment Gates had heard expressed: "'But . . . she has gone into man's work; let her take what comes.'" Women had gained "better hours" and the sympathy of employers who were "either voluntarily abandoning" or being forced to give up "starvation wages." Still, challenges remained, particularly for those whose jobs required them to work late. Gates suggested walking behind "any young woman who is leaving her work after nightfall": "You will observe that, for the most part, she is looked at with evident suspicion by escorted women who cannot discriminate; by too many men she is given glances that are questioning, or significant, or leering."[20]

Compounding all of this was the difficulty of finding a place at night to eat. Restaurants and cafés may have welcomed women by themselves during the day, but fears surrounding prostitution led owners to prohibit "unescorted women"—those hoping to enter without male accompaniment—after a certain hour, often eight or nine o'clock but sometimes as early as six. These policies were defended as necessary for keeping out disreputable women, who, it was believed, were the only kind who habitually went out at night alone. One restaurateur opined that if figurative bars "should be let down entirely," then upright female customers "would soon clamor to have them up again." In 1897, the manager of Dorlon's, a restaurant on Twenty-Third Street and Broadway near the southern end of the Tenderloin, cited the policy as "an absolute necessity in our present location," adding that "respectable women do not, as a rule, come to our restaurant alone after 9 o'clock, and the few who do invariably accept our explanation pleasantly and go quietly away."[21]

Not all women, however, proved as acquiescent as those in the manager's account. In at least four cases women, forced out of establishments at night and unable to find a place to dine after attending a show or working a long day, initiated legal proceedings intended to spotlight a condition they viewed as unjust. Those ejected often felt ashamed by the implication that they, as lone women, must be immoral. Every time such a situation made the papers, Oscar or one of the other Waldorf representatives—who by now had acquired the status of authority—was asked his opinion. In 1897, Boldt's manager, Thomas Hilliard, commented on one such lawsuit with disbelief: "I thought the practice of excluding from hotels and restaurants women who come unattended by men was given up long ago. It is a relic of the Middle Ages."[22]

Most restaurants, even those located in neighborhoods far from the "white light" entertainment district of Broadway and the Tenderloin, did not feel the same way. One of the first lawsuits to gain citywide attention was the abovementioned 1897 case, brought by lawyer Clara Foltz against the proprietor of a hotel and restaurant in Harlem. Foltz and her daughter had been attending a scientific lecture and exhibition. About 9:40 it started to rain heavily, and, seeking shelter, the women ducked inside Hollander's on 125th Street, hoping to call a cab. Thinking it discourteous to occupy the space without ordering food, Foltz tried unsuccessfully to summon a waiter, even though, according to one report, "plenty of them" were "standing around." Evidently the restaurant hoped the women would become frustrated and leave on their own; when this didn't happen, a waiter approached them, explaining, "I am sorry, lady, but you cannot be served here after 9:30 o'clock." He then insisted, according to Foltz, "you must get out" and pulled the back of her chair, while others in the restaurant sat laughing. Embarrassed and angry, Foltz found another man, either a manager or Hollander himself, who casually backed up the action of the waiter: "Oh, that's all right. . . . Them's his orders."[23]

Foltz, a recent New York arrival, already enjoyed a reputation in California, where she had successfully challenged state prohibitions to become the first female lawyer on the Pacific coast. Married at fifteen, she separated from her husband and raised five children while building a career that encompassed lobbying for women's suffrage and the right of the accused to a public defender. That rainy night at Hollander's in 1897, Foltz vowed to sue if the restaurant did not agree to change its policy; the manager, little concerned with such threats coming from a woman, took her business card without looking at it. Later, he revised his opinion, for the next morning Foltz received a visit from the restaurant's lawyer, who, in her words, claimed to "regret the occurrence of the night before" and tried to dissuade her from "the idea of a suit." Describing the meeting in a letter to Hearst's populist *New York Journal*, Foltz stated wryly, "I never got so much free advice from an attorney before in my life."[24]

Foltz filed suit against the restaurant and hotel, seeking $5,000 in damages. In support of her claim she referred to the section of New York's Penal Code, providing that anyone who "carries on business as an inn-keeper . . . and refuses, without just cause or excuse, to receive and entertain any guest . . . is guilty of a misdemeanor." Still, there was the qualification of "just cause or excuse." Could not the keeping out of undesirables be just cause? Editorial responses varied: some aligned with Foltz against the keeper of the "medieval restaurant," while others, such as a writer for the *Albany Morning Express*, believed that a hotel and restaurant owner deserved to enforce "such rules as he may make . . . for the maintenance of the moral standard which respectable patrons have a right to expect." As part of an epistolary exchange with the newspaper, Foltz pointed out the contradiction of assuming all women who entered with men were not prostitutes: "I cannot see why a street wanton with a betrousered escort is a better guest than a respectable woman who has the misfortune to be alone."[25]

In her use of "betrousered," reducing male diners to their outer, sartorial aspect, Foltz may have been hinting at an early activist tactic of women finding "any man," be he a livery driver, mechanic, or someone pulled off the street, to gain entry to a restaurant. In this they put a challenge before owners: Which boundaries are more important to preserve, those related to gender or class? In such cases, managers of expensive cafés looked on helplessly as roughshod men—but men, all the same—dined on terrapin with ladies in silks. Obviously, this technique, while provocative, was insufficient as a means of bringing about change. In the years after Foltz, other women filed, or announced plans to file, similar suits. Invariably their efforts failed. Still, what one newspaper referred to as the "moth eaten subject" of women "being kept out of the best restaurants at certain hours" would not go away. As larger numbers of women began to find enjoyment, during the years after the turn of the century, in theatergoing parties and postshow gatherings, more lawsuits appeared. In 1901 Oscar, while acknowledging that women unknown to the establishment might be turned away, explained that strict enforcement of prohibitory rules would be impossible because of the hotel's female guests: "Well, we serve them, certainly. We are compelled that this should be so. What would a hotel be that did not do this?"[26]

Oscar's suggestion was that hotels, unlike restaurants, had obligations to their overnight guests. If a woman was staying at the Waldorf-Astoria, then she must have already been classed as respectable—and, if there was a slip in the hotel's judgment, Joe Smith and his detective staff would find it. Therefore, no reason existed for denying women a spot at the table. But places of accommodation could not always be described as more liberal than restaurants: Hollander's, where Clara Foltz suffered the experience that led to her suit, was also a hotel. What was the dividing line between where women were allowed and where they were not? Further, in a new era of visibility, with women emerging into the public sphere as workers and consumers, did the old signifiers of wholesomeness still carry weight? How could men be counted on as judges? Flirting and other forms of indecorous behavior, while unacceptable in polite society, did not necessarily signify lustful intent: women and men, moving through a less segregated urban realm, enjoyed new and numerous opportunities for visual and verbal interaction. What if overeager hotel employees made mistakes in judging a woman's character?

Through her studies of trade journals, historian Cocks has suggested that hotel proprietors evinced signs of becoming, in the first decade of the twentieth century, increasingly ambivalent about their role as moral enforcers. An additional set of lawsuits, related to cases such as that of a "hapless night clerk" who "confused Martins and Mortons" and deduced incorrectly that a couple was unmarried, instilled a feeling among owners that maybe it was time to be less concerned with the "private transgressions of their patrons." At some point, it was feared, the contradictory efforts innkeepers were required to balance—offering guests unquestioned hospitality and policing them at the same time—would be forced into the open.[27]

When this happened, it came through an incident that carried the battle against extramarital sex and cohabitation, one that generally unfolded in private guest rooms, out into the public world of the restaurant. On December 4, 1906, what became known as the "Englishman letter" appeared in the *New York Times*, reprinted from a dispatch sent the previous day to London's *St. James Gazette*. In the letter, an unidentified British man described the insulting treatment he had received at the hands of "what is generally considered the best hotel, in Fifth Avenue." The man claimed he had been visiting the United States on business, from London. The "wife of an old friend" was traveling to Yokohama to join her husband, "and the latter asked me to escort her as far as San Francisco." They checked into the unspecified hotel under separate names, were assigned rooms on different floors, but, as would be expected of friends, made plans to dine together. On the evening of their arrival they sat in the restaurant, having dinner, when "a shabby looking individual" walked up to them and asked, "in loud, insolent tones," if they were husband and wife.

"On receiving a curt and indignant reply in the negative," the writer continued, "the man shouted out, so that any in the room could hear him: 'Then I guess you will have to clear out of this.'" The outraged visitor asked for the hotel's manager, who confirmed, "'I guess I can't interfere. That is one of our hotel detectives.'" By this time, the female friend, "fearing even greater insults in less world-renowned establishments," begged to leave for the West Coast, "which we did under conditions of the greatest discomfort." The letter was couched as a "warning to those deluded mortals who contemplate a so-called pleasure tour in the United States of America" and asserted that such abrogation of personal liberty was "by no means an unusual occurrence in the best New York hotels." Little surprise, the man added, that "England is an earthly paradise to the rich American." Then he closed with a postscript: "The New York hotel referred to is quite on a par with the Carlton and Savoy Hotels in London."[28]

Naturally, fingers pointed to the Waldorf-Astoria. Oscar, visited by a reporter for the *New York Times* later in the day, "read the letter through carefully," shrugged his shoulders, and said, "'It never happened here.'" To the *World* he averred that if a man and woman "of respectable appearance" arrive together with separate baggage and register under different names, then they would be given "rooms on different floors" and could eat together "as often as they like." Inadvertently, though, Detective Joe Smith, speaking to the *World*, implicated himself by recycling the arguments hotel owners had long put forth to support moral surveillance. Stating his belief that no occurrence "as the Englishman described ever took place in a Fifth avenue hotel," he added that managers of the Waldorf-Astoria "protect our guests" and insisted that women "are safer in New York hotels than they are any-where else in the world." In another article that appeared on December 16 (with the embarrassing headline "Are American Hotels Run by Prudes?"), a Washington hotel manager both implicated the Waldorf and defended it, claiming, "It's perfectly evident to anyone, to what hotel the Englishman refers, and it's one of the best managed in the country."[29]

In all probability the incident *did* take place at the Waldorf-Astoria, how-ever much the letter writer may have overstated certain details. House detectives, in the Waldorf's case, were not employees of a private firm of investigators; rather, they were licensed New York City police officers with individual shield numbers. Each season, hotel management applied directly to the police department for a renewal of officers' plainclothes permits. In other words, when detectives acted anywhere within the Waldorf, it was with municipal authority: for this reason, managers were inclined to give them freedom. Although Oscar told the *World* that, in case of suspicion, an offend-ing party would be "called into the manager's office and asked to explain," evidence indicates that this was not always the case. Both of the Waldorf's surviving logbooks contain references to detectives removing people from one of the hotel's public spaces, summarily and without discussion. What probably happened is that the English man and woman had, earlier that afternoon, transgressed the rules against in-room visitation, not necessarily

The Waldorf's Palm Garden, ready for service, ca. 1902 (Library of Congress).

for romantic purposes. Smith or one of his detectives may have noticed an infraction but wasn't able to catch up to the pair until dinnertime. The "loud, insolent tones" were likely an exaggeration.[30]

This was something new for the hotel industry. There had been editorials written against hotels and restaurants that barred unescorted women, along with others written in support of the Russian writer, Maxim Gorky—who, in 1906, had been ejected from several Manhattan hotels for staying with a woman to whom he was not legally married. But there had never been an open letter written by a patron who was falsely accused of having extramarital relations. The effects were immediate. The night after the letter appeared, George Boldt was hosting a dinner at the Waldorf for the New York State Hotel Association. The keynote speaker, Colonel Archie Baxter of the State Assembly, took the opportunity to lecture the gathered proprietors, good-naturedly, on being "less suspicious of women who go to hotels." Baxter suggested tempering zealous efforts "with a good deal of restraint and discretion." In response, Boldt, when it was his turn to speak, attested to the respect with which women had always been treated at the hotel and recalled an incident in which Louise had witnessed two unaccompanied women being turned away from a top restaurant. At the time she had remarked, as Boldt described it, "George, if you ever do that sort of thing, I'll not speak to you again." Perhaps memories of Louise (who had died three years earlier), coupled with feelings of remorse for those times the hotel may have been hasty in coming to a negative interpretation of its guests' behavior, inspired Boldt's next move.[31]

At some point during the first week of 1907, not long after the "Englishman" episode, Boldt directed his managers to post the following notice on the Waldorf-Astoria's bulletin board:

Ladies without escort will be served in the restaurants hereafter at any hour.[32]

Simple as it was, this single line, placed in the lobby where all could see it, was unprecedented. Never had a New York hotel or restaurant made so public an announcement in favor of women's autonomy. A woman, the notice implied, did not require the accompaniment of a man for validation of her character or personhood: she could be alone without being thought of as intrinsically *less*. The prohibition itself, varying from establishment to establishment with little consistency as to hour or circumstance, had never been stated as "policy" for the benefit of those entering. Because of this its boundaries and applications were always mysterious. Through this action the Waldorf-Astoria exposed an unwritten rule for purposes of effacing it. The posting bore a visual and conceptual impact that was quickly noticed. Oscar, now promoted to a new job as one of the hotel managers, gave a reporter his explanation: "Yes, we will serve women. What else can you do in a hotel? . . . You cannot have a rigid rule that women unattended cannot be served in the dining rooms after 6 o'clock. Of course, we shall continue to be careful.

We must use some discretion. But any woman or women who come here at any time and have the appearance of being respectable will be welcome to dine in any of the restaurants."[33]

As overseer of the hotel's catering and banquet operations, Oscar was in an ideal position to make observations about the changing habits of the women he not only served but met with to arrange plans for parties and luncheons. Suggesting in 1898 that American women were "as busy as the men," he had noted how it was customary for female patrons to "come in in a hurry, take a quick lunch as a man does down town [*sic*], and go off again." Two years later, addressing the rise in popularity of drinking among women, he had seen fit to clarify, in a moment of candor, "It's not soda cocktails they order." Now, asked about motives behind the Waldorf's "ladies without escort" statement, he answered in a way that evinced an understanding of the "New Woman" and her social influence: "Ah, the women are being heard from nowadays. They are found in every business, and in some they lead the men. It was not so a few years ago. . . . But the bars are down now."[34]

All the same, Oscar's comments about continuing to be "careful" and limiting openness to women of "respectable" appearance suggested the barriers had not been completely removed. A *New York Times* reporter observed how the "notice at the Waldorf-Astoria was taken to indicate that the 'new' woman had conquered." But noting that the sign had specified "ladies," rather than the more general "women," he set out to make the rounds of hotels and restaurants to determine wherein, exactly, lay the difference. The night manager of Delmonico's attested that "a lady is one you can tell easily . . . by the way she sits, by the way she orders, by the way . . ." A Waldorf manager, not Oscar, temporized ("Why, my dear Sir—why, a lady, my good fellow, is a—um—lady"), while the proprietor of Shanley's restaurant demurred, "Well, far be it from any man to discuss such a delicate subject."[35]

"Unfortunately," the *Times* writer concluded, "it did not seem to be a question of a woman's right to dine when and where she pleased, but rather one of her eligibility and right to the title of lady." The "extent of feminine supremacy" inferred by the Waldorf's policy was narrow. For all its implied acceptance, something about the sign, the writer intimated, felt insincere. What he didn't state, but surely knew, was that managers were uncomfortable making a reference to prostitution in so public a forum as a newspaper. Much, in an era typified by the separation between outward propriety and what went on beneath the surface, had to remain unspoken. "Ladies" were welcome, but all women were not. Looked at in this way, the Waldorf-Astoria's action, while removing certain limitations based strictly on gender, reinscribed others related to appearance and behavior. As such, it both evened out the playing field—women, in theory, could now dine as the equals of men—and left it open for future battles.[36]

In early twentieth-century New York, roof gardens flourished as carefree accompaniments to a summer evening. Pitched atop hotels, theaters, and restaurants, the "gardens" cooled parties of men and women, weary of the smells and sounds permeating the horse-clogged streets. The Waldorf-Astoria's, set against gables and turrets, made a fairy-tale picture; it was dappled with electric lights resembling, as one observer put it, "clusters of glow-worms." Music—waltzes from Victor Herbert, a pizzicato rustling of strings and harp—surged beneath the clinking glasses and chatter. Eating clams, cucumbers, boneless pigeon in jelly, young couples would cast romantic glances to the purplish clouds turning black past the river, on the Jersey side of the Hudson. Ladies wore hats designed by the likes of Madame Virot—feathery white tulle, clusters of roses, green silk leaves—and wrapped their low-necked dresses in colorful scarves and satin foulards. After a long day working in the heat, with an open window and electric fan the sole relief, New Yorkers delighted to bask in the fourteenth-story winds that dried the sweat from temples and brows.[37]

It was into such a scene that Harriot Stanton Blatch, a women's rights activist and the daughter of suffragist Elizabeth Cady Stanton, entered on July 12, 1907. The place was the roof garden at the Hoffman House, Oscar's first hotel employer, still in business nearly twenty-five years later. Blatch and a female friend had just finished a meeting in nearby Madison Square and wanted refreshment on a warm night. What followed was the by-now customary refusal, with the same explanation that the escort rule was designed to keep out "objectionable women," of the type, the head waiter explained, "you would not like to have dining with you." This time, however, the unescorted woman, Blatch, had a response that was immediately quoted and which lent fervor to discussions of her subsequent lawsuit: "I have never been bothered by objectionable women. When I have been annoyed it has been by men. Do you make an effort to keep objectionable men out of your restaurants? I do not think that you do."[38]

Blatch's comments during the run-up to trial indicated how much she had been thinking of the Waldorf-Astoria's formalized policy regarding women, which had been placed on the bulletin board some six months earlier. Speaking to the *Evening World* and other publications, she explained her intention of forcing a citywide discussion of the escort rule's arbitrariness. A woman, she pointed out, "may dine at the Waldorf without trouble." But in more informal establishments in Harlem and other middle-class areas of the city, "a woman must starve if she has no escort." What was the "dividing line"? Blatch concluded that it was "an exceedingly crooked one." Her arguments were notable for their emphasis on behavior rather than character, with what for the time was a striking suggestion that all women, even those who supported themselves through prostitution, deserved fair treatment: "It is to be inferred that there are occasions when the women of the underworld go into a restaurant purely and simply because they are hungry and give themselves entirely to the business of eating without disturbing any one, and under such circumstances there seems no good reason why they should not be served."[39]

Although the jury decided against Blatch, her case led to favorable developments. Much argument in court hinged on the question of whether Blatch and her friend had been offered an alternate space—be it dining room or café—within the Hoffman House. On this point defendant and plaintiff gave conflicting accounts. But, as one of Blatch's associates pointed out later, the judge had determined, irrespective of the verdict, that women could not be turned away completely. Restaurants and hotels were required to serve all, even if managers still exercised discretion regarding space and location. Further, on the day of the verdict, February 6, 1908, Louis Cuvillier, a member of the New York State Assembly, introduced a bill—inspired by Blatch's experience—guaranteeing to "all persons, including women, whether alone or accompanied by escort," the right of "full and equal accommodations, advantages, facilities and privileges of inns, restaurants, hotels, [and] eating houses." Given that he used nearly identical wording, Cuvillier's evident hope was to take the New York State "Malby" law of 1895, seen widely as a symbolic victory for African American residents (by invalidating, at least on paper, discriminatory entrance and seating policies), and reframe it with women at the center.[40]

Cuvillier's bill was never officially considered by the assembly, perhaps because its language encompassed such traditionally male provinces as "bath houses" and "barber shops." The assemblyman may have simply wanted to make a point. But, in the bill's stated goal, it foreshadowed later struggles over discrimination at institutions such as the New York Athletic Club, which would not admit women until 1989. Growing out of the debate over women's access to recreational space, it also suggested the degree to which the Waldorf had moved, after fifteen years, to a position of influence within American society. More than a business, Boldt's hotel was now a social institution: it set policies that other establishments were pressured to follow. Though the issue would continue to be debated in other states and localities, New York City never witnessed another lawsuit related to the rights of unescorted women in hotels and restaurants. Blatch and her colleagues, assisted by the Waldorf's discreet but visible support, had lifted awareness of the discriminatory rule to the point where those guilty of practicing it would have been targets of scorn. After Blatch, the old escort rule became an embarrassment, and women grew accustomed to dining where and when they pleased.

The proscription against unmarried couples occupying hotel rooms survived, but it was enforced with less rigidity, especially after expensive lawsuits such as the one that entangled the McAlpin, a large tourist hotel not far from the Waldorf, in 1915. In another case of an overzealous hotel detective coming to incorrect conclusions, the plaintiff contended that she was broken in upon while her husband was giving her a doctor-prescribed enema treatment. According to case reports, the husband checked his wife into the hotel, under her name, before leaving to attend to some work. The front desk knew he would be returning, but evidently not everyone on staff received the message. After the chief house detective threatened, upon knocking, that the door would be "broken in," he accused the couple of "prostituting this hotel" and of "using this place for a whorehouse." The enema was halfway done, and the husband protested, "This lady is my wife; I am giving her douches." As if this had been an admission of some outré sexual practice, the detective replied, "So much the worse." A doctor later confirmed that the woman was left in "a very nervous, excitable, and hysterical condition" and had also suffered emotional and physical pain because of the experience. A letter of apology from the McAlpin's manager, L. M. Boomer, did not prevent the couple from filing suit and being awarded the then-considerable sum of $8,000. The McAlpin appealed and lost.[41]

By this time other forces were in play to diminish fears about prostitution within the vicinity of the Waldorf-Astoria and nearby hotels. Chiefly, the Tenderloin, which since the 1870s had operated in the shadow of elegant Fifth Avenue, was dying. Brothels, gambling houses, dance halls—all the "resorts" that once lent the vicinity its flagitious character—had closed, forced out of business by the actions of citizens' groups, civic authorities, and, finally, corporate power (the latter was symbolized most visibly by the opening in 1910 of Penn Station, whose construction had effaced much of the Tenderloin's northern part). Like gambling, which took on a looser, more private character—away from the fixed addresses of brownstones and into private hotel rooms—Tenderloin prostitution grew more diffused in the years after 1910. Places like the Haymarket, viewed by moral crusaders as the most "notorious" of Tenderloin dance halls (once so popular that a Waldorf-Astoria bartender named a drink after its owner), closed or were otherwise cleansed of their illicit elements. Prostitution, of course, still existed in the 1910s, but area hotel operators likely felt relief that it was no longer so brazenly outside the door.

For George Boldt, though, this was not necessarily the good news it might have seemed to be. For, along with the Tenderloin went the theater district.

By 1908, few of the city's top showplaces remained south of Forty-Second Street: New Amsterdam, Victoria, Republic, Lyric, Liberty—these were the new theaters that helped transform Longacre Square (after 1904, Times Square) from a shabby district of carriage manufacturers into the center of American entertainment. Restaurateurs, music publishers, and café operators all followed the northward migration, along with, naturally, audiences and patrons, eager for a taste of the white lights, for the glare of marquees and fifty-foot ads for Budweiser. After-theater patrons, counted on to fill bars and restaurants, largely skipped the Waldorf. Ten blocks south of the action, Boldt's palace was no longer convenient for them. With this drop-off in traffic came the first signs of physical decline and, with it, several cracks in a veneer heretofore thought unbreakable.

"Not until 1910 was it that Boldt began to realize that something was wrong with his hotel," Albert Crockett observed. The Waldorf-Astoria, with its restaurants, ballroom, lobbies, corridors, expensive carpets and elevators, required daily maintenance. Public areas remained tidy, but the guest rooms suffered. Soon, patron complaints mounted to the point where they were impossible to ignore. At the same time, a cluster of new hotels—among them, the St. Regis, Knickerbocker, and, especially, the Plaza, unveiled near the southeastern corner of Central Park in 1907 (replacing an earlier Plaza on the same site)—began to compete for Boldt's wealthier patrons, who sought something newer and, by now, more fashionable. He invested money in rehabilitation, firing his chief housekeeper and striving to improve general conditions, but the onset of war in Europe diminished some of his overseas business. When Boldt died of a heart attack in December 1916, after several years of laboring to bring the hotel back into profit, friends and family blamed the effects of overwork. Crockett observed how Boldt's attempt "to keep his personal oversight over everything . . . found a man of his age [he was sixty-five] unequal to the effort."[42]

Boldt's son, also named George, had been designated as successor, but to most people the Waldorf-Astoria was unimaginable without the bespectacled man who, in the words of one former housekeeping manager, "decided every important detail like a prudent, stern but kind father." Others spoke of Boldt's charitability and drew attention to the volunteer work he performed as a trustee of Cornell University in Ithaca, New York, where, eventually, a residence hall and tower would be named for him. Storied proprietor Simeon Ford, described as the "Mark Twain of the hotel industry" for his skills as a raconteur and wit, also recalled how Boldt, never threatened by competition, had sought amity among his colleagues: "One of the first things he did when he reached town [in 1893] was to invite all the leading hotel men of Manhattan to have luncheon with him at the Waldorf. We were too thunderstruck to refuse."[43]

As president of the Hotel Association, Boldt had honored Ford with a luncheon upon the latter's retirement in May 1914. At the time, George had no way of knowing that one of his cochairs on the event committee would, several years later, assume his position as leader of the Waldorf, in a way that equaled and, arguably, surpassed his own contributions. This was a figure who would usher the Waldorf-Astoria into modern times—overseeing its closure on Thirty-Fourth Street and rebirth on Park Avenue—and, in the process, become one of the most celebrated hotel managers in American history. His name, already referenced as proprietor of the Hotel McAlpin, was Lucius M. Boomer.

CHAPTER 3

"Boom Centre"

Lucius Boomer brought new standards of efficiency to the field of hotel management. For all his success, George Boldt had essentially been an old-fashioned family innkeeper. Ever-present, "on duty" (as Oscar would recall) "from nine in the morning until two the next," he presided over the Waldorf as if it were his home. To patrons he was the kindly, somewhat eccentric gentleman standing by the front desk, ready to offer salutations or a loan. To employees he was a paternal figure, cultivating respect through an environment that was disciplined yet supportive. One internal memo, dictated in 1906 by Oscar (who changed his peremptory tone when writing on the behalf of Boldt), points to a formal brand of civility that would be unthinkable in the twenty-first-century American workplace: "It is the wish of Mr. Boldt that every head of a department carry a memorandum pad in his pocket, so that when he receives verbal instructions from Mr. Boldt, or from another head of a department, he may jot such instructions down, as in this way the instructions are more likely to be carried out. You will find that this is far better than relying on one's memory. Mr. Boldt attaches great importance to the carrying out of this rule."[1]

By contrast, Boomer was brash and focused. Unlike his distrait predecessor at the Waldorf, he came on with a directness that could be intimidating—especially to those meeting him for the first time. He didn't possess much in the way of lightness or humor. In the observation of public relations specialist Edward Bernays, hired by Boomer as a consultant for the Waldorf, his client could be "sarcastic when he felt someone was not particularly bright." A number of people, Bernays recalled, found him "supercilious." Though Bernays felt this conception was inaccurate and somewhat unfair, there was no question that Boomer's style and bearing—he was always "meticulously dressed, a trait he consciously adopted to make his employees aware of what he expected of them"—inspired respect and even fear. Howard Meek, founder of Cornell University's School of Hotel Management in Ithaca, recalled an encounter in 1923, when Boomer showed up early—6:00 a.m.—in preparation for a lecture he had agreed to give. The hotel school was new and, evidently, its location not well marked: "I heard a stomping and a tapping of a cane down the hall. . . . Somewhat irate, [Boomer] said, 'Where do you keep yourself? How does anybody know there is any hotel department here? Nobody has ever heard of you. I have spent a half an hour trying to find you.'"[2]

Later, Boomer, always a proponent of hygiene, visited the home economics cafeteria and was "upset," in Meek's recollection, by the presence of crumbs, the result of a system that allowed visitors to toast their own bread. His complaints didn't end there, as evidenced by a letter written to a colleague several years later: "Another point that I make regarding the work at Cornell is that discipline seems to be completely lacking. Students wander into classes five or ten minutes late. They seem to lack any real respect for authority and the whole atmosphere is one of easy democracy, which is not altogether the atmosphere of business."[3]

Boomer's 1925 book, *Hotel Management: Principles and Practice* (Meek called it "a monumental work in the field"), is packed with charts and graphs supporting the economic value of "scientific organization" in the running of hotels. To run a hotel "intelligently," Boomer wrote, it was necessary "to go deep into details and not be satisfied merely to glance at lump figures of earnings and expenses." There are descriptions of egg boilers, electric toasters, special cutting machines "effective in controlling the amount of butter supplied to a patron"; discussions of toilet seats and the extent of tile to apply to a bathroom wall; suggestions on how to minimize cost through exterior window panes that "never require painting." In ways that presaged the standardization policies of later corporate chains, Boomer (who at one point managed no fewer than five hotels, including the Waldorf) recommended using "one pattern of table linen instead of several," reducing stationery to "a single style and kind," determining a limited set of designs for glassware and china, and removing hotel-specific monograms from dinner plates. This last effort could reduce the cost by "thirty cents a dozen without affecting quality or attractiveness."[4]

George Boldt had been generally relaxed when it came to matters of expense. Wealthy patrons departing by ocean liner often found their cabins stocked with various delicacies, compliments of the Waldorf-Astoria. One 1906 letter, dictated by Oscar at Boldt's request, called for "Half dozen of selected Grapefruit," "Six bottles of milk," "cream," and "specially selected Cherries," among other items, to be put on the steamer of Mrs. C. G. Emery, millionaire wife of a cigarette manufacturer. When Lucius Boomer took control, he did away with some of Boldt's extravagance while ensuring that, in Bernays's description, the surface "amenities of the Victorian era" were preserved: the doorman still "tipped his hat to arriving guests . . . the bellboy hung up the guest's hat and coat after he deposited his hand luggage in his room." Boldt had been a lavish and generous host; Boomer, while wanting to preserve the hotel's reputation for luxury (to the extent that it was profitable), was an accounts-minded businessman.[5]

Still, those who spent any length of time with Boomer came to appreciate him. Beneath the demanding exterior lay a man with finely developed ideals and principles. Howard Meek found him to be "exacting" but "sympathetic." Stocky in build, with thickly handsome features—large oval head; smallish mouth; straight nose; wide, fleshy chin—he exuded a force and decisiveness that made him seem taller than the five feet, eleven inches he once listed on a passport application. Running a hotel endowed Boomer, in his own view, with responsibilities that went beyond the financial: he had taken it upon himself to become, through his profession, a social leader. As community institutions, he wrote, "our great hotels have done much toward promoting the scientific use, combination and concentration of resources." Hotels were more than places to stay; they were "important in solving modern living problems," essential responses to the overcrowding that was characteristic of urban life. He was among the first to establish the concept of hotels as cities within cities, models of social organization in which the varied drives and desires of a metropolis—food, shopping, health, recreation—could be supplied under one roof. Boomer's writings are marked by references to the Waldorf-Astoria as the exemplar of a "New Way of Living"; some even claimed he was the first to connect hotel life with the now-ubiquitous phrase "a home away from home."[6]

Lucius Messenger Boomer came from a line of visionaries and eccentrics. The utopian language he drew upon, frequently and with an idealist's sense of mission, was a product of his familial history—one that would have surprised even those who thought they knew him well. His great-uncle, George Boardman Boomer, was the founder of Castle Rock, an 1850s attempt to build a model New England village, devoted to abolitionist values, in what was described as the most "unprogressive" section of remote southern Missouri. Lucius's grandfather, Lucius Bolles, was a pioneering bridge builder whose works included the first structure to span the Mississippi River as well as commissions for General Grant during the Civil War. Born in Poughkeepsie, New York, in 1878, Lucius Messenger grew up under the tutelage of his father, Lucius Sylvius, who had also entered the family profession as an engineer working with steel. Lucius Junior's was an eventful childhood, marked by frequent changes in residence according to the demands of business: in 1889, while living in Johnstown, Pennsylvania, the family survived a flood that killed more than 2,200 people. All the while, Lucius was surrounded by his father's books—William Smith's *History of Greece, An Introduction to Natural Philosophy* by Denison Olmsted—as well as the teachings of Charles Taze Russell, whose *Millennial Dawn* series prophesied an imminent Second Coming followed by Armageddon.[7]

"Both Mr. and Mrs. Boomer had from childhood an intense interest in religious movements," wrote Lucius Messenger's mother, Berthaldine (referring to herself in the third person). Now settled in Chicago, the Boomers, around 1892, fell under the sway of a messianic leader named Cyrus Teed, who called himself "Koresh" and believed he was the reincarnated Christ. Like many cult leaders before and since, Teed attracted his followers through a progressive stance that, on the surface, at least, touted social and racial justice alongside millenarian appeals to "scientific colonization" and the creation of a "New Jerusalem" that would (according to one pamphlet) welcome the "millions of men, white and black, in the United States and in other countries, ready to enter into the united life system." The Koreshans, as members of the sect came to be known, believed in the potential for immortality through "conservation of the sex energies" and, more significant for the molding of young Lucius's values, the reconciliation of Christian theology with discoveries in science. This last goal inspired Cyrus Teed's most unusual teaching, one that became the epistemological foundation of Koreshanity: all things—humans, animals, vegetation—live not on the surface of the earth but *inside* of it. The world, as one bemused newspaper writer described it, "is a hollow globe." In the words of historian Lyn Millner, Koreshanity "comforted" followers (who numbered, at the order's peak, around 200) with the knowledge that they "lived in a finite world they could understand."[8]

By 1894, sixteen-year-old Lucius Messenger, known to his family as "Louie," was teaching music as part of the newly founded "Koreshan University," established at the group's Chicago compound in Washington Heights (Louie was, by all accounts, a skilled violinist). Later he served as chief engineer of what was to become one of Teed's grand projects: using science to prove the convexity of the earth's surface. Carrying a massive, T-framed device known as the "Rectilineator," Louie, in February 1897, traveled with a team of fellow Koreshans to then-remote Naples beach, in southwest Florida. Working long days in the subtropical climate, Louie and his colleagues battled "rain and storm," winds and nautical accidents, as they slowly, section by section, extended the Rectilineator along the level beach. A sequence of mahogany posts would be planted in the sand; then, heavy crossbars were laid at right angles along a line halfway up the vertical posts. Since there were only three sections of crossbar, the entire process—at the end of which, if Teed's convex theory held, the Rectilineator would hit the upturned surface of beach—was bound to take time.[9]

Lucius Messenger Boomer ("Louie"), front row, second from right, with
the Koreshan Unity orchestra, ca. 1895 (State Library and Archives of
Florida/Alamy).

Before it ended, Louie, who had begun to have doubts about the Rectilineator's accuracy, was called back to Chicago, along with younger brother
Harry: their father, Lucius S., who had funded the whole Florida expedition,
was dead of a heart attack. For a time, it looked as if Louie might stay within
the Koreshan fold. Professor Ulysses Morrow, the project's "Astronomer and
Geodesist" (and inventor of the Rectilineator), attested in a letter written
from Florida that he had heard from Louie, and that "Master [Teed, who was
in Chicago] has helped him and Harry much." But, although he continued
to visit sister Bertha and his mother, Berthaldine (both of whom had moved
permanently to Estero, Florida, site of Teed's New Jerusalem), Lucius appears
to have left the Koreshan "Unity," as the group was known, upon finding
employment in the hotel world. In this he followed the path of many who

grow up in religious environments: as an adult he no longer identified himself as a member of the Unity, even if the group's philosophies (especially
those related to housing and social organization) would continue to bear an
influence. To Berthaldine, who suffered the death of Cyrus Teed in 1908 and
believed sincerely that he would come back to life, Lucius's departure was
hard to swallow. "I want Louie to salt.[as in "put away"] a little bit of his
'hard-earned filthy [lucre],'" she wrote to a fellow Koreshan in 1911, as her
son was beginning to prosper. "I want to turn it to the Unity's and his own
account by making him lay up his treasure in the earthly heaven to be."[10]

She had no way of knowing just how successful Louie would become.
Unsurprisingly, Lucius never mentioned his former Koreshan life to inter-
viewers. A group that made headlines by keeping its leader's dead body in a
Florida bathtub for more than a week, certain it would momentarily resume
breathing, did not exactly fit the life narrative he wished to promote. The
official Lucius Boomer story, repeated with minor variances, began as fol-
lows: Penniless after his father's death, he went to work as a stenographer in
Chicago. Unable to afford an overcoat for the coming winter, he took a train
south, where he found work as a bookkeeper in the Flagler chain, largely
responsible for crafting Florida's popular image as a vacation paradise.
"I didn't know one thing about bookkeeping," he later stated to a newspaper columnist, "but I accepted the job at once . . . [then] went out and bought
a book and studied like the dickens." In the manner of successful Americans who downplay their accomplishments through a self-effacing pose—
one whose surface humility can obviate the revelation of uncomfortable
details—he added, "It must have been a good book, for I made a fair bookkeeper. Eventually I became the head bookkeeper and cashier for a hotel
at St. Augustine."[11]

The hotel was Flagler's Alcazar, a palatial Spanish Revival building designed
by the New York firm of Carrère and Hastings (later the architects for the New
York Public Library on Forty-Second Street). While working at the Alcazar,
Boomer took advantage of the Florida off-season by managing summer hotels
such as the Queen's Royal in Niagara-on-the-Lake, just over the Canadian
border. By 1907 he was in New York, working as the "right-hand" man to Fred

Sterry, partial owner of the new Plaza (designed, like the Waldorf, by Henry Hardenbergh). Later he became treasurer for a company that managed the Lenox, Tuileries, and Empire hotels in Boston. In 1909, thirty-one-year-old Boomer entered into his first venture as a leaseholder, paying (with funds no doubt supplied by investors) a total of $765,000 to occupy the Hotel Nassau in Long Beach, on New York's Long Island. But the biggest development in this phase of Lucius's career arrived at the end of 1912, when his company, Merry & Boomer, came in to manage the giant new McAlpin, located near Macy's department store at the shopping nexus of Herald Square, Thirty-Fourth and Broadway, in Manhattan.[12]

Touted in ads as "A City in Itself," the McAlpin rose twenty-five floors above the street: "so high," the *New York Times* observed, "that the hotel seems isolated from other buildings." Boomer, who not only managed but sat on the board of directors for the governing corporation, used the McAlpin as an incubator for what he described as "progressive" concepts associated (in an example of how Koreshan ideals could be applied within the secular realm) with "community living." Night workers had the benefit of their own floor, on which silence was preserved during all hours of the day. Elsewhere parents could deposit children in a staff-monitored playground. In response to lingering societal ambivalence over the legitimacy of unaccompanied women, and to help female guests themselves feel safe, Boomer created a special floor with its own reception desk accessed by a separate elevator. Women made up the entire floor staff, which included desk clerks, attendants, and restaurant managers. In a statement that no doubt pleased his suffragist-minded mother, Boomer wrote, "There are no real barriers, so far as the [hotel] business itself is concerned, to women achieving whatever positions and whatever success they really *want* to achieve."[13]

Boomer also sought to make the McAlpin a place that was, in his words, "progressively valuable to the worker." Employees had access to health insurance, bonuses, and a savings bank paying 6 percent on deposits, along with social programs designed to reinforce the hotel as a community: athletic and theatrical clubs, an employee-run periodical, English classes for those new to the United States, business instruction in hotel operation, an at-cost grocery store. While the Koreshans were disappointed at Boomer's perversion of their communistic philosophy, tainted by application to a capitalist system, they could at least take comfort in knowing it had an influence. During these years Lucius continued to send money to the settlement in Estero, and Berthaldine felt certain that her son's success had been good "in an indirect way to the cause." Still, for all the conviction of his beliefs, Boomer was first and foremost a businessman, and progressivism could only go so far. In 1918 he rejected the idea that McAlpin waiters who had gone on strike would be reemployed ("We are not sorry they struck," he asserted). Whenever conflicts rose between his mother's egalitarian beliefs and bottom-line questions of economics, the latter prevailed. If one side of Boomer's outlook was shaped by Koreshanity, the other drew upon the ideas of Herbert Hoover, who, in the words of political historian Robert K. Murray, "became the spokesman for the new emerging business age" of the early 1920s: "Secretary of Commerce and, as one critic said, 'assistant secretary of everything else,' [Hoover] popularized not only business prosperity but also the need for business responsibility. His own successful career had not been built on the ruthless individualism of a savage economic past, but on the humanitarian-oriented individualism of a cooperative economic system in which all could share."[14]

Like Hoover, Boomer believed in what Murray described as a "'modern progressivism' of business expansion and scientific efficiency." In the hotel field, which saw enormous growth during the early 1920s as more and more properties were being funded and built, Boomer found an ideal vocation. By the time he arrived at the Waldorf in 1918, he was managing not only the McAlpin (where he would remain, seemingly omnipresent, until 1922) but the Claridge on Forty-Fourth Street and Broadway. Financially, the Waldorf-Astoria had not been doing well. Although it was just one block from the McAlpin, the contrast between Herald Square and Fifth Avenue was greater than simple geographic distance would imply. The former, close to Pennsylvania Station and the cluster of department stores of which Macy's was the centerpiece, was a destination for the middle and working classes. To many of these people, there was no reason to venture as far as Fifth Avenue, which, though growing more commercial, held on to its patrician standing with the Waldorf-Astoria and B. Altman's, a department store considered so exclusive that it did not need to display any sign. The Waldorf was stuck: too elite for denizens of Herald Square, but no longer elite enough for the patrons who had moved north to the St. Regis and Plaza, farther up Fifth Avenue. In 1914 it had lost $60,000; in 1916, close to $240,000—nearly $5.7 million in contemporary figures.[15]

For a time after George Boldt's death, the Waldorf was led by George Jr., described by one observer as "an amiable young man, but not 'heavy' enough to run a big institution like the one which his able father so successfully built up in New York." Junior himself agreed, confessing how the "strain that goes with handling the multitude of matters connected with the Waldorf-Astoria has been very great." Boldt's estate, initially appraised at a minimum of $12 million, had shrunk (after deduction of unpaid debts, losses at the Waldorf and in coffee speculation, plus now-uncollectable loans for which the generous proprietor was known) to a net value of just over $1.1 million. Even the redoubtable Oscar was having problems: after celebrating the marriage of his son, Leopold, to Florence Gerken, wealthy daughter of one of the country's top horse breeders, he was forced to suffer the public humiliation of a divorce suit in which the younger Tschirky was charged with "cruel and barbarous treatment." A manager interviewed in 1918 for the *National Hotel Reporter*, a gossipy trade publication, summed up the general feeling: "There is no gainsaying the fact that for the past several years . . . the big hyphenated hotel has been on the wane."[16]

In stepped General Coleman T. du Pont, who took over the Waldorf's lease and, in an illustration of one of his personal maxims ("I don't do much . . . I pick other men to run things for me"), installed Lucius Boomer as manager. Du Pont, virile captain of industry, highway builder, Republican senator, child of privilege whose wealth did not prevent him, as a youth, from working as a mule driver and blacksmith in one of his family's mines, had a talent for spotting young men of what he described as "whole-souled ambition." By this point, du Pont—one of three cousins who had taken over the family's decrepit powder factory and, through competitor buyouts, transformed it into a leading manufacturer of explosives—had branched into ownership of hotels. Boomer was his protégé, "very able, most practical, a good business man, an honest, hard worker," who, du Pont claimed, was "scrupulously fair, always." He added that Lucius, who, in addition to running the Claridge and McAlpin, had also managed du Pont's Hotel Taft in New Haven, "made good in every hotel proposition he has ever been responsible for." Others agreed that the financier had made the right choice.[17]

"Lucius M. Boomer is a big man mentally," one insider commented. "I don't think there is another hotel man in the United States who has shown so much originality and initiative." Lucius, who once compared managing a hotel to captaining a large passenger vessel, immediately worked to streamline operations at the Waldorf, implementing what had already become known within the industry as the "Boomer system" of accounting, with its forms and charts. From the public's vantage little changed, although women soon became more prominent on staff: in compliance with the government's wartime "work or fight" order, all types of employment deemed nonessential were barred to men of draft age. By June 1918, the Waldorf and Claridge, which Boomer continued to manage, had installed fifteen female elevator operators; Beatrice Foley, chief housekeeper, assumed a position behind the Waldorf's information desk. Lucius reported that all the women newly employed as waiters, historically a man's occupation, were doing good work. Indeed, only one restaurant position still required filling by males over draft age: under state regulations, women were not allowed to serve alcoholic drinks.[18]

As it happened, this last proscription would not matter for much longer, though its removal pointed to a complication rather than an improvement. In his book *Last Call,* Daniel Okrent identified multiple contributors leading to the Volstead Act, which created national Prohibition: decades of lobbying by "dry" forces (representing a motley alliance of suffragists, Protestant fundamentalists, and progressives); the influence of Wayne Wheeler and his powerful Anti-Saloon League; the implementation of federal income tax, which made up for the funds the U.S. government would lose through the absence of a liquor excise; and, finally, wartime anti-German sentiment directed against brewers and their companies. Less generally known, however, is that what could be termed a "dry run" of Prohibition began on July 1, 1919—some six months before the Eighteenth Amendment to the Constitution made it permanent. For a time, restaurateurs, saloon owners, and hotelkeepers felt certain that President Wilson would rescind his Wartime Prohibition Act, which outlawed the sale and manufacture of any beverage containing more than one half of 1 percent alcohol. After all, the armistice had been signed back in November 1918. What need was there for a Wartime Prohibition Act, purportedly designed to conserve resources of fruit and grain, if there was no longer a war?

Wilson remained silent, however, and, across the country, Americans imbibed over the course of what they feared would be a last night of revelry, June 30, 1919. In New York, a double procession formed on Manhattan's Tenth Avenue: one line of people held empty bottles with candles, the other held bottles that were "full when the parade started and empty when it finished." Free hands carried, between the lines, a coffin lid, plodding into Broadway and Times Square. In the Bronx, one group of neighbors held a "prohibition party," complete with jazz music, sandwiches, beer, and wine. Supplementing the *New York World*'s "obituary" for "John Barleycorn," they, too, had a funeral: at midnight, several people lugged a coffin to a vacant site and buried it, "with due and proper ceremony." Many feared the night would outlast available supplies of liquor: at Forty-Second Street's New Amsterdam roof garden, home of the long-running Ziegfeld Follies, ushers and elevator operators were unable to get patrons—who wanted to remain where they knew liquor was plentiful—out of the nine o'clock and into the midnight shows. Elsewhere people just drank whatever they could before the city-mandated closing time. "The crowd isn't trying particularly to have a good time," one hotel manager observed. "Everybody seems to have but one idea and that [is] to get as full of liquor as possible before 1 o'clock."[19]

In the words of historian Michael Lerner, "Wartime Prohibition gave New York City its first glimpse of life under a legal ban on alcohol." Still, with no clear system of enforcement at the federal or municipal level, the law could easily be ignored. Indeed, many bars and saloons continued to operate, "figuring," as Lerner explained in *Dry Manhattan*, "they had little to lose before the Eighteenth Amendment [*real* Prohibition] took effect and put them out of business for good." Only hotels, Lerner pointed out, "readily complied with the wartime dry regulations, unwilling to risk their entire businesses for the sake of liquor sales." As in the earlier fight to distance themselves from Raines law hotels, establishments such as the Waldorf-Astoria wanted to be perceived as respectable and law-abiding. Unlike saloons, furthermore, hotels were large organizations composed of multiple departments that required top-level coordination: alcohol would either be served fully, throughout the premises, or it wouldn't be served at all. Given that Prohibition, whether it arrived in July or January, was a certainty, members of the New York Hotel Men's Association decided they might as well make the necessary operational adjustments and get used to it. On June 30, Lucius Boomer sent the following memo to department heads at the McAlpin, Claridge, and Waldorf: "For your information and guidance: At midnight . . . we will discontinue the sale of all beverages with alcoholic contents. This means literally what is stated and includes wines and beers."[20]

But this *didn't* mean he was happy about it. As a youth Lucius had been exposed to the temperance beliefs of his mother, who once, in a pamphlet, reminded applicants to the Koreshan University that "abstinence from profanity, tobacco, intoxicants, and licentiousness will be required of all students." Later, though, coming of age in the hotel business, he had learned to be tolerant of alcohol and even to enjoy it himself. Returning from a 1923 trip to Europe with his Norwegian-born wife, Jorgine (whom he had married three years earlier), he described conversations with leaders of champagne firms, who "are all unable to comprehend what they are pleased to term the 'hypocrisy of America.'" By "hypocrisy," he, and the champagne producers, referred to the illegal distribution network, created at the start of Prohibition, that allowed Americans—at least those with sufficient incomes—to drink as freely as they had before. "I was told," Boomer added, "that 'buyers' for the United States are doing business on such a scale that they find it necessary to send representatives to Rheims, Epernay and the other centres of the champagne district."[21]

In this system, the largest and most prominent of leisure establishments suffered. Encouraged by the laxity of overseas officials, who had no interest in enforcing what they viewed as the ridiculous laws of a puritanical country, a cadre of enterprising "rumrunners" (in Jazz Age terminology) built fortunes by paying export duties to town governments and loading their ships with alcohol at ports such as Nassau, which grew prosperous as a result. Sailing north, these entrepreneurs deposited their goods in "floating warehouses," situated just outside the three-mile coastal line demarcating American territory, before heading back to the Caribbean for further loads. As Daniel Okrent related, the "mother ships," remaining stationary for months at a time, offered smaller bootleggers (as well as private citizens who owned boats) a "waterborne version of big-city shopping." Customers could sail from ship to ship, select their purchases as if they were at a market, then scurry back to port under cover of night, using signals to avoid detection by the Coast Guard. Eventually, the alcohol, sometimes pure but often diluted with chemicals and dyes, found its way to the tables of small restaurants whose proprietors had discovered that federal enforcement agents, paid little more than what would later be considered minimum wage, were happy to augment their salaries with extra income.[22]

"Everybody who gets about New York," Boomer told a reporter in January 1922, "knows that the restaurants in the central hotel district are supplying the lack of liquor that hotel patrons feel." Dining rooms inside the Waldorf and other hotels were now patronized, he added, "only for necessary meals." In corroboration Ralph Day, Prohibition director for New York State, admitted how "big hotels are helping the prohibition department . . . standing by the law, and losing business as a result." Ironically, what Day referred to as the "best people," the wealthy patrons who had once made the Waldorf a bastion of propriety, were now "furnishing the upkeep of all the little eating places where liquor is sold." While Day promised to boost his staff—which, in early 1922, consisted of little more than 300 agents for the entire state—Boomer and his colleagues at the Hotel Association grew increasingly frustrated at what they considered an inattentiveness and lack of enforcement. According to one estimate, liquor-related losses at Boomer's New York hotels (which, by now, included the Waldorf, McAlpin, Claridge, and Martinique) were exceeding $4 million annually.[23]

"Closing the bar," asserted Roy Carruthers, Boomer's new second-in-command at the Waldorf, "was like taking the most profitable department away from the storekeeper." Desperate, Boomer and other members of the New York Hotel Association wrote a letter to U.S. President Warren Harding, pleading with him to intercede on their behalf by augmenting enforcement and clamping down on Times Square speakeasies. The letter, reprinted in city papers on June 8, 1922, brazenly went over the head of Prohibition director Day, who, in retaliation, dispatched a squad of agents to raid the Claridge less than a week later—an open act of harassment that, expectedly, uncovered nothing alcoholic. In response, an angry Boomer shut down the hotel, leasing it to a real estate operator who converted it to stores. Although other defunct hotels, including the Holland House and Knickerbocker, had been rumored to be victims of Prohibition, the Claridge was the first in New York to shutter for that formal reason, as stated by Boomer on June 25: "Unequal enforcement of the Volstead act by prohibition officers has forced me to lease the Hotel Claridge for business purposes."[24]

Given its larger size, the Waldorf, Boomer explained, could partially make up for the lost revenue through room rates, which had been increased between one and three dollars per night. In addition, he discovered potential in unused space: a portion of the Waldorf's storied wine cellar, once among the largest in the city, was fitted up with weights, running track, and showers and turned into a gym. At the same time candy, pastries, and soft drinks emerged as profitable answers to the craving of a stimulant-hungry public, to an extent that would have appalled later generations of health advocates. As if in discovery of silver linings, *Hotel World*, a trade periodical, even touted the similarity of effect: "Candy chemically is converted into alcohol in the human system, and even the Prohibitionists can't stop this conversion by statute . . . !" In the same issue the author of a cookbook, *Candy for Dessert*, reinforced this point by citing sugar as "one of the most easily digested foods that satisfy." The Waldorf did its part by installing a confectionary and soda counter, where, beginning on July 1, 1919, the old cocktail menu

Lucius Boomer at the peak of his career, early 1930s (Frank Rust/Associated Newspapers/Shutterstock).

was demobilized and a new one, offering one hundred sweet concoctions, slipped into its place. While the names, sprinkled with "fizz," "punch," and "cooler," were similar to those of their alcoholic predecessors, no one was fooled.[25]

"The night life was dead," observed architectural historian H. I. Brock. "No hotel since prohibition has been as heartily a part of real life in this great city as it used to be." Writing in the third person, Brock (from the vantage of 1925) recalled visiting the Waldorf's roof garden soon after Wartime Prohibition took effect. His drink, he bemoaned, "was something in a glass pitcher called a 'cup'": "He remembers still the look of the familiar headwaiter who ventured to propose it—his look as he brought it on like that of a dog who has been killing sheep. And the desperately disappointed expression of the young person of the opposite sex who shared the beverage. After a brave sip or two the pitcher stood neglected. The conversation languished."[26]

For many, the end of the original Waldorf-Astoria was symbolized by an event during the last week of January 1920, when, "piece by piece," the hotel's bulky four-sided bar—revered as the inventing place of the Bronx Cocktail as well as concoctions with names like "Baby Titty"—was, in the words of the New York Herald, "carried away to drawing rooms and parlors throughout New York." A structure many had thought would last forever was now revealed, with the "tearing away" of the "great mahogany elbows and joints," as destructible, "tucked . . . under arms and beneath coats to keep the rain and snow from damaging it." Many of the souvenir hunters were "gray haired men," old denizens who stood waiting until "every piece" was gone and a giant hole facing Peacock Alley took its place.[27]

"The Waldorf, though it is still an institution," claimed Brock, "does not touch . . . the life of New Yorkers . . . so nearly as it used [to]." Prohibition, among other unintended effects, was responsible for an illicit flowering of city nightlife, one pushed out of public view and into the secluded domain of brownstone cellars and private "clubs," whose "members" were issued numbered cards. With a single piece of legislation, old patterns governing hangouts like the Waldorf bar (which remained, to the end, an exclusively male preserve) were broken down. Women, who had fought so hard for equality in the open-air roof garden, now found themselves accepted as one of the boys. In the new demimonde, social barriers related to gender and (in the case of certain Harlem speakeasies that catered to an integrated clientele) race, gave way. Hidden on side streets, generally thought to be safe from raids due to liberal exchange of protection money, Prohibition-era nightspots gave New Yorkers an idea of all the things they could do when no one was looking. In short, Jazz Age Gothamites, living in what was regarded as a "wet" city (i.e., one where alcohol was easily procurable) at a time of artistic creativity and the liquor that went with it, were not going to choose a hotel soda fountain for their gathering spot.[28]

After the onset of Prohibition, Brock wrote, the Waldorf began to seem "foreign"—*in* New York but not of it. This was a startling change for an institution that had built much of its fame through balancing the tastes of New Yorkers with out-of-towners' appetites and desires. During the 1920s the Waldorf-Astoria, though still a popular site for meetings and banquets, lost much of its local patronage: few people, any longer, chose to visit its dining spaces unless they were staying there. But one event, the Democratic National Convention in the summer of 1924, proved the old hotel still had the capacity to bring diverse groups together, at a time when New Yorkers and their fellow Americans seemed more opposed than ever. In the last great moment of the old hotel's life (aside, that is, from its colorful destruction), it played host to two warring forces. They were fighting over Prohibition: the cause of the missing bar, much of Lucius Boomer's financial trouble, and all the drama that ensued.

In October 1923, Boomer was one of hundreds of city leaders, marshaled by real estate mogul Joseph P. Day, to serve on a nonpartisan committee organized to convince the Democratic Party to hold its 1924 national convention in New York. For the Waldorf and other hotels whose revenues had suffered under Prohibition, this could be a boon: one week or longer in summer (still considered a soft time of year for hotel traffic) at full capacity for rooms and restaurant tables. In fact, so hopeful was the New York Hotel

Association that its members raised their entire quota, part of the $250,000 total anticipated as necessary to win the bid, within two weeks of the committee's inception. They further pledged not to increase room rates for the thousands of delegates expected to stream into town for what would become, without question, a historic event: New York had not hosted a national political convention since 1868. As its social and cultural prominence increased during the years after the Civil War, a mounting sense of the city's separateness from the rest of the country had given rise to the idea, framed positively or negatively depending on perspective, that New York was not really America. Hosting the Democratic National Convention would, in Day's summation, give the city a chance to prove it was a place for all; not "New York, N.Y." but "New York, U.S.A."[29]

By early 1924 the bidding had narrowed to four cities: New York, Chicago, St. Louis, and San Francisco. Boomer sent his chief manager, Roy Carruthers, to Washington as part of a small but diverse delegation including Ralph Pulitzer, publisher of the *New York World* (which credited itself for first proposing the convention plan), boxing promoter and Madison Square Garden proprietor "Tex" Rickard, and Eleanor Roosevelt. On January 13, representatives of the cities offered their pitches, one by one, to the Democratic National Committee (DNC). San Francisco, host of the Democratic convention in 1920, touted benefits of climate for the "average delegate" who was over the age of fifty, turning off DNC members who, in the words of the *World*, resented the suggestion that delegates would be "decrepit candidates for old men's homes." St. Louis simply didn't have the money, and Chicago, it was felt, could use a rest: it had hosted one of the parties in every convention year since 1896. Finally, New York offered a lot of money: the total of $255,000 in combined cash and a guaranteed portion of concession sales at Madison Square Garden, where the convention would be held. For a financially strapped DNC, still operating under a deficit of $180,000 from the 1920 convention, New York was the obvious choice: it won unanimously on the third ballot.[30]

With that, reported the *World*, offering readers the kind of "inside" political view for which the paper was known, "the curtain settled on as harmonious if lively [a] session as ever the committee held." The upbeat mood would not last. Decades later, historians would still be analyzing the complicated mix of factors that made the 1924 Democratic Convention the longest and most rancorous in American political history. A party bifurcated along regional lines—nativist, agrarian Protestant South and West versus urban, industrial North with its large Catholic and Jewish immigrant base—struggled to reconcile deep social divisions born out of conflicting attitudes on race, equality, and religion. United in opposition to the Republicans and what William Jennings Bryan, standard-bearer for the populist Democratic wing of southern politics, railed against as "the demands of Wall Street," Democrats in 1924 often seemed to agree on little else. In the political climate of the early 1920s, it was possible for a Democrat to support women's suffrage yet turn a blind eye to the growing political influence of the Ku Klux Klan, which had been revived in the wake of D. W. Griffith's racist 1915 film epic, *The Birth of a Nation*. At the same time, eastern Democrats, united under the scrappy but amiable banner of New York governor Al Smith (onetime Lower East Side Catholic schoolboy), openly derided Prohibition and made religious freedom a rallying point. Soon these conflicts would manifest themselves at the Waldorf, which became Madison Square Garden's unofficial annex: site of the "Waldorf Convention," as one columnist described it.[31]

"I cannot speak too highly of the attitude and position of [Waldorf manager] Roy Carruthers," exclaimed a Democratic official, "in the arrangements made by his hotel." Carruthers, it was implied, gave an affordable deal on rent: within days of New York's winning bid, it was announced that the Waldorf-Astoria would become, for the duration of the convention, Democratic National Committee headquarters. Soon managers and representatives of the various state candidates, eager to be as close to the offices of the DNC as possible, rushed to acquire space in the hotel's many suites. Ohio's James Cox, who had lost by a wide margin to Warren Harding in the 1920 presidential race, arrived first, setting up quarters in a former brokerage office on the main floor. Then, in a bit of irony noted by newspaper columnists with fond memories of earlier days, John Davis of West Virginia, former U.S. ambassador to Great Britain and a "dry" in favor of Prohibition, was assigned the exact spot the Waldorf's legendary bar once occupied. Next, a partition was constructed, and Alabama's Oscar Underwood, a "wet" fierce in his opposition to the Klan, moved into the barroom's old seating area. With the final addition of secondary headquarters for Al Smith himself, directly facing Underwood and Davis across Peacock Alley, the Waldorf's street level came to resemble a map of opposing armies. Among major candidates, only William McAdoo, a suffragist dry widely known as the Klan's choice (he never encouraged the KKK, but he didn't repudiate it either), chose a different hotel, setting up lavish quarters on a floor of the nearby Vanderbilt, at Thirty-Fourth Street and Park Avenue.[32]

"The Waldorf-Astoria will be the boom centre," proclaimed the *Times* on June 19, 1924, employing a term that first surfaced in the 1870s to describe lobbying for a particular political candidate: to "boom" for someone meant to rally support. Early on, supporters of McAdoo (who, with his pro-labor, dry stance, appealed to progressives in the West and South) voiced concern about New York as a convention city; they would, many feared, be ganged up on and bullied by advocates of the enormously popular Al Smith. To some extent their fears were justified. Despite his two unsuccessful presidential bids, Alfred Smith—addressed with a "Hello, Al!" by friends and strangers alike—was one of the most beloved political figures in New York. Upon arrival, Smith's managers stretched an enormous banner across Thirty-Fourth Street in front of the Waldorf; everywhere they went, delegates encountered Smith's distinctive *New Yawk* visage (one writer described him as a "homely man with sun-burned face and tousled hair") on posters, buttons, and signs. Franklin Delano Roosevelt, nominating Smith for the presidency in what became known as the "Happy Warrior" speech for its allusion to Longfellow, spoke of his candidate's everyday appeal: "If you would know what the hearts of the masses hold for him, ask anyone; when you leave this session, ask the woman who serves you in the shop, the banker who cashes your check, the man who runs your elevator, the clerk in your hotel."[33]

The 1924 convention was notable for being open to the public, another source of concern for McAdoo, who had emerged as Smith's chief competitor. The moment Roosevelt voiced his nomination for Smith, Madison Square

Garden became, in the words of Robert Murray, "a cauldron of sound and movement." High in the galleries, where the Smith rabble was at its most bumptious, fire sirens hitched to portable batteries let out a terrifying blare that endured for close to forty minutes. Smith, chewing cigars, spent most of his convention time off-site, in an armchair at the Manhattan Club, adjacent to the Garden. But whenever he ventured out, to Waldorf-Astoria headquarters, pandemonium ensued. Once a cameraman made the mistake of asking people to pose with Al on the Waldorf sidewalk: the crowd lunged with such ferocity that the camera was overturned. A reporter for the *Sun* wrote of how Smith was "nearly smothered" at the Waldorf by "enthusiastic friends," as the "yelling, perspiring mass . . . set up a great ovation." Marching bands tromped down Peacock Alley, eschewing Irving Berlin's new composition, "We'll All Go Voting for Al," in favor of the longtime Smith theme song, "Sidewalks of New York." During one such Waldorf procession, what the *World* described as a "big good natured appearing man" decided to have some fun with the crowd, shouting, "Three cheers for Wayne B. Wheeler," the much-loathed (in New York) head of the Anti-Saloon League: "a howl went up from hundreds of throats" as a "rush was started for the man."[34]

As the convention proceeded, the Waldorf took on the appearance of a train station, active around the clock. Bellboys, known at the Waldorf for their eagerness to dispense with helpful touristic information, were overheard explaining to English visitors, stopped on the elevator in front of DNC offices, "These are all Democrats getting out." Reporters jabbed at how delegates "from the rural sections if clothes are a criterion" tried to maintain some semblance of "home hours" by getting back to their rooms around ten o'clock, in an "imitation rush hour." Other delegates, more culturally inclined, would give elevator operators a "busy time" between midnight and one o'clock as they returned from the theater. Even later, small groups would "form in the corners" of the lobby or else remain on the sidewalk, talking in the June night until the "dark before the dawn" arrived and they, too, disappeared "into the elevators." Notorious personages, including Harry Thaw, killer of architect Stanford White, appeared in the Waldorf lobby, as did a "tall, slender young man" later revealed to be Milton Elrod, editor of the Klan publication *Fiery Cross*. New Yorkers approached them with irreverent humor. In one Waldorf scene an Indiana delegate pontificated, "What this country needs is a return to fundamental principles." Referencing Governor Ralston, Indiana's favorite son candidate (and, it happened, a favorite of the Klan), the man went on: "What the Democratic Party needs is contact with the soil so that, like Antaeus after renewed contact with his mother Earth, it may rise revivified for the coming campaign. What the party needs is a rustic candidate like Sam Ralston. He was born and bred between two rows of corn."

"Oh, a pumpkin," someone interrupted. It was a "New Yorker with an 'Al' Smith button on the lapel of his coat." Humor masked anxiety: at the time, a group of Klansmen had set up headquarters in a suite at the McAlpin, where they circulated copies of the anti-Catholic newspaper *Fellowship Forum*. Then, on Independence Day, an estimated 20,000 Klan members gathered in Long Branch, New Jersey (ironically, known at the turn of the century as a liquor and gambling resort), to protest Smith's candidacy. Beneath the surface conviviality—food, picnics, weddings—lay a threatening element. One speaker, a Klan leader from Indianapolis, told of how he had just returned from *"Jew* York," asserting that, much as Smith supporters would like to see their candidate win, "there will not be anybody but a Protestant as President or Vice President." One vending shack had been set up with an effigy of Smith, clutching a whiskey bottle: "Keep Al Smith out of the White House," a sign read, "3 shots for 5 cents." "For hours," reported the *Times*, "men, women and children [cheered] the throws of those whose baseball found the eyes of the effigy." By the end of the afternoon, Smith's caricature had been "pounded to a battered pulp."[35]

To the Klan, which reached a peak of membership and political influence during 1924 and 1925, Al Smith—urban, Catholic, of immigrant background—was dangerous and foreign. Through verbal attacks the likes of which would be familiar to later generations, a presidential candidate's basic Americanness was questioned. The 1924 convention, meant to be an expression of unity, instead exposed the fissures separating groups of citizens along social and economic lines. To many observers, it appeared as if the

Democratic Party no longer had the power to hold its diverse constituency (what one columnist referred to as its "many-colored cloth") together. The political system Americans trusted in was breaking down: each day, delegates submitted ballot after ballot in a futile attempt to nominate an electable candidate. The convention environment didn't help: poorly ventilated, stifling in midsummer, riddled by demonstrations from fans of both Smith and McAdoo, cavernous Madison Square Garden had become inimical to the solving of problems. After the seventy-seventh ballot, candidates' representatives (including Franklin D. Roosevelt, who was managing Smith) decided it was time for what they called a small "harmony" conference, to be held in more favorable surroundings.[36]

"Room 310 of the Waldorf Hotel now holds the fate of the Democratic Party," proclaimed the *Louisville Courier-Journal* on July 6, 1924. By now, Al Smith and William McAdoo were deadlocked: neither had achieved the two-thirds majority required to win the nomination, but each held on to enough votes to prevent one of the remaining "dark horse" candidates from ascending. The Waldorf harmony conference, which the *Chicago Tribune* described as "the convention in miniature," proved to be, like its larger companion, ineffectual. Smith indicated that he would withdraw from the race, but only if McAdoo pulled out at the same time. McAdoo, who had more votes than any other candidate, resisted. Already, many of the delegates, exhausted and out of funds, had gone home, and an irritable mood had descended on much of the city. One western delegate, believing he had been overcharged by six cents on a telegram, blurted to the clerk, in a fit of overreaction, "This is the last convention New York will ever see, let me tell you!" McAdoo supporters derided the "tactics of New Yorkers and the assaults by a hostile press," while the Smith camp charged its opponent with spreading rumors that delegates were being bribed with "women and liquor." One delegate, believing Democrats were already "beaten," summed up the situation and his feelings about it: "We are in a family row over a religious issue.... I'm disgusted."[37]

To an extent, the very publicness of the Garden and the Waldorf, both of which had opened their doors to newspapers and radio networks (the latter had still been in their infancy during the 1920 convention), fueled the conflict and inhibited its resolution. Delegates, scrutinized and made fun of with every new report, became self-conscious, digging deeper into their positions out of fear of being viewed by their constituency as spineless. One Fifth Avenue department store owner noted this phenomenon in ways that pointed to the burgeoning influence of media during the twentieth century: "The delegates have never had laid before them such voluminous accounts of their own doings in convention. . . . This tends to magnify and place in a strong light all dissensions and disputes. It doesn't allow the delegates to do the amount of forgetting that is necessary when their business is to compromise and get together."[38]

In the end, through late-night meetings held in "smoke-filled" rooms at the Waldorf and other hotels, both Smith and McAdoo were persuaded to step down. The deadlock broken, a compromise candidate, West Virginia's John Davis (the "dry" whose headquarters had occupied the old Waldorf bar), quickly secured the nomination. In a speech to convention delegates on the evening of July 9, 1924, Al Smith affected bonhomie as he promised to take off his "coat and vest" and work toward Davis's election. He even claimed, unconvincingly, that if he were to confess disappointment, "it would not be true." Notwithstanding these efforts to come off as a good sport, Smith's self-aggrandizing tone—in the speech he extolled his gubernatorial achievements on everything from workman's compensation to water power while boasting of New York as "the greatest city in the world"—gave some indication of his true feelings. Biographer Christopher Finan has suggested that Smith, whose gruff appearance contrasted unfavorably with that of erudite Davis, was "angrier than he was willing to admit." Indeed, Finan observed, Smith's "pride had been stung."[39]

Smith's resentment gave extra meaning to events that took place five years and three months later, when Al stood on the roof of the Waldorf-Astoria and posed for photographers. In a temporary break from politics, he had assumed directorship of the corporation that would oversee development of a new skyscraper—eventually known as the Empire State Building—to rise eighty-five stories on the old hotel site. That morning, October 2, 1929,

Al held one end of a rope that had been lassoed around a piece of fancy Beaux-Arts cornice—hopelessly outmoded in an age of steel and gleaming lines—and pulled. As if enjoying the chance to punish the Waldorf for being part of his humiliation and defeat, a smiling Al Smith—onetime gambler, denizen, and bar patron—delivered the opening blow in its destruction.

Two months after the convention, in September 1924, Boomer, still in partnership with Coleman du Pont, arranged for purchase of the Waldorf-Astoria building and land, which had remained—over the course of twenty-seven years—in the hands of the two Astor estates. The Waldorf's economic future, it was determined by Boomer, having observed the success of the former Knickerbocker and his own Claridge (both of which had been converted to offices and stores), lay in retail. Accordingly, "a number of high-class shops and possibly a banking establishment" were announced for the ground floor spaces that had, only recently, housed political candidates. At the time, ownership appeared like a wise move: it gave the new Waldorf-Astoria Realty Corporation, which Boomer had organized, control over "one of the largest single pieces of centrally located property in the city." But it also created a burden: among New York hotels, the Waldorf-Astoria bore the distinction of receiving the highest tax assessment. For 1926, this leaped to $12.6 million—more than five times the city average.[40]

"The shrewd foresight of the Astors in selling the property is now plain," a Waldorf corporation lawyer would state in 1936, five years after Boomer and his partners initiated a suit against the city to recover payments on taxes that had, they argued, been overassessed. "Although [the Astors] sold before the top of the market was reached, they saw the signs of the local change certain to affect their hotel." By the late 1920s, only a handful of first-class hotels remained below Forty-Second Street. The Metropolitan Opera House, filling an entire city block at Thirty-Ninth and Broadway, survived as a relic of nineteenth-century splendor; otherwise, much of the area surrounding the Waldorf was now given over to factory buildings comprising the Garment District, which maximized revenue through stacking twenty or more floors onto tiny parcels of ground. The Waldorf was simply too short and too wide to be profitable: its operating losses grew in size for each year from 1925 onward. Boomer alluded to all of this in a memo he sent employees on December 20, 1928: "You will realize that in the Waldorf-Astoria there are great areas of unproductive space which the more modern hotel has avoided. Nevertheless, all of this space is subject to enormous tax, has to be heated, lighted, &c."[41]

For some time, rumors had floated within the real estate industry that du Pont and Boomer were preparing to sell. However, room occupancy at the Waldorf remained generally high, even as restaurant business declined. The hotel's workers, 1,400 in number according to one estimate, were therefore shocked when they read further and came to the main point of Boomer's memo: "Commencing with the losses through prohibition, which destroyed a highly remunerative branch of our business, without compensation, the increased cost of operation and numerous taxes have become so burdensome that it is no longer justifiable to continue the hotel." The closure, remarked the *Times*, would mean "more than the passing of a hotel"; it would mark "the passing of an American institution, for the Waldorf-Astoria occupied a unique position in American life."[42]

On May 1, 1929, the old Waldorf witnessed so much activity that visitors—middle-aged couples returning to the scene of honeymoons, the "rich men, poor men and beggar men" who "streamed in and out of the lobby doors"—may have been able to trick themselves, for a moment, into thinking the glory days were back. Garrulous bellhops led curiosity seekers on tours of the rooms where presidents and potentates once slept, while guests, including Fred Muschenheim, Hotel Astor proprietor and the Waldorf's rival, attended multicourse meals for breakfast, lunch, or dinner. Meanwhile, a gavel sent staccato shots across the terrace of the roof garden, where mahogany tables and upholstered chairs passed into the arms of winning bidders, alongside rugs, mirrors, and gooseneck lamps. Peacock Alley, relinquishing its elitist pretensions, became a bargain hunter's paradise: one Miss M. J. Lange, of Baraboo, Wisconsin, had the honor of walking away with the first batch of ashtrays, saucers, and cups. While most expressed regret for the passing

Golden age: demolition workers at the original Waldorf-Astoria, 1929
(Library of Congress).

of a landmark, few visitors would have thought to argue against the forward march of progress: the idea that city government might step in to protect a historic structure was decades away. Still, one happy note prevailed
within an otherwise subdued celebration: Boomer had decreed that all
proceeds from the hotel's final day, May 1, would be donated to a benefit
fund for employees.[43]

"The Waldorf-Astoria did not go gladly," observed Empire State Building chronicler John Tauranac. Demolition took four and a half months. The
Waldorf had been constructed with solidity and heft; as architecture, it was
designed to last longer than the thirty-six years claimed by its oldest section. By December a rubbish wagon, its sides packed with debris, sat in the
lobby, resting atop wooden floorboards that had been stripped of tilework.

Workers, poking fun at the reputation of the place they'd been hired to destroy, posed for reporters in Edwardian attire, accessorizing their dust-filled overalls with top hats and monocles while using shovels for canes. A large bronze statue of an ethereal female, swathed in robes and pulled from its original cornice perch, had been repurposed as a coat rack: derby hats slanted rakishly above flowing locks and an impassive classical face. One worker took his lunch in a porcelain bathtub, lounging with a pipe and newspaper, while downstairs, in part of the basement, others came across a stash of empty wine bottles and liquor crates. Wooden box sides announced the names of forgotten whiskey brands, including the one that stood out most prominently: GOLDEN AGE. The words jumbled alongside another—GRAND—in a toppling pile.[44]

Meanwhile, a long plot of real estate, improbably set above track lines for the New York Central Railroad, was slowly being cleared some fifteen blocks to the north. It was here, on a once-grubby stretch of Park Avenue dominated by a boiler plant, that Lucius Boomer was realizing his dream for a new Waldorf-Astoria.

CHAPTER 4

Temporary Storms and Stress

While Lucius Boomer was generally admired, there were a few, from time to time, who questioned his judgment in matters of business. One such skeptic was Robert A. Taft, future senator and son of the former U.S. president. In 1922, the younger Taft sat on the board of the corporation that ran the Hotel McAlpin. Boomer, then in the process of resigning as manager after a scuffle with the board chief, was, in Taft's view, no longer the best person to run the McAlpin, having weakened his energies through the oversight of too many properties and becoming "a kind of financier." Since partnering with Coleman du Pont in 1918, Lucius had directed a greater amount of time toward establishing corporations, bringing together the names and fortunes that would run the Waldorf and other ventures. Boomer's sincerity was never in question, but the finer points of what would happen later, once projects got underway, were not always worked through with the kind of attention that had initially secured his reputation in the industry. This could have been a natural consequence of his increased responsibilities: as Boomer himself wrote in *Hotel Management*, the chief executive of a hotel needed to be "relieved of detail duties" in order to have "a detached view of his enterprise as a whole." In any case, when it came to his decision to purchase the Waldorf hotel and property in 1924, Boomer had evidently not considered the likelihood of enormous taxes, previously borne by the Astor estates, along with higher tax assessments based on the addition of retail.[1]

"Personally," Taft wrote his father in 1922, "I should not be afraid if Boomer left[,] for [the McAlpin] can afford to employ the best hotel man in the country. And I think there are better than Boomer." One story in particular reveals Boomer's strengths alongside his weaknesses. On the evening of April 12, 1927, the tower of the unfinished Sherry-Netherland, a new hotel Boomer was financing with du Pont near the southern edge of Central Park, caught fire. A furnace used to heat rivets for construction earlier in the day had likely been allowed to simmer, emitting sparks that fell onto sawhorses and other temporary structures left behind by workers. Flames spread to the wooden scaffolding of the tower, which shot, in one description, "blazing timbers ten feet and more in length," to the corner of Fifty-Ninth Street and Fifth Avenue, "revolving like gigantic pinwheels as they descended." As many as 100,000 people, gathering in the "ringside streets," risked injury from crashing beams as they watched the fire, which lasted ten hours and could be seen as far away as the Bronx. The whole situation, observed the city's fire commissioner, was an example of the "folly of putting up framework scaffolding around a building thirty or forty stories high." Once a fire started "in such a place," the commissioner noted, there was "no way of fighting it."[2]

At the time Boomer and his builders were criticized, by the New York Board of Fire Underwriters, for not having constructed "a wholly enclosed elevator suitable to carry a forty-gallon chemical fire extinguisher on wheels." Had they done so, the underwriters stated in a report, the fire "probably could have been easily extinguished in its early stages." The fact that no major damage had been inflicted on the Sherry-Netherland's main structure, as Boomer would proclaim, had really been "a matter of luck more than anything else." Yet, while Boomer undoubtedly could have taken steps to avoid the ordeal, no one could fault the quiet perseverance he displayed once it started. Lucius was no stranger to disaster: beyond his childhood survival of the Johnstown flood of 1889, he had suffered months in a Florida hospital, after getting his first hotel job, battling typhoid fever. Whatever happened, he had been through worse. Describing the Sherry-Netherland fire, in 1927, journalist Niven Busch noted how Boomer had merely "stood in the crowd for three or four hours" that evening, "looking up." It didn't appear as if this "man watching [his] skyscraper . . . blaze like a wax match" felt "any particular emotion."[3]

The story of the Sherry-Netherland, which managed to open just seven months after the fire, is useful for appreciating Lucius's coolheaded manner during the troubled early years of the new Waldorf-Astoria, plans for which were revealed to the public in March 1929. To some, a block-sized hotel, projected to cost more than $28 million ($420 million in current figures), would seem to defy standards of prudence. Since the early 1920s, bankers, real estate professionals, and those within the hospitality field had been warning that too many hotels were being constructed throughout the United States. Lumping hotels with "office buildings" and "apartment houses," banker S. W. Straus asserted, in 1927, that after "five years of very heavy building," American cities had "reached the saturation point in these . . . types of structures." The year before, hotel magnate E. M. Statler had been more direct, arguing that the building of new hotels "should be based on facts—not hopeful fancies." Statler acknowledged the risk of being classed as part of a band of "unwelcome prophets"—the kind who "pull long faces and utter solemn warnings to people who at the time are prosperous and happy"—when he cautioned of the "wasteful over-production" that could threaten "the entire hotel industry."[4]

Not all of Statler's industry colleagues were as pessimistic. Buoyed by profits connected with the auto trade, one Detroit hotel operator, speaking in 1925, pointed to how the Ford company was producing "9,000 cars a day" and "breaking all records." The head of Chicago's Palmer House enthused how "millions" were "being spent in new hotel construction" in that city "because of the demand for accommodations"—one that reflected "the country's prosperity." While Prohibition had undoubtedly cut into hotel profits, some within the industry felt there had been a silver lining to the loss of liquor. Speaking in 1927, one hotel expert indirectly credited Boomer when he asserted that the move toward "more scientific methods" in the operation of hotels—already "well underway in 1919"—was "speeded up and pushed ahead many years by the peremptory demands that prohibition

brought about at that time." Profits resulting from a more economical operation were augmented by the high occupancy that came with greater numbers of people traveling for business and pleasure. As a result, hotels were
able to raise their nightly room prices. The industry, averred one manager,
was simply ramping up to meet a public need: "We would not be able to
develop and increase as we have done . . . except that the hotel business and
general business are so flourishing." By 1928 the boom was showing no sign
of abatement: that year, thirty-seven hotel plans were filed in Manhattan
alone.[5]

Hotels were part of a larger construction wave that transformed American downtowns in the 1920s. In New York, entire neighborhoods—among
them, the Midtown district of which the new Waldorf would be part—were
made over into skyscraper cities-within-cities. Skyscrapers, with frames of
light, durable steel, promised a high return on investments by making the
most of small parcels of land. And, by the early years of the decade, new
developments in elevator technology were allowing them to grow taller and
taller. What one British architect described in 1928 as "[America's] greatest
contribution to world development" would not have been possible without
the teams of aerial workers—the press dubbed them "sky boys"—who, in
apparent defiance of fear, regularly traversed girders just inches wide as they
added to a building's frame, piece by piece. It was the sky boys—many were
from seafaring backgrounds and had worked on the masts of ships—who
became responsible for one of the most widely recognized photographs in
Waldorf-Astoria history. In it, two construction men straddle a hovering
beam, as a Waldorf meal arrays itself on the low table between them. Behind
each diner stands another worker, dressed in full waiter's uniform (black
jacket, bow tie) and balancing a tray of bottles and foodstuffs in his hand.
One of the seated men looks down at the expanding city, the roofs and ter-
races whose height the Waldorf, in 1930, was already surpassing.[6]

The photo, accompanied by a short promotional film in which the "waiters" could be seen getting their customary instructions from Oscar before
being hoisted skyward, feet nesting in the bends of metal hooks, echoed that
of the previous year, when workers similarly donned elegant hats and took

afternoon tea amid the wreckage of the old Waldorf kitchen. Only this time, the gag had been set up to portend a lofty future—the hotel's renowned service taken to new heights—rather than to memorialize the lustrous, now-crumbled past. The new Waldorf was to be the world's tallest hotel: in July 1929 the *Herald Tribune* had announced it would contain "14 Palaces in [the] Sky," served by a kitchen "200 feet up in the air": "Each suite will have a bathroom like that of a Roman villa, with marble floors and wainscots. The boudoir baths, as the hotel elects to call them, are to be fourteen by nineteen feet and will form a suite in themselves."[7]

The Waldorf was being designed by the New York–based architectural firm of Schultze & Weaver, whose earlier commissions included Boomer's Sherry-Netherland, as well as sprawling hotels for the Biltmore chain in Atlanta, Los Angeles, and Coral Gables. As described in the *Herald Tribune*, the Waldorf-Astoria's ballroom would be, "virtually, a built-in opera house," with "two levels of boxes" and "a public address acoustic system to make the orators heard in the remote parts." Because the hotel was "expected to contain a population of 4,000 or 5,000 wealthy persons," it would be lined with "two or three . . . shopping arcades at the street level and on the lower floors." The "palaces with vaulted roofs"—what became, in final form, the suites of the Waldorf Towers—would be "numerous enough to house all the royal families at once," the paper suggested, but would not be "held in reserve for foreign visitors." Readers were assured playfully that "industrial kings, cattle kings, home-run kings and all the domestic royalty" would be able to stay in them too. The hotel, Boomer explained, would be modern without embracing the cool austerity of the modernistic: "When the old Waldorf-Astoria was built, it was the model of hotels all over the world. . . . We want the new one to do what the old one did—not to copy other styles, periods or existing hotels, but to be original all through and create new international hotel standards. That is our ambition . . . and we are ready to go the limit to achieve it."[8]

Covering an entire city block, the new Waldorf-Astoria was made possible through a remarkable series of maneuvers, both above ground and below.

Chief among them was the development of Park Avenue, north of Forty-Second Street, as a luxury commercial district. When industrialist Cornelius Vanderbilt opened his Grand Central Terminal on Forty-Second Street in 1871, he predicted it would be adaptable enough to last a century. However, within two decades the terminal was outdated. Its train yard, described by historian Donald Miller as "the largest in the Western Hemisphere," fed a line of visible tracks extending all the way up Park Avenue to Fifty-Sixth Street—an expanse that was only passable, east to west, through an insufficient sequence of pedestrian and traffic bridges. A gruesome accident in January 1902, when poor visibility, created by smoke buildup in the tunnel north of Fifty-Sixth Street, led the engine of one train to crash into the rear of another, only reinforced what many had long been saying: New York's steam-driven train system—the cause of noxious gases and, in this case, horrific loss of life—was due for an overhaul. In 1903, the state legislature issued the following mandate: all of New York's passenger trains must, within five years, switch from steam to electric power.[9]

Credit for devising the "air rights" concept that would transform a grimy stretch of Park Avenue goes to William Wilgus, chief engineer for the New York Central Railroad. Wilgus observed that conversion from coal-burning to electric engines would diminish the need for ventilation. Now, once-open tracks could be paved over and built upon. It took some work, but Wilgus—who also helped design the new Forty-Second Street terminal—finally convinced the New York Central board of his idea's soundness: massive steel columns, sunk into Manhattan bedrock, could support revenue-producing buildings that would bestride the train tracks without impeding passenger service. By the time Grand Central Terminal opened in 1913, two of these structures, a post office and exhibition hall, had already been built, in a monumental Beaux-Arts style intended to conform with that of the station. Park Avenue, which had formerly ended at Fiftieth Street (the start of the old train yard), was now extended down to the northern border of Grand Central at Forty-Fifth Street. All the land in the middle, property of the railroad, was leased to private developers in an arrangement beneficial to both sides. Grand Central retained ownership and a degree of control over how the land was developed; lessees were given ready-made parcels at a time when full blocks, during the expansion that accompanied early twentieth-century Manhattan, were becoming increasingly difficult to find.

Louis J. Horowitz, aggressive chairman of the Thompson-Starrett Company, New York's premier builders (Manhattan's "Skyline Is Thompson-Starrett's Byline," its brochures read), claimed the idea for a new Waldorf-Astoria was his. In an oft-repeated story, Lucius Boomer was vacationing in Florida at the end of 1928, days after announcing the old Waldorf's imminent closure, when he received a telegram from Horowitz, whose specialty had become, in his own description, financing "schemes" for new construction projects. Lucius, who had been entertaining thoughts of retirement, looked at Horowitz's words and discussed them with his wife, Jorgine. He then decided to take a train back to New York. "If you run it, I'll build it," the telegram had read. Horowitz later explained that he had believed the Waldorf "stood for something that deserved to live," and that the telegram had been inspired by sentimental feelings for his friend, Boomer's business partner Coleman du Pont, now battling cancer of the larynx. The truth, however, was that Boomer had been thinking about a new location for some time, as evidenced by his official closing announcement for the old hotel, issued on December 20, 1928: "We retain all rights to the name of Waldorf-Astoria Hotel for future use." By February 1929, Oscar Tschirky, whose on-the-job guardedness rarely extended to his public statements, had let it slip that "I do think there will be another Waldorf-Astoria, and Oscar will be in it."[10]

One week prior to Boomer's announcement in December 1928, Thompson-Starrett had been reorganized into a new company led by a directorate of prominent figures, including auto executive Walter Chrysler and bankers Robert Lehman and Charles Hayden, along with the chewing gum magnate William Wrigley Jr. Correctly, Louis Horowitz, as chairman, predicted the new board would represent "many potential building jobs," and that its powerful members could be used "like the great big hitch of horses that pull a heavy circus wagon across a muddy lot." In his telegram and subsequent communications, Horowitz told Boomer that the banking firms represented at Thompson-Starrett would be willing to finance the "land, building, equipment, and working capital for a new Waldorf-Astoria." Next, Horowitz approached the New York Central Railroad about one of its real estate parcels, convincing executives that "a well-known hotel so close to Grand Central would be a distinct asset," generating business "along with a fat ground rent." The only problem was that the site, a full block bounded by Park and Lexington Avenues, between Forty-Ninth and Fiftieth Streets, was already occupied by a YMCA and, more challengingly, a power plant and boiler system generating heat and electricity for a large section of the Grand Central neighborhood.[11]

In order to make space for the Waldorf-Astoria, the New York Central offered to move the entire plant, at its own expense, to a substation, 250 feet long and 60 feet wide, that had been carved out of bedrock four stories below the Graybar Building on Forty-Third Street. The operation, described by an engineering observer as "one of the most intricate and difficult pieces of work ever undertaken in this city," was completed in three phases. First, five cylindrical steam water heaters, each weighing twenty tons, were released from service at the old plant on May 27, 1929, then hauled underground seven blocks and attached to a new system of pipes and hot water mains—all in time to meet the deadline of September 20, when steam heat would be required for twenty-four neighborhood buildings. Next, eight rotary converters, each a ten-foot wheel with supporting metal base, had to be taken apart at Fiftieth Street, lowered piece by piece through a hatchway onto a sequence of flat cars, and then pulled along tracks to Forty-Third Street. There, the converters were lifted down to the substation floor with the help of rope blocks and cranes. All the while, trains continued to pass into and out of Grand Central. Any slip as pieces were being taken out of the Fiftieth Street power station—no basement separated it from the railroad activity below—and a 3,000-pound shaft might have crashed onto passengers.[12]

But perhaps the most delicate phase was the third, involving transfer of a backup battery designed to offer power in case of system failure. Each of the battery's 160 cells was a rectangular tank, seven feet long, filled with lead plates that were submerged in corrosive acid. Given that the Waldorf's lease stipulated clearance of the battery by November 1, 1929, there was no time to ensure worker safety by removing the acid prior to transportation. Each 4,550-pound tank was therefore clamped as securely as possible and lifted whole from its supporting frame by an automobile jack. With care so as not to crack the tank's glass base (the sides and top were of metal), its movers then lowered it fifty-five feet by tackle onto a ramp alongside the train tracks, where it was placed on a trailer and hauled by electric tractor to Forty-Third Street. This "unprecedented experiment," as described in the *New York Times*, was characteristic of an engineering project that had implemented "every possible short-cut."[13]

By the end of October, everything had been completed to prepare for the new Waldorf save removal of the physical power plant itself. Again, train service would continue while the giant structure—marked by two smoke towers ascending 250 feet—was to be dismantled, piece by piece. With just two and a half months to complete the job, the Albert Volk Company, demolition specialists, agreed to a contractual provision that served as both negative and positive incentive. One thousand dollars would be added to payment for each day that work was completed ahead of schedule; conversely, for each day behind, $1,000 would be deducted. In addition to the smoke towers, eight concrete coal bins, each weighing one ton, would have to be removed, along with the steel trusses that supported them. Although the plant was barely two decades old and, therefore, "modernly constructed" (as pointed out by Albert Volk), none of its materials would be salvaged due to lack of time. Volk, remarking on the building's "fortresslike construction," explained how workers would use "compressed air machines, acetelyne [sic] torches and heavy lifting equipment"—all to service one of the most "difficult" demolition jobs the company had ever undertaken.[14]

This final phase was just getting started when larger events threatened to derail the entire project. By 1927 the rise in the stock market, underway for several years, had reached a new peak, with averages climbing in all but two months. Then, in the spring of 1928, the market began to show signs of instability: huge jumps were followed by equally significant decreases. Still, the mood was speculative, as more and more middle-class Americans became tempted by the lure of profit during what industrialists such as Andrew

Foundation for the new Waldorf on Park Avenue in late 1929, prior to demolition of the power plant. Train tracks running from Grand Central Terminal are visible below ground level (FPG/Getty Images).

Mellon assured them was a time of boundless prosperity. Buying of securities only increased after the presidential win, in November 1928, of Herbert Hoover, who, despite his own private concerns about the market, was widely perceived as a symbol of the philosophical, economic, and even moral rightness of American capitalism. Despite a mild attempt by the Federal Reserve Board to pull in the reins, speculation continued, with a great number of customers buying on margin—that is, with loans from brokers. In the summer of 1929 prices, along with the rate of brokers' loans, rose almost every day, but confidence began to slip in the autumn. Investors, their loans no longer sufficient to cover the decline in stock value, started getting calls from brokers for more cash, just to stay in the game. As historian John Kenneth Galbraith explained, a "fortunate speculator" who had resources to answer one call, "presently got another and equally urgent one": "The singular feature of the great crash of 1929 was that the worst continued to worsen. What looked one day like the end proved on the next day to have been only the beginning."[15]

Thursday, October 24, brought the onset of a panic, as nearly 13 million shares sold at low prices. That afternoon a group of bankers met at the Wall Street offices of J. P. Morgan and decided to infuse money into the market. The benefits resulting from this example of what financial insiders termed "organized support" were only temporary: by Monday stock prices had fallen again, and this time the bankers determined there was nothing more they could do. The market would have to be left to its own forces. "Black Tuesday," October 29, became (until 1987) the single worst day in stock market history, with more than 16 million shares traded. Reasons behind the timing of the crash would be long debated, but overall the scholarly consensus was that America's economic bubble had risen to the point where breakage was inevitable. Given the preponderance of brokers' loans, it was the middle-class investor who took the first hit. While tales of a suicide wave that followed the crash were later exposed as myth, the image of desperate men, poised at the edge of windowsills, found its way into the realm of hotels— reputed since the nineteenth century as ideal locales for self-termination. According to Galbraith, hotel clerks near the financial district in downtown

Manhattan were rumored to be asking guests, in a bit of dark humor, if they wanted the room "for sleeping or jumping."[16]

Back at the Thompson-Starrett office, caught in the middle of Waldorf-Astoria preparations, a joke was circulating that the company's "initial dynamite blasting"—preparatory work for a steel frame to be placed above the Park Avenue tracks—"had caused what happened down in Wall Street." Soon Horowitz, vacationing in Europe, began getting "frantic cables" from his New York real estate broker, telling him that "the hotel deal was in danger." As Horowitz later explained, the bankers who funded the new Waldorf-Astoria had a "bomb-proof shelter" in their agreement, a clause "which might have been interpreted as giving them the right to withdraw from the deal if they deemed the time was somewhat less than ripe to sell securities to the public." Horowitz, a Jewish immigrant from Poland who started his New York career as a shoe salesman, had built a reputation at Thompson-Starrett for the kind of persuasive energy that generated, during his early tenure with the company, lucrative contracts such as the one for the 1905 Sears plant in Chicago. Back in New York, he called a meeting of the bankers and convinced them that if they backed out, the New York Central Railroad, having just completed the costliest segment of its work—all on the Waldorf-Astoria's behalf—would be left "holding a most expensive bag." To their credit, Horowitz attested, the bankers "stuck to their bargain," even as they faced "a loss they could see before they started."[17]

Horowitz's suggestion—backers knew they were going into a project that likely wouldn't make money for a long time—could be used to illustrate the hotel's history over the next two years and, indeed, through the early 1940s. The Waldorf-Astoria became a white elephant. Still, it would be unfair to assume that Boomer and his fellow board members went ahead blithely, knowing that, since the money had already been raised, there was no turning back. During the fall of 1929 few could have been aware of just how long the economic downturn—what eventually was termed "depression"—would last. Indeed, by November the market had stopped falling. Then President Hoover stepped in to reduce both corporate and individual taxes, in a move widely seen as restorative ("Just think," quipped comedian Will Rogers, "lower taxes and not on a Presidential election year"). Through March 1930 the market continued to recover. In fact, not until early summer 1930 did stock prices begin falling again in large amounts. By then, steel construction on the Waldorf was well underway and 216,000 bags of cement had been ordered for concrete flooring. One contract, for ornamental bronze, iron, aluminum, and nickel work, had been awarded to the General Bronze Corporation of Long Island City; another, for 400 carloads of face brick, was given to Continental Fiske, Inc., of Darlington, Pennsylvania. The brick was designed to match the Waldorf's limestone base in a new color designed especially for the project: Waldorf Gray.[18]

Through the spring of 1930, therefore, Boomer, his backers, and the American public still had some cause for optimism. Total cost for the Waldorf-Astoria was estimated at just over $28 million, to be funded by the sale of bonds and a block of common stock, as well as a $10 million contribution from the New York Central Railroad, which would receive rent of $300,000 per year. Bonds were secured through an $11 million bank mortgage, contracted in the early days of October 1929 but recorded, by coincidence, on October 29, Black Tuesday. Prior to the crash, in early October, the new Waldorf-Astoria Corporation had taken out an advertisement in newspapers across the country, emphasizing the names of board members: in addition to Boomer, Horowitz, and Charles Hayden, there were Francis du Pont, General Motors president Alfred P. Sloan, and the magazine publisher Condé Nast. Men such as these, the ad had implied, would never lend themselves to a frivolous enterprise. Now, many of the same men sought to ensure the public, through the various channels at their disposal, that the Waldorf's financial footing was as solid as the building itself. Given that John Prentiss, of the investment firm Hornblower & Weeks, also sat on the Waldorf board, it was not surprising that Hornblower's December investment review would identify Waldorf-Astoria bonds as one of six "sound investments at most attractive prices."[19]

In the report Hornblower & Weeks further assured readers that "fundamental conditions" remained "sound," even if "sustained improvement" was not likely to be observed until the "late Spring." This statement was in keeping with what historian Galbraith characterized as a program of "organized reassurance"—optimistic statements issued during the early part of the Depression by top figures in American business and government. Initially, John D. Rockefeller, in what Galbraith cited as his "first public statement . . . in several decades," volunteered the information that he and his son had been buying common stocks. Then, in November, a Waldorf-Astoria Hotel Corporation board member, General Motors' Alfred Sloan, numbered among the industrial leaders who met with President Hoover as part of a series of highly publicized "prosperity conferences" at the White House. These were, as Galbraith observed, strictly "no-business" meetings, called by Hoover not because there was "business to be done" but because it was "necessary to create the impression" that business was being done. After one such conference on December 5, Hoover took to NBC radio to explain how business leaders were working, as an Associated Press story described it, toward "maintenance of prosperity."[20]

At the Waldorf, Lucius Boomer was doing his part to cast the hotel as an institution that would honor tradition while embodying Hoover's promise for the American future. On March 24, 1930, in a ceremony documented by the *Herald Tribune* and other papers, he stood with Oscar Tschirky in the open space that would become a new Peacock Alley. Also in attendance was another old-timer, Augustus Nulle (once George Boldt's private secretary), who was to return to the Waldorf as treasurer. After taking off their hats, the three men stood reverently as Charles Hayden, citing the event as "another milestone of progress" in the history of New York, drove the Waldorf's first rivet into a vertical steel beam: "I feel that I am driving home the fact that the tangible realization of a wonderful dream is underway." In skyscraper construction, a rivet—Donald Miller described it as a "small steel cylinder with no threads and one round head"—is the piece used to fasten two beams of a structure into place. The rivet takes a connection that has been temporarily sealed with bolts and makes it permanent. This one, reported the newspapers, was gold-plated.[21]

One of the most complex tasks engineers faced in realizing Schultze & Weaver's design lay in construction of the ballroom, which was to rise multiple

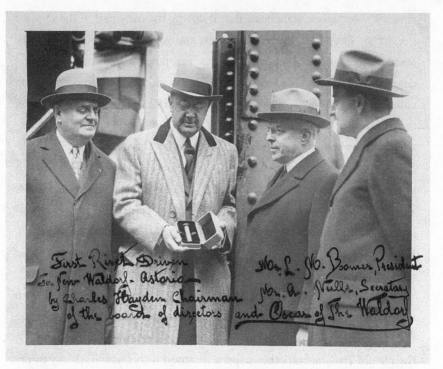

First rivet driven at the new Waldorf-Astoria on March 24, 1930, with (left to right) Oscar Tschirky, Lucius Boomer, Charles Hayden, and Augustus Nulle. The handwriting is Oscar's (Oscar Michel Tschirky Papers, Division of Rare and Manuscript Collections, Cornell University Library).

stories in the center of the hotel. Devoid of interior columns (the insertion of which would have blocked views), the 10,000-square foot ballroom created an enormous hole that somehow needed to support the weight of a full thirty-seven stories above. To implement the engineers' solution to this problem, three crews of steel erectors labored for a week in the early part of July 1930, hoisting into place a sequence of giant trusses—each weighing between 20 and 63 tons—as curious crowds gathered at the corner of Fiftieth Street and Park Avenue. This structure was then covered by a horizontal "top chord," well over one-third the length of a north-south Manhattan block, weighing 74 tons. Cited by the *Herald Tribune* as the largest of its kind ever used in a New York building, the truss system would serve to divert

4,500 tons of weight off to the ballroom's sides. In a further article of January 4, 1931, the paper displayed its willingness to reproduce the statistical issuances of the Waldorf's press department, which had, evidently, found a quotable source in the census data from a section of northern New York lying completely within the Adirondack Park. The ballroom, in addition to containing a stage suitable for a "symphony orchestra," would be large enough to host more than the entire population of Hamilton County.[22]

By the end of summer 1930, the skeleton of the Waldorf's first fourteen floors was in place, along with much of the lower facade. As the Waldorf rose, architectural observers could discern how greatly this new structure differed from Schultze & Weaver's earlier hotels, whose exteriors had incorporated an eclectic 1920s mix of Spanish Revival, neo-Georgian, Italian Renaissance, and other elements. Indeed, early plans for the Waldorf, which the firm's chief designer, Lloyd Morgan, had drawn up at the end of 1928, called for a tower adorned with neo-Gothic finials. By construction's start, however, ornamental touches had been, in Leonard Schultze's words, "eliminated as largely as possible," and uncluttered Art Deco had emerged as the building's dominant style. This shedding of twenties-era motif was in keeping with Boomer's mandate, set early in the design process, to be "original all through." While *New Yorker* writer Lewis Mumford criticized the "dull limestone lower façade which," in his view, turned into "an equally dull brick wall," most critics were more generous. The federally sponsored writers of the *WPA Guide* would praise the "well-proportioned series of setbacks" on the upper floors (the result of city codes for tall buildings), while another observer wrote approvingly of the way in which the "showiness of 1893," evident in the old Waldorf, had been scaled back to "the restraint of 1931."[23]

Inside, Schultze & Weaver built upon the facade's modern aesthetic through consistent use of reflective metal surfaces—especially nickeled bronze. Elevator doors had a polished texture that made them shine hazily. For one set, Louis Rigal designed a circular frieze whose willowy classical figures—elongated women playing lyre and mandolin—were spread across the gap between doors. With each opening the figures moved apart then slid together. One third-floor corridor, part of the assemblage of hallways and

Nickeled bronze elevator doors, with Louis Rigal's frieze at center
(Timothy A. Clary/AFP via Getty Images).

meeting spaces designed to feed into the Grand Ballroom, was described by
the hotel as the "Silver Gallery." Here, mirrors extended nearly to the ceiling, and visitors opening doors could watch their reflections in a multitude
of glass panels. Upon approach, no other space in the hotel appeared so
sleekly modern. But those with memories of the original Waldorf could look
up and recognize a series of murals by impressionist painter Edward Sim-
mons. The works had been transplanted, in their original order, from the
Fifth Avenue building's Astor Gallery. Schultze & Weaver thus infiltrated one
of the most contemporary rooms of the hotel with antiques from the nineteenth century. In this way the firm visually interpreted Boomer's promise,
made in late 1929, that the new Waldorf-Astoria would "glorify and carry
on the traditions of the old."

On the afternoon of September 29, 1931—twenty-four hours before guests
were set to arrive for the hotel's official "preview"—maids dusted surfaces
while janitors mopped. In the ballroom, workers tested the movable stage,
raising and lowering it to be even with the floor, as a musician played snatches

of classical melodies on the adjacent organ. Three hundred waiters in starched white shirts formed a line on the ballroom floor, where they were inspected for hygiene and correctness of posture. In the kitchen, Alexandre Gastaud, head chef and a veteran of the old Knickerbocker, stood watching as a sequence of forty-gallon urns—each could transform water into coffee within ten minutes—rotated slowly. Garry Henry, chief steward, talked with a reporter, enumerating the items that would constitute some 6,000 meals to be served the next evening: 1,200 lobsters; 200 gallons of soup; 10,000 oranges, pears, and apples. In the Park Avenue lobby, a doorman checked his gold-braided uniform in a large mirror and blew his whistle. Meanwhile, reported the *Times*, "detectives backed by special patrolmen" kept guard over the hotel's "half-dozen entrances." They were augmented by "squads of bell-boys," sent to protect the Waldorf from intrusion by their less-fortunate peers, the "scores of job seekers who idled outside."[24]

Twelve thousand had been invited to the preview on September 30, but, given that each pass was good for two people, more than 20,000 attended. In the words of one account, "All of New York was represented": mature men in old-fashioned cutaway jackets (dusted off, perhaps, from earlier visits to the Waldorf), women in satiny dresses affixed with gardenias, younger people in business suits, rumpled from the workday, and still younger ones in school uniforms. Peacock Alley, now a wide corridor running side to side between the Park Avenue and main lobbies, was a particular site of interest. There, reported the *Chicago Tribune*, "Dowagers, young society girls, pink-cheeked old beaux and a lot of people who did not appear to fit into the scenery" made themselves comfortable in a variety of settees and chairs. Also present throughout the hotel were notable figures from the country's political, financial, and artistic realms: New York City mayor Jimmy Walker; the ubiquitous Al Smith, having finished his Empire State Building some months earlier; film actress Mae Murray, who ordered the first meal in the Sert Room; as well as Walter Chrysler, RCA president David Sarnoff, publisher George Doubleday, and a sampling of Astors, Roosevelts, Vanderbilts, Fishes, and Whitneys.[25]

Given that he and the Waldorf had been, as the *Times* put it, "insepara-ble from the beginning," it was Oscar Tschirky who stood at the top of the

Park Avenue lobby stairs, receiving visitors. For some time, in Edward Bernays's view, Oscar had been little more than a "peripatetic, lumbering professional host whom guests had transformed into a potent nostalgic symbol." Nonetheless, Oscar had "persuaded himself that he was indispensable to the successful running of the hotel." His chief value to Boomer, who otherwise possessed little affection for the man Bernays dismissed as "supercargo," lay in his role as a "handshaker" and the recipient of "much human-interest publicity." Now a testy sixty-five, Oscar grimaced when one woman, small and elderly, pinned a flower to his lapel. He didn't enjoy being fussed over. Later Oscar retreated to the back of the Grand Ballroom, where Estonian-born conductor Ernö Rapée (still one year away from what would be his career-defining job as head of the Radio City Music Hall orchestra) played turn-of-the-century airs.[26]

At six o'clock all music in the Grand Ballroom stopped. Speakers arranged throughout the hotel emitted an electronic hum; then a voice emerged: "The opening of the new Waldorf-Astoria is an event in the advancement of hotels. . . . It carries on a great tradition in national hospitality." Even if they hadn't already known what was happening, guests would have recognized the steady, cadenced voice of President Herbert Hoover, speaking from the White House in an address broadcast across the nation via NBC radio: "The erection of this great structure at this time has been a contribution to the maintenance of employment and is an exhibition of courage and confidence to the whole nation." It was rare for a sitting U.S. president to involve himself in the opening of a private structure, though not unheard of. In May, Hoover had formally dedicated the Empire State Building, but that event had been limited to his pressing a button (from Washington) that switched on the lights of the skyscraper's lobby, along with a congratulatory telegram sent by the president but read aloud at the ceremony by Al Smith. Then again, the Empire State, for all its remarkability, was in the end an office building; hotels could claim an entirely different place within American society: "Our hotels have become community institutions. They are the center points of civic hospitality. They are the meeting place of a thousand community and national activities. They have come to be conducted in far larger vision than mere profit earning."[27]

In the speech Hoover also managed to work in a bit of hospitality history, speaking of how "137 years ago . . . the first so-called great hotel was opened in New York—the old City Hotel," which at the time had been "heralded as an immense establishment and which comprised seventy-three rooms": "It was visited from all parts of the country as one of the fine exhibits of our national growth. A long line of constantly improving hotels from that day to this has marked the measure of the nation's growth in power, in comfort and in artistry."[28]

The Waldorf, Hoover suggested, was both the City Hotel of the twentieth century and a testament to how far America had come in what he saw as the realization of its ideals. On December 2, 1930, the president had delivered an address to Congress in which he acknowledged how, during the past year, the United States had "suffered with other nations from economic depression." At the same time, he assured Americans that "the fundamental strength of the nation's economic life" was, in his view, "unimpaired." Insisting the Depression could not be "cured by legislative action or executive pronouncement," Hoover asserted that "economic wounds" could only be healed by "the action of the cells of the economic body—the producers and consumers themselves." For a commander in chief who sought to assure his constituency that America's depression was temporary ("Our immediate problem is the increase of employment for the next six months"), an endeavor such as the Waldorf-Astoria reflected one of "the many factors" to which he had pointed in his congressional address as providing "encouragement for the future."[29]

At the end of Hoover's speech, Boomer took to the stage of the Grand Ballroom and, in an address that was also broadcast nationally, visited the same themes. The Waldorf could be counted among "the notable achievements" that had "marked America's material and artistic progress." More than celebrating the finish of a "wonderful building," the preview of September 30 was designed to pay "tribute to the traditions, the genius and the enterprise" that the new hotel represented: "We of the Waldorf-Astoria have built with confidence in our country's growth and prosperity and, looking beyond temporary storms and stress, we feel sure of the successful career of this great hotel."[30]

The next morning, October 1—official opening day—it looked as if Boomer's roseate prediction might come true. "At 7 a.m., when the clerks went on duty," wrote the *Herald Tribune*, "guests already were waiting in the lobby with their luggage." The newspaper quickly corrected itself: in the Boomer lexicon, drilled into staff, there were no guests, only *patrons*. These neither checked in nor out but, in terminology designed to reflect luxurious ease, simply *arrived* and *departed*. The American fascination with races and contests surfaced in an unofficial competition among members of the public to be "first." Learning that Waldorf-Astoria board member Charles Hayden had already been awarded the honor of first patron, one A. E. Kusterer, investment banker of Grand Rapids, shipped his luggage to the hotel a week in advance, then arrived by train to stay just one night, September 30. Leaving in the early morning hours, he became the first to depart. Another man, an occasional guest of the old place, sent a payment well before opening and was mailed in return a certificate on which was printed, "MR. WARREN ROSS . . . FIRST ADVANCE PAID PATRON."[31]

October 1 was also the day on which those who hadn't possessed connections necessary to secure a ticket to the preview could make their inspection of the Waldorf premises. In reporter Edward Angly's description, they "thronged the lobby, strolled and sat in Peacock Alley and rubbernecked their way through all the public rooms." Easily numbering "another 20,000," Angly believed, the crowd could only be compared in density to that which had populated the old Waldorf "in the long, hot summer days of 1924 when the Democrats were trying to choose a candidate for President." Although these people could be classed as lobby-sitters who were "merely on sightseeing missions," Angly pointed out that there were also more than a thousand guests "sleeping under the Waldorf-Astoria's roof," and that, for dinner the first evening, "every chair in every dining room of the building was occupied." Much of the opening day's attention, conceded Angly, could be

Irving and Sam Browning, *Exterior View of the Waldorf-Astoria Hotel, 301 Park Avenue, New York City*, ca. 1930s (PR 009, Browning Photograph Collection, New-York Historical Society).

chalked up to the "human desire to see something new before one's neighbor has seen it"—a desire that made for a "booming business day," even in the hotel's barbershop. After the hoopla of opening day quieted down, however, and the public's rush to see the new hotel began to subside, Waldorf management had to face a difficult truth: 2,000-plus guest rooms, nightly, would not be easy to fill.[32]

Signs of concern appeared immediately. Prior to opening, the Waldorf's newspaper advertisements had emphasized familiarity. One notice, which had run extensively in late August, urged readers: "Address reservations once again: 'Waldorf-Astoria, New York' . . . and feel content." While a small line at the top explained how rates started at just six dollars per day, "as at the old Waldorf," most of the ad's space was taken up with a list of the "former key personnel," such as Oscar, Boomer, and Augustus Nulle, who had been "retained." As early as October 2, 1931, however, newspaper ads began to stress affordability, in ways that suggested a fear that the hotel's longtime efforts to cultivate an elite reputation had succeeded too well: "There is something about the new Waldorf-Astoria that immediately indicates luxury . . . and implies high price. The indication is correct, but the implication is not."[33]

Even in a solid economic climate, hotel managers rarely projected capacity sales. Occupancy rates might vary according to season, month, or night of the week. A rate that hovered around 75 percent was generally thought of as ideal, when combined with income from restaurants and other services (which could make up as much as half a hotel's total income), for keeping an establishment in the black. Throughout the early 1930s, occupancy at the Waldorf rarely exceeded 50 percent. Faced with weak patronage, at a time when many Americans could not afford to travel, Boomer had no choice but to bring the Waldorf's $10 rooms down to what had been the base $6 per night price (just over $100 in contemporary figures). Certain rooms were reduced further, to $5. This step, while it helped with occupancy, lowered revenue. In 1932 the Waldorf-Astoria Corporation posted a net loss of more than $3.1 million. That October, Boomer, always emphasizing the positive, told a reporter that he had been "amazed" by the "volume of business." No doubt, the customary fall increase in banquets and catered dinners had provided a small boost. Still, the corporation's net losses for the first six months of 1933 totaled nearly $1.5 million.[34]

"Virtually two-thirds of New York City's 329 hotels are bankrupt." So began a sobering article by Barrow Lyons in the *Nation* of October 4, 1933. "Either their mortgages have been foreclosed, or are about to be, or their management has passed into the hands of financial backers—mostly savings banks and insurance companies." Other reports served to verify Lyons's claim. Newspapers revealed that the Hotel Dixie, opened on Forty-Third Street in April 1930, was in foreclosure by October 1931. The Carlyle, unveiled in 1930 as a residential hotel (like the Waldorf Towers, intended for long-term occupancy), went into receivership the following year; the Pierre, lucky by comparison, lasted two years before going bankrupt in 1932. "Few of the hostelries," Lyons added in the *Nation*, "are more than half filled," with managers "taxing their imaginations to the limit to earn enough to pay interest on their mortgages, city and federal taxes . . . and other fixed charges." In this climate, the writer suggested, old rules governing male and female behavior in the private spaces of hotels were being relaxed: "Many of the establishments which appeal to traveling men permit them to bring their 'wives' without additional charge, and one of the newer large hotels [Lyons hinted it was the New Yorker, not far from Penn Station] is reputed to permit open prostitution."[35]

At the Waldorf-Astoria, issues were complicated by one of the methods through which construction had been financed. Leasehold bonds (those secured with payments made by a building's lessee—in this case, the Waldorf-Astoria Corporation) had become a popular form of investment in the early decades of the twentieth century because, in theory, their value would be certain to grow with that of the expanding real estate market. On its surface, the new Waldorf had appeared like a good investment: the structure was to be located in an area of Manhattan where property values were rising dramatically. The locking in of a fixed ground rental for a period of twenty-six years and eleven months (as noted in the corporation's bond advertisements, which had appeared in newspapers during the early part of October 1929) meant that investors could look forward to steadily increasing returns.

Furthermore, it had become industry standard, as a measure of security, for holders of leasehold bonds to possess the right of action, ahead of the lessor, in cases of default by the lessee. Prospective Waldorf investors were further assured by language in the "Security" section of the bond ads: "When the mortgage securing these Bonds [sic] is recorded, the term grant from which the leasehold is derived will be free of all liens . . . and should any subsequent mortgage be placed upon either land or building, it will not affect the leasehold and the mortgage securing these bonds."[36]

The ads had made it seem as if the bonds were secure, as Lyons wrote in the *Nation*, "under all circumstances." Left unmentioned was a clause in the rental agreement through which the lessor, New York Central Railroad, would have the right to take physical possession of the Waldorf if the lessee defaulted on payments. And, by the fall of 1933, as Lyons reported, the Waldorf-Astoria Corporation's yearly rental was "considerably in arrears." As part of a reorganization plan worked out between New York Central and the hotel in the spring of 1932, the railroad would defer rent provided that investors agreed to switch their holdings to income bonds—that is, bonds for which interest would be contingent upon the Waldorf having reached a specific level of earnings. One group of bondholders, frustrated by the likelihood of not seeing any payments under the new plan, attempted to protect its investment with an action (filed in New York State Supreme Court) for the appointment of a receiver. Speaking to the *Times*, Boomer insisted the bondholders' petition was unnecessary and that fortunes would soon improve: "While the hotel has had to contend with the adverse conditions general to all business . . . a rapid and substantial increase must occur with the return of normal conditions of travel and business in general." After lawyers for the New York Central declared in court that any attempt to put the Waldorf in receivership would force them to make use of the possession clause—an event that would leave the bondholders with nothing—the suit was withdrawn.[37]

"The story of the Waldorf-Astoria," observed Lyons, ". . . could hardly be called [one] of downright chicanery, for unquestionably some of the 'big' men who engaged in that operation thought it would succeed." It was unlikely that people such as Hayden, Sloan, and Boomer "would consciously lend their names to a gigantic swindle." Nonetheless, Lyons suggested, "some elements in the deal" had an appearance of being "hardly straightforward," and for the investors, looking ahead to the prospect of many years without dividends, the results were "virtually the same as if [they] had been swindled." Bondholders were trapped: because New York Central Railroad, as landowner, had decided on a position of "forbearance," they had no choice but to go along. In agreeing to the reorganization plan, New York Central may have been motivated by more than a willingness to show patience and good faith: in 1931, it had advanced the Waldorf over $4,750,000. The question of what would become of that money, were the hotel corporation to dissolve, no doubt weighed on the railroad's mind. Whatever the motives behind its creation, the arrangement—one in which the customary protections given investors were subverted by the railroad's larger powers—kept the Waldorf-Astoria Corporation intact as an entity and helped it ride out the worst years of the Depression. And, by the end of 1933, Boomer and his associates had a new reason for feeling a small degree of hope.[38]

On December 5, 1933, Benjamin de Casseres, a critic and satirist described as the "scourge of Riverside Drive," sat beside a news ticker that had been specially wired for him inside the Waldorf-Astoria. He had risen early, declared himself "ready and fit," and made his way to the Waldorf around three o'clock in the afternoon. The wire, set up by the United Press as a relay from its New York office, ensured that de Casseres, in his words, would not be foiled by "legislative horse feathers" in the attempt to remain "law-abiding." So, as dusk overtook the winter afternoon, he waited for news from the West. His mission: to be the first person to buy and consume a legal drink in the United States since the end of 1919. At 5:33, as de Casseres sat with stopwatch and highball, word arrived: two minutes earlier, at 5:31, Utah had become the thirty-sixth state to vote for repeal, establishing a three-quarters majority. Prohibition, which the writer compared to a "13-year jail sentence," was dead. He took the highball and "flung it head-on" at his "teeth."

Immediately the press service sent a correction: Utah's vote had actually occurred at 5:32:30. Reportedly beating out hot dog king Oscar Mayer, who competed from Chicago, de Casseres thus proclaimed himself as "law-abiding" by just thirty seconds.[39]

De Casseres had chosen the Waldorf-Astoria because, thirty-six years earlier, arriving from Philadelphia, he had taken his first drink in New York at the old Waldorf bar, standing with one "foot on a rail." But, in a piece of historical irony, what had arguably been the original hotel's most emblematic feature was nowhere to be seen in the new Waldorf, opening at the moment it did. After the 1932 election of Franklin Delano Roosevelt, when repeal began to seem imminent (FDR had adopted an anti-Prohibition platform during his campaign), Boomer, along with executives of other hotels built during the 1920s, had to determine how to construct bars and wine cellars in facilities planned without them. For the Waldorf, built over tracks, the question posed a special challenge: even if underground space could somehow be found, the rumble of trains would create, dining experts believed, vibrations inimical to the storage of fine wine. The Waldorf's solution was to build a "cellar" on the fifth floor, where thermal controls were installed to keep wine at the proper temperatures. Downstairs, off Peacock Alley, carpenters worked throughout Thanksgiving of 1933 to fashion a new "Cafe-Lounge" that, in the words of the *Daily News*, seemed to "run for miles."[40]

Pauline Sabin, an anti-Prohibition advocate who, in her career as a prominent interior designer, had worked on a number of suites inside the Waldorf Towers, urged Americans to "justify by their conduct" the new freedom this "great victory" had granted. For New Yorkers, at least, Sabin's trust was well-founded: in contrast to the bacchanalian final night before Wartime Prohibition, more than fourteen years earlier, the first night *after* Prohibition was notably restrained. Several thousand people stood in Times Square on the afternoon of December 5, their gazes fixed upward to an electric sign: "Utah voting!" The only sound, reported the Associated Press, was a "policeman's horse" as it "pawed the pavement." Then: "Prohibition is dead!" The crowd "whooped a few 'Hoorays,' but it didn't roar." Instead, for the rest of the evening, it was "a playful throng." Acting out of habit, perhaps, celebrants first went to the old speakeasies, which (now operating with licenses) were "jammed" early in the evening. Within a "few hours," though, people appeared to have moved "elsewhere to catch a drink of legal liquor." Some, in fact, made their way to the Waldorf-Astoria—where, in another publicity move, John O'Connor, hardy veteran of the original bar, served drinks while Oscar opened bottles.[41]

CHAPTER 5

No More Junior Proms!

An immediate effect of Prohibition's repeal was the move of city nightlife out of the speakeasies and back into restaurants and hotels. For almost fourteen years, New Yorkers looking for a drink had been forced into basements and private clubs, which, however romanticized by images from Hollywood films—the flapper in short skirt and long pearls, doing the Charleston on tabletops—often fleeced patrons with high prices and alcohol of uncertain purity. Indeed, fear of "poison liquor" was cited as a reason for the Manhattan public's sudden abandonment of speakeasies in December 1933. For a while, old places such as the Merry-Go-Round, famed for its rotating, carousel bar, tried to stay commercially relevant, displaying liquor with the government excise seals turned outward (as proof of authenticity) and emphasizing a "personal touch to their patronage" that large hotels could not provide. A few, like the 21 Club, survived through conversion into legitimate restaurants. Most, however, were undone not only by changes in public taste but new state regulations, which mandated that "interiors" of any establishment selling liquor "be kept free from screens, blinds, curtains or anything to obstruct a clear view." This clause, intended to discourage illegal activity, invalidated the very setup of most speakeasies, which were often cramped, den-like by nature. By the end of 1933, it had been "more or less conceded," in the judgment of *Variety*, that the "speaks" were "doomed."[1]

Meanwhile, the Waldorf-Astoria and other hotels, having suffered under the twin calamities of the Depression and Prohibition, began to glimpse signs of a turnaround. By the middle of December, bids for Waldorf securities had risen 4 percent. Claiming, prematurely, that repeal was "taking class hotels out of receivership," the show business periodical *Variety* credited the new "boom times" to nostalgia for "the glory of a yesteryear Broadway." Younger New Yorkers, who had never known what it was like to order a drink legally, romanticized the Gay Nineties and the lost ideals of extravagance associated with them: "So much post-prohibition reminiscence concerning . . . Delmonico's, Sherry's, the Waldorf, Knickerbocker, etc., has been publicized . . . that with repeal everybody of any consciousness or sophistication immediately sought haunts approximating these glamorous antecedents." At the same time, Depression-era pricing ensured that what the *Brooklyn Eagle* described as "impecunious young men," college students escorting their dates, could afford the martinis, which cost thirty-five cents at the Waldorf's Empire Room—"Quite a drop from the old 'speak' prices of 75 cents and a dollar each, and no knowing what was in 'em." A Biltmore hotel representative, speaking to the *Chicago Tribune*, could not restrain his excitement: "Will I talk to you about our business under repeal? I'll say I will! This will give you an idea: on Monday, Dec. 4, the day before repeal . . . the Biltmore served 210 luncheons. On Wednesday, the first full day of repeal, we served 779 luncheons. Yesterday we served more than eight hundred. How's that?"[2]

The Waldorf, whose managers said they were "swamped" during the week after repeal, met their reported 25 percent increase in dinner patronage by hiring five new dance bands, spread throughout the cafés, restaurants, and the Empire Room and Sert Room (located to the right and left, respectively, of the Park Avenue lobby, near the hotel's main entrance). Men and women in evening attire bobbed to the orchestra of Spanish-born, Cuban-raised Xavier Cugat and his hit theme song, "My Shawl," in a polite manifestation of the rhumba fad sweeping America. Alternating with Cugat was his fellow Catalonian, Enrique (Enric) Madriguera, who interspersed Latin numbers with catchy popular ballads such as "Lovable": the melody, pushed along on willowy strings, conjured images of women in satin dresses, gliding past the Empire Room's beveled mirrors. By March 1934, in a celebration of the hotel's forty-first anniversary, Lucius Boomer announced that occupancy had increased by "more than 60 percent" over the previous winter: "We confidently look forward not only to increasing prosperity but to a resumption of the fine social life of pre-depression years." *Variety* again capped the ebullient mood, repeating a story heard "around New York" that repeal had brought the Waldorf "out of the red," and that the hotel was "doing the best of its career, even dating back to the old Waldorf (34th and Fifth) days, strictly on the cocktail trade."[3]

In truth, neither the higher occupancy rates nor restaurant patronage was substantial enough to bring the hotel a profit. Still, Boomer's upbeat message was not lost on the hundreds of workers employed in the Waldorf's lounges, bars, and restaurants, or the various unions competing to represent them. Since the onset of the Depression, workers' salaries across the industry had been lowered as hotels struggled to make payments to investors and banks. The U.S. Department of Labor reported wage cuts, among cooks and waiters, of 25 percent. Further, many hotels, the Waldorf included, had taken to charging employees for uniforms and laundry. In a manner reflective of Oscar's frequent proclamation that everything ran "like clockwork," the Waldorf became known among waiters for its "speed-up" system, which, according to the Communist newspaper the *Daily Worker*, required a waiter to "always have a mop or a dish in his hand and be on the run." Those in the ice department were said to have it the hardest: their jobs required them to "run to and fro from the cold ice room into the warm dining room." Another grueling job was that of banquet waiter, hired on a recurring basis or for a night, to work the large catered dinners that kept the Grand Ballroom and adjunct spaces filled many evenings of the week. Here, waiters did not have the chance to earn individual gratuities and were further subjected to imperious directives, as outlined in the "Banquet Services" employee guide from 1935. Though enforcement was by now relegated to assistants, the rules bore unmistakable signs of Oscar's originating hand:

> An offensive breath is an abominable thing for anybody, and especially in a waiter. It is preventable and cannot be tolerated. The same is true of body odors.
>
> Six extra rolls for each table on second service and NO MORE.

The hardest job: ice room worker at the Waldorf (Alfred Eisenstaedt/The LIFE Picture Collection via Getty Images).

Return all unserved food to the serving station, the Chef is the one who decides on its disposition—NOT YOU.[4]

Regular waiters, those who worked full-time in one of the restaurants, were in a better position, though soon they too faced a cut in their incomes— through measures that, ironically, had been created to improve conditions for American workers. In the summer of 1933, President Franklin Delano Roosevelt launched the National Recovery Act (NRA) as one component of his New Deal legislation, the scope of which was unprecedented within American history. With an aim of providing—for the first time in the United States—a federally mandated minimum wage, as well as of apportioning work across a broader swath of the labor force, the NRA established a standard forty-hour maximum workweek with a $15 minimum weekly salary. A total of $60 monthly (around $1,200 by twenty-first-century standards) would not have provided an existence far above the poverty line for many New Yorkers. Still, during the worst years of the Depression, a small minimum was better than nothing; and, given the generally low cost of living, some people—such as those fortunate enough to live in "model tenements" like the Lavanburg Homes on the Lower East Side, where three-room apartments cost $7.50 monthly—would have been able to provide for necessities and have money left over.

As an additional component of the NRA, employees were given the right to "organize and bargain collectively through representatives of their own choosing." This section of the act also stipulated that workers would be "free from the interference, restraint, or coercion of employers . . . in the designation of such representatives." As Joseph Rayback explained in his *History of American Labor*, the NRA, in seeming to create an "invitation to form independent unions under governmental protection," inspired a "sudden revival of labor unionism" throughout the country. Unions with declining membership now "quickened into life, forming new locals." At the same time, industry began discovering methods through which to subvert the NRA. To implement the act, Roosevelt's NRA administrator, General Hugh Johnson, had announced that each branch of industry would be given its own code, to which all related businesses would be subject. Soon the restaurant industry, claiming a forty-hour week was "not feasible or practicable," lobbied successfully for a modification to fifty-four hours. The restaurants' gain opened the door for other industries, each of which sponsored its own code committee, to follow suit, citing the need for exemptions based on special conditions. By the end of 1933, the codes, meant to be standard, had become so unevenly applied that labor organizers began to claim the NRA stood for "National Run Around."[5]

As head of the hotel committee, Lucius Boomer took the restaurants' lead and, during hearings in Washington in December 1933, also submitted a code with a maximum of fifty-four hours per week, at twenty-eight cents per hour. This worked out to the same amount of money per week—fifteen dollars— as first outlined in the president's NRA plans, but with an additional fourteen working hours thrown in. It was clear, with this step, that Lucius, like other business leaders, hoped simultaneously to comply with the system and resist it. As a member of the Sons of the American Revolution who could trace his ancestry to a lieutenant in the Continental Artillery, he thought of himself as patriotic and cooperative (NRA compliance was largely voluntary, but participating businesses were able to display insignias of a blue eagle, wings outstretched, alongside the slogan "WE DO OUR PART"). Privately, though, he was opposed to the concept of what former president Herbert Hoover had warned against, in his 1929 inaugural speech, as "government ownership or operation" in "relation to business." Edward Bernays recalled being invited by Boomer for luncheon with Hoover, by this time a resident of the Waldorf Towers, soon after Roosevelt's inauguration in 1933: "We ate in Mr. Hoover's huge high-ceilinged dining room. . . . Mr. Hoover seemed truly disturbed. Throughout lunch he emphasized that the United States had fallen on evil days. 'Soon there will be no private hospitals or private universities left in the country,' he said ominously. At one point . . . Hoover placed his finger ten inches from the edge of the table, moved it slowly along the tablecloth to the edge, let his finger drop, and stated funereally, 'Shortly we will be over the precipice.' Boomer agreed."[6]

Beyond his hostility to government control over business, Lucius was "adamant in his objection to labor unions, which he felt were going to ruin the country." Bernays viewed these attitudes as flaws in an otherwise admirable character: "Reason could not affect his fervor against Roosevelt and the New Deal." Like Hoover, Boomer was a mixture of progressive and conservative. The utopian ideals of his Koreshan upbringing rechanneled themselves, in adulthood, through an adherence to welfare capitalism and the theory that American business and not government held the responsibility for providing social services. Few other 1930s hotel workers were offered the range of benefits Lucius set up at the Waldorf: in addition to vacation pay and health insurance, employees had access to YMCA memberships and an in-house library, as well as classes in French, German, cooking, financial planning, and (for those interested in advancing their careers within the hospitality field) management, purchasing, and front office procedure. Employees were also encouraged to offer feedback through suggestion boxes placed throughout the hotel: "There is only one key to these boxes and Mr. Boomer has it," the employee manual assured. Undeniably these initiatives, like the academic program Boomer helped establish at Cornell, were rooted in humanistic sincerity. Nonetheless, the 1930s Waldorf was in such a precarious state that Lucius—even had he sympathized with Roosevelt—would have been angered by any mandate to hire more people than he felt necessary.[7]

As the months passed, additional flaws in the NRA system, which Roosevelt's administration had initially created to encompass mainly large-scale, interstate industries (like manufacture, rail transportation and shipping), began to show. For example, how could a code be applied to the same categories of business in two cities with widely different economies? And what about service workers, whose incomes were not always based on a fixed salary? One particular sticking point had to do with the factoring in of gratuities for waiters. For owners of hotels and restaurants, a minimum salary for waiters was "too burdensome an innovation"; consequently, in a revision of the hotel code submitted for President Roosevelt's signature, the twenty-eight cents hourly minimum for general hotel workers was reduced by half for waiters, who were expected to make up the difference in tips. Alarmed by the idea of depending on the whim of a dining public (many of whom might mistakenly believe that those who served them were already being provided for, under the NRA), waiters in Boston assailed the code as "inconsistent and un-American."[8]

New York City waiters, backed by the American Federation of Labor (AFL), were equally concerned: during the third week in December, they threatened a New Year's Eve strike if the new code was not modified. As this would be the first New Year's celebration freed from Prohibition, and patrons in hotels and restaurants across the city were expected to spend large sums in order to have a good time, the NRA acted quickly. It directed Mrs. Elinore Herrick, New York State mediator in charge of collective bargaining, to negotiate a settlement between waiters and their employers. Presided over by two officials of the AFL Local 16 chapter, the discussions yielded an agreement that waiters' wages would remain the same as they had been, even if the president were to sign the revised code. There were, however, additional points of contention—the fifty-four-hour week, salary deductions for meals—that Herrick's agreement overlooked, leaving many waiters frustrated.

After a large buildup, the strike threat ended quickly—too quickly, it seemed to those who felt they'd been sold downriver in what one account termed the AFL's "bluff." Resentment continued into the New Year and provided an opportunity for smaller, less established unions to gain a foothold in attracting dissatisfied workers. In contrast to the AFL, which emphasized a "craft" orientation designed to unite workers of the same trade, the newer unions, attracting support from left-wing political organizations, stressed the importance of an "industrial" approach that would unite the entire rank and file, from dishwashers, porters, and icemen to the highest-paid chefs. Determined to keep out unions of any kind, hotels responded to the new labor climate by cobbling together a number of preexisting craft societies (such as the Geneva Association, a longtime waiters' club) into something called the Federation of Hotel and Restaurant Guilds, which they encouraged workers to join. Labor organizers quickly assailed the guild as a "company union"—that is, one giving the appearance of being led by employees but controlled, in reality, by corporate heads—and a "fraud."

Meanwhile, organized labor had begun responding to the NRA's inadequacies, through what Rayback described as a "wave of strikes" that "spread through the nation"—to the point that, by 1934, "almost one-seventh of the total [American] labor force . . . became involved in industrial conflicts." In New York, strikes extended across multiple industries and even, at various times during the 1930s, took place on top of one another. At one point, a subway strike of construction workers completing the IND line overlapped with one made by cleaners and dyers in the garment industry—which was followed some months later by the first-ever strike of New York burlesque performers. At the Waldorf, a harbinger of trouble arrived on January 19, 1934, when Oscar assembled the kitchen and restaurant workers to ask about their union affiliation. Discovering that many were connected with the Amalgamated, one of the new left-wing unions, Oscar said nothing further but ended the meeting in what observers recalled as a state of consternation.[9]

Four days later, on Tuesday, January 23, 600 of the Waldorf-Astoria's staff—waiters, cooks, busboys, and others—left their posts at the height of the dinner hour, seven o'clock, and walked off their jobs. Diners in the Sert Room, some of whom had already finished one course and had napkins spread across their laps in preparation for another, grew restless and began to leave, while the orchestra, in the words of leftist commentator Herbert Solow, "played on as when the Lusitania sank." The "industry's flagship," the Waldorf-Astoria, was going down. Solow reported that one waiter, in response to a diner who begged not to be starved, shot back, with a French accent, "We have starrrved for yearrrs; trrry it forrr one meal." Others delighted in stories that executives had been recruited to fill in for missing cooks and waiters. "Boomer waited on tables," invented the left-wing *Militant* paper. "And Oscar tried his fat hands at cooking. But the diners couldn't get so much as a hamburger-on-rye. It was very, very sad." In truth, with national unemployment exceeding 20 percent, the Waldorf had plenty of reserves. By the next day, Boomer reported that waiters from as far away as Philadelphia had applied for jobs, and that as many as 200 of the defectors had come back. The AFL local even sent the Waldorf a letter offering help— a move guaranteed to arouse further suspicion of the "legit" union's motives. As far as Boomer was concerned, service at the hotel was back to normal and business was "even better than usual."[10]

Then he added, with premature confidence, "The strike is broken."[11]

During the five weeks of battle that followed the Waldorf walkout, no one could point to a specific event that had triggered such a subversive act on the part of employees, whom the corporation liked to portray as part of a big family ("*We* are glad you are an employee of The Waldorf-Astoria," beamed the handbook. "We hope *you* are"). Most believed it was the dismissal of a sous chef, Andre Fournigault, known among workers for his militant unionism. Sometime during the afternoon of January 23, the truculent Fournigault had had an argument with Oscar or another of his superiors. In a statement to the press, Boomer explained that representatives of the Amalgamated Food Workers then appeared in his office to demand shorter hours, higher wages, and, above all, union recognition—along with the reinstatement of Fournigault, a French native who had worked at the hotel since its 1931 opening: "They indicated it was their purpose to require that this employee be retained in his position because the representatives of the Amalgamated Food Workers had decided he was competent. . . . They were informed that the matter of employment in the Waldorf-Astoria is a question of individual skill and merit and involves satisfaction given by employees to patrons of the hotel."[12]

The merit question had been a stumbling block for Boomer in his negotiations with administrators of the NRA and their insistence that employees be given the right to bargain collectively. Wary of anything that might imply acceptance of labor unions (which generally function as workers' representatives during the collective bargaining process), Boomer had insisted on the inclusion of a clause stipulating that hotel proprietors could hire and fire "on the basis of individual merit subject to the fluctuating conditions of the business." The NRA disagreed. When President Roosevelt signed the hotel code in November 1933, neither side was happy. Boomer resented the exclusion of the merit clause, along with the idea that he might be forced to retain an employee such as Fournigault, whom he would describe as "unsatisfactory." Labor representatives, for their part, were angered that the workweek had expanded from forty to fifty-four hours without a corresponding increase in the fifteen-dollar minimum wage. They also protested the retention of practices such as the "split watch," in which waiters were required to work both lunch and dinner but received no compensation for the space in between. For Boomer, then, dismissing Fournigault was an assertion of his rights as a proprietor; for the Amalgamated Food Workers, pushing for union recognition exploited the one hopeful spot (collective bargaining) in a code so troublesome it made that of the steel industry, notorious for its promotion of company unions, appear, in the words of Herbert Solow, "like a labor charter."[13]

On January 25, the walkout turned into a general strike after Boomer and his colleagues at the New York City Hotel Association refused—or, more accurately, given their insistence that service was normal, ignored—the Amalgamated's demands. By the next day the strike had spread to more than a dozen hotels as newspapers warned of a "crisis." Speaking from union headquarters in a dim Eighth Avenue tenement, B. J. Field, the Amalgamated's secretary, proclaimed that as many as 30,000 were "ready to respond to the strike call," though hotel officials insisted on a number closer to 800. As was often the case with these kinds of estimates, issued at a time when labor disputes tore at the city on such frequent basis, the union overstated while business owners underreported. Nonetheless, an investigation made by the *New York Times* suggested the strike was indeed having an impact. At the Park Central, Fifty-Fifth Street and Seventh Avenue, 65 out of 150 waiters took off their aprons and left, forcing managers to scramble for replacements. In the meantime, hungry diners offered to go into the kitchen and serve themselves ("some of them did," reported the *Times*). The Savoy-Plaza's entire wait staff walked off, along with 16 cooks at the Roosevelt, 30 waiters and busboys at the Brevoort in Greenwich Village, and 20 employees of the Essex House.[14]

Still the Waldorf, as New York's most influential hotel, remained, in one description, the "storm center." There, an estimated thousand men in raincoats crowded the sidewalks on Lexington and Park Avenues, carrying signs that denounced "UNION DISCRIMINATION." One pedestrian, decked in top hat and evening attire and headed, in all likelihood, for the Empire Room, became an unintentional sympathizer when he found himself carried along by the strikers in a manner that, according to the *Times*, "added to the general hilarity." Much humor came from the way protesters latched onto the Waldorf's elite reputation as something irrelevant during these times of

Striking waiters at the Waldorf, January 1934 (author's collection).

widespread poverty. One youthful picketer, part of a "particularly noisy group," carried a sign whose words suggested nothing less than a demolition of the rarefied ideals that George Boldt, Oscar, and, in his less utopian moments, Boomer had upheld as essential to the hotel's social significance—through the years of Albert Morris Bagby, blueblood horse shows, and debutante balls: "No More Junior Proms at the Waldorf!"[15]

New York hotels had long been known for their resistance to unionization, which they maintained over the course of several strikes in the late nineteenth and early twentieth centuries. The first of these was in 1893 and arose in part as a response to the insistence of some proprietors—George Boldt among them—that waiters shave their beards. Waiters also protested against sixteen-hour days and the system of having to pay for their own uniforms (a onetime cost of forty-five dollars, at a time when monthly salaries averaged sixty dollars). Others were angered by charges imposed for small offenses for which it would have been hard to fix definite blame, such as the kind indicated in a memo Oscar once wrote to the Waldorf's chief housekeeper: "In future, I wish you would send me all bills for cleaning dresses which have been soiled in diningrooms [sic], as I have decided to make the waiters pay the cost of cleaning all dresses damaged through their negligence."[16]

On April 16, 1893, forty waiters associated with the newly formed International Hotel Employees Society "flung down their napkins" at the Holland House, "just as the hotel's guests were beginning to think about dinner." The strike then spread to the Waldorf, which Boldt had opened just four weeks earlier. Boldt, who made it clear that "I object to my men joining a union, and they know it," nonetheless sent word that he was open to discussions for the sake of maintaining peace. In a move typical of his qualities as a leader, at a time when the Waldorf was a comparatively small concern—a business, not yet a corporation—Boldt, it was reported, "called all the employés [sic] . . . together late in the evening and promised that all their just demands would be met." With this "assurance," the waiters were content to have the strike "declared off."[17]

According to economist Morris Horowitz, reporting in his 1960 study, *The New York Hotel Industry*, efforts to organize the entire rank and file of hotel workers were hampered by the dominance of small local unions that had "no incentive to expand." These locals kept out the competition through prohibitive initiation fees and other means that allowed them to hold "absolute control" over most of the city's top dining establishments (Horowitz quoted labor leader Hugo Ernst as characterizing the setup as a "job trust," rather than a union per se). The International AFL had just two locals in New York City, one in Manhattan and the other in Brooklyn. Both were "composed principally of . . . craftsmen, waiters and bartenders," and neither local showed interest in "organizing the larger group of semiskilled and unskilled workers in the hotels and restaurants," many of whom were ambivalent when it came to questions of union representation. In his 1956 book, *Union House,*

Union Bar, writer Matthew Josephson described the bind in which many hotel workers found themselves: "On the one hand the employer offered [the worker] the company union through which he could 'protect' his rights by permission of the management. . . . On the other hand were the free and legitimate trade unions with representatives of the workers' own choosing, but to join them often meant the loss of one's job."[18]

Organized on an industrial basis in 1921, the Amalgamated Food Workers' Union led its first New York strike, a successful effort involving pastry chefs at the Hotel Plaza, just two years later. In April 1929 it started what Horowitz described as a "long and bitter" strike against cafeterias in the Garment District. Without support from the AFL locals, this more ambitious strike, in contrast to its predecessor, was "doomed from the start." Cafeteria proprietors obtained injunctions against picketers, and Amalgamated leaders were arrested and jailed. The Amalgamated's influence among the rank and file of workers remained strong, however, and by early 1934 the union had attracted the support of the Communist League of America. This, contrary to its name, was actually an opposition splinter group, formed in 1928 by former Communists who were loyal to expelled Soviet leader Leon Trotsky. After the aborted New Year's Eve strike led by the AFL, the "Trotskyists" sent in B. J. Field, a former Wall Street analyst who had undergone a political reawakening, to confer with the hotel waiters, many of whom spoke only French. Soon, according to Trotskyist leader James Cannon, who chronicled his version of events in a book of printed lectures, the waiters insisted that the French-speaking, intellectual Field represent them as the union's secretary. As a result, Field, well-intentioned but impulsive and egotistical, inexperienced in union affairs, found himself leader of the Waldorf-Astoria uprising, which by now had expanded to become what, at the time, was the largest hotel strike in New York City history.[19]

Inflated by the overnight media attention, in which his dark-haired, mustachioed image appeared, as Cannon wrote, "in all the New York papers," Field soon made enemies of his fellow Trotskyists, some of whom were alarmed at his refusal to cooperate with rival political organizations (including a group of Communists who offered support through their own paper, the *Daily Worker*) in ways that would have presented a unified front. Instead of "organizing the militancy of the ranks from below," Field sought support from the NRA's Elinore Herrick, whom the Trotskyists viewed as a "government shark" whose only goal was to "knife the strike." But the tough-minded Herrick did not think much of Field either. At a hearing on February 6, she rebuked the Amalgamated leader for calling the strike in the first place: "You know that we have many times taken up the discharge of one man because of his alleged union activities. . . . Why did you not come to this board when [Fournigault] was discharged at the Waldorf and before the walkout there?" In the meantime, Paul Coulcher of AFL Local 16 had further damaged the Amalgamated's credibility by going to court in an attempt to restrain it from picketing restaurants in which the larger union had agreements. This was, in the words of Matthew Josephson, "an action that few union officers would have cared to take even under the circumstances of jurisdictional rivalry."[20]

Local 16 had every reason to want to curtail the Amalgamated, especially once the latter's members began directing efforts toward smaller restaurants, those not associated with hotels. Though details wouldn't become known until a widely publicized trial in 1937, Coulcher and several of his AFL associates (the same men who had "negotiated" the calling off of the New Year's Eve strike) were in league with the well-known gangster Dutch Schultz. Working with Schultz's henchmen, they set up a dummy union, the Metropolitan Restaurant and Cafeteria Association, whose sole purpose was to extort money from owners in return for protection. Those who resisted the Association's high initiation fees were visited with pickets and, in some instances, stink bombs. Then, Coulcher and his fellow racketeers would come back, negotiate a smaller fee, and the bombs and pickets would disappear. Amalgamated, portrayed by Local 16 as a rogue—"We are not cooperating with the Amalgamated in any form," asserted Coulcher—further diminished its standing when, on February 5, a thousand strikers descended on the Waldorf-Astoria. A few of them became unruly and fought with police, who responded by issuing a riot call. The wife of one worker, it was charged, bit an officer's thumb, breaking the skin, while someone else allegedly caused a pedestrian to fall and shatter his kneecaps. Meanwhile, Boomer continued to insist the strike was nonexistent.[21]

Clearly, the Amalgamated—to say nothing of its strike effort—was in trouble. But, quietly and behind the scenes, sympathy toward the workers and their struggle had been building within certain quarters. Much to the Waldorf's eventual distress, help for the strikers was on the way.

———

February 1934 was a turbulent month in New York labor affairs. Brooklyn laundry workers, some making as little as sixteen cents an hour, picketed for the right to a minimum wage, while, in a citywide taxi strike, nonstriking drivers had the doors and windows of their cabs smashed. Some were dragged out and beaten by union members. Despite their resort to violence in a few cases, the taxi strikers could claim what newspaper editorialists saw as a legitimate grievance: the city wanted to pocket, rather than share with drivers, a fare tax that had been collected but later nullified in court. Still, the taxi strike never attracted prominent support from social and political figures, most of whom had the money to ride in private cars. Hotels were different. Many left-leaning celebrities resided in them, ate frequently in their restaurants, and thus faced the moral dilemma of being served by underpaid workers on a daily basis. After waiters at the Hotel Algonquin, known for its "Round Table" of quip-spouting literati, left their posts on January 29, actress and singer Elsie Janis, who lived at the hotel, offered to take their place. Fellow Round Table wits, among them the caustic *New Yorker* writer Alexander Woollcott, lent assistance in an effort to keep hotel managers from hiring strikebreakers. Soon, other notables joined the cause: picketing outside of Greenwich Village's bohemian Hotel Brevoort, the playwright Susan Glaspell (best known for founding the Provincetown Players) lent vocal support, telling reporters that she had visited Amalgamated headquarters and walked away "convinced the strikers are right."[22]

On February 6, Glaspell and her fellow sympathizers, a group now expanded to include columnist Heywood Broun as well as Theodore Dreiser (whose 1925 best-selling novel, *An American Tragedy*, had dealt graphically with class divisions in the United States), scored a victory. Eleanor Roosevelt was planning to attend a Waldorf luncheon the following day, in order to sew the NRA's insignia into a hat—part of a launch ceremony, sponsored by the Millinery Code Authority, for clothing marked with the blue eagle label. Pointing to the Waldorf as "the heart of the dispute," the protesters convinced Roosevelt to have the event moved to a different hotel, the Governor Clinton, one of several on the Amalgamated's "white list" of places where no strike was in effect. The telegram further made clear that the Waldorf deserved to be singled out and boycotted for its symbolic importance: "by absenting yourself . . . from Waldorf-Astoria," the First Lady would "avoid appearance of acquiescing in anti-union attitude of hotel corporations." Later that afternoon the group, now augmented by several Algonquin Round Table writers, met at the home of Norman Thomas, Socialist Party presidential nominee and former Presbyterian minister, to review plans for a new act of disturbance scheduled for the same night. The self-appointed leader would be a twenty-five-year-old poet and magazine editor named Selden Rodman.[23]

Rodman was long and sinewy, the ideal person to stage a demonstration in which height would provide a crucial asset. The place was the high-ceilinged Empire Room of the Waldorf-Astoria, where orchestra leader Meyer Davis's swooning music, delivered with a surfeit of strings and lack of brass, could have been a soundtrack to an early 1930s romantic movie—the kind in which millionaires fell for astonished shopgirls after a night of delirious dancing that felt, as the young women would proclaim, "like a dream." This particular night, however, there was an additional presence, born not of Upper East Side cotillions but of the grimy streets of Hell's Kitchen: a squad of house detectives, wielding blackjacks and positioned at strategic points along the room's perimeter. Outside, in the Park Avenue lobby, reporters and cameramen waited for the moment they'd been promised by Rodman and his cohorts. Only, it didn't come. Rodman had spread the word to such an extent that everyone—from the press in the lobby to the hotel's house staff to Meyer Davis—was prepared. For the orchestra members, this meant playing as long as they physically could, in the evident hope that, after an hour of uninterrupted music during which no demonstration could take place, the plotters would get tired, give up their plan, go home to their armchairs and practice socialism there.

That moment didn't come either. Rodman, pale in a black dinner jacket, was determined to make a speech. By this time, his courage had been bolstered not only by the consumption of several cocktails but by the arrival of Woollcott and fellow Algonquin wit Dorothy Parker, both of whom gave what the papers described as "moral support." Finally, the exhausted musicians stopped playing and Selden climbed atop his upholstered chair. Stocky detectives tensed. "There is a strike in progress at this hotel," the former Yale student announced. "The manager of the hotel—." Selden disappeared as his chair, pulled from under him, flew across the room. Tables overturned, sending china to the floor. Blackjacks fell and satin sleeves, grabbed by meaty fists, tore from jackets. "Is this a private fight?" Dorothy Parker asked, borrowing an old boxing term. "Or can anyone get in [bet] on it?" Young women in ruffled dresses gazed widely, startled by the sight of such hooliganism at the Waldorf-Astoria. Others, including the novelist Mary McCarthy, shouted encouragement as Selden's disheveled head bobbed up and down like a cork. Somehow his accomplice and coeditor at *Common Sense* magazine, a senator's son named Alfred Bingham, managed to get up for another round and speak: "We urge every self-respecting man and woman in this room to join our protest and leave the dining room with us. We also urge the waiters here to walk out—"[24]

Bingham was down, as the field widened into a circle of tables knocked over like set pieces in a Marx Brothers movie farce. Davis marshaled his players back to the dais for a reprise of his version of 1933's big song, "Did You Ever See a Dream Walking?" ("it's too, *too* divine!"), while claques of people began to leave, some willingly, others not. Rodman and Bingham, yelping from bruises, were yanked by what remained of their collars along a side corridor and thrown to the street. Two other young men, supporters who were less active in the protest but unfortunate enough to be standing in the line of fire, were arrested by detectives, taken to the Fifty-First Street station, and charged with disorderly conduct. Parker and Woollcott simply left the

Empire Room, "chatting gaily." The next day, twenty-six-year-old Norman Burnstine, one of the men arrested, would charge the hotel with using excessive violence during what had been intended as a peaceful demonstration. Responding to charges that detectives had swung blackjacks and billy clubs, Lucius Boomer, the "chief enemy of the striking waiters," offered angry denials: "These people just tried to stage a show." Still, when news of the outbreak appeared, the photo-heavy *Daily News* printed evidence: an image of a Waldorf house detective brandishing a club as he moved in on a wincing Norman Burnstine.[25]

Enter New York City mayor Fiorello La Guardia. In an older day of iron fists—under the 1920s mayoralty of Jimmy Walker—hard-handed police tactics would have been overlooked, if not rewarded. But the short-tempered former congressman from Italian Harlem, a progressive Republican who had scarcely been in office one month, was determined to fight for the rights of labor—even if it meant angering his chief of police, who eventually resigned over mayoral-prescribed limitations in the handling of taxi and hotel pickets. Indeed, La Guardia's greatest achievement as congressman had been the passage (after a nine-year fight) of the Norris–La Guardia Act, outlawing notorious "yellow dog" employment contracts that required workers to agree not to join a union. La Guardia was no stranger to bullying. His biographer Thomas Kessner wrote that "few politicians were more adept at the creative use of interpersonal terror." But La Guardia's sympathies naturally gravitated toward the underdog—in this case, members of the working class and their right to a decent living. As another biographer recounted, La Guardia during his years in Congress had become a champion of the Eskimo people, whom he believed were "innocents, exploited by everyone who crossed their path." An illustrative story went around that once, after securing benefits for an Eskimo tribe so remote that the Department of the Interior couldn't locate them to disburse the funds, La Guardia pointed out: "That just shows how neglected they've been, . . . They can't even be found."[26]

Privately, La Guardia was a terror. Believing it the ideal method of getting the most from his employees, he berated and insulted in ways that could degenerate, as Kessner observed, "into abuse for the sheer pleasure of it." At the same time, this man who more than one observer characterized as Napoleonic, so short his feet often didn't touch the floor when he sat, was hypersensitive when it came to himself. La Guardia hurt others' feelings, but his ego was prone to being wounded by any slight, real or imagined. As New York's first Italian American mayor, immigrant member of an ethnic group often visited with prejudice and discrimination, La Guardia believed he had a lot to prove. His was a crusade to improve the city, win federal funds and help the economy, beat down long-standing city patterns of corruption and favoritism, and root out what was left of Jazz Age immorality (most strikingly, for the last effort, through his obsessive fight against gambling and slot machines). "Our indefatigable mayor," wrote the *New York Times* sardonically, in February 1934, "takes his duties not only seriously but comprehensively." All of these factors—La Guardia's thin-skinned temperament, his regard for organized labor and the working class, the rashness of his actions—combined to bring trouble for Lucius Boomer and his associates in the New York hotel industry.[27]

Two days after what some papers were calling "The Battle of the Empire Room," La Guardia received a letter from Jean Bamford, a young "sympathizer with the NRA labor codes," which, she asserted, "the Waldorf-Astoria [had] willfully violated." Bamford, who lived in Greenwich Village and moved in artistic circles, described how she "took part in the demonstration of protest" at the Waldorf and had personally witnessed "hired thugs of the management, armed with blackjacks and dressed in evening clothes." These men, Bamford charged, had "assaulted" peaceful demonstrators who, "having voiced their protest," were leaving the Empire Room "quietly": "If violence on the part of strikers is reprehensible, it is even more reprehensible on the part of supposedly reputable interests who hire . . . strong-arm men and racketeers to uphold their position of defiance to the NRA codes."[28]

Bamford then reaffirmed her support for the mayor and implored him to help the strikers: "Far from having lost my belief in your liberal and humane viewpoint, I feel sure that you will devote every effort to guaranteeing fair play to those championing the rights of justice and collective bargaining. . . . I feel that the management of the Waldorf-Astoria deserves a public rebuke

Mayor Fiorello La Guardia at the Waldorf, 1940, in a rare lighthearted
moment (author's collection).

for the way it handled the situation on Tuesday night, and I am sure that you,
who have ever been noted for your courage, will not hesitate to make it."[29]

La Guardia did not criticize the Waldorf publicly—yet—but a reference
in his files to an attached "letter from Hotel Waldorf-Astoria Corporation,
to Miss Jean Bamford, relative to waiters strike," suggests he forced the hotel
to issue a written response. He also moved to involve himself in the strike
for the first time. On Saturday afternoon, February 10, a few hours before
strikers embarked on a new round of disruptive activity (one threw a rock
through the window of the Hotel Taft, where it sailed past teatime patrons
to land on the cocktail bar), the mayor announced that, in labor disputes
affecting the well-being of citizens, his administration would "take whatever
steps it could to restore normal conveniences to the public." La Guardia, a
strong admirer of Roosevelt, wanted to ensure New Yorkers of his support
for the president's New Deal legislation. Further, he was prepared to employ

all the legal tools in his command as executive for the purpose of upholding the common good. Stating his desire for hotels to "get together with their employees and end the present differences," the mayor also mentioned, as an aside—hotel managers should have seen it as a warning—that he had closed two strikebreaking Brooklyn laundries, nailing them for unpaid water taxes.[30]

Meanwhile, Norman Thomas and his celebrated friends kept up their efforts, sending telegrams to La Guardia, as Elinore Herrick worked to fashion a settlement. On February 16, newspapers made an announcement: the strike was over. Thanks to a conference between the NRA's Regional Labor Board, hotel representatives, and Field (who was still criticized by his Trotskyist allies for putting too much trust in Herrick), a four-step settlement called first for the removal of pickets; second, for hotels to reemploy individual workers "so far as conditions permit"; third, for the union to send representative groups of workers to each hotel in order to facilitate said reemployment; and, fourth, for the establishment of hearings to investigate hotel working conditions, which, Herrick admitted, were characterized by "abuses." However, in their rush some newspapers misreported the terms, leading to confusion for the strikers and their putative champion, Mayor La Guardia. In truth, only the first two provisions were part of the actual settlement; point three, regarding the workers' committees, was merely an idea that had been discussed—one the hotel representatives would never agree to formally, as it would have implied recognition of the Amalgamated union. As soon as Field learned that the representatives sent to hotels had been turned away by managers, he cried foul, claiming he'd been duped by the Labor Board, and immediately called back the pickets. By the next morning, February 17, the strike was on again.[31]

A key part of the Amalgamated's effort was its stipulation that the Waldorf agree to rehire Andre Fournigault, who boasted to *Herald Tribune* reporters, "I am the symbol of the strike. . . . They'll have to take me back." Not so, said Boomer, who brushed off the suggestion as preposterous. Things were looking hopeless for Field and the Amalgamated: Herrick's efforts to mediate had become, in the words of James Cannon, "a noose for the strike,"

with the workers subject to an agreement that made the question of reemployment up to the hotels, "as conditions permit." But La Guardia was not
finished. At the time, he likely felt pressure to reassert his support of working men and women, due to problems that had developed with another of
President Roosevelt's recovery projects, the Civil Works Administration
(CWA). Federal CWA funds, for which La Guardia had lobbied even before
he entered office, were being held up through administrative inefficiencies
on the national level, with the result that a percentage of the 56,000 workers
hired by the mayor's new parks commissioner, Robert Moses, to construct
recreational spaces throughout the city now faced the prospect of a layoff.
Clearly, this would have been a bad time for the mayor to be portrayed as
reneging on campaign promises. After receiving another telegram from Norman Thomas, whom La Guardia regarded as a close political associate, the
mayor stepped forward to the press once again, issuing a simple message to
hotels and the union: work it out.[32]

"The hotel strike has gone on long enough now," he insisted to reporters
for the *World-Telegram,* "that its termination has become a matter of general public interest." Unfortunately, La Guardia was still confused about the
exact terms worked out under the auspices of Herrick and the Labor Board.
As part of his statement, which was also printed in the *New York Sun,* he
directed the Amalgamated to cease picketing immediately and send out
committees of strikers to the managers of affected hotels to discuss a settlement. This was exactly what Boomer and his colleagues had insisted they
would not do. When the committees arrived, naively brandishing copies of
the mayor's statement in the papers as a directive for both sides to follow,
they discovered that the hotel managers (who kept up steady communica-
tion with one another through the offices of their association on Fifty-
Seventh Street) refused any substantive discussions. At the Waldorf, the
"secretary went in and when she came out she told us that Mr. Bloomer [*sic*]
would not see any committee from the union." Mr. Enderly, Boomer's head
of personnel, asserted that "no mass reinstatement would be made, only
by single application": "We asked him if the strikebreakers would be dis-

charged and he said at no time would that happen. He also said that we would not find any hotel who would do that."[33]

The various committee reports, one for each hotel visited, were sent directly to La Guardia on February 19 and featured comments that could have been deliberately fashioned to rouse the mayor's ire. When reminded that the hotel's response was "to be reported to Mayor La Guardia," John Barres of the Brevoort claimed that "it made no difference" and that "he had nothing to talk about." A clerk at another hotel told employee delegates that he "did not care what the Mayor said," while someone at the Savoy–Plaza added that "a statement in the press was of no value to him." Most galling was the manager of the Park Central, who, after being told the committee had come to see him "by request of Mayor La Guardia," responded that he "didn't know" the mayor and that, anyway, "Mayor La Guardia wasn't running the hotels." This was a direct challenge to authority, made worse by the next day's headlines: "Mayor Intervenes in Hotel Strike" and, embarrassingly, "Mayor Fails." Lambasting the managers for their "arrogant" attitude, La Guardia threatened that if they refused to "settle this vexing strike," they would have to take "full responsibility." Then he added, ominously, "The Mayor will act to protect the public."[34]

———

Tuesday, February 20, would have seemed an unlikely evening for surprise attacks. The city, having suffered one of its coldest winters in years, was digging out from a blizzard that had demobilized much of it and caused further hardship for those out of work. Diners in the Waldorf-Astoria's restaurants were no doubt looking forward to a warm meal, irrespective of whether it was served by union waiters. In short, no one was prepared for what happened around seven o'clock, when five city health officials turned up at the Park Avenue entrance, demanded to see Mr. Boomer, and immediately launched into an inspection of the kitchens, pantries, and the entire 500-member corps of cooks, food handlers, and waiters. In Boomer's words, they "turned the place upside down." Men were taken in groups to the house physician's office and examined for signs of tuberculosis, scabies, and any other potential threat to, as La Guardia had put it, "the public welfare." The process, which froze dinner service for most of the evening, lasted all the way to midnight and even had to be continued the next day. Similar "health raids" took place at the Roosevelt, the Park Central (which had just been fully inspected and passed the week prior), the Astor—all the hotels, in fact, that had rebuffed the mayor's directive. Any doubt the inspections were conceived as anything other than punishment evaporated when an official admitted he'd been told to arrive at dinnertime. "All in a day's work for the Health Department," La Guardia said, cheerfully.[35]

As for what the inspectors found, La Guardia called it "astounding, startling, shocking, and revolting." If conditions weren't "immediately corrected," he would be forced to take "drastic methods to protect the public." Then, in a remark calculated to hit Park and Fifth Avenue proprietors where it hurt, he added, "These are not Bowery hotels that I am referring to." In truth, little had been discovered beyond a number of employees who were working without official health department cards. These workers, hotel owners insisted, had already been certified by a physician, but their cards had not yet arrived, there being a standard delay between approval and documentation. Most people saw through the theatrics. "Informed persons," observed the *Sun*, "are not likely to believe that managers of our great hotels permit conditions broadly described by Mr. La Guardia to exist in the places where they live and on which their reputations and fortunes depend." Still the mayor had made his point. On February 22, nearly one month after the strike had begun, Lucius Boomer and two other hotel representatives initiated a meeting with La Guardia at City Hall, where they indicated their readiness to settle.[36]

By now, though, even supporters were criticizing the mayor. A painter named Langdon Gillet sent La Guardia a telegram denouncing "the utterly scandalous and unwarranted clubbing of our hotels through the means of the Health Department." The *Sun* called the raids "a political attack of a kind unparalleled in this city," while the *Times* noted correctly that such strong-arm tactics were "precisely the methods" employed by the corrupt Tammany-aligned mayoral administrations whose ways the new mayor had vowed to change ("he ought to be able to see that extreme abuse of the right to inspect or regulate ought not to be resorted to for any ulterior purpose"). AFL Local 16's Paul Coulcher, whose connection with Dutch Schultz and his mobsters had not yet come to light, reminded La Guardia that "legitimate organized labor" was not supporting the Amalgamated union or its strike. Elinore Herrick, meanwhile, informed the mayor that he'd been mistaken in his interpretation of the earlier settlement terms: indeed, she explained, hotel managers had never agreed to meet with union representatives. The result was that, by the time of a second meeting with Boomer on February 23, La Guardia was starting to weaken in his resolve. Three days later, he told reporters he was ready to move on. Announced the *Times*, "MAYOR TAKES HANDS OFF HOTEL STRIKE."[37]

La Guardia's about-face puzzled some observers while angering others. The *Daily Worker* expressed resentment at the mayor's decision to "wash his hands of the whole affair," calling out, in particular, his seeming lack of interest in going after the detective and employment agencies that had often hired, during this strike and others (the paper charged), thugs and strongmen to intimidate workers. To the *Brooklyn Citizen*, a paper that had taken a position against the hotel strike, La Guardia's sudden silence was easy to explain. The thin-skinned mayor simply "could not stand the criticism by his own newspaper organs for his actions in having the Health Department 'crack down' on the hotels." It was all in keeping, the paper opined, with the nature of a bully—one who knew how to throw punches but, in the end, lacked the personal equilibrium to "take it on the chin."[38]

Now foundering under the leadership of B. J. Field, who had lost support from the Trotskyists (they took the rare step of expelling him for insubordination, midway through the strike), the Amalgamated had no choice but to go back to the terms Herrick had negotiated two weeks earlier: hotel owners would reemploy strikers "so far as conditions permit." Those who couldn't be rehired immediately would be put on a "preferential list." On this basis, a humbled Field announced on February 28 that the Amalgamated had called off the strike. The union's one gain was that hotels agreed to let go of strikebreakers—that is, nonunion members who had been hired since the strike began—but the absence of an imposed schedule allowed managers to take their time with this. By the end of March, according to the *Herald Tribune*, "many hotels were not living up to their promises." The industry felt itself under no legal obligation: when Herrick appointed the Hotel Association's secretary, Mark Caldwell, to a five-member committee for purposes of investigating labor conditions, he refused to serve. The committee moved forward anyway but later disbanded in frustration after hotel managers ignored requests to submit documents or appear at a hearing. According to the committee's final report, hotels had exhibited "complete defiance."[39]

In December 1934, New Yorkers celebrated the one-year anniversary of the repeal of Prohibition. Interviewed for the *Times*, Oscar spoke of a "general improvement in the hotel business" with the return of liquor, while George Boldt's old competitor, Fred Muschenheim (still in charge at the Astor), attested that hotels were "looking forward to rather a prosperous year." These were optimistic pronouncements: in truth, alcohol was subject to heavy government taxes, and its sale was not enough to lift hotels out of the red. The Waldorf-Astoria by the middle of 1934 was two and a half years behind on rent; its corporation had liabilities of close to $5.5 million and liquid assets of just over $550,000. In the 1920s, hotels had been able to offset losses by increasing room rates, but now, given the general economic climate, raising prices was no longer an option. For the industry at large, then, survival was tied closely to the effort to keep down labor costs. This in turn led hotels to take an increasingly hostile stance toward the NRA and its codes. A hotel executive summed up the general feeling, one of being lost in a world that business leaders of the Hoover era couldn't recognize: "Washington has done everything for labor. Now we feel that Washington must do something for capital."[40]

In September, hotel officials proposed another modification of the NRA code, this time with a 25 percent cut in the minimum wage. NRA officials in Washington, noting the minimum was already fifteen dollars for a fifty-four-hour workweek, claimed this would "bring pay to just about the lowest for any Blue Eagle code." Further, the American Hotel Association requested an executive order that would exempt any member from code provisions if it was unable to earn "operating expenses, taxes, interest and insurance charges." As the association was well aware, this would have applied to the majority of New York City's hotels. The NRA was "stumped," as the *Herald Tribune* put it. It couldn't approve the changes, but at the same time it admitted there was little that could be done to enforce "full code compliance," due to the fact that only "2 percent of the hotel employees" were unionized nationally. The failure of the New York strike had only reinforced how the right to bargain collectively meant little if businesses refused to acknowledge employees' representatives. Meanwhile, hotels across the country went on ignoring the codes. "Frankly speaking," the association's president summed up in early 1935, "there are no such things as a restaurant or hotel code. They are dead."[41]

As it turned out, this wasn't far from the truth. At the end of May 1935, deciding a case related to the New York poultry industry, the U.S. Supreme Court ruled that the federal government had no right to regulate trade within the boundaries of a state. Its powers were limited to interstate commerce, a category into which most businesses did not fall. Thus, in one ruling, the Court wiped out the entire NRA and its system of codes. At a luncheon of the Merchants Association held at the Hotel Astor, industry leaders praised the decision, claiming it "returned business to the business man." The *Times* reported that "every mention of the Supreme Court's NRA decision" brought forth "waves of handclapping." Introducing Chamber of Commerce president Harper Sibley as keynote speaker, the head of the Merchants Association, Louis Comstock, summarized the prevailing attitude—one that, in its critique of gigantism as a source of hardship, could just as easily have been used by the other side, and, indeed, by anyone grappling with economics in America as a whole: "The colossal nature of the undertakings at Washington since March, 1933, though thought in some degree reasonable and mitigated by the times, recalls a line from one of the Greek dramatists, 'And ever shall this law hold good: Nothing that is vast enters into the life of mortals without a curse.'"[42]

As the Waldorf worked to subvert one federal program, it was benefiting from another. Section 77B of the new Federal Bankruptcy Act of 1934 allowed corporations to reorganize without first getting unanimous approval from holders of securities. Within weeks of the act's passage, numerous companies that had been threatened with foreclosure—from McCrory five-and-dime stores to tile manufacturers—made petitions to the federal courts. Lucius Boomer, applying for the Waldorf-Astoria, documented how the corporation had worked to reduce operating costs as well as workers' salaries—including his own, which he had agreed to drop to $36,000, from $60,000. The U.S. District Court judge, given the option under the act to either appoint a trustee or allow the Waldorf to continue operating with its current management, chose the latter. This was a decision the Waldorf's lawyer praised as beneficial for maintaining the hotel's image and reputation: "Since October 1931, the Waldorf has had no tag on it, and we have been able to operate under our own steam thus far. . . . A trustee's name on the hotel's letterheads and checks would be a deterrent [to recovery]."[43]

Under the reorganization plan, approved in early 1936 after nearly two years of discussions, the New York Central Railroad forgave the Waldorf-Astoria Corporation its unpaid rent in exchange for a limited degree of ownership: various hotel furnishings would now be the railroad's property, which it would lease back to the hotel. Bondholders, meanwhile, were forced to exchange their unpaid interest for debentures (unsecured bonds) and a greater allocation of stock. The new plan thus allowed the Waldorf to start over, financially, by eliminating its main sources of debt. At the same time, overall business was given a spur after the Interstate Commerce Commission mandated, in the summer of 1936, the lowering of East Coast railroad fares from 3.6 to 2 cents per mile. This move brought tourists to New York in numbers that boosted the Waldorf's room occupancy, in 1936, by 7 percent. In 1937, receipts in hotel bars across New York increased by more than 15 percent; that year, the Waldorf-Astoria Corporation was able to make its first-ever interest disbursement. A modest 1 percent, the *Wall Street Journal* nonetheless pointed to its significance, calling it "the first tangible result of the improvement now under way in the hotel industry."[44]

With this came a new push to organize workers in city hotels. To labor leaders, it seemed contradictory that Lucius Boomer, who had always empha-

sized his progressive achievements in the field of employee relations, would
devote so much energy to fighting the approach of unionism. "Mr. Boomer,"
observed the writer of one publication, "always took pride . . . in his reputation as a liberal leader among hotel owners." Still, when Boomer's former
allies in the American Hotel Association began negotiating a member-wide
collective bargaining agreement for New York in 1938, Lucius took the
unusual step of resigning from the association. By the early 1940s, the Waldorf was viewed as "an impregnable anti-union fortress," one of the last of
New York's major hotels to avoid signing a contract. A flyer distributed by
the New York Hotel Trades Council, an advocacy group working to organize Waldorf employees, featured a drawing of thirteen chairs set around a
table on which had been placed a turkey labeled "CONTRACT BENEFITS."
The chairs, occupied by maids, chefs, and bellmen cutting into their meals,
bore names of all the hotels that had been unionized: Vanderbilt, Pennsylvania, Park Lane, New Yorker, and others. Only the chair captioned Waldorf-
Astoria was unoccupied; it faced an empty plate and sat at a distance from
others at the feast. "TAKE YOUR RIGHTFUL PLACE," the flyer urged
Waldorf workers.[45]

"Management of the Waldorf-Astoria is not anti-union," Boomer insisted
in a letter to a dissatisfied employee in 1945. "Never has a condition of employment been non-membership in a labor union." Indeed, unionization "has
not been the preference of the majority of Waldorf employees." In this
Boomer was alluding to a vote taken in December 1942, when the hotel's
workers decided against union representation, 925 to 473 (the Hotel Trades
Council would later charge Waldorf management with intimidating workers in order to influence the outcome). But elsewhere in the letter Boomer
addressed what he saw as the danger of allowing an "outside organization"
to influence hiring decisions: "I am sure you do not intend to charge our
Management . . . with the thought of replacing the security of good business
with the insecurity of poor business." To Boomer, having convinced a judge
that the Waldorf could be run without trustees, good business meant the
continued avoidance of contracts with organized labor. Speaking to his
industry colleagues at a hotel convention in 1937, he asserted that "through

unionization, we are in danger of very radical wage demands, which, in my opinion, the business cannot bear." The same year, all Waldorf workers received a pamphlet, in which Boomer explained that "pay of employees will be better as business improves": "Thus far, we have not been able to pay a satisfactory return to capital; in fact, we have paid almost no return to investors. . . . *We can only divide what we can earn.*"[46]

Meanwhile, organizers for the Hotel Trades Council intensified their efforts. Stationing themselves at the Waldorf's employee entrance, they handed out newspapers, leaflets, and invitations to what would eventually number more than 300 meetings. In December 1945, employees again voted on representation, and this time the union won by a large majority. Three months later, the Waldorf-Astoria and AFL's Hotel and Club Employees Union Local 6 signed an agreement that established a fixed base salary, wage increases of up to three dollars per week, and other benefits for all 2,100 members of the hotel's staff. In what Trades Council president Jay Rubin described as "one of the greatest victories of the city's organized hotel workers," the Waldorf was now the 144th hotel in New York City to become fully unionized.[47]

This time, Boomer did not protest; in the nine years since the reorganization plan went into effect, many things had changed. After the "King of Swing," clarinetist Benny Goodman, headlined two successful engagements with his band in 1938 and 1939, the Empire Room began to throw off its fusty reputation and embrace young people's music ("no one expected a swing band to do that well at the Waldorf," recalled Goodman's lead vocalist in 1939, Louise Tobin). In 1943, after a temporary name change to Wedgewood Room, the Empire took a chance on an up-and-coming vocalist named Frank Sinatra, cementing a relationship that would endure, both professionally and personally (Sinatra later moved into the Waldorf Towers), for much of the singer's life. But the biggest change at the Waldorf-Astoria was monetary: after fourteen years on Park Avenue, the hotel was finally making a profit.[48]

CHAPTER 6

Weekend at the Waldorf

In 1945, moviegoers could experience Waldorf glamour without ever leaving Flint, Macon, or King of Prussia. *Week-end at the Waldorf,* an MGM comedy-drama that became the sixth-highest-grossing American film that year, showcased a roster of big names: Ginger Rogers, Van Johnson, Lana Turner. But the greatest star of the movie was undoubtedly the Waldorf-Astoria itself, which had been brought to life with verisimilitude, room by room, on a Hollywood studio lot. Eschewing any question of an on-location shoot, MGM drew upon original Schultze & Weaver hotel blueprints, along with thousands of still photographs, to design reproductions that were so meticulous the Waldorf's publicist, Ted Saucier (who had been hired as technical adviser), observed that upon visiting the sets he had "the weird experience of being at home—though I knew perfectly well it was 3,000 miles away!" The film, a listless reworking of an earlier MGM moneymaker, 1932's *Grand Hotel,* was most successful when detailing the myriad behind-the-scenes activities that made the Waldorf run: bellboys dashing into position and lining up as they prepared for inspection at the start of the day, teams of floor polishers whisking giant brooms across the *Wheel of Life* lobby mosaic, coiffed switchboard operators plugging and unplugging phone extensions with the rhythm of a typist. *Week-end at the Waldorf* was, above all, a giant commercial: as the *New York Times* observed, "Mr. Lucius Boomer's elegant boarding house sure has hit the publicity jackpot."[1]

Still from *Week-end at the Waldorf*, 1945, with Lana Turner standing
in the main lobby—re-created, piece by piece, on a Hollywood set
(Photofest, Inc.).

In the opening scene, a pair of newlyweds arrives by taxi and enters the
Park Avenue lobby, gazing shyly, peering into the Wedgewood Room and
spotting Xavier Cugat (one of several Waldorf characters playing themselves
in the film). Upon reaching the check-in desk, the man, a soldier on leave, is
informed there are no available rooms, whereupon the young woman, played
by 1930s child star Cora Sue Collins, blurts out, "But we came to stay at the
Waldorf!" Soon her voice rises to a petulant cry: "We just can't go anyplace
else. We just *can't!*" This fictional crisis, resolved when a sympathetic businessman offers his permanent Waldorf quarters for the weekend, speaks to
a real-life situation: the scarcity of hotel rooms during wartime. Indeed, far
from the oversupply that characterized the Depression years, the 1940s witnessed a sharp increase in occupancy—to the point that, by 1945, New York
hotels were operating with vacancies of 2 percent. Not only were more servicemen in town, waiting to be sent overseas, but their numbers were mul-

tiplied by the families and loved ones wishing to see them off. Other factors added to the crowding: department store buyers, for example, accustomed to staying several days, now took up rooms for weeks at a time, due to the shortage of goods. By 1944, hotels had set up what one account described as "a cooperative central system," through which overflow guests were directed to other establishments, sometimes in what would have seemed (to anyone looking for the excitement of Manhattan) disappointing locales. "I've placed people in White Plains, Newark, and Coney Island," one hotel manager confessed.[2]

For the Waldorf-Astoria, of course, this came as a welcome development after years of financial struggle. In 1941 the corporation had lost $772,902. By the following year the loss had gone down to $337,472. Nineteen forty-four saw a profit of $502,032, which increased to $828,181 in 1945, the year *Week-end at the Waldorf* was released. Wartime rationing, to which hotels were subject alongside private households, only increased profits by limiting the portion size and variety of food served ("Whatever they ask for," said another manager about a group of banquet clients desiring steak, "they'll get chicken"). Behind the assuring figures, however, lay concerns about what would happen after the war. As Boomer and others pointed out, repairs to the Waldorf and other hotel properties were of necessity minimal, due to a shortage of labor and governmental limits placed on construction expense. Costs were piling up in subtle but important ways: lighter "Victory" models of vacuum cleaners, for example, did not remove dirt as effectively, resulting in faster disintegration of carpets. Boomer, in arguing for the establishment of an industry "rehabilitation fund" (not allowable under tax law), explained how "ostensible annual hotel profits" gave an inflated sense of "our true profits." Clearly, if the Waldorf's financial prosperity were to continue, it would need a safeguard against higher costs and the inevitable drop-off in postwar occupancy. This it found through a revenue-generating young employee named Claude Philippe.[3]

Born in England, Claudius Charles Philippe—or, as he was known by everyone from dignitaries to harried assistants, Philippe—had a modest yet colorful background. His father was a popular French chef who had worked at London's upper-crust Carlton Club and who later opened his own restaurant, Chez Philippe, in the medieval French town of Grenoble. Young Philippe spent his teenage years at the Hotel de Crillon in Paris, where, as a member of the room service staff, he learned the importance of tact and discretion: on one occasion, he skillfully arranged the tray of a well-known military general (who, as a *New Yorker* profile later explained, was "unmarried but not unaccompanied") to make it look as if the two full breakfasts it contained had been prepared for a single person. Immigrating to the United States in 1929, at age eighteen, Philippe first worked at the Sherry-Netherland hotel and, later, the Central Park Casino, a glamorous nightspot that closed soon after the onset of the Depression. With employment scarce in 1930, Philippe found an outlet for his aggressive personality through the selling of Fuller brushes, door to door. Finally, drawing upon earlier connections, he landed at the Waldorf-Astoria, five days after it opened, where he was hired as an assistant to Oscar Tschirky. For the next twelve years, he worked in anonymity, "astute enough," wrote Edward Bernays, "to curb his ambitions in the face of Oscar's own overweening desire for the spotlight" and waiting for a chance to make a reputation of his own.[4]

In April 1943, that chance came: after years of threatening to retire, Oscar—who, at seventy-seven, had been with the Waldorf for a full half century—finally did it, stepping down to assume, officially, what had long been his primary function, that of symbolic "host." Promoted to manager of the banquet department, Philippe would tussle with Boomer, who, in the former's recollection, "fired and rehired" him three separate times. Philippe's achievement—and the source of frustration for Boomer, who often felt the hotel's capabilities were being taxed—was a dramatic increase in the number, size, and complexity of in-house catered events. Once, against Boomer's wishes, Philippe booked a breakfast for 6,000 female employees of New York Telephone ("I'm always inclined to fight, and ask permission later," he explained). On another occasion he convinced the Ford Motor Company to showcase dozens of its new models in the Grand Ballroom, which had to be cleared of cars after ten in the evening and reset for corporate meetings by nine o'clock the next day. At times, in Philippe's eagerness to fill every available space, he would overbook. Speaking to columnist Ward Morehouse III in the 1980s, a former hotel executive recalled the story of a host who arrived for her function at the Starlight Roof, only to find that Philippe had bumped it for a Yankees celebration: "The woman fainted dead away in the lobby." Still, the financial results were hard for Boomer or anyone at the Waldorf to argue with. Notwithstanding those important factors related to the surge in wartime occupancy, it's significant that the Waldorf's initial year of profit, 1944, coincided with the first full year of the Claude Philippe regime.[5]

It wasn't long before Philippe became known, in the press, as "the new Oscar of the Waldorf," though, as Geoffrey T. Hellman observed in the *New Yorker*, Philippe's job had "not only swallowed up Oscar's but taken in extra-Oscarian fields." One former Philippe assistant described his boss as a modern race car, next to Oscar's Duesenberg: the latter, still under the influence of George Boldt's distaste for pushy sales tactics, did not seek new business but allowed it to come to him. Philippe, by contrast, began each day with a keen perusal of newspaper clippings from the society pages, dictating letters to organizers of events that he felt should have been held at the Waldorf instead of at other hotels ("I like to think that everybody tries here first"). A slim, charismatic man with slicked hair, tailored clothes, and horn-rimmed glasses, Philippe was married several times and had a daughter, Claudia, but—during the workweek, at least—had little life outside the hotel domain. The *New Yorker*'s Hellman trailed him as he ran from a lunch hosted by Firestone tires to a March of Dimes event, then to a gathering of the American Trucking Association before winding up at a reception for the Pan American Society, chumming with executives and chastising busboys along the way. Eventually Philippe and his banquet department, which catered as many as ten events per day, would be responsible for a full three-quarters of the Waldorf's annual profit.[6]

Through the better part of the 1940s the hotel's banquet department, spurred by an overachieving Philippe, was a veritable factory. Daily it turned out events for a cornucopia of groups, paying little attention to the social or political views that might have been espoused by the organizers. Dinners for the National Council of American-Soviet Friendship followed communion

Claude Philippe in action, 1961 (Yale Joel/The LIFE Picture Collection via Getty Images).

breakfasts sponsored by the anti-Communist Holy Name Society. A non-partisan stance was good for business and also conformed to Boomer's views regarding the expansive role of a hotel within society. During the years immediately following the war, however, as the United States' oppositional focus shifted from Fascism to Communism and new fears emerged over the extent of Soviet political involvement in American life, the Waldorf found itself under increasing pressure—from the press, segments of the general public, and from colleagues within the hotel industry—to bar its doors against anything that might be labeled anti-American or subversive. In this the hotel's resolve was to be tested: inevitably, with so many comings and goings, Boomer, Philippe, and their Waldorf associates would come under fire for what was perceived, in certain quarters, as a tolerance for organizations—in particular, those with suspected Communist ties—they should have been prepared to turn away.

The anti-Communist Red Scare that, to a dramatic extent, permeated American life and discourse after the close of the Second World War was shaped in part by events that took place at the Waldorf-Astoria. On February 28, 1946, Secretary of State James Byrnes, addressing the Overseas Press Club at a Waldorf dinner, alluded to tensions with the United States' recent wartime ally, the Soviet Union. Indirectly criticizing the USSR for its purported removal of Japanese industrial equipment from Manchuria (which the Soviet Union had invaded in August 1945), Byrnes asserted that no country had the right "to help itself to alleged enemy properties in liberated or ex-satellite countries before a reparation settlement has been agreed upon by the Allies." Going further, Byrnes insisted the United States would not agree "to any one power deciding for itself what it will take from these countries," before closing with a statement that, in its suggestion of the potential for future hostility, bore dark implications: "We do not want to stumble and stagger into situations where no power intends war, but no power will be able to avert war." Byrnes's speech at the Waldorf, according to historian R. B. Levering, "alerted the political elite" (identified by Levering as "public officials in Washington and the news media") of a "fundamental shift in U.S. policy toward Stalin's government."[7]

A second event occurred soon after, on March 15, when Winston Churchill, former British prime minister, arrived at the Waldorf-Astoria. Churchill had traveled, by way of Washington, from Westminster College in Fulton, Missouri. There, in the company of U.S. president Harry Truman, he had delivered the address known, ever since, by its introduction of a phrase that became synonymous with Communist repression: "Iron Curtain." Churchill's Fulton speech, with its reference to secret "fifth columns," instilled the notion many Americans would come to develop of the Soviet Union's hidden influence, one that, "far from the Russian frontiers and throughout the world," worked covertly for purposes of undermining "Christian civilization." Communism, in this troubling suggestion, was not limited to what could be *seen*; its insidiousness lay in a skill for operating undercover, through initiatives that would appear, on their surface, every-day and benign. Now, at the Waldorf, during a supper hosted by the City of New York, an unrepentant Churchill set out to defend his earlier comments: "I do not wish to withdraw or modify a single word." Citing Soviet military activities in Persia ("or if you like to call it Iran, tho you'll run a great risk of confusing it with Iraq"), Churchill warned Russian officials that if they failed to "take advantage" of the "widespread sympathy" existing throughout "the English-speaking world" for their country's suffering and loss during the war, "the responsibility will be entirely theirs." With these speeches—one by Byrnes and two by Churchill—the Cold War, in the words of Levering, "clearly was underway." The United States and Soviet Union, through one of the most abrupt reversals in American political history, had taken a giant step along the path from allies to enemies.[8]

Indeed, so sudden was this reversal that it took time for many in the United States to catch up with it. A Gallup poll conducted near the beginning of March 1946 indicated that 35 percent of Americans still believed the Soviet Union would cooperate with the United States in world affairs. Churchill's warning of a Communist Russia bent on "the fruits of war and the indefinite expansion of . . . power and doctrines" appeared to contradict the promise inherent within the new United Nations, whose charter President Truman had lauded, in June 1945, as "a declaration of great faith by the nations of the earth . . . that war is not inevitable." Over the next several years—the labile period between Japan's surrender and the onset of the 1950s—the Waldorf-Astoria became a meeting ground for two opposing responses to Communism. One side emphasized vigilance and battle; the other, dialogue, restraint and compromise. Eventually the ideological forces represented by these sides, driven to combat by the fears and tensions of the early Cold War, would move to a showdown the likes of which the Waldorf, accustomed to more locally oriented battles, had never seen.[9]

———

In the fall of 1946, Lucius Boomer initiated what would be his last and argu-ably greatest move as a public figure: giving up his entire apartment, suite

37A of the Waldorf Towers, to the U.S. State Department for the final session of the Council of Foreign Ministers conference. The conference was
established at the State Department's suggestion the previous summer, for
the purpose of bringing together the major Allied powers—the "Big Four"
of England, France, the United States, and the Soviet Union—to draft peace
treaties for the defeated Axis countries. Through the course of long and
difficult sessions, in which Secretary of State Byrnes grew increasingly frustrated with what he perceived as the Soviets' filibustering tactics, the ministers had convened in London, Moscow, and Paris without achieving much of
substance. Now, given that the same ministers were planning to be in New
York for the United Nations General Assembly of October and November,
Byrnes proposed an attempt to finish what they'd been unable to complete in
the other cultural capitals. This would be the first peace treaty negotiated on
U.S. soil since 1905, when the Treaty of Portsmouth (New Hampshire) had
formalized the end of the Russo-Japanese War. As such, and particularly
because of its connection to the United Nations (whose General Assembly
meetings would be held in temporary quarters, in a retrofitted structure left
over from the 1939 World's Fair in Queens), the Council of Foreign Ministers
reflected New York's ascent as the de facto capital of the United States, the
city most emblematic of American achievement and ideology.

The only problem was space, a shortage of which Undersecretary of State
Dean Acheson described, in a telegram dated October 24, 1946, as "critical."
In terms of infrastructure, New York was not prepared for the international
level of responsibility thrust upon it after the war; resultingly, the State
Department had to scramble in order to obtain housing for the conference
ministers and their official delegations. Frank Ready, Boomer's second-in-
command at the Waldorf, pulled together the requisite number of rooms,
sixty for offices and seventy-five for living quarters, through (as a grateful
State Department put it) "outright eviction of clients and cancellations of reservations"—all with less than one month's notice. Three additional hotels,
the Belmont Plaza, Barclay, and Lexington, came up with smaller allotments.
Earlier the Waldorf had turned away guests in the patriotic spirit of wartime; now, it did the same for what Acheson, in a letter posted for the

benefit of patrons inside the Waldorf's lobby, vaunted as "the future peace and security of the world." Apologizing for "the inconvenience which will necessarily be caused," Acheson assured management that the "disappointment of your prospective guests will be more than compensated for in the knowledge that the accommodations they had hoped to obtain in your hotel" were being used to further what was "unquestionably the most critical effort in which our world statesmen are today involved."[10]

But the larger problem—where to hold the meetings themselves—was not solved, in James Byrnes's recollection, until Lucius and Jorgine Boomer "generously" turned over their apartment, stripped of furniture but otherwise retaining the colorful tapestries and decorations associated with Jorgine's Norwegian girlhood. Ensconced in the Boomer drawing room, surrounded by bric-a-brac such as a drinking cup whose inscription read, in translation, "Wine in the dish gives you marrow in the bones," the four ministers negotiated issues such as control of the Danube and war reparations owed by the smaller Axis powers. Tensions were high on both American and Soviet sides. Days prior to the first session, during an address before the UN General Assembly, the Soviet minister of foreign affairs, Vyacheslav Molotov, attacked the "selfishness" of American policy on atomic energy and its "desire to secure for the United States the monopolistic possession of the atomic bomb." Then, on November 3, with the conference set to begin, President Truman reaffirmed his plan to maintain U.S. control of Pacific islands captured from Japan ("Mr. Truman could not have chosen," voiced one British correspondent, "a worse time for the reiteration of this policy"). For his part, James Byrnes, an otherwise upbeat man with long experience at various levels of American politics, was "depressed as well as exhausted" from the earlier conferences, during which Molotov had repeatedly shot down majority decisions by indulging in his use of the veto. By the start of the Waldorf sessions on November 4, many people, wrote columnist Ivan Peterman, were "becoming skeptical of the Big Four," and the conferees themselves were "getting on each other's nerves."[11]

Still, Byrnes did not believe the situation was hopeless. "As long as men meet socially and continue to discuss their problems," he wrote in his 1947 memoir, *Speaking Frankly*, "there is a chance to solve them." During the fourth week, he invited Molotov to his Waldorf suite and feigned a desire to break up the conference—without finishing any treaties. "A year from now," he recalled saying, "other individuals may find it possible to agree," since, after all, "time is a great healer." Molotov, who in spite of his defiant tactics did not want to return home without finishing the job (the Soviets were set to receive benefits that would commence with the treaties' completion), replied that he felt Byrnes was being overly "pessimistic." In her book *The Threat of Peace*, historian Patricia Dawson Ward characterized this story as an exaggeration, citing a State Department account of the Molotov visit in which Byrnes issued no threat of adjournment. Regardless of what was actually said at the meeting, negotiations improved afterward. On the following day the four ministers (in addition to Byrnes and Molotov, they were British foreign secretary Ernest Bevin and the French deputy Maurice Couve de Murville) quickly worked through what had been one of their stickiest disputes from earlier sessions: rival Italian and Communist Yugoslav claims for the Adriatic port city of Trieste. So genial did proceedings become that *Life* magazine reported how "Jimmy" Byrnes ended the sixth and final week in "linked arms" with the other ministers, singing a round of "For He's a Jolly Good Fellow."[12]

Throughout the nearly two-month conference the Waldorf had been fortified with what for the hotel was an unprecedented level of security: 50 military guards and 150 policemen ("one would think," observed columnist Peterman, "that Tojo and A. Hitler were hiding under the table"). As a measure, though, of how truly international the hotel had become, Waldorf employees shrugged off any hint of being impressed by the presence of foreign ministers. "In this shop the biggest are every-day customers," observed the in-house florist. "We are serving dukes, duchesses, queen of this country, boss of that country." Robert Remacle, a room service waiter living in Queens, explained that his primary interest lay in collecting autographs: "'Who I am waiting for here is Molotov.' His accent was on the last O. 'That's the guy nobody got. . . . I want him the worst.'"[13]

Despite these and other blasé reactions—"I don't turn my head for any of them," a porter boasted—few could deny that the Council of Foreign

Ministers was a defining moment in the history of the Waldorf-Astoria. Never before had an official State Department event been held in a New York hotel. For Boomer, the coming together of representatives from different nations, working through international problems in clean, peaceable surroundings, was the fulfillment of his conception of the Waldorf, stated back in 1931, as "a civic institution in the broadest sense." The Waldorf, as host to the Council of Foreign Ministers, moved beyond the sphere of local and national affairs to occupy a position of influence on the world stage. For a time, as the ministers and UN delegates prepared to head home in advance of the December holidays, there prevailed, in the words of *Life*, "an atmosphere of optimism, a sense of real progress, a feeling that the world was measurably closer to a workable peace." None of it would last.[14]

By November 1947, James Byrnes was back at the Waldorf, in a surprise new role as legal counsel to the motion picture industry. Having resigned as secretary of state shortly after the Council of Foreign Ministers conference, Byrnes published his book of memoirs and quickly stepped into private life, opening a Washington law office with the long-established firm of Hogan and Hartson. Meanwhile, the American movie business, as represented by its trade organization, the Motion Picture Association of America (MPAA), was in need of help. General box office receipts were down 20 percent, in the first part of 1947, from what they had been during the war; sales for individual movies were fluctuating, and studio executives voiced private concern that American consumers had become finicky in their tastes. International film exports had diminished because of high taxes, particularly those levied by Great Britain. Religious groups protested the release of *Forever Amber*, a splashy historical romance whose depiction of morals earned it the Roman Catholic Legion of Decency's "Condemned" rating—which meant the nation's more than 25 million Catholics were instructed not to view it. Finally, the looming presence of television signaled, in the words of film historian Thomas Doherty, that "Hollywood's monopoly on screen entertainment was coming to an end."[15]

But none of these factors was as urgent as the need for Hollywood to defend itself against the charge of being a stronghold of Communism. Accusations of a Red influence within the film colony went back to the 1930s, when numbers of stars donated money to causes that also happened to be supported by the U.S. Communist Party: in particular, the struggle against General Franco's Nationalists in the Spanish Civil War. In 1938 a witness for the Dies Committee, Congress's first investigation into Hollywood and Communism, made the following assertion: "Almost everyone in Hollywood except Mickey Mouse and Snow White has been signed up by the Communists at one time or another." Congressional inquiry paused after the 1941 Nazi invasion of Russia and America's entry into the war, but it resumed as part of the general climate of suspicion informing the late 1940s. In spring of 1947 the House Committee on Un-American Activities (abbreviated as HUAC), led by a crusading politician named J. Parnell Thomas, announced plans for a new investigation into the extent of subversive behavior within America's movie capital. Incensed, the MPAA's publicity-minded president, Eric Johnston, vowed to fight back, using, as one account put it, an "outstanding foe of censorship," James Byrnes (who, as secretary of state, had supported a UN covenant on freedom of the press). Emboldened perhaps by Byrnes's support, Johnston lashed out at HUAC when called to testify in October. Government, he vowed, shall not "tell the motion picture industry, directly or by coercion, what kind of pictures it ought to make."[16]

Such defiance was hard to maintain in light of larger developments. On March 12, 1947, President Truman had appeared before Congress to request $400 million in aid to the governments of Turkey and Greece, both of which were engaged in conflicts against Communist-led forces. Truman's address to Congress formed the basis of what became known as the Truman Doctrine, advocating direct U.S. involvement "to support," in the president's words, "free peoples who are resisting attempted subjugation." Combined with additional statements made by the new secretary of state, George Marshall, the Truman Doctrine signaled a further deterioration of the U.S.-Soviet relationship. At the same time, anti-Communist sentiment was intensifying within the public and private sphere: the New York City Board of

Education, for example, voted on a resolution that would have banned Communist groups from meeting on school property. A businessmen's group voiced agreement with George Marshall that the Soviets were engaged in a "supreme effort to win control over the minds of the people of the world through skilled use and distortion of all the weapons of modern psychology." Red-baiting Hollywood columnist Hedda Hopper played on movie studios' fears by warning that "paying customers will gladly sacrifice an evening's movie entertainment rather than support what they consider the Commie menace." In short, when ten Hollywood writers and directors were threatened with contempt of Congress by refusing to answer, during the October HUAC hearings, whether they had ever been members of the Communist Party, Johnston and the MPAA knew that a face-saving plan was necessary.[17]

A brief article in the *New York Times* of Saturday, November 22, 1947, reported that Johnston would be calling an "emergency conference" of studio executives for the following Monday, November 24, to be held at the MPAA's New York offices on West Forty-Fourth Street. Monday came, however, and the location had changed to the fourth-floor Perroquet Suite of the Waldorf-Astoria. Assuming the veracity of the initial *Times* report, the last-minute switch to the Waldorf was a sign of the industry's need to defend itself with a public statement—one that would not have earned as much attention had it come from a private office. However, even without the fillip of a locale known by members of the press (who, though not invited to the meeting itself, were given an on-site briefing by Johnston), the MPAA conference would have qualified as an exercise in public relations—a field that remained, in the words of one observer, "the basis of all movies." Unanimously, it was reported, the studio heads (among them Paramount's Barney Balaban, Fox's Harry Cohn, and Nicholas Schenck of MGM) voted during the conference to suspend all members of the "Hollywood Ten," without pay. It was an action, voiced the *Times*, "unprecedented in American industrial fields." Further, the MPAA issued what became known, infamously, as the "Waldorf Declaration," mimeographed copies of which were handed out to press members assembled at the hotel after a second meeting. The declaration read, in part: "Members of the Association of Motion Picture Producers deplore the action of the 10 Hollywood men who have been cited for contempt by the House of Representatives. We . . . will not re-employ any of the 10 until such time as he is acquitted or has purged himself of contempt and declares under oath that he is not a Communist."[18]

In his 1979 memoir, *Heyday*, Dore Schary, producer for RKO, recalled that it was James Byrnes who stepped in, after rounds of bickering among conference participants, to offer an argument for firing the Hollywood Ten. Byrnes, more than anyone present, understood the degree to which the anti-Communist viewpoint (one that, with his initial Waldorf speech in February 1946, he had had a role in creating) now informed administrative policy in Washington. In Schary's remembrance, Byrnes said he "doubted that any government official 'would argue with the decision of the industry to get rid of [Communists].'" Already, as Byrnes was aware, the U.S. Supreme Court had declined to review the case of a federal employee who had been dismissed for membership in an organization suspected of being a Communist "front." Further, according to Byrnes, "the [Hollywood Ten] could be relieved of their jobs because of the contractual 'morals' clause," long written into studio talent contracts, "on the basis that their behavior had brought disrepute on the industry." It was for this reason that termination notices received by members of the Hollywood Ten contained references to "actions, attitudes, and public statements and general conduct [which] have . . . violated your employment agreement with us." But it was another section of the Waldorf Declaration that would most accurately portend the course of future events: "We will not knowingly employ a Communist or a member of any party or group which advocates the overthrow of the Government of the United States by force or by any illegal or unconstitutional methods."[19]

With this, the Waldorf unwittingly played host to the launch of the Hollywood blacklist, a system that, over the course of its nearly fifteen-year existence, barred hundreds of film performers, writers, and directors from employment. Some careers would not recover until the 1960s; others never did. From the beginning, though, a number of organizations mobilized to assist the Hollywood Ten and raise money for their legal defense. One of these was the National Council of Arts, Sciences and Professions (NCASP), a group that had come into being as the Hollywood Democratic Committee (HDC) in order to lobby, in 1943, for the reelection of President Roosevelt. As such, the HDC had acquired early celebrity support from movie stars such as Danny Kaye and Olivia de Havilland. Over time, and through a sequence of alignments and mergers with (and subsequent dissociations from) similar groups, the NCASP emerged in the spring of 1948 with a new "Policy and Program," vowing to fight for not just the Hollywood Ten but for a broad range of causes, among them the rights of minority groups and women, universal health insurance, rent control, teachers' salaries, the easement of restrictions on cultural exchange, and freedom of speech: "We call on all Americans to fight for the Bill of Rights as the foundation of our political and cultural life."[20]

But the most prominent spot on the NCASP's agenda was reserved for international peace, which, the organization stated, could only be achieved by "exposing and stopping the bi-partisan attempt to split the world into two camps, embodied in the Truman Doctrine." Over the coming months the NCASP became increasingly preoccupied with the idea of a large-scale peace event; and, by autumn of 1948, the Waldorf-Astoria, associated with the Waldorf Declaration, one of the most publicized manifestations of the Red Scare to date, had emerged as the organization's ideal location. If the Waldorf could be used by movie studios to promote intolerance, it could just as easily be used to promote a countering stance, one of receptivity and openness. The resulting Cultural and Scientific Conference for World Peace, described in a modern CIA report as "one of the strangest gatherings in American history," would carry the Waldorf to a new level of controversy. In the process the hotel would be forced to take a stand in the conflict between duty and ideology, the innkeeper's mission of hospitality and a need to appease those who believed that mission—Boomer's foundational emphasis on "every station in society"—was being taken too far.[21]

In early April 1948, Professor Harlow Shapley, Harvard astronomer and chairman of the NCASP, received a letter from his scientific colleague Albert

Einstein. The famous physicist, connected in the public's mind with the E equals mc squared equation that laid (to an extent that has long been debated) the theoretical foundation for American development of the atomic bomb, had recently editorialized in the *Atlantic Monthly* about a general disinterestedness in the threat posed by atomic power: "The public, having been warned of the horrible nature of atomic warfare, has done nothing about it, and to a large extent has dismissed the warning from its consciousness." Now, in his letter to Shapley four months later, Einstein, a committed pacifist who would eventually express regret about his role in President Roosevelt's decision to fund atomic research at Los Alamos in New Mexico, voiced fears that the urge to keep other nations from developing atomic weapons would be used as justification for a "preventive war" to be launched by the United States against the Soviets: "I feel now sure that the people in power in Washington are pushing systematically toward preventive war. I have the impression that it is the duty of the leading intellectuals of this country to launch a strong appeal to the American public to vitalize strong opposition to this development before [members of the U.S. government] have driven it so far that irrevocable steps have been taken and nobody can stop anymore the course of events. What is your opinion . . . ?"[22]

Beyond his pioneering contributions toward modern understanding of the size of the Milky Way galaxy, Shapley was a lifelong advocate of progressive causes, vocal in his denunciations of racism, U.S. foreign policy, and, most notably, the House Committee on Un-American Affairs. In November 1946, he was subpoenaed before HUAC in relation to campaign donations made by the Massachusetts chapter of a voters' group with which the NCASP, in an earlier incarnation, had been briefly connected. Shapley's angry denunciation of HUAC as a "secret inquisition" and his refusal to hand over financial records of the voters' group made him a target of the Federal Bureau of Investigation. Since the war the FBI had expanded its spying program, widening the definition of what constituted a threat to "national security" in order to encompass the political activities of ordinary citizens. Using what it termed "technical surveillance" (likely a hidden microphone planted on the body of an informant), the FBI learned, on January 7, 1949, that Shapley and the NCASP were planning a "peace conference" to be held at the Waldorf-Astoria at the end of March. The conference, which had already attracted a roster of left-leaning sponsors, including composer Leonard Bernstein and the African American educator Dr. W.E.B. Du Bois, would surely, in the words of a confidential FBI report on Du Bois, be part of a "world-wide Communist-inspired 'peace' propaganda campaign."[23]

At the time, "peace" was increasingly being viewed by the FBI as a euphemism for "Communist." August 1948 had seen the World Congress of Intellectuals in Defense of Peace, organized in Wrocław, Poland. Nominally led by a group of Polish and French intellectuals, the congress was widely believed, by members of the American press, to have been directed by Stalinist operatives from Moscow. This charge became more believable after the Congress's chairman, Soviet author Alexander Fadeyev, used his opening speech to rail against American political leaders as imperialist warmongers, who co-opted the pens of "reactionary writers" in order to advance their plans for "world domination." During his closing remarks, Fadeyev boasted that "the work of the Congress was only beginning." Later, when the *Daily Worker*, house organ of the Communist Party in the United States, became the first publication to make an official announcement of the Waldorf-Astoria conference (on January 10, 1949), it appeared that Fadeyev was making good on his promise. Investigators looking for Stalinist involvement only needed to point to the Waldorf conference's invitations, whose mastheads listed as "sponsors" several known Communist sympathizers (among them African American performer Paul Robeson and the novelist Howard Fast) who had also attended the notorious Wroclaw Congress. Any remaining question was dispelled by the name of the Hollywood Ten member who had been the first to refuse to answer (in a grandly arrogant manner) questions put forth by HUAC: openly Communist screenwriter John Howard Lawson.[24]

The Cultural and Scientific Conference for World Peace was, in the report of a confidential FBI informant "of known reliability," a direct "follow-up on the World Congress of Intellectuals held in Wroclaw, Poland." Based on this single assessment, elicited in connection with surveillance methods of questionable legality (as evidenced by the attorney general's periodic disagreements with the FBI and its spying efforts), a fantastical narrative developed around the Waldorf conference. Right-wing labor columnist Victor Reisel, who demeaned intellectuals as "long-hairs and glamor boys and girls," told his readers the conference had been planned by Fadeyev and another Soviet operative in Paris at the end of 1948, as part of the "Comrades' [plan] to treat this country like an overgrown nursery." Harry Schlacht, writer for the anti-Communist Hearst organization of papers, urged Americans to "throw a shield of protection around our Flag so that no godless ism may find lodgment on our shores." In the view of these scribes, here were the warnings intoned by Churchill, in Missouri and at the Waldorf back in 1946, made terrifyingly manifest: atheistic fifth columns, hitting at "Christian civilization." Communists, as another Hearst columnist, Ruth Alexander, put it, were "masters of lies and deceit" that used "Fronts" like the NCASP—organizations that seemed innocuous—to draw "unsuspecting liberals" into toeing the "Communist Party line," which was moving "with the precision of a giant and evil watch, calculated to clock the destruction of the Western world."[25]

What neither the FBI nor the columnists realized was that the NCASP had been working on the conference for nearly a year, since the time of Einstein's April 1948 "preventive war" missive to Harlow Shapley. While a number of conference sponsors, among them the playwright Lillian Hellman, were overtly sympathetic to the Communist cause, most could be categorized as concerned liberals like Hellman's young theatrical competitor Arthur Miller, who questioned "the sharp postwar turn against the Soviets." Rather than being the directive of Soviet chieftains who got together in Paris to plot, as Reisel suggested, a bigger and better version of Wroclaw, the Waldorf conference was a homegrown effort—this in spite of the fact that it would feature, like the event in Poland, delegates from countries that included the USSR. Minutes of a meeting held on March 2, 1949, revealed that the NCASP's treasurer "had been able to borrow" the $5,000 deposit needed to secure the Waldorf-Astoria. In addition to sales from tickets to the conference, which included a main dinner that would cost what at the time was a hefty $10 per plate, money would be raised through an "art auction" of donated works. The NCASP organizers had budgeted to come out even, with hopefully a small amount of money left over. As administrative director Jack Kamaiko explained to the *New York Times*, the NCASP possessed, as of March 25, a total of $35,000 in the bank and had spent $50,000 on the conference. The $15,000 debt could be made up, Kamaiko asserted, through "solicitations" to be made at the dinner, as well as during adjunct events to be held at Madison Square Garden and Carnegie Hall: "Small voluntary contributions and membership fees are our only source of income."[26]

By then the NCASP had been forced to deal with concerns that its host, the Waldorf-Astoria, would get cold feet. *Counterattack* was a newsletter-style publication, circulated in urban centers throughout the United States but most prominently in New York, offering its readers "Facts to Combat Communism." It had been founded in 1947 by American Business Consultants (ABC), a group that included former FBI agents who had access to confidential information selectively leaked from the bureau's vast holdings of files on private organizations and citizens. Each week, a new issue would appear with late-breaking news underlined in a typewritten script that, with its appearance of being pounded out in haste, only added to the urgency ABC wished to inspire. *Counterattack* issue number 92, on February 25, 1949, opened with the announcement that "HIGH COMMUNISTS FROM MANY COUNTRIES" were planning to descend upon the Waldorf-Astoria for a "big propaganda powwow." Denigrating Harlow Shapley as "the Number 1 scientist in the leadership of Communist fronts," the writers went so far as to claim that the conference would be "under general supervision of Cominform," the Soviet information bureau created in 1947 to propagandize Communism internationally. *Counterattack* always ended with an action item: WHAT TO DO. This time, it was "*Burn up the wires* to Washington with phone calls & telegrams" to urge the State Department not to admit known Communists. Further, "Urge the Waldorf-Astoria Hotel to cancel the meeting and thus avoid embarrassing its non-Communist guests."[27]

Panicked, Hannah Dormer, a journalist and political activist who served as vice chairperson of the NCASP, called the managers of the Waldorf, who assured her they "had no intentions of breaking any contracts with NCASP,"

especially since the organization had already paid a deposit. For the Waldorf, though, the pressure to cancel the booking moved beyond questions
of contracts and deposits. In December 1947, President Truman had published a list of organizations deemed by the attorney general's office to be
Communist in nature. The list, known as AGLOSO (Attorney General's List
of Subversive Organizations), was only intended for use by the U.S. government as a way of checking the backgrounds of federal workers. An effect of
publication, however, was its adoption by private companies to screen both
prospective and current employees. In March 1948, the president of the
Statler chain of hotels announced in an employee newsletter that there was
"no room" for Communists in his organization. Then, sometime in early
1949, incoming president of the American Hotel Association, Harry Gow-
man, initiated a new program for creating, as the trade publication *Hotel
Monthly* explained, "a greater awareness of appreciation among hotel employees for the American Way of Life." Concurrent with this program was a
directive (based on the understanding that "hotels are natural meeting places
for all kinds of people") that AHA members check the AGLOSO list prior
to booking organizational conferences or meetings. For convenience, the
AHA supplied a copy of the list, whose "publication," asserted *Hotel Monthly*,
"had its desired effect."[28]

The NCASP, at this time, was not on the AGLOSO list. Nonetheless, as
weeks passed and the peace conference, scheduled to begin on March 25,
drew closer, the Waldorf found itself under increasing pressure to explain
how an organization branded as a front for the Cominform could have
finagled its way into what Reisel called the "swank Waldorf-Astoria ballroom." Much was made of the supposed hypocrisy of the Soviet delegation
(which included as its main ambassador the composer Dmitri Shostakovich) stuffing down a dinner that would include what the *World-Telegram*
described as "(capitalist-grown) fresh fruit" and "Key West turtle soup, well
flavored with dry sack," which, the paper added sardonically, "should go
down without too much difficulty." Others, such as *New York Sun* columnist H. I. Phillips, took swipes at what they portrayed as the drabness of
Soviet cuisine: "There is no need for immediate hysteria. . . . Borscht can't

be popularized as a Park avenue dish on only one week-end effort." *Counterattack*, meanwhile, charged that the Waldorf had become a dupe for a Communist front seeking to legitimize itself with "the luster of luxury, expensiveness, dignity . . . and thus make it immune from attack." After all, the newsletter added, "People with so much money can't be Communists, can they?"[29]

Meanwhile, the hotel continued to insist that there was no way it could cancel the conference. "The Waldorf-Astoria, in this instance," explained an unidentified spokesperson, "is, as a public institution, playing the role of serving the public." Another manager pointed out that the NCASP had never been added to the Attorney General's List of Subversive Organizations. Claude Philippe further explained the hotel's position to the *World-Telegram*. Yes, he had read what had been written about conference participants in the newspapers; yet, "we will treat them all as guests of the house. . . . We are hospitable to all our guests, unless they are traitors. . . . But then none of these people could be classed as traitors since there was no objection to the conference from the State Department."[30]

Still the attacks continued. Next in line was Walter Winchell, the rabble-rousing columnist and commentator whose weekly program had, several months before, edged past that of competitor Jack Benny to become the most listened-to in radio. With his breathless, staccato delivery, pitched against a clattering aural backdrop meant to simulate a telegraph, Winchell became, in the words of biographer Neil Gabler, "an anxiety-monger who brilliantly captured the national mood in times of uncertainty." Born to a Jewish family in Harlem, Winchell had challenged the pro-Nazi German American Bund organization in the late 1930s ("It is the likes of you that will cause a clean-out of Jews in the U.S. within *10 years*," read one piece of hate mail Winchell received) and denounced Fascism throughout the war. Later he drew upon his close friendship with FBI chief J. Edgar Hoover as personal and ideological support for a self-propelled anti-Communist initiative, through which he routinely hurled inflammatory words at those he perceived as being soft on Reds. Attacking the Waldorf conference on his program of Sunday, March 13, Winchell directed his ire toward the U.S. attorney general, Tom Clark, who had recently granted visas to Shostakovich and other members of the Soviet delegation, among them the same Fadeyev who had shocked Western visitors with his vituperations on American culture at the Wroclaw Congress: "I say that Shastakovich [sic] isn't coming here as a musician, he's coming as a Communist propagandist. Therefore, if the United States Attorney General . . . sees no objection to 7 imported Communists at the Waldorf Hotel in New York, surely the New York Mayor O'Dwyer will not object to Walter Winchell asking 70,000 members of the American Legion to picket on Park Avenue."[31]

The American Legion, founded by veterans in 1919, had grown by the end of the Second World War to include more than 3 million members. In addition to lobbying for benefits (it was instrumental in drafting the G.I. Bill, signed by President Roosevelt in 1944), the Legion worked to promote an ethic of "Americanism," through activities as diverse as the picketing of movies associated with blacklisted artists, advising readers of its *Legion* magazine on "the way you can fight Communism," and promoting anti-Communist loyalty oaths for workers in both the public and private sectors. The Legion's Americanism Commission, an influence behind the Good Citizenship program created by the American Hotel Association, also functioned as a private unofficial counterpart to the FBI, keeping files on suspicious organizations and infiltrating their events to provide reports from within. On March 25, the commission dispatched its research specialist, Karl Baarslag, to cover the Waldorf peace conference for an article in one of its newsletters, *Summary of Trends and Developments Exposing the Communist Conspiracy*. In criticizing the "1,800 pro-Soviet banqueters" as "a hard-looking lot" whose faces "reflected shifty-eyed cunning, hard-bitten cynicism, smug self-satisfaction, arrogance, and typical Communist conceit," Baarslag exposed what he saw as the irony of a socialist gathering being held in the plush Waldorf-Astoria: "Clothing, women's coiffures and wraps and their general mien and bearing showed the mob to be almost 100 percent middle class and upper middle class. Probably less than one in a hundred had ever worked with his hands or ever undergone suffering, poverty or social degradation. Upper class scum and decadent intellectuals describes this mass of Stalin's stooges."[32]

Meanwhile, the protesters arrived to do their part in what the *World-Telegram*, playing on the four-year-old movie title, promised would be "a Big Week End at the Waldorf!" Winchell's adjuration to the American Legion had been seconded by leaders of other patriotic groups, among them three separate sets of war veterans (Catholic, Jewish, and Disabled) and the ad hoc People's Committee for Freedom of Religion. These in turn were augmented by the Ancient Order of Hibernians; the Knights of Columbus; American Gold Star Mothers; the Marine Corps League; members of various parishes of the Orthodox Church (traveling from as far as Trenton); anti-Soviet Americans of Russian descent; and representatives of Poland, Lithuania, Croatia, and other countries that had come under Communist rule. All through Friday, as temperatures lingered below fifty degrees, women in native costumes—scarves, shawls, colorful aprons, and embroidered skirts—knelt on the Waldorf sidewalk, chanting prayers and holding signs that read "Stop Stalin! Save Slovakia" and "Genocide Is the Red Peace." For many, the protest grew out of personal experience with brutality: one man, an escapee from a Siberian labor camp, told reporters of how he had witnessed a priest turned into "a human icicle," frozen to death with buckets of water thrown over him, as "2,000 other prisoners were forced to watch." Others, however, expressed their distaste for the conference in xenophobic terms, finding ammunition in the reported extravagance of the Waldorf's dinner menu. "Let them eat strawberries," shouted one young man. "They'll eat black bread when they get back!"[33]

With hecklers urging them to "go back to Russia!" conference attendees and panelists had to display what one observer characterized as "a good deal of fortitude" just to make it through the Park Avenue doors. Bowing to pressure from the American Legion and other groups, the Police Department announced it would remove limitations on pickets: any number would be allowed, provided the doors themselves were not blocked. Arthur Miller, hosting a panel on the Starlight Roof (while the main dinner was held in the Grand Ballroom, sessions took place throughout the hotel), dryly recalled the "big news in the press that every entrance of the Waldorf-Astoria would be blocked by a line of nuns praying for the souls of the participants, who

Protesting against the Cultural and Scientific Conference for World Peace, 1949 (Keystone-France/Gamma-Keystone via Getty Images).

had been deranged by Satanic seduction." Beyond the human barrier that extended down Forty-Ninth and Fiftieth Streets to surround all sides of the hotel, resistance now appeared from another source: members of the anti-Communist left (what remained of the 1930s Trotskyists) who had, with funding later rumored to have been given by the CIA, set up offices in a Waldorf bridal suite in order to counter Shapley and the NCASP on their own turf. With membership that included novelist Mary McCarthy and Nicolas Nabokov, composer and cousin of writer Vladimir, this new group, American Intellectuals for Freedom (AIF), busied itself with what Nabokov recalled as "frenzied activity": "There was a perpetual flow of visitors. 'Freedom lovers' of varied sizes and genders squeezed their way in and out of the cluttered premises. Some chatted excitedly, others buried their faces in reading matter that the two secretaries or the attendant of the mimeograph machine provided from its bathroom-paper heap."[34]

The long battle over the conference the *New York Times* called "one of the most controversial meetings in recent New York history" now moved to a finish inside the Waldorf, as the NCASP struggled to defend itself against the attacks led by AIF. The counterintellectual group had been organized with the goal of waging a fight that would be effective but at the same time would not appear, in Mary McCarthy's words (as reported by Nabokov), as if it had been "staged by [red-baiting Senator] Joe McCarthy." Such a distinction was impossible to maintain: from its tenth-floor Waldorf "office," AIF sent a barrage of press releases filled with unverifiable information—for example, the claim that two members of the Soviet delegation were actually secret Russian police agents sent to "protect" Shostakovich from "anti-Soviet contacts"—that was then picked up and reprinted, sometimes verbatim, by newspaper editors as a way of inciting the mostly right-wing picketers that surrounded the hotel (some of whom waved copies of the front pages of the *World-Telegram* and *Journal American*). The NCASP fought back with its own statements, issued from temporary headquarters on the fourth floor, but "with rare exceptions," recalled one observer, these were "ignored or buried in the press." Meanwhile, the prayerful tone of the initial demonstrators gave way to a violent current: during the adjunct conference session held at Madison Square Garden, one attendee claimed to have been harassed with shouts of "Christ killer" and "Dirty Jew," while the *Daily Mirror* printed a photo of a middle-aged female protester holding an insecticide gun, smiling. Attached to her overcoat was a handwritten sign: "EXTERMINATE THE DIRTY-RED RATS."[35]

The furor was so loud—one researcher counted sixty-two "emotionally charged words or phrases" about the conference in a single issue of Hearst's *Journal American*—that it precluded almost any consideration of the sessions themselves. These were made up of panels organized by theme ("Education in a Disunited World," "The Screen, the Radio and the Press") and led by a who's who of global intelligentsia, among them former vice president and Progressive Party candidate Henry Wallace; physician Ernst Boas; young novelist Norman Mailer; and Mirta Aguirre, a Cuban writer and critic. Of the conference delegates, only Dmitri Shostakovich, as keynote speaker and member of the Fine Arts panel, received significant attention in the press: music historian Terry Klefstad observes that this was due not only to the enormous popularity of Shostakovich's symphonies in the United States but also to American awareness that his works had been prohibited in the USSR on the grounds of Formalism, "alien to the Soviet people and its artistic tastes." Because of this, anti-Communist Americans, especially those on the left, were inclined to view him with a degree of sympathy, as one of what Nabokov called the "Soviet sacrificial lambs" sent to the Waldorf as mascots: "tortured, innocent creatures saying things they did not mean and could not believe."[36]

At the same time, Shostakovich's February 1948 apology at a conference in Moscow (echoed in his speech on the Starlight Roof of the Waldorf, where the composer acknowledged departing "from big themes and contemporary images" and thus losing "contact with the people") made him the object of derision as a Soviet puppet. Disembarking at La Guardia Airport, he had been treated to shouts of "Hey, Shosty, look this way!" from newspaper photographers. Later, at the Waldorf's opening dinner, he was photographed looking boyish and pale, timidly eating a strawberry dessert the captions insisted it was hypocritical for a Russian to enjoy. Meanwhile, picketers urged him to "jump out the window," in reference to Soviet schoolteacher Oksana Kasenkina, who the previous year had become a cause célèbre after leaping from the third floor of the Russian consulate in New York, in order to avoid being sent back to the USSR. The treatment continued in press editorials, including one from the *World-Telegram* of March 25: "The Russians, in addition to raising hell generally, also raise a lot of beets for borscht. But frankly, how can you get culture from a beet? How can the Soviets bring something they haven't got?"[37]

By contrast, the Waldorf's administration was generally given a pass: it had, in the view of the *Daily Mirror*, accepted the Cultural and Scientific Conference for World Peace "at face value," and now (despite the lack of any apologetic statement from the hotel) was "up to its ears in innocent embarrassment." Other than explaining that to pull the conference would have been, as reported in the *Mirror* and *Times*, a violation of state antidiscrimination laws, the hotel remained silent once sessions began. Hiding behind its characteristic restraint, the Waldorf behaved as if the quickest way to dispel controversy was to comment on it as little as possible. On the other hand, certain guests, discovering they were housed "under the same roof" with what the *Journal American* called "Stalin stooges," expressed "disgust and anger." One visitor, a "bronzed oilman" from Amarillo, "slapped his sombrero against his knee in an expression of futility," claiming that he couldn't understand "'how our country can put up with stuff like this'": "'They ought to take these Commies down to the waterfront and ship them out, including the so-called Americans playing footsie with them. . . . One thing I'm sure of—we wouldn't stand for stuff like this in Texas.'"[38]

Eleanor Roosevelt, writing in her "My Day" column, lamented what she perceived as the "rather depressing" newspaper reports and "melodramatic" picketing methods that were "not really helpful in getting to the public a calm and unbiased review of the things that were actually being said." The former First Lady expressed a wish that "we had treated the 'peace' meeting more casually." Arthur Miller was bemused that "a meeting of writers and artists could generate such widespread public suspicion and anger," adding that the Waldorf conference "ended in futility, except for its setting a new and higher level of hostility in the Cold War." The National Council of the Arts, Sciences and Professions would last several more years, but in 1955, after receiving word from the attorney general that it would finally be designated as subversive, it voted to disband. For much of the general public, the impression that remained of the peace conference could be summarized by a drawing, captioned "The Wake of the Red Itch," that appeared in the *Daily Mirror* on March 28, 1949, the day after sessions ended. In it, the Waldorf-Astoria's twin Deco spires appeared in conversation, the inward-facing walls supplanted with tearful eyes and wheezing cartoon noses. "I *STILL* SMELL SOMETHING!" complained the north tower, leaving its southern counterpart to respond, "FUMIGATING, NO DOUBT!"[39]

———

As it turned out, Lucius Boomer missed all the controversy for which, through his success in making the Waldorf-Astoria a place of international attention, he had been largely responsible. On June 26, 1947, Lucius and wife

Jorgine were vacationing in Norway, en route to a house they owned in the scenic Bøverdal valley. Driving through the town of Hamar, Boomer noticed a hotel by the name of Astoria and, thinking he would find out if it had any postcards he could send to friends, decided to stop. He made it as far as the lobby, where he collapsed in a chair and died instantly of a heart attack, aged sixty-eight. The next day, according to his wishes, Jorgine had his body cremated and the remains shipped back to the Waldorf in New York. Nick Racz, one of Boomer's assistant managers, recalled holding the ashes, exclaiming, "Can you imagine, that's Mr. Boomer?" It seemed impossible that a man so powerful could be reduced to a box.[40]

In his final correspondence with Howard Meek of Cornell University, Boomer offered a rare hint of personal insecurity when he inquired about an honorary diploma that had been awarded him during a visit to the School of Hotel Administration in April 1947. Like most hotel executives of his generation, Lucius had entered the business without a degree from an institution of higher learning. Now, writing to the director of the academic program he had helped create, Boomer expressed anxiety over the whereabouts of the diploma (which Meek had offered to hold for safekeeping): "Hope the certification that I am now a college man (of a sort) hasn't been misplaced, and that it will come along in due course." While self-deprecating, Boomer's tone points to the seriousness with which he viewed education, from his early years teaching music with the Koreshans to his later influence as a writer and organizer of classes for hotel employees. This focus extended to his own standards of learning: Boomer remained open to new ideas, even as he insisted on the primacy of his own. Much of what made the Waldorf a success under Boomer's leadership came from his willingness to consider the slightly unorthodox: he leaped at odd opportunities and used them to build the reputation of the hotel in accordance with his expansive goals. He had carried the eccentric inquisitiveness of his Koreshan youth into the American mainstream.[41]

From the perspective of everyone at the Waldorf, Boomer would be impossible to replace. For two years Frank Ready assumed the top management spot, while Claude Philippe built his popularity as the hotel's public face. He also continued to book a parade of events, in keeping with his "ask permission later" philosophy. At last, Philippe overstepped: in November 1949 the hotel hosted another dinner for the National Council of American-Soviet Friendship, a past client that, by now, could be counted among the most blatantly Communist of organizations branded as "subversive" by the attorney general. Again, the hotel came under fire from *Counterattack*: "What excuse can the Waldorf offer for this?" This time, however, a new Waldorf president stepped in to clarify matters: "*I have seen your issue of Nov 18*, calling attention to party held at the Waldorf-Astoria, by National Council of American-Soviet Friendship. I don't know how this outfit got into the hotel. We have just recently purchased controlling interest in the hotel and the reservation was not made since we took it over. . . . I assure you that neither this nor other subversive organizations are welcome in our hotels."[42]

The new president's name was Conrad Hilton.

CHAPTER 7

Little America

For decades, a visitor to any Hilton hotel would find, tucked inside the night-stand drawer, a paperback copy of *Be My Guest*, Conrad Hilton's 1957 memoir. Those expecting rote policy statements or how-to discussions of management were surprised to discover a revealing account of the hotelier's choppy rise, starting with his early life as a merchant's son in late nineteenth-century New Mexico and moving through forays into banking, politics, and—during one especially unsuccessful period—management of a female vaudeville trio. Inside the pages were candid assessments of his relationship with his father (who increasingly viewed the younger Hilton as a business rival) and his own "doomed" second marriage, to Hungarian beauty Zsa Zsa Gabor. Most vivid were the memories of a youth spent traveling New Mexico Territory, as representative of his father's trading concern; in one passage, Hilton described the low-lying tamarisk trees as "feathery plumes of bluish-green topped by sprays of pink blossoms." Fluent in Spanish since childhood, young Conrad (or "Connie," as he was known to family and friends) would journey by mule-driven wagon for weeks at a time, sleeping in the "fine old canopied beds" of aristocratic haciendas. There, he developed the firm but gracious standard of negotiation that he would later cite as a personal hallmark: "Custom demanded a polite interchange . . . inspection of the *rancho*, several glasses of wine, before any hint was given that business was afoot." This was all part of a "leisurely" long-established tradition: "Finally we would go and look at the cattle, or mohair, or hides.... Whereupon, couched in language as flowery as spring itself, we would settle down to a garlanded but most hard-headed bargaining bout. Wares changed hands in a flutter of bows and courtesies."[1]

It was fitting that the date of Conrad's birth, in 1887, happened to be December 25. Brought up within a large Roman Catholic family, Hilton moved comfortably among three distinct cultural groups—Spanish-speaking ranchers, Native Americans, and white settlers—while adhering to the beliefs instilled by his devout mother, for whom prayer, he wrote, was "precisely as necessary and life-giving as food or air." Over the years much would be made of Hilton's religiosity: as a real-life character on season 3 of the fictional TV series *Mad Men* (2009), he was portrayed, in one scene, calling ad executive Don Draper in the middle of the night after experiencing a business "revelation" through divine contact. While staunch in his devotion to Christian principles, Hilton also professed respect for other religions, each of which, he wrote, offered a pathway to "the one God." In contrast to his Waldorf predecessor, Lucius Boomer (rumored, among the few non-Gentile staff members, to hold a private distaste for Jews), Hilton spoke often at meetings of interfaith charities. One of his favorite childhood stories concerned Santa Fe's cathedral, built between 1869 and 1886. According to legend, the Roman Catholic archbishop in charge of the cathedral ran out of funds and could only complete it after his friend, a Jewish merchant who had financed the project, offered to tear up the promissory notes in exchange for permission to add one word above the entrance. Hilton would write of visiting the cathedral as an adult and being "moved by its beauty. I was equally moved to see over the arch the part Abraham Staab [the merchant] had played in its building. There were the Hebraic initials, JVH, symbolic of the word 'God' of the Christian faith, 'Jehovah' of the faith of the Jews."[2]

Hilton's own success came as the result of similar partnerships, faith in those of different backgrounds, and, most significantly, a willingness to act on unexpected opportunities. In 1919, at age thirty, Connie set out for Texas with the intention of buying a bank. Reaching Cisco, "a cowtown gone crazy" with oil profits, he offered the $75,000 asking price on the first bank he found for sale (intending to raise the money through investors), only to have the owner send him back a peremptory telegram from Kansas City: *"Price up to $80,000 and skip the haggling."* Incensed at the man's rudeness, feeling taken advantage of for having agreed on the price too quickly, Hilton walked off, informing the telegraph operator, "He can keep his bank." Hoping to rest before setting out to find another bank, he decided to stop at a small red-brick hotel named the Mobley. Inside, all was confusion: "The milling press in the hotel lobby acted like sardines clamoring to get into the can. From behind, from the sides, the crowd tried to push into the tiny funnel around the desk clerk. Since I was tall, in excellent condition and determined to get a room, I plunged right into the spirit of the thing and was within speaking distance of the clerk, when that harassed individual slammed his book shut and hollered: 'Full up!'"[3]

After conversing with the owner, who claimed that he longed to make *"real"* money" in the oil fields instead of herding bodies at a "glorified boarding house," Conrad came to a decision: rather than buy a bank, he would buy a hotel. The Mobley became the "first" Hilton property, in 1919. Over the next five years, Connie settled into the pattern of his early career: buying run-down Texas hotels and refurbishing them with "a platoon of scrub women, a company of window washers," and "a division of painters and carpenters." Along the way, he survived tragedies and close calls. In one incident, his manager in Dallas, a good friend, was shot and killed by a deranged former partner. Later, in 1924, he launched construction on the first Hilton hotel built from the ground up, also in Dallas, only to run out of money. Forced to choose between paying the bank loan and the contractor, Hilton was saved when a Jewish friend, Harry Siegel, surprised him with a loan of $30,000: "Pay 'em both, Connie. . . . I trust you." This gesture, Hilton wrote, reminded him of the story of the Santa Fe cathedral and filled him "with a living gratitude for a country where we can all work together as children of one Father." It became the inspiration for Hilton's pro-America philosophy, one that viewed religious tolerance as key to the furthering of mutual goals: "Men like Harry Siegel and Abraham Staab, any man of any faith who tries to do his daily business . . . in God's way, is, to my mind, a pioneer of peace."[4]

In 1929, Conrad announced plans for the El Paso Hilton, newest in a chain that already included hotels in Fort Worth, Dallas, Waco, and Abilene. Soon after, the stock market crashed. El Paso's Hilton managed to open on schedule, in 1930, but by then the entire industry had been hit: "People weren't traveling." Now married and with two sons, Hilton "went broke by inches" as he struggled to keep hold of properties. Sheriffs posted judgments in his lobbies, while a furniture company to which he had originally owed $100,000 sued him for the last part of the balance—$178. Humiliated and half a million in debt, Hilton was "rushing from one hotel to another . . . always trying to raise a dollar here, a dollar there." His marriage suffered during the "frenzied effort" to keep the family "fed, clothed and housed." At his lowest point, unable to buy groceries, one of his bellboys surprised him with a loan of $300, the young man's entire savings, for "eating money." Even then, however, Connie allowed himself a flash of the optimism that he viewed as intrinsic to American enterprise. Near the end of 1931, he came across a magazine photo of the new Waldorf-Astoria, whose flag, Hilton wrote, flew "confidently in the face of adversity." For Connie, who by now had lost control of all his hotels, the Waldorf symbolized "high mountains, the wide horizons" that were visible even from the depths of "the valley." The photo offered a promise of better times and inspired a personal goal that would take Connie eighteen years to fulfill: "I clipped it and put it in my wallet."[5]

Hilton described the next few years as being like "the slow recovery from an operation." His first step was to regain management of his hotels by making a deal with the wealthy Galveston family that had taken them over. Next, he raised a total of $30,000 to buy back his El Paso hotel, whose corporation he then reorganized under Section 77B of the 1934 Bankruptcy Act—the same law that Lucius Boomer drew upon for the Waldorf. Then he did something similar for Abilene. In 1938, having rebuilt his Texas chain, Hilton expanded to San Francisco and acquired the Sir Francis Drake, a luxury hotel that had fallen on hard times. This became Connie's practice for the next several years: searching for hotels that had gone into receivership during the Depression and then purchasing them at bargain prices. By 1943, he had bought the Town House in Los Angeles and two hotels in Chicago (including the world's then-largest, the Stevens), along with his first New York hotels, the Roosevelt and the Plaza. Meanwhile, following one of his "hunches," he began buying shares in the Waldorf-Astoria Corporation—one year, as it happened, before the hotel began realizing a profit. In November 1949, the trade publication *Hotel Monthly* announced that Conrad Hilton had secured 68 percent of the corporation's stock. Now in control, he installed himself as board president and brought in a genial war veteran named Joe Binns, formerly of the Stevens in Chicago, to manage.

The Waldorf-Astoria, having lacked a strong leader since Boomer's demise, was now a Hilton hotel.

———

Notwithstanding his disavowal of Communism, whose "essence" he described as "the death of the individual and the burial of his remains in a collective mass," Hilton generally promoted a tolerant view of social groups with backgrounds different from his own. This openness extended beyond questions of religion. By the 1950s, a period during which few leaders in the hotel industry were willing to take a stance against discrimination, Hilton's corporation had become known, in the words of one African American travel writer, for extending "its hospitality to all races of people." Speaking to television host Art Linkletter in 1954, at a time when the Hilton chain was expanding internationally, Conrad asserted that American hotels in countries like Egypt and Turkey gave people a chance to "rub elbows" with one another, in the hope that "prejudices may erase." In 1952, Hilton arranged for an excerpt from one of his public addresses, "The Battle for Peace," to be reprinted as a full-page color supplement to *Life* magazine. The insert, which featured a drawing of a red, white, and blue–garbed figure representing Uncle Sam—hands clasped, kneeling—linked anti-Communism and pro-Americanism with an inclusiveness based on religion and ethnicity. Proclaiming that "America now knows it can destroy communism," Hilton urged "Our Father in Heaven" to "Inspire us with wisdom, all of us of every color, race and creed."[6]

The Red Scare of the 1950s united Republicans like Hilton with centrist and even left-leaning Democrats, due to the fact that America's contradictory

Conrad Hilton in front of "The Greatest of Them All," 1949 (Martha Holmes/
The LIFE Picture Collection via Getty Images).

positions on race—the hypocrisy of a country that proclaimed liberty while allowing segregation—had become a favored rallying cry for Communist leaders. Speaking at a Paris conference in 1948, Soviet delegate Alexander Fadeyev (the same Fadeyev who later addressed the Waldorf peace assemblage) included racism among the evils of an American culture that reeked "with the stench of decay." One Soviet propaganda poster, from 1948, depicted an American man of color bound with ropes beneath an image of the Statue of Liberty and the Manhattan skyline. "Under Capitalism," the caption read. In 1944 no less a conservative than J. Edgar Hoover, the FBI's Red-hunting chief, used a speech at the Waldorf-Astoria to lament how the "baseless rumors and hates started by one bigot" can reach "floodtide proportions" in the form of "rackets" such as the Ku Klux Klan. Prejudice, insisted Hoover, was incompatible with an "American tradition" that was "wholesomely democratic." Two years later, the actor Raymond Massey, also speaking at the Waldorf, summed it up: the "entire world," he pronounced, was "watching America and the way it handles its racial and religious minorities."[7]

"Our international prestige," Massey added, "is dependent upon our ability to deal with our national issues." This perception of racism as a stain on the United States' image—now, in the light of American postwar dominance, on display to an unprecedented degree—consumed officials at the highest levels of government. Beginning in 1947, President Truman's Justice Department issued a series of amicus (or "friend of the court") briefs to the Supreme Court, arguing for decisions that would outlaw segregation. Its brief of December 2, 1952, demonstrated how "the existence of discrimination against minority groups in the United States has an adverse effect upon our relations with other countries": "The United States is trying to prove to the people of the world of every nationality, race and color, that a free democracy is the most civilized and most secure form of government yet devised by man. . . . Racial discrimination furnishes grist for the Communist propaganda mills."[8]

As lawyer Ian Fagelson explained in an article for the *Journal of Supreme Court History*, after each amicus brief, the Court "ruled unanimously in favor of the position argued by the Justice Department." The most celebrated of these decisions was made in the case of *Brown v. Board of Education* (1954). While actual implementation was postponed for one year, the Court, in ruling that segregation of children in public schools was unconstitutional, overturned decades of "separate but equal" legislation in the southern United States and delivered what American newspapers cited as a "Blow to Communism." The *Brown* ruling was also a victory for the National Association for the Advancement of Colored People (NAACP), whose chief counsel, Thurgood Marshall, had argued one of the five separate cases into which *Brown* was combined. *Brown*, in the words of historian Mary Dudziak, allowed the NAACP to "argue that its work promoted, rather than undermined, the nation's Cold War interests," at a time when it and other civil rights groups were regularly being labeled as communistic by the segregationist White Citizens Councils of the South. After February 22, 1956, when the *New York Times* published an article suggesting that the Communist Party had plans to "inject itself into . . . civil rights struggles," the NAACP grew particularly defensive. "The Negro has never been other than moderate," insisted African American diplomat Ralph Bunche during his remarks at a Waldorf-Astoria dinner held May 17, 1956, in honor of the second anniversary of the *Brown* decision:

> This has been true of his leadership as represented by the NAACP, despite some grievously false current attempts to portray the NAACP as being at one extreme, with the White Citizens Councils at the other. The Negro American knows that he is entitled to point with pride to the fact that through all these long years of injustice and imposed racial handicap, in his struggle upward he has always fully appreciated the meaning of democracy and has never failed to respect its institutions.[9]

Keynote speaker at the dinner was twenty-seven-year old Dr. Martin Luther King Jr., free on bail after having been arrested by Alabama officials for his leadership of the Montgomery bus boycott. King used the Waldorf speech, titled "A Realistic Look at Race Relations," to discuss the boycott's goal: initially crafted to ameliorate conditions on Montgomery buses for African Americans, it had now expanded to include full integration of the city's bus system. He spoke of the effectiveness of "passive resistance," through which "the Negro is saying to his oppressors, 'I don't like the way I am being treated . . .' in vociferous terms." Referencing the "little brown man in India," King praised Mahatma Gandhi for deciding to "confront physical force with soul force" in the effort to "free his people from . . . the economic exploitation and the humiliation inflicted upon them by Britain." King also summarized two responses to race relations: that of the optimist "who would conclude that the problem is just about solved," and that of the pessimist who, by pointing to "the determinative effects of habit structures," would insist that prejudice is "permanent and inflexible." Then, getting to the "realistic look" built into the speech's title, King advocated a third response, one that "seeks to reconcile the truths of two opposites and avoid the extremes of both," in the manner of Hegelian philosophy: "We have come a long long way, and we have a long long way to go." To avoid becoming "victims of an optimism which would blind our eyes to the true realities of the situation," activists would be called upon to continue the struggle: "If democracy is to live, segregation must die."

> The underlying philosophy of democracy is diametrically opposed to the underlying philosophy of segregation, and all the dialectics of the logicians cannot make them lie down together. Segregation is a cancer in the body politic which must be removed before our democratic health can be realized.[10]

After the May 17 Waldorf address, African American columnist Louis E. Martin observed, Dr. King was now "a national figure"; he would "never again belong exclusively to Montgomery, Alabama." For the NAACP, too, the *Brown* anniversary dinner, described by executive secretary Roy Wilkins as "one of the best affairs" the organization had "ever given," marked the onset of a period of success and challenge. Due in part to its decision to provide legal support for King and other leaders of the Montgomery bus boycott, the NAACP was sued by the Alabama attorney general on June 1. Subsequently, a state judge ordered the organization to suspend operations in Alabama. The resultant legal costs and lost revenue precipitated what regional director Franklin Williams called a "financial emergency" that continued long after the victory of December 20, 1956, when the U.S. Supreme Court ruled that segregated forms of public transportation were unconstitutional (the NAACP could not legally resume operations in Alabama until 1964). To raise funds, Williams came up with a plan for a $100 per couple event, to be held in the NAACP's home base of Manhattan. Given the Waldorf's reputation and track record with benefits, it was natural that Williams would try to secure it as host for the affair, to be known as a "Freedom Fund" dinner. But the attempt to book New York's most prominent hotel would throw the NAACP into a different kind of battle, one centered around the prime Manhattan commodity of space.[11]

"Every important function that was over a thousand people was booked at the Waldorf," recalled restaurateur and former employee Tom Margittai, "partially because of its Grand Ballroom and partially because it was the best for prestige and getting people to pay the $50, or whatever it was, to participate." But if the NAACP needed the Waldorf-Astoria, the Waldorf also depended on the NAACP and organizations like it: as noted, the hotel's banquet and sales department, led by the domineering Claude Philippe, was responsible for three-quarters of its profit during the mid-1950s. The nation's bumpy path toward desegregation would inform the relationship between these long-standing institutions—the Waldorf and the NAACP—each of which promoted an optimistic ideal, one stressing the core fitness and propriety of American life. From its inception the Park Avenue Waldorf exemplified strength and opportunity: with these values in mind, Conrad Hilton had written "The Greatest of Them All" across the photo he slipped into his wallet and, later, under the glass of his desk in Texas. In acquiring the Waldorf, Conrad built on a personal and professional narrative. Each hotel, he wrote in Be My Guest, was conceived as "a little America," offering evidence of "the fruits of the free world." But if Hilton hotels represented America's best, there were occasions where they showed up its worst. Now part of

Hilton's chain, the Waldorf discovered that if it took credit for the one, it would have to bear responsibility for the other.[12]

Historically, the Waldorf-Astoria's relationship with segregation could be described as inconsistent and, at times, contradictory. In June 1895, "three black men," as reported in the *New York World*, "went into the café of the Hotel Waldorf . . . and had drinks," while George Boldt and a group of "indignant" friends watched from a nearby table. This event, unprecedented in the two-year history of the hotel, was conceived as a "test" of New York State's new Malby Act, which—one year before the *Plessy v. Ferguson* Supreme Court decision that gave legal sanction to segregation in the South—mandated that African Americans receive equal treatment by operators of hotels, theaters, restaurants, bathhouses, and railways. Around the same time, another "colored man," who, in the words of the *Tribune*, "had evidently read the law and understood its meaning," was granted service in the Waldorf's café and "went his way rejoicing." When questioned about these occurrences—would "colored people . . . be received as guests in the restaurant," and not just the cafe?—George Boldt replied that he "preferred to climb the mountain when he reached it." To another reporter he voiced frustration over the first group of men, who "were obnoxious because they were ill-bred": "Without saying that I dislike negroes I must insist that this Malby law is an outrage, as it prevents us from making any selection of our patrons. A man who runs a first-class hotel must respect the wishes of his guests as to the sort of people that he entertains, and the law should not dictate to him."[13]

Boldt's distress would be temporary. After the tests succeeded in proving that, when forced to do so, proprietors of restaurants, theaters, and Turkish baths would admit people of color, New York's recreational life settled into a period of de facto segregation that would last for decades. In the Tenderloin this meant, in effect, the existence of separate "white" and "black" establishments only blocks or even doors apart. African American counterparts to the sporting figures, stage personalities, and gamblers who populated the Waldorf bar could be found at Tenderloin establishments like Nat Edwards's

Sixth Avenue saloon, where white patrons were, for the most part, admitted only if they happened to be known to the management. Meanwhile, hotels including the Waldorf discovered simple ways to preserve an all-white clientele. Speaking to a *Tribune* reporter after the Malby Act's implementation in 1895, the manager of Hoffman House suggested that the "good sense of the colored people would keep them from intruding where they were not welcome." Head waiters were instrumental in ensuring this would be the case. "From the hints which they dropped," reported the *Tribune*, "it is safe to say that [waiters] will serve [people of color] when they come, but they will probably do it in a manner to make a second visit improbable."[14]

For the remainder of the "first" Waldorf-Astoria's history, African Americans were sometimes welcomed as guests if they arrived as part of a larger, predominantly white, organization. In January 1928, NAACP president Mary McLeod Bethune lectured at the Waldorf under auspices of the National Council of Women, which was holding a conference. Bethune arrived with a group of nine African American women, who were, in the words of one report, shown "every courtesy" as guests of the hotel. Urging her listeners to "open the doors," Bethune asked members of the council "not to forget" their "Negro sisters here in America" as they worked to improve conditions for women around the world. Meanwhile, southern-style segregation was occasionally practiced at the Waldorf, behind the scenes. The following January, in 1929, white and black employees were separated at the hotel's annual staff reception. As described by a Baltimore newspaper, the *Afro-American* (in an account that, tellingly, was not contradicted by Waldorf management), "whites were served a regular seven-course dinner" in the main ballroom, while the "colored employees," some fifty to sixty workers, were given "only a plate of salad, ice cream and cakes" in a room "far removed from the main events." Given that receptions during previous years had been integrated, it was likely that the Waldorf, in this case, acceded to a request from the predominantly white staff. "None of the hotel officials," claimed the paper, "would assume responsibility for the 'jim-crowing' of the colored help."[15]

After the new Waldorf opened in 1931, African Americans became more visible as luncheon attendees, performers, and, in certain instances, overnight guests. In the progressive spirit of Mayor La Guardia's New York, with racial equality a much-publicized administrative concern, unwritten policies of segregation were difficult for hotel and restaurant owners to maintain. Still, the Waldorf occasionally relegated African Americans to less visible areas, in ways suggesting that the hotel's public rooms—as sites of commingling activity—did not, in the view of management, constitute a single, level field. In March 1932, Hunter College hosted an integrated "Senior Hop" on the Starlight Roof. But, two years later, Gimbel's department store (at the time, chief rival to Macy's) suffered embarrassment when it decided to open its annual ball, previously held just for executives, to all employees. For this Gimbel's rented the Grand Ballroom, only to discover that the Waldorf-Astoria did not, in the words of the *Afro-American*, "allow colored [persons] to enter [it]." By that time, the "large number of colored persons, working in the store as porters, kitchen help and elevator men," had already been invited. How to uninvite them? Eventually the store manager explained that, "although it hurt him," the African American workers would have to return their invitations. To compensate, he offered them theater tickets for the night of the party, "so they would not feel 'out of things.'"[16]

Performers of color often observed how their artistry helped create greater tolerance within the general American social climate. By the end of the 1930s, barriers at the Waldorf had begun to dissolve, largely through the presence of the African American entertainers who appeared there. Not long after opening the new Waldorf, Boomer signed a contract with MCA (then the largest music talent agency) to book nationally recognized as well as up-and-coming performers into the Empire Room and Sert Room. On October 26, 1938, "Swing [music]," in the words of columnist George Ross, "crashed the hallowed halls of the Waldorf-Astoria," as Benny Goodman and his orchestra settled into the Empire Room for an engagement that proved how "the citadel on Park Avenue" could adapt to the vigorous dancing tastes of young "jitterbugs." Beyond opening the Waldorf to the latest in popular music, the engagement was notable for another reason: Goodman's band featured three African American musicians, among them arranger Fletcher Henderson and drummer and vibraphonist Lionel Hampton. It was the first integrated band to play major American hotels. Speaking to the *Pittsburgh Courier*, Hampton voiced awareness of the booking's significance: "In a spot as important as the Waldorf, I am sure it will have a far reaching [*sic*] effect and will mean much in the future towards the breaking down of racial prejudice, not only in the musical profession, but others as well."[17]

Ultimately, what signaled a change in the racial environment at the Waldorf-Astoria, from the perspective of both performer and guest, was America's entry into the Second World War. With crowds of people from diverse social backgrounds filling their lobbies, hotel proprietors had no choice but to loosen barriers to some extent. At the same time, café and nightclub patrons began to grow more familiar with the idea of African American performers in what had formerly been all-white settings. Because it viewed "greater acceptance of Negroes as part of winning the war," President Roosevelt's administration, as reported in a 1943 *Billboard* article, had "publicly urged [the entertainment] industry to give Negroes a break." The first entirely African American band to play the Waldorf was that of John Kirby, a native of Winchester, Virginia, who, in 1935, had appeared as bassist on several recordings of singer Billie Holiday. Kirby played one of the Waldorf's lounges for a week in October 1942. Meanwhile, both the Waldorf and its competitor, the Savoy-Plaza on Fifth Avenue, believed they had been promised the hotel debut of a rising star who, in the words of theatrical columnist Billy Rowe, "blazed a new trail for both her and her race": Lena Horne. The singer and actress, coming off a prominent role in the Hollywood film *Cabin in the Sky* (featuring an African American cast), eventually went with the Savoy-Plaza, due to signed agreements. However, as biographer James Gavin recounted, that engagement's financial and critical success was not enough to shield Horne from racial indignities: "The Savoy-Plaza gave her a room for dressing, but wouldn't let her sleep in it. Each night after work she went home to [Harlem's] Hotel Theresa."[18]

Within the span of four years, such arrangements had become increasingly uncommon in New York's top hotels. Back in December 1931, shortly after the Waldorf's opening, the writer Langston Hughes had published a caustic poem in the Marxist magazine *The New Masses*. Titled "Come to the Waldorf-

Astoria," the poem took the form of a mock adjuration, one that castigated the hotel's promotion of luxury at a time when so many Americans were suffering: "Listen Hungry Ones! / See what **Vanity Fair** says about the new Waldorf-Astoria: 'All the luxuries of private home . . .' / Now, won't that be charming when the last flophouse has turned you down this winter?" With a sarcasm implying that their presence would not be appreciated, Hughes had urged African Americans from Harlem to "Drop in at the Waldorf this afternoon for tea . . . Give Park Avenue a lot of darkie color—free—for nothing!" Now, writing fifteen years later, he observed the change in his column for the African American newspaper, the *Chicago Defender*: "In recent months, out of town colored people whom I know—not celebrities either—have stopped at the Waldorf-Astoria, the Pennsylvania, the Commodore."[19]

It's significant that Hughes made his observation in the summer of 1946, some months after Lucius Boomer entered into discussions with representatives of the new United Nations about holding official events at the Waldorf. A former UN counsel once confessed to author Charles Abrams that, initially, "the problem of accommodations for colored personnel and delegates had worried the secretariat"—this being a time when both de jure and de facto segregation were emerging as factors that could complicate the United States' postwar role as host to foreign dignitaries. The counsel explained how "the Waldorf agreed to accept UN guests and dignitaries without considering their complexions" if, in return, "the UN promised to favor the Waldorf with its recommendations." This relationship no doubt encouraged the Waldorf to move more quickly than many other hotels when it came to admitting guests of color in general. Regardless, as Abrams explained, the "most discriminatory" New York hotels were generally the ones that ranked "just below the status of the Waldorf and the Pierre"—that is, those who felt less secure in their social and economic footing and therefore believed they would have more to lose by letting down racial barriers. Abrams cited the case of one establishment, "east of Times Square, catering to an intellectual and literary clientele," that "decided to take all comers on the theory that [its] regular guests were opposed to discrimination." But, after "increased applications from Negroes" led it to fear "the effects of a disproportionate balance," the hotel (likely, the Algonquin) "went back to [its] old policy of limited Negro registration."[20]

Notwithstanding the development of a more racially inclusive environment in the 1940s, there were still people who continued to think of the Waldorf as a "white" hotel. In early 1946, two young African American women, Red Cross volunteers who had been nursing soldiers in Europe, returned to New York and were taken, along with several white coworkers, to the Waldorf in one of the organization's red-and-white-painted vans. Upon reaching the hotel a woman, presumably a Red Cross representative already inside, ran out and apologized: the African American women would have to go elsewhere. The Waldorf, she said, would not allow them to stay there. Suspecting the Red Cross might be "helping to foster bias," the left-wing *Peoples Voice* newspaper called a Waldorf manager and received the following response: "'We do not discriminate against Negroes and never gave the RC or any other organization any reason to believe that Negroes could not stay here. We have 4 or 5 Negroes staying here now.'"[21]

Meanwhile, African American social groups and organizations began looking to the Waldorf as a host for their affairs—to the eventual detriment of Harlem institutions such as the Hotel Theresa. As Harlem social arbiter Gerri Major commented in March 1949, "Time was when a lady who stopped in the Waldorf's Peacock Alley for an afternoon pick-up . . . thought she was putting the nuts on the cake"—that is, living it up. No longer. The following year, African American columnist Dan Burley could proclaim, satirically, "Move Over White Folks, Here We Come!" Harlemites, wrote Burley, seemed "to have gone Waldorf-Astoria-Savoy Plaza crazy," in a way that emphasized how "we can go there just as well as [whites]." Initially, the trend of what Burley described as "Negroes . . . outdoing one another trying to crash . . . famous places" had been limited to clubs and charities with little connection to an overt political agenda. That began to change in 1944, after the United Negro College Fund (UNCF; like the NAACP, an organization with a racially diverse directorate) decided to use the Waldorf's Perroquet Suite for a board meeting. According to historian Marybeth Gasman, the UNCF's secretary had made several unsuccessful attempts to reserve the room when Walter Hoving, chairman of Tiffany and Company and a leader within the UNCF, called Lucius Boomer directly. Suddenly, the room that had been "unavailable" for three different dates became open. Waldorf managers still had hesitations over the word "Negro," however. As Gasman recounted, when the board members got to the hotel, they noticed that the sign read, "Hoving-Rockefeller Education Meeting": "When Walter Hoving saw the sign, he tore it in two. . . . After several more meetings, the name of the organization appeared on the sign outside the meeting room. . . . The secret was out—the hotel whose name was synonymous with upper-crust white America was now hosting a meeting about the future of black colleges."[22]

By the 1950s, the Waldorf was hosting so many events that a joke emerged to the effect that civil rights organizations could never relocate to the South—not while the Waldorf-Astoria remained in the North. Prize location for dinners and benefits was the Grand Ballroom, with its large capacity. Securing the ballroom, however, was not an easy matter: aspirants had to get past its gatekeeper, Claude Philippe, characterized by Tom Margittai as "absolutely the dictator of space for these functions." As a "master of sales and booking," Philippe was "playing politics with the various organizations" in hopes of extracting maximum revenue from the Waldorf's multiple event spaces. His toughest ongoing challenge was filling the Starlight Roof, which no one liked because its narrow rectangular layout created poor sightlines and acoustics. NAACP representatives would discover evidence of what they called Philippe's "dickering" when attempting to make plans for their second Freedom Fund dinner, scheduled for November 1958. On January 11 of that year, Philippe sent the NAACP a letter documenting its "tentative reservation" for the Grand Ballroom on one of three potential November evenings. In the letter he stipulated a "minimum guarantee of 1,000 persons." Next to each of the dates for the Grand Ballroom, one of Philippe's many secretaries had typed, without explanation, "or 2nd option."[23]

"The Waldorf held us off until February 19," NAACP executive secretary Roy Wilkins explained in a letter to a board member, "and then sent us a complete contract for—the Starlight Roof!" Pointing to business conditions associated with the overall economic downturn of 1958, Philippe offered "his solid and immovable opinion" (in Wilkins's sarcastic account) that the NAACP would not be able to meet the 1,000-person minimum required for the Grand Ballroom. "What he meant, of course," continued Wilkins, "was that he was dickering for another affair which he thought *could* fill the ballroom at greater profit to the hotel." In a follow-up letter, Philippe continued his efforts to persuade Wilkins's assistant, John Morsell, to take the Starlight Roof, at first name-dropping royalty: "Having served over 900 for the Dinner in honor of Her Majesty Queen Elizabeth II [in the Starlight], I am quite frankly, [*sic*] at a loss to understand [the NAACP's] lack of enthusiasm for one of New York's most beautiful ballrooms." Then, in a response to Morsell's suggestion that they begin looking at dates in the Grand Ballroom for 1959's dinner, Philippe made what an NAACP staff member characterized, in pencil in the letter's margin, as "the threat": "As the general availability for the Ballroom on a Sunday night in 1959 will still represent the same problem because of the many Annual Dinners that have been with us for over twenty years, I would very much appreciate if you would prevail upon Mr. Wilkins and your associates to . . . come to The Waldorf next November."[24]

Accept the Starlight Roof now, Philippe implied, or you can forget about ever making it to the Grand Ballroom. Fed up with Philippe and not wanting to hold a dinner in what Wilkins described as "a bad room," the NAACP decided to take a chance. It pulled its business away from the Waldorf and arranged for the 1958 Freedom Fund dinner to be held at the Hotel Roosevelt instead. Even then, Philippe did not give up: in a new letter that inspired someone at the NAACP to write double exclamation marks in the margin, he emphasized how "Waldorf prestige" would "draw a larger attendance" and suggested the organization renege on its commitment to the Roosevelt ("it is early enough . . . they still have time to resell the date"). Philippe's words, with their hint of anxiety over not having all the banquet rooms filled, suggested it would be relatively simple to get back in his favor. In learning how to navigate the Waldorf's tricky political currents, the NAACP had discovered a valuable tactic, one it would be called upon to use again—for a very different reason.[25]

In November 1954, the Waldorf-Astoria made one of its most publicized race-related moves to date: it invited singer, actress, and dancer Dorothy Dandridge (who had recently made history as the first African American Best Actress Oscar nominee, for her performance in the movie musical *Carmen Jones*) to headline at the Empire Room. The invitation, which, according to press reports, was made at Conrad Hilton's personal behest, came with a difficult provision: Dandridge, as a last-minute replacement for French singer Patachou (sick with a case of the flu), would have just over one week to prepare her act. As biographer Donald Bogle explained, Dandridge "agreed to perform and immediately began rehearsals," but soon "the strain and pressure proved too great." Neurotic and insecure, the beautiful star felt the Waldorf was "too important—and socially significant—a booking" to undertake without feeling completely prepared. In a move that drew criticism from African American columnist Bill "Izzy" Rowe, she pulled out. Fortunately, in the words of Bogle, "the Empire Room was so eager to have her perform" that it invited her back, this time "at *her* schedule." When the opening of her seven-week run finally came, in April 1955, the press viewed it as another example of the Waldorf's fulfillment of an American vision.[26]

"Democracy, grace and beauty entered the Empire Room of the Waldorf-Astoria," wrote Izzy Rowe, having forgiven Dandridge for her earlier letdown. "We looked upon [Dandridge] with great pride and boundless enjoyment." Conrad Hilton, part of the first-night audience, was, in the opinion of columnist Earl Wilson, "to be congratulated for this great advance." Composer Noble Sissle compared Dandridge's engagement to "Jackie Robinson breaking into major league baseball." As *Billboard* had noted back in 1943, hotels represented "the toughest jobs to get for Negro talent," expressly because hotel managers were afraid that "use of Negro musicians and floorshows [would] attract Negro patronage." In truth, by 1955, nonhotel nightclubs in Manhattan had long welcomed African American headliners: the

Waldorf, in this respect, was behind the curve. But its initiative in hosting Dandridge represented the start of a movement to remove what had been, along with television, one of the last barriers for performers of color in New York. Soon after Dandridge ended her run, it was announced that her costar in *Carmen Jones,* young actor and singer Harry Belafonte, would continue the Waldorf's "democratic note" by opening at the Starlight Roof. Then, in 1956, the Empire Room's chief competitor, the Persian Room at the Hotel Plaza (no longer owned by Hilton), announced *its* first headliner of color, Eartha Kitt. Meanwhile, the Waldorf continued to book African American artists, among them—fourteen years past the date it had originally intended for her—Lena Horne.[27]

Philippe, whom daughter Claudia believed was "ahead of his time in terms of race," deserved much of the credit for the change in the Waldorf's direction. After the Hilton Corporation arrived in the fall of 1949, it installed Merriel Abbott, longtime entertainment booker for Chicago's Palmer House (also a Hilton hotel), as talent overseer for the Empire Room—even though she would maintain headquarters in Chicago. Abbott had broken down barriers of her own: born in 1893, she rose to prominence first as a dance instructor and then as a producer of floor shows (her all-female "Merriel Abbott Dancers" appeared in multiple Hollywood films). By 1950 she was booking more talent than any other person in the entertainment business. Eventually, she would become head of booking for all hotels in the Hilton chain—this at a time when female, Jewish executives were unheard of in the hotel industry. After the summer of 1955, however, she decided to scale back her operations to focus exclusively on the midwestern hotels. Now over sixty, she needed a rest, she explained. She had also clashed with Philippe, who sometimes hired acts on his own for the Starlight Roof—in defiance of Abbott's "exclusive booker" title. On the surface, Abbott's withdrawal meant that Joe Binns, Hilton's even-tempered manager at the Waldorf, took over bookings for the Empire Room; however, as Tom Margittai attested, "[Philippe] was running the Waldorf-Astoria, not Joe Binns."[28]

Margittai once observed how, unlike Oscar (who, for all his celebrity acquaintances, never forgot that he was, in the end, a servant), Philippe

"Democracy, grace and beauty": Dorothy Dandridge at the Empire Room, 1955 (Walter Carone/Paris Match via Getty Images).

"appeared as an equal . . . to all the presidents and chairmen of the board and greats of his day." No longer bound to the nineteenth-century European traditions that Oscar had exemplified, Philippe could realize his ambition to influence Manhattan society and not just serve it. In 1952 he launched what would become his most famous contribution to New York's social life, the annual April in Paris ball, held at the Waldorf as a benefit for various Franco-American charities. In its first year, April in Paris transformed the Grand Ballroom into a miniature Gardens of Versailles, featuring what the *Times* described as "long, broad streamers of pale blue satin . . . simulating the appearance of a cloudless summer sky." After a dinner "in the famous Parisian tradition . . . with vintages from French vineyards," actors Sir Laurence Olivier and Rex Harrison portrayed Francois I and Henry VIII in one of a series of historical tableaux. The final tableau, reported the *Times*, "included a revue of costumes designed by several famous couturiers of France, worn by well-known women of society and the theatrical world." With guests including Brooke Astor, Mayor Vincent Impellitteri, and Prince Aschwin of Lippe-Biesterfeld, the April in Paris ball was a return to the Waldorf's elite 1890s beginnings, the kind of event George Boldt would have approved as offering a "haven" for the "well-to-do."[29]

By 1956 the affair had grown even more elaborate: party planner and bon vivant Elsa Maxwell (a longtime Waldorf Towers resident) rode into the ballroom on one of eight elephants on loan from the circus, while guests bought raffle tickets for door prizes that included what the *Times*' Meyer Berger described as "automobiles, [a] diamond necklace," and a "full-length natural mink coat." The souvenir program, nearly two feet long, included "color reproductions of works by Picasso, Braque and Rouault, among other masters." But if, through devising April in Paris, Philippe catered to high society, indulging its taste for the lavish and extreme, elsewhere—through his work as a talent booker—he tested society's limits.[30]

In 1957, facing down what Earl Wilson claimed were objections from certain hotel guests, Philippe brought in the Waldorf's first entirely African American orchestra since the 1942 John Kirby engagement, inaugurating a summer music festival on the Starlight Roof that featured Count Basie and Sarah Vaughan in June and then, through July, Lionel Hampton with Diahann Carroll. Sales were so strong that Philippe brought the initial pairing of Basie and Vaughan back in August. By the end of 1958, *Variety* could point to the fact that the Waldorf had hired "a Negro headliner" for its high-profile New Year's Eve booking three years in a row. Further, as it had with its policies toward "unescorted" women in the early 1900s, the hotel bore an influence beyond Park Avenue. After the Waldorf's success with "Negro stars," Earl Wilson noted, formerly segregated hotels in Chicago, Miami Beach, and Las Vegas "fell in line." Social change revealed itself through small, seemingly offhand gestures. Referencing a 1956 Empire Room engagement, Wilson noted how the brassy vocalist Pearl Bailey crossed another line when, at one point during her performance, she engaged in a bit of "dancing with two white prep school boys."[31]

As it happened, Bailey's Empire Room appearance during May 1956 was concurrent with the *Brown v. Board of Education* anniversary that brought Martin Luther King Jr. to the Waldorf-Astoria for his "A Realistic Look at Race Relations" speech (marking the first of at least six visits King made to the hotel as a guest). The evening of May 17, as Bailey sang of "irresistible force" meeting an "old immovable object" in her rendition of "Something's Gotta Give" at the Empire Room, Dr. King was upstairs on the Starlight Roof, reminding his NAACP listeners of how "old man segregation" lay "on his death bed." Later, two separate groups converged on the Waldorf's ground floor. Columnist Jimmy Booker, of Harlem's *Amsterdam News*, described the scene playing out on both sides of where he stood. In the main lobby, set against the Columbian Exposition clock topped with the Statue of Liberty, Dr. King held "the center of attention." A "small group of whites," wanting to know "something about the protest movement" that had roused "Negroes throughout the country," surrounded the young minister from the South, asking him questions. Meanwhile, in the adjacent Park Avenue foyer, Virginia native Pearl Bailey chatted about "the race question and other subjects." Bailey, who had worked in African American nightclubs before going overseas to entertain troops during the war, sat outside the Empire Room, "warmly greeting each person who came over" for an autograph or signed publicity photo.[32]

"You know," reflected Bailey, "in many ways this kind of thing does a lot for race relations too." In a reference to African American pianist and crooner Nat "King" Cole, who had recently been criticized for telling reporters he would continue performing for segregated audiences in the South, Bailey observed how "entertainers can't afford to be as open as the leaders." Still, she asserted, "These people [coming for autographs] remember and it has impact." The scene, playing out for all to observe, came together spontaneously—an example of people interacting through space.

Martin Luther King Jr. at the Waldorf, 1964, with Coretta Scott King, Hubert
Humphrey (center), and Mayor Robert Wagner at microphone (New York City
Municipal Archives).

And the hotel's unwritten but consistent policy of allowing all visitors, both
guests and nonguests, to wander its lobbies and hallways, meant that the
chance to observe, listen, and learn would not be restricted to those who
had bought tickets to the NAACP dinner or the Empire Room. It was at
moments like these that the Waldorf exerted its most significant influence
over metropolitan life, in ways that went deeper than April in Paris or the
willingness to hire performers of color—a development that, however beneficial for Horne, Dandridge and others, took a long time to arrive. As a
public forum, where a Harlem reporter could "look across the lobby and
watch a Rev. King" while simultaneously observing "Pearl Bailey have them
rushing to get her autograph," the Waldorf came closest to fulfilling Lucius
Boomer's mission: a community center in the broadest sense, open to all.[33]

———

Given Claude Philippe's arrogance, there were many at the Waldorf who secretly longed for his downfall. In October 1958 their hopes were realized, when Philippe was indicted by a federal grand jury on five counts of tax evasion. Over the course of four years, the indictment charged, Philippe had failed to report nearly $150,000 of income. Further, according to the fifth charge, he had not been honest about the extent of his tips. As Tom Margittai recalled, Philippe "controlled all the money that came in from the gratuities, and he charged 15 percent for gratuities on everything—printing, music, flowers": "He gave the service staff 12 percent and he kept back 3 percent. He automatically included me because I was part of the banquet department. He distributed cash—he didn't give or get receipts."[34]

As a result, the Internal Revenue Service spent months interviewing current and former employees in an attempt to figure out "how much money [Philippe] held back." According to Margittai, Philippe had also been the beneficiary of monetary tributes, which clients were happy to pay if it meant their banquet or wedding reception would be favored with the master's touch:

> I happened to be in [Philippe's] inner office, which was very large and had two secretaries sharing it. In front of him sat the father and mother of the bride. They were just about finishing the conversation of the booking of the wedding, and the father said, "Mr. Philippe, we would be very grateful for your personal attention during the function and every aspect of it," and handed him an envelope [reading that it contained] $500. Philippe said to one of the secretaries, "Tell Charlie Ohrel to come in." Charlie came in, and [Philippe] gave him the envelope and said to the couple, "Mr. Ohrel is my number one assistant. He will take care of you." What he meant was, "Five hundred dollars I don't take; I only take a thousand dollars and up."[35]

Joe Binns, for once more voluble than the man who had been his inferior in title only, tried to establish distance from the tax controversy by pointing out, in a statement made to the *Times,* that Philippe had been connected to the Waldorf "long before it was acquired" by the Hilton Corporation. For his part, Philippe claimed he was "innocent" and had "never evaded" the payment of taxes. Eventually, he was able to avoid a jail sentence by pleading guilty to one count of evasion and paying a $10,000 fine. But the scandal damaged Philippe's reputation, and, in the view of Margittai, "nothing worked out [for him] after that." He was allowed to remain at the Waldorf long enough to complete his involvement with the 1959 April in Paris ball; then, according to the *Herald Tribune*, he "resigned" to work as an "executive consultant" for the Zeckendorf real estate corporation, which was planning a new hotel for property it owned north of Rockefeller Center. That hotel was never built, and in early 1961 Philippe announced a new relationship with the Loew's Corporation, then building the Americana Hotel on Fifty-Second Street and Seventh Avenue, in the populist environs of Times Square. As journalist Ward Morehouse III recounted, Philippe characteristically found a way to make "the lesser into the best," by describing the Americana as "'east of Seventh Avenue' to enhance its location."[36]

Upon opening in September 1962, the modernistic, fifty-story Americana was the first new Manhattan hotel with more than 1,000 rooms since 1931, when the Waldorf had been completed. The Americana also had its own nightclub and a 3,000-capacity ballroom with a hydraulic-powered rotating stage. It also had Philippe, who remained, in the assessment of Waldorf executive vice president Frank Wangeman, a force "to be reckoned with" when it came "to hustling and selling"—even "with all of his shortcomings." For these reasons, Wangeman and Conrad Hilton expressed private concern about the Americana and its potential to harm the Waldorf. Writing from his office in Beverly Hills, Hilton told Wangeman of an invitation he had received for a ball at the new hotel, observing how "it does seem that [the Americana] must have a terrific organization for they are taking business away from you." Hilton also noted that singer Eddie Fisher had arranged for a luncheon at the Americana and that the Saints and Sinners Club, a circus-performers' benefit group that had been meeting at the Waldorf since the 1930s, was leaving too. "So, if you don't look out," Hilton intoned, "the Americana will steal the whole hotel from you."[37]

It was into this situation that the National Association for the Advancement of Colored People was pulled when arranging its Freedom Fund dinner for 1963. After he left the Waldorf-Astoria, Philippe had tried, naturally, to take as many clients with him as he could. This included the NAACP's John Morsell, with whom Philippe made a reservation for the Americana's as-yet-unbuilt Imperial Ballroom in March 1961—more than two years in advance of the targeted 1963 banquet date. One year later, Morsell wrote Philippe to say that the NAACP had decided to stick with the Waldorf for 1963: the rights organization was committing to a two-year agreement, one that would provide it with "leverage in terms of service, etc." Aggrieved, Philippe demanded an in-person visit with Morsell, writing with a tone of insistence that he never would have resorted to in earlier, better days: "I am certain you will agree that we [at the Americana] are more than entitled to such a meeting." Regardless, the NAACP had made a decision: the 1963 Freedom Fund dinner would be held in its usual place, the Waldorf-Astoria. There it would have remained had it not been for two events that would force the issue of hotel segregation—so long thought to have been resolved within tolerant New York City—back into the national spotlight.[38]

In January 1962, an African American man, George Weaver, arrived at Houston's Shamrock Hilton and was told by managers that the hotel had "no record" of his reservation. Weaver, assistant secretary of labor under President Kennedy, was a frequent Hilton guest and longtime member of its credit card program, Carte Blanche. After presenting a written copy of his room confirmation, he got the same response—even though, as Weaver later attested, he could "see before [the room clerk] a reservation card" with his "name and title." Eventually he gave up and arranged to stay with a friend. That evening, Weaver would throw away the speech he had prepared for the Houston Negro Chamber of Commerce and launch instead into a critique of American segregation. Having returned from an international trip, he pointed out that U.S. racial policies were attacked frequently during sessions of the UN and reminded his audience of what civil rights advocates had long

insisted: "As the strength and might of America grow, America's responsibilities grow," and "our collective actions today are not only of concern to
the local community but also to the rest of the world." Speaking to Houston
newspapers in the days following the incident, Weaver insisted that he had
never, until then, been turned away by a Hilton hotel—even in Dallas. In
fact, he admired the company for being one of the first to "break the color
barrier." Meanwhile, the Shamrock's manager, Houston native Porter Parris, insisted that "Hilton hotels go along with local custom . . . I know of no
hotel in Houston where Negroes are admitted—at this time. However, when
this custom is changed, the Hilton hotels will change too."[39]

For Conrad Hilton, there was immediate backlash. A Houston minister
telegrammed him, claiming that the city had been "GREATLY EMBAR-
RASSED" by the Weaver incident and expressing "HOPE" that Parris
would "MAKE IT CLEAR THAT THE HILTON HOTEL DO [sic] NOT
TURN AWAY NEGROS [sic] BECAUSE THEY ARE NEGROS." The hotel
magnate was also copied on a letter sent to Parris from a Houstonian who
considered himself "neither a right-wing radical or a left-wing liberal" but
who nonetheless felt "this type of incident" would "give the city a black eye"
and contribute to "the spread of Communism around the world." Evidently
believing the problem lay with the old-boy regime of Porter Parris (described
in another letter as "very well thought of in Houston"), Hilton acted quickly.
By the beginning of March, it was reported that Parris would be transferred
to the new San Francisco Hilton and that Conrad's youngest son, Eric, would
assume managerial responsibilities at the Houston Shamrock. The next
month, papers announced that "major Houston hotels," including the Shamrock, had "integrated their room and restaurant facilities." Each hotel, it
was shown, had "accepted at least one Negro." Quietly, the Hilton Corporation had worked with hotel owners to integrate properties without drawing
attention from the White Citizens Council or other racist groups. As the *New
York Times* noted, Houston "newspapers and radio stations had been asked
not to mention [integration] unless there were incidents."[40]

Three months passed without controversy. Then, on July 1, 1962, Thomas
Allen, an African American delegate to the annual NAACP convention in

Atlanta, arrived at that city's Hilton Inn with two associates and, like Weaver in Houston, was refused accommodation. Two weeks prior, his guest room in Atlanta had been confirmed by the Hilton Corporation's New York reservations service, a one-stop office that enabled patrons to make travel plans for Hilton hotels in any city around the world. But hours before his train's scheduled departure on June 30, Allen had received a note directly from the Hilton Inn, Atlanta, that rooms were "sold out complete for the period of July 2nd through the 8th." After speaking with an agent at the reservation office in New York (where he lived), Allen had been advised to head south anyway: according to records, his hotel booking was indeed confirmed, and the New York agent promised to call Atlanta to clarify. Now, standing at the check-in desk of the Atlanta Hilton, Allen was again informed that his party's reservation had been canceled. Lloyd Farwell, the hotel manager, came forward and, without making any "allusion" to "race or color" (as a complaint filed by the NAACP would later note), promised that the Hilton Inn "would assist in rehousing the group." This did not happen, and the three delegates wound up walking with their luggage in ninety-degree heat because taxis refused to pick them up. Later that morning a fellow delegate, still in New York, called the Hilton reservations office and explained the situation to a Miss Diaz, who lamented, "It's not right."[41]

Dr. Eugene Reed, president of the NAACP's New York state branch, moved quickly to punish the Hilton Corporation for the discriminatory practices of its Atlanta hotel. On August 3, responding to an invitation for a dinner the local Williamsbridge (Bronx) branch was planning to hold at the Waldorf, Reed pointed out that "the Waldorf-Astoria is a Hilton hotel." He would not, on principle, "participate in anything" that would "bring revenue to the Hilton chain" until it was willing to "take a stand acceptable to the [NAACP] with regard to discrimination." Two weeks later the New York NAACP, meeting with presidents from ninety-five local branches, voted to "withhold patronage from all Hilton Hotels including the Waldorf Astoria." Reed, in a letter addressed to the Hilton office at the Waldorf, underscored the connection between the local and national: "We do not absolve northern branches of business establishments from responsibility for patterns of discrimination and segregation carried on by their southern counterparts." In his acquisition of the Waldorf (and, earlier, the Plaza), Conrad Hilton claimed to have taken pains to ensure the hotel's historic and cultural identity would be preserved. His fear, he explained in *Be My Guest,* was that he would be seen as a marauder: "Genghis Khan or, at the very best, Tom Mix about to shoot his guns off in the lobby." Now, in an irony that confounded Hilton executives, the company was being penalized for *not* bringing all hotels into corporate line, for its inability to override the local conditions that made each Hilton establishment a distinct community with its own social patterns and rules.[42]

"The policy of the Hilton Hotels Corporation," explained the Waldorf's Frank Wangeman, writing to New York Governor Nelson Rockefeller at the beginning of September, "is to welcome all persons as its guests regardless of race, color, or creed." However, there were "two exceptions" then "beyond [the company's] control." One was the Hilton in New Orleans, where Louisiana law prohibited "the housing of white and Negro guests in the same building." The other was the Atlanta Hilton Inn, where "local custom" had "thus far prevented" executives from "fulfilling [their] wish to accommodate Negro guests." Wangeman admitted how the "unfortunate experience of Mr. Thomas Allen and his party in Atlanta" was "of great embarrassment" and expressed regret over the Hilton Corporation having been "obliged to take the action" it did. Referring in part to the Houston incident from earlier in the year, Wangeman assured Rockefeller that the company was working as quickly as possible to change local policy, as it had "successfully so done in certain cities during the past decade." In the meantime, however, it seemed "scarcely fair to penalize the great majority of our properties whose records of observing human rights" could not "be questioned." Finally, Wangeman told Rockefeller that the "Atlanta problem" would be discussed at the next gathering of the Hilton Operating Committee, "a group of top executives." The committee, promised Wangeman, would "try to find some new, positive approach that [would] alleviate the condition in Atlanta."[43]

Governor Rockefeller had become involved on August 25, when the state NAACP asked him to pull an upcoming Republican convention from the

Hilton in Buffalo. The governor refused, explaining that it was "too late, frankly, to consider making a change of the location of the convention." But, in a gesture intended to show support "of the efforts on a national basis for bringing about equal opportunity for all," Rockefeller invited Eugene Reed and other NAACP leaders, along with executives from Hilton, to a meeting in his Manhattan office. After the conference, which took place on September 10, Reed agreed to "temporarily rescind" the Waldorf boycott, with the understanding that Hilton would review its "discriminatory policies" and work to eliminate them by the start of November. Reed's concession drew immediate fire from an editorialist at the *Amsterdam News*, who asked:

> What do you think would happen if Conrad Hilton picked up the phone in his offices and called the manager of Hilton Inn in Atlanta, Ga. [sic] and said: "Dr. Martin Luther King will be in your lobby in a few minutes. I want you to rent him whatever available suite he is able to pay for, and from now on I want you to rent rooms to any qualified Negro who asks for a room and has the money to pay for it." We'll tell you what would happen: As of that moment the Hilton Inn in Atlanta would become an integrated hotel. . . . It would be that simple.[44]

Justine Priestley, a liberal white woman who wrote for the *Amsterdam News* under the pen name Gertrude Wilson, also criticized the NAACP for what she perceived as its excessively soft attitude toward the "Hilton chain": "Conrad Hilton is the same man in Atlanta, Georgia, when he stands up to Mr. Allen, a Negro, and says he can't accommodate him, as he is here in New York welcoming him to the Waldorf Astoria to banquet after banquet . . . happy to have Mr. Allen's money."

Drawing comparisons to the New York boycott against Woolworth five-and-dime stores, whose southern outlets would not allow African Americans to occupy lunch counter seats, Wilson reminded readers that the decision to avoid patronizing "businesses which discriminate" was one of the "few weapons which the Negro [could] draw upon in his fight for equality." As with Woolworth, anyone "who cared"—African Americans as well as white sympathizers—should continue the boycott: "Do we have to go to the

Waldorf for our luncheons? Do we have to hold our political conventions in their meeting rooms and parlors? We do not."[45]

November came, and the Hilton Hotels Corporation, as promised, sent a letter to the New York State Commission for Human Rights, copying Rockefeller and Eugene Reed. Aside from instructing local hotel managers that "particular care" should be taken in ensuring that there would be "no exceptions" to the Hilton policy of welcoming "all guests regardless of race," the Operating Committee had failed to accomplish much. Indeed, with respect to Atlanta, "the situation [had not] changed particularly" since early September. All the same, manager Lloyd Farwell had been "requested to do his utmost to convince the hotel interests of [Atlanta] that their local custom [was] contrary to today's philosophies on human rights." The letter implied that Farwell himself wanted integration but was encountering resistance from the Chamber of Commerce and managers at other hotels. Emphasizing how "we cannot do this alone," the Hilton Corporation pointed out that "a hotel is a part of the community where it is located." Atlanta, a city that had only begun desegregating its movie theaters in May 1962, less than six months earlier, would have to be a "continuing project."[46]

Clearly, Eugene Reed had been hoping the Hilton Corporation's stance would be similar to that of Rudolf Bing, manager of New York's Metropolitan Opera, who had recently threatened to cancel Atlanta engagements of its national tours until African American patrons could buy tickets in traditionally "white" sections of the Fox Theatre, a local landmark (as a result of Bing's position, the Met Opera had held its first performance before a desegregated Atlanta audience in April 1962). The Hilton Corporation's evident unwillingness or inability to do the same meant, from Reed's perspective, that the hotel boycott would resume. On November 3, he led a picket line outside the Waldorf-Astoria, where state NAACP members turned the tables on Conrad Hilton by questioning the patriotic ideals he had most ardently promoted: "KHRUSHCHEV" could stay at Hilton hotels, one sign read, but "AMERICANS" were "UNWELCOME." Connie's cherished notion of his hotels as little Americas, symbols of unity, was dissolving in the face of inequality. How could Hiltons promote "the fruits of the free world" when America's commitment to its own democratic values was in question?[47]

In early December, the national NAACP became involved for the first time, requesting a conference with Hilton officials. It looked as if the boycott, previously confined to New York state, might extend to Hilton hotels across the country. At the Waldorf-Astoria, executives grew increasingly frustrated. Writing to Boston business leader and civil rights activist Kivie Kaplan, the Waldorf's director of catering, Clyde Harris, pointed out that "we, in the Hilton Organization, probably engage more personalities such as Lena Horne, Pearl Bailey, Duke Ellington, etc., than any other Hotel Organization [sic] in the country." Presumably referring to the 1940s UN agreement (in which the Waldorf agreed to house all delegates regardless of color), Harris also wished "to go on record as saying that The Waldorf-Astoria was the first hotel in this City to show a definite interest in the deplorable problem of discrimination." Lastly, Harris reminded Kaplan that there were "approximately twenty-one other Hotels [sic]" in Atlanta that were also segregated: "Why Hilton Hotels Corporation should be singled out . . . is far beyond me. . . . Don't you honestly believe that this is discrimination?"[48]

On March 4, 1963, the NAACP delivered the blow it had been holding in reserve. With just over two months' notice, John Morsell of the organization wrote the Waldorf's John O'Reilly (a onetime Philippe assistant now running the banquet department), informing him that it was "herewith cancelling its reservation with the Waldorf-Astoria for the 1963 Freedom Fund dinner, scheduled for next May 19th": "We delayed reaching this decision for as long as we could, in the hope and expectation that the Hilton Hotels Corporation would by now have seen its way clear to end the racially discriminatory policy in effect in its establishments in Atlanta and New Orleans. . . . This continued stain on the otherwise good Hilton record is painful to us as it must be to you, and leaves us with no choice but the one announced here."[49]

Even worse, in an action Philippe no doubt perceived as a victory—his revenge against the hotel that had forced him to resign—the NAACP announced it was moving the dinner to the Imperial Ballroom of the Hotel Americana. By now the Waldorf was suffering doubly, as it fought a separate, simultaneous boycott initiated by the Congress for Racial Equality (CORE), which sought to gain employment for African Americans and other minorities in nonmenial positions (out of 400 food and beverage workers at the Waldorf, CORE reported, there were only 4 African American waiters and no waitresses or bartenders of color). During several days in which it led "nightly" pickets of the Waldorf, CORE sent letters to multiple organizations, urging them to "refrain from holding affairs" at the hotel, out of solidarity. In response, the Urban League, citing its long-standing policy of not crossing picket lines "where racial justice was believed to be involved," called the Waldorf and—with only three days' notice—canceled a banquet that was to be held in the Grand Ballroom.[50]

In the midst of this crisis—a financial blow for a hotel already aching from the effects of competition—Hilton executives sent the Atlanta hotel's manager, Lloyd Farwell, a letter on April 12, insisting that the Hilton nondiscrimination policy "be complied with." This time, perhaps because Atlanta hotels were starting to lose convention and banquet business of their own, something changed. On May 1, Millicent Smith, an African American social work supervisor from Chicago, reported in a letter to the NAACP's Roy Wilkins that she had recently stayed at the Hilton Inn, Atlanta, for two days and was "the recipient of the utmost in courtesy, cordiality and service." In a handwritten postscript, Smith added that she "also had dinner in the hotel dining room"—a significant observation, given that the majority of Atlanta restaurants would not begin desegregating, on a trial basis, until the end of June.[51]

The NAACP waited until its Freedom Fund dinner was completed at the Americana. Then it sent a press release confirming that the Hilton Inn, Atlanta, had been "accepting Negro guests for the past several weeks." Not stated explicitly—but implied in the acknowledgment that two of the NAACP's own staff members had also stayed at the inn—was that the Hilton boycott would be dropped. On June 21, the *Atlanta Constitution* announced that fourteen of the city's "leading hotels and motels" had agreed to accept some form of integration. While the decision applied only to "conventions

with a limited number of Negro delegates," such distinctions were soon leveled out by a greater event: the passage in July 1964 of the Civil Rights Act
(initiated by President Kennedy and signed by his successor, Lyndon B. Johnson), which, among other provisions, established "injunctive relief against
discrimination in public accommodations."[52]

Within days the act's constitutionality was challenged by one of the few
Atlanta establishments unwilling to join that city's integration effort, the
Heart of Atlanta Motel, in a case that went to the United States Supreme
Court. As historian A. K. Sandoval-Strausz reported, the Heart of Atlanta's
owner drew upon an argument that resembled George Boldt's complaint of
nearly seventy years earlier, challenging Congress's right to "take away the
liberty of an individual to run his business as he sees fit in the selection and
choice of his customers." In contrast to its 1935 decision on the National
Recovery Act, which excluded hotels from consideration as "interstate"
industries, the Supreme Court, in this case, ruled that "Congress' power over
interstate commerce" extended to "the regulation of local incidents thereof
which might have a substantial and harmful effect upon that commerce."[53]

In other words, the Heart of Atlanta, 75 percent of whose patrons came
from out of state, was, according to the Supreme Court, "interfering significantly with interstate travel" by refusing rooms to African Americans. Travel
was a form of commerce, and "under the Commerce clause" of the Constitution, Congress had the power to "remove such obstructions and restraints" as
put into place by the Heart of Atlanta and other discriminatory hotels. The
Supreme Court's reasoning took into consideration the nature of transportation in 1960s America: "The sheer increase in volume of interstate traffic
alone would give discriminatory practices which inhibit travel a far larger
impact upon the Nation's commerce than such practices had on the economy of another day." In ruling against the Heart of Atlanta, the Supreme
Court effectively put a stop to officially sanctioned hotel segregation in the
United States. The improved climate for African American travelers (who,
no doubt, continued to face illegal discrimination in certain places and settings) was reflected in two developments of 1966: first, Harlem's Hotel Theresa, once considered an uptown equivalent to the Waldorf and other luxury

hotels, began converting its guestrooms into offices. Second, the *Travelers Green Book*, an annual guide for African Americans desiring a "Vacation without Aggravation," published the final issue of its thirty-year history.[54]

In later years, the NAACP returned to the Waldorf as a scene for dinners and events. Celebrating its eightieth birthday with a star-studded bash at the hotel in 1989, the organization drew upon support from celebrities such as Stevie Wonder, who filled the Grand Ballroom with the lurching rhythms of his hit "Master Blaster (Jammin')" as attendees swayed in ballgowns and tuxedos. By now the NAACP had grown accustomed to withstanding charges that, in its embracement of and by the cultural mainstream, it had become irrelevant—out of touch with the continuing struggles of African Americans. Keynote speaker at the Waldorf that night was announced (until illness forced his cancellation) as President George H. W. Bush, who, during his earlier tenure as vice president, had addressed the NAACP on three separate occasions. Still, few would have denied the relevance of comments made by executive director Benjamin Hooks as he rose to the Grand Ballroom's stage, surveyed the audience and surroundings, and recalled how there had been a time, not many years earlier, when the only African Americans to be seen regularly at hotels like the Waldorf-Astoria were those serving "white folks." Then he added, "We've come mighty far, haven't we?"

———

In the sequence of narratives and counternarratives that shape the essential dichotomy of American life, the social gains as represented by the Civil Rights Act were followed by losses: the death of Martin Luther King (who, three years before his assassination, had again spoken at the Waldorf, in a strongly worded denunciation of the Vietnam War), murders of civil rights activists, riots that destroyed large sections of African American neighborhoods, urban renewal policies that further displaced minority citizens, and the ascendance of a new conservatism that found its mainstream apotheosis in the 1968 election of Richard Nixon as president of the United States. When Nixon rose to power, the Waldorf was ready: the soon-to-be commander in chief would issue his acceptance speech from the hotel's ballroom stage,

where he assured Americans that his motto would be the words of a sign he
claimed to have seen held aloft by a teenager in Deshler, Ohio: "Bring Us
Together." Faced with a sinking economy and recession, America under
Nixon would instead become more fractious. The Waldorf-Astoria, centered within a swirl of speeches and political protests, again offered a
forum for the airing of differences that seemed, at times, unbridgeable.
Behind the scenes, though, in a controversial moment, it moved beyond its
role as host for polemical exchange by making its own stamp on the era's
social debates—suggesting in the process a new interpretation of the hotel
man's creed. If a hotel was meant to embrace "every station in society," then
why wouldn't the less fortunate, in addition to the well-to-do, be welcome?

CHAPTER 8

The Waldorf Belongs
to the People

On January 15, 1964, Arizona senator Barry Goldwater, having recently announced his candidacy for the Republican presidential nomination, stepped inside the Waldorf-Astoria's Grand Ballroom and proclaimed, "We don't know of starvation in this country today." The occasion was a black-tie dinner of the Economic Club of New York, an organization made up of some of the city's top figures in business and finance. An elaborate Waldorf meal—lobster bisque, roast prime rib of beef au jus, brandied Arizona dates—had been the opener for a speech in which Goldwater lambasted President Johnson's new initiative to fight poverty through $1 billion in federal spending. The poor, suggested Goldwater, in an articulation of the views that had made him a bête noire of liberal America, were largely to blame for their own problems: "In a society where the vast majority of people live on a standard that is envied by all other nations, it must be appropriate to inquire whether the attitude or action of the small group not participating in the general prosperity has anything to do with the situation." Arguing that welfare recipients, "if physically able," should be "put to work to earn their benefits at a specified rate per hour," Goldwater further criticized government programs that "reduce the incentives for enterprise and abolish the consequences of inertia." The harshest polemic, however, came from a section of the address that had been cut and therefore was not delivered at the Waldorf. Nonetheless, newspapers would report it as part of the prepared text: "We are told . . . that many people lack skills and cannot find jobs because they did not have an education. That's like saying that people have big feet because they wear big shoes. The fact is that most people who have no skill have had no education for the same reason—low intelligence or low ambition."[1]

The address, reported the *New York Times*, was "interrupted by applause 10 times"—an early display of the support that would, during the Republican National Convention that July, lift Goldwater to the top ranks of his party, as official nominee for president of the United States. But despite his visual appeal—in magazine photos he appeared as a handsome western cowboy—Barry Goldwater proved an unwieldy candidate, liable to handing what adviser J. William Middendorf described as "fat, juicy, unscripted sound bites" to the media. To Americans grasping for stability in the months after President Kennedy's death, Goldwater was too mercurial: a champion of personal liberty who had integrated his family's chain of department stores, but who later voted against the 1964 Civil Rights Act on the grounds that it infringed on states' rights. In the view of Middendorf, Goldwater's "off-the-cuff" comments on Social Security (a program the senator criticized as an arrogation of federal power) were part of what "sank his candidacy before it even left the dock." Goldwater would, in the general election that November, carry his own Arizona and just five states of the Deep South; Lyndon Johnson's share of the popular vote, 61.1 percent, became the largest in twentieth-century American history.[2]

Johnson's victory proved, in the words of an overseas commentator, that the "majority [of the American people] is against extremism" and that there would be "no going back to a dreamland of the past" when it came to questions of social justice. Still, Goldwater and his views on wealth and poverty intensified a debate that would only grow more contentious as the 1960s progressed. What to make of the 7 million people who, in 1964, through a seeming contravention of American ideals—hard work, initiative, self-sufficiency—looked to the government for relief in the form of welfare payments? Should the United States continue to offer, as it had since the administration of Franklin D. Roosevelt, monetary support for the less fortunate? Or should social welfare be a "private concern," as Goldwater voiced in his 1960 treatise, *The Conscience of a Conservative*, one "promoted by individuals and families, by churches, private hospitals, religious service organizations, community charities and other institutions"? Was there a way to separate deserving welfare recipients from those who merely sought to bilk the system? Perhaps, even, that very system didn't go far enough in redressing the injustices, both racial and economic, that had forced people on welfare in the first place.[3]

A short review of welfare in the United States is useful as context for the Waldorf-Astoria's involvement with discussions surrounding public relief. "Welfare," as Americans came to understand the term, originated during the Great Depression, when President Roosevelt announced his ambitious plans to stimulate economic recovery through the National Recovery Act and other programs of the New Deal. More than a set of initiatives, the New Deal was an expression of philosophy, one rooted in the specific question: What does a healthy system of government owe its citizens? In a speech to the Associated Press at the Waldorf-Astoria in April 1934, Secretary of State Cordell Hull attested to the "potent remedies" the government had already applied in order to "stay panic conditions," with the result that "the more acute ravages of the depression" were being "checked." He was referring, of course, to the establishment of the Federal Emergency Relief Administration (FERA), which created jobs for millions of Americans; the Civil Works Administration (CWA), the Federal Deposit Insurance Corporation (FDIC), and other agencies. At the same time, Hull, in declaring that the Roosevelt administration would "propose to care for the unemployed and unfortunate," offered a hint that further New Deal initiatives were to come. These, asserted Hull, would be in keeping with the government's moral obligation to right the failings of the Hoover administration, which had permitted the "outrageous financial manipulations of stock markets" that "stripped millions of individuals of their life savings": "When aid for the unemployed, social justice and social welfare constitute a first lien on our civilization, how could deliberate neglect to direct attention to these unequal and distressful conditions of those who toil be justified?"[4]

Hull's emphasis at the Waldorf on "those who toil" was significant: the subsequent Social Security Act, signed into law by President Roosevelt on August 14, 1935, centered firmly, both in spirit and application, on the American worker. While there were sections establishing state grants for care of the elderly, dependent children, and the unemployed, the act's centerpiece was Title II, Federal Old-Age Benefits. Title II established a contribution in the form of a percentage tax on both employers and their employees. This tax, deducted from each wage payment, was then put into a reserve account operated by the U.S. Treasury. Upon retirement at the age of sixty-five, workers could look forward to receiving a monthly pension whose size was proportionate to their total lifetime earnings. The notion of retirement as part of a distant but attainable future reflected the country's emotional climate as it lumbered past the rough years of the Depression. A drawing from the *St. Louis Dispatch* reflected the larger mood: in it, a caravan of human figures moved, slowly but inexorably, toward a sequence of three faraway mountains labeled "Old Age Pensions," "Unemployment Insurance," and "Economic Security."[5]

While the Social Security Act benefited millions of Americans by offering them a safeguard against the inability to work during their senior years, it also had significant problems. In an omission that was formally protested by the NAACP and other groups, Title II excluded in-home domestic workers, on the grounds that keeping track of wages paid by private householders (as opposed to, say, owners of department stores or factories) would be too difficult. What this meant, in practical terms, was that African Americans, a large percentage of whom worked as maids and servants, were often cut out of Title II benefits. Nor did farm and agricultural workers, among the country's poorest residents, qualify for Title II. Despite these flaws, Social Security was a landmark achievement that even the conservative *Wall Street Journal* hailed, in 1935, as "one of the foremost social measures of the age." The act's retirement portion would eventually become so fixed in the American consciousness that any attempt to meddle with it was akin to political suicide. In 1982, both *Newsweek* and the *Boston Globe* would quote an unnamed Democratic aide who compared Social Security to the dangerous "third rail" that gave him nightmares after riding the subway as a child: "Anyone who tries to touch it gets electrocuted."[6]

The Aid to Dependent Children section of the Social Security Act—Title IV, establishing what most people came to describe as "welfare"—would encounter a more ambivalent public reception. Title IV's origin lay in the system of "widows' pensions" created by multiple states beginning in the early 1910s, with the goal of freeing indigent mothers from the need to work outside the home. Aid to Dependent Children (ADC) established federal support for the continuance of these pensions while broadening eligibility: the former emphasis on "widows" gave way, under Title IV, to a more liberal awareness of the existence of single mothers. In 1939, however, amendments to Social Security allowed widows to claim eligibility for their husbands' retirement pensions. This development, known as Survivors Insurance, shifted wives of deceased workers to the more respectable domain of Title II. In a reflection of the male breadwinner concept on which Social Security had always been based, widows were now reclassified as productive members of society, extensions of their late working husbands. Aid to Dependent Children, meanwhile, became the province of an increasing number of African American recipients, many of whom had been ineligible for Title II retirement benefits to begin with. Initially just 3 percent of ADC funds were administered to African Americans; by 1948, as historians Premilla Nadasen, Jennifer Mittelstadt, and Marisa Chappell observed in their study, *Welfare in the United States*, "non-white families constituted 30 percent of ADC clients nationally."[7]

A consistent quality of American welfare was its tendency to absorb and reflect psychological fears endemic to the larger society; in this way, welfare became a lodestone for postwar anxieties surrounding Communism and the rise of the Cold War. As the United States moved into a more prosperous economic phase during the late 1940s, civic leaders and politicians voiced greater skepticism over the ADC program and welfare recipients in general.

The idea of getting something for nothing, of able-bodied people sitting back to gather benefits while the majority worked, went against the standards of "Americanism" that were being propounded—through initiatives such as the 1947 "Freedom Train," a privately funded locomotive displaying the Bill of Rights and other documents—as an antidote to socialist threats. During the period in which the Waldorf-Astoria was averting demands to cancel the supposedly pro-Communist Cultural and Scientific Conference for World Peace, it was also playing host to a range of speakers who castigated the Truman administration's welfare programs. In one 1949 Waldorf address, George Craig, national commander of the American Legion (and future Indiana governor), spoke against the "growing tide of economic and political dependence" that bucked "self-reliance and initiative" and gave a boost to Communism and Socialism. America was in danger of becoming, Craig advanced (using a general term that had come to refer to all forms of government assistance), a "welfare state."[8]

Truman's vice president, genial septuagenarian Alben Barkley, used the Waldorf to make a defense. At the annual Democratic National Committee fundraising dinner, held at the hotel in December 1949 (the first time the DNC had ever hosted this event outside of Washington), Barkley denounced those who "regard every tree frog as a roaring lion and every innocent angleworm as a spreading adder." It was nonsense, Barkley insisted, for "hitching post devotees" to suggest that Democratic social policies were "leading us . . . on the last mile toward collectivism in America." Not everyone in Barkley's party agreed: Virginia Democratic senator Harry F. Byrd, an avowed segregationist and promoter of strict "pay as you go" economic policies (i.e., those emphasizing avoidance of government debt), posed a rhetorical question to newspaper publishers gathered at the Waldorf in April 1952: "If the President is opposed to Socialism why is he constantly advocating an extension of the number of those who receive payments from the Treasury of the United States?" Casting himself as "not a Truman Democrat" but a "TRUE Democrat," Byrd decried the "orgy of Federal spending and waste" that had begun, in his view, with the Roosevelt administration. By creating a "population of government dependents," welfare subverted American standards

Nixon supporters at the Waldorf, November 5, 1968: "They were not very good at being ecstatic" (Bernard Gotfryd/Getty Images).

of free enterprise, portrayed by Byrd as "the greatest deterrent in the world to Russian aggression": "As I see it, the welfare state, about which we have been hearing so much in recent years, is that state of twilight in which the glow of democratic freedoms is fading beyond the horizon, leaving us to be swallowed in the blackness of Socialism, or worse."[9]

In November 1952 Americans elected their first Republican president in two decades, former Allied commander and war hero Dwight D. Eisenhower. Many expected that Eisenhower, who had campaigned on a strong anti-Communist platform, would gradually lead the federal government away from welfare programs. Indeed, Eisenhower's vice president, former California senator Richard Nixon, suggested as much during a Waldorf-Astoria address to the American Newspaper Publishers Association in April 1953, three months after inauguration. The "task" of the new administration, asserted Nixon, who had built his political reputation as a crusading member of the House Committee on Un-American Affairs, would be to "reverse the process of the last twenty years" through promotion of an ethic of "general welfare," one that would aim "to help, not control": "There is a difference between the general welfare and the welfare state. In the welfare state the government absorbs the citizens and private groups. It may smother them with honey, but none the less it smothers them. They are regulated from cradle to grave."[10]

Instead, Eisenhower, a moderate Republican who would, on occasion, reveal progressive tendencies when it came to social issues, solidified the government's commitment to relief programs through the establishment, in 1953, of the new cabinet-level Department of Health, Education, and Welfare (HEW). Promoted as a means of increasing efficiency and saving money in the long run, the department's creation drew fire from conservative southern Democrats (many of whom, like Senator Harry Byrd, had long voiced opposition to welfare), as well as newspapers such as the *Chicago Tribune*, whose editorial page assailed HEW as "a disposition to put welfare in politics and keep it there on a permanent, organized basis." Over the course of the next decade, the number of Americans said to be "on welfare" grew exponentially, even as the economy (notwithstanding a few dips) continued to thrive. From its beginnings as a relatively small and underfunded component of the 1935 Social Security Act, ADC had grown, by 1960, into the federal government's largest and most expensive assistance program, with more than 3 million recipients.[11]

The increase in what was often referred to as the welfare "rolls" came largely as a result of industrialization and the decline of agriculture. As greater numbers of unskilled laborers in the rural South were replaced through mechanization, they continued to migrate to urban centers. There, they found the range of available work to be limited: there were more people than jobs. Expansion of welfare programs also swelled the rolls. In 1950, midway through Truman's second term, Congress had passed funding to cover the needs of caretakers as well as dependent children. A 1956 amendment provided additional services, such as family counseling. Then, during the Kennedy administration, a new provision allowed states to admit jobless married men, otherwise ineligible for unemployment benefits, into the ADC program for the first time (the federal government administered ADC through a system of state grants). Certain observers, among them sociologists of both liberal and conservative bent, also pointed to what they saw as the decline of the traditional family unit and the increasing tendency for single parents to be women who had never married. In any case, by 1964, when Barry Goldwater gave his "big feet" address at the Waldorf, the idea that private charity might somehow resume its earlier role as the main provider of cash relief had become, in the words of *Time*, "an 18th century solution for a 20th century problem."[12]

In August 1964, President Johnson spoke at the Waldorf-Astoria, addressing 3,000 members of the American Bar Association. As Cordell Hull had done in the same spot thirty years earlier, Johnson framed the Democratic purpose in moral terms, both domestically and from the viewpoint of international mission: "It is right that the strong should help the weak defend their freedom . . . that the wealthy should help the poor emerge from their hunger." It had been a blistering summer, in ways unrelated to temperature. On July 2, the president had signed the Civil Rights Act, outlawing racial discrimination in the public sphere. Within weeks, the bodies of three young civil rights workers, missing since June, were found near a pond in Mississippi; they had been beaten and shot by local members of the Ku Klux Klan. Also in July, a series of riots, fueled by longtime tensions between police and African American residents, broke out in Rochester and New York's Harlem. During the Waldorf speech, Johnson threw an apparent jab at his Republican presidential opponent, Goldwater, by claiming that those "who would hold back progress toward equality, and at the same time promise racial peace, are deluding themselves and the people." Then he launched into a passionate defense of the Civil Rights Act, while denouncing both the riots and the Klan murders: "The Congress has passed the law. The President has signed the law and the President will enforce the law. . . . Neither demonstrations in the streets nor violence in the night can or will restrain us from seeing to it that laws rightly passed will be justly observed."[13]

Despite Johnson's sureness that American dedication to "legal order" would "keep . . . peace in this land," violence stemming from race-related conflict continued to scar the hope-filled but unstable 1960s. As it had with

Communism during the postwar years, the ADC program—now attacked from both sides, by supporters as well as opponents of the welfare system—bore the weight of larger antipathies directed against low-income African Americans. Welfare also symbolized what many felt was wrong with America and New York City, as both struggled to deal with the effects of rapid change. The lawyers gathered for President Johnson's address, along with those who continued to use the Waldorf-Astoria for debutante parties, charity balls, and other events, likely thought of the hotel as one of the few places that would always be the same, an establishment citadel. But, during an era in which protest threatened the security of even the most elite institutions, the Waldorf proved to be more a reflection of American life—its failings and controversies—than anyone would have expected.[14]

The 1964 Harlem riot, triggered by the police shooting of an African American teenager in the predominantly white Yorkville neighborhood of Manhattan, offered an indication that New York was no longer the place of harmony as represented by the coming of the United Nations, the Council of Foreign Ministers, and other signposts of postwar optimism. In early 1965, the *Herald Tribune*, long associated with the liberal wing of the Republican Party, published a series of articles with the title "New York City in Crisis." Later printed in book form, the articles spotlighted a host of problems ranging from middle-class flight, traffic congestion, and rising crime to the stultification that came from a one-party government controlled by the Democratic political machine ("When in doubt, don't!" the paper quoted Senator Robert Wagner advising his son, now the mayor, on the subject of how to deal with city crises). Taking the form of what *Herald Tribune* editors described as "a sweeping indictment," the articles and book attacked New York's welfare program for its enormous cost: more than $502 million, or 13 percent of the total city budget: "[New York] is a city in which half a million people, more than the number living in the states of Alaska, Delaware, Nevada, Vermont, or Wyoming, are now receiving welfare with no solution in sight. "'There is not a single thing we can do to keep this figure from increasing,'" says one Welfare Department worker. 'For every case we close, another three or four are added to the rolls.'"[15]

Inextricably tied to the problem of welfare was that of housing. Since the early years of the La Guardia administration in the 1930s, the clearance and rebuilding of slums had been a key government initiative, one advanced by progressive concepts of health and hygiene. Early urban renewal projects were relatively modest in size: Vladeck Houses, begun in 1939 on the Lower East Side, consisted of four six-story buildings on a plot of just over two acres. Later projects, such as the privately funded construction of Lincoln Center for the Performing Arts (for which ground was broken in 1959), wiped out entire neighborhoods or else large portions of them. As part of condemnation proceedings, the city government was required to find housing for all residents whom such projects displaced. The problem was that, during the late 1950s and early 1960s, destruction of old tenement districts was taking place faster than new housing projects could be built. By 1965, some 520,000 people resided in New York City public housing, but the list of those waiting to get in had grown to 660,000. Further, in the effort to keep low-income areas from being overrun by people on assistance, the city had placed a ceiling on the number of welfare recipients allowed into housing projects. Welfare workers, meanwhile, found it increasingly difficult to find apartments for their clients, especially those displaced as a result of fires and other emergencies. Around 1960, the city quietly began placing welfare recipients in hotels when there was no other option. It would be a full decade before this practice came to receive wide public attention.

In November 1965, New Yorkers elected a new mayor, one whose future seemed as promising as that of any figure within national politics. John Vliet Lindsay was young (in his middle forties) and handsome. His movie-star looks, elegant bearing, and colonial Dutch ancestry led many to describe him as "patrician," in a way that was at first approving and later, by his second term, derogatory. A Yale graduate and former congressman, Mayor Lindsay symbolized the goals and viewpoints of what was then known as the liberal "East Coast wing" of the Republican Party, a group led most prominently by New York governor Nelson Rockefeller. East Coast Republicans, in con-

trast to the western, Sunbelt contingent of Barry Goldwater, were historically tight when it came to financial matters but progressive on many social
issues. Spurning what he portrayed as the indolence and inaction of his predecessor, three-term Democratic mayor Robert Wagner, Lindsay won on a
reform platform, one highlighted by what was then an unusual campaign
tactic: with the help of a creative group of advisers, Lindsay the candidate
embarked on "walking tours" of struggling neighborhoods in Harlem and
other parts of the city. The image of Lindsay as *man of the people*, taking off
his jacket to explore city streets and chat with ghetto children, contributed
in no small part to his mayoral win. Days after the election, the cover of *Time*
featured a watercolor of the blue-eyed Lindsay, alongside his campaign pledge
to "make our great city once again the empire city of the world."[16]

Lindsay fell into trouble from the start. His initial days in office were consumed with a transit strike that froze subway and bus service across the
city. Over the next two years, from 1966 to 1968, the mayor strained under
pressure from additional strikes (including one by sanitation workers that
left stinking mounds of garbage throughout the city), more riots and near-
riots after the death of Martin Luther King Jr., and a standoff at Columbia
University, where student radicals took possession of most of the school's
academic buildings and held its dean hostage. Determined to eschew the
quid pro quo system of favors on which, historically, much of the city's politics had rested, Lindsay found himself, by the middle of his first term, lacking support from those who could best help him accomplish his goals. The
police force, in particular, disliked and resented him, believing he too often
sided with the opposition (African Americans and other minorities) in its
fight to maintain order. While many of Lindsay's problems stemmed from
his naivete in thinking he could transform New York almost single-hand-
edly, they also reflected larger events over which he had no control: always
there were reminders that the city's unrest was the nation's.

On February 23, 1966, having been in office a little over one month, Lindsay met President Johnson at Kennedy International Airport and escorted
him to the Waldorf's Grand Ballroom. The occasion was a dinner organized
by a liberal but anti-Communist organization, Freedom House, to honor the

president for his contributions to civil rights. As Johnson launched into his speech, James Peck, a longtime antiwar activist who had infiltrated the event, stood on a chair, tore open his tuxedo shirt, and shouted, "Mr. President! Peace in Vietnam!" (*Newsday* recounted one "matron" as sighing, "Some obstreperous people . . .") before being carried away by Secret Service agents and handcuffed. Meanwhile, the streets outside the Waldorf filled with close to 4,000 picketers chanting, "Hey, hey, LBJ, how many children did you kill today?" A photo published in *Newsday* unintentionally captured the night's merging of local and national issues: in it, a protest sign was dumped inside a New York City trash can, the metal rim meeting handwritten words: STOP BOMBING. Just below, pasted onto the can as an urging against the behavior that had given the city a reputation for dirtiness, was another sign: "JUST A DROP IN THE BASKET HELPS KEEP NEW YORK CLEAN."[17]

The idea of an America coming apart—of cities broken by crime and violence; of minorities flouting the deference traditionally accorded police; of rioting on campuses, where students no longer displayed respect for authority—took political shape in the 1960s, as signs emerged of a pushback against the liberal Kennedy/Johnson social agenda. During the 1966 congressional elections, Democrats lost forty-seven seats in the House and three in the Senate. Richard Nixon, returning to politics after a break of eight years, jumped into the 1968 presidential race with a campaign stressing the restoration of "law and order" to American life. In this the Waldorf-Astoria played no small part: political writer Leonard Lurie observed that Nixon "always had a fond place in his heart" for the hotel after delivering a successful speech to New York State Republicans there in 1952 (indeed, it was during this event that New York's then governor, Thomas Dewey, had informed the young senator that he would be Eisenhower's vice presidential nominee). During the run-up to Election Day, a Waldorf suite was transformed into Nixon's press headquarters, where reporters grappled with the inconsistencies of a candidate who, in the view of *Boston Globe* columnist James Doyle, skillfully manipulated his conservative base: "On the issues of crime, civil rights and Vietnam he will raise the fears of his audiences, then he will immediately plead not guilty."[18]

Nixon, in preparation for election night, November 5, 1968, temporarily vacated the Upper East Side apartment he lived in with his family and rented a suite in the Waldorf Towers. At 12:30 on the morning of November 6, he "fairly flew onto the stage of the Grand Ballroom," as reported in the *Globe*, "shooting up both arms with the fingers splayed apart in the victory sign." Proclaiming his desire to "bring the country together," the president-elect displayed his adroitness with the era's mod rhetoric: "We want to bridge the generation gap and the gap between the races." Despite Nixon's emphasis on inclusion—"This will be an open administration, open to ideas, to different viewpoints"—many political observers were skeptical. Writing in the *Observer*, British journalist Anthony Howard looked across the Waldorf's ballroom and noted that "the only black faces visible anywhere were [workers] on the bandstand." The Nixonites gathered on the floor represented, in Howard's view, "members of what has been called 'the no change coalition,' the people for whom life has been generous enough for them to be determined not to have it threatened." Howard further suggested that the "restrained plaudits of [Nixon's] followers" gave evidence of their intrinsic complacency, their desire not to upset the social order: "They were not very good at being ecstatic, if only because their nature is basically placid and docile. For most of them, even coming into the massive, opulent hotel on the corner of 50th Street and Park Avenue had been an outing, even an adventure. The city is not their home, and its agonies are not their anxieties."[19]

Significantly, Howard pointed to the closeness of the election—in which Nixon won the popular vote by just a little over 500,000—as a sign that never before had "the two Americas been quite so precisely and surgically divided." The two Americas to which Howard referred broke down along racial and economic lines: white and black, wealthy and poor, urban and (in reflection of the continued decline of U.S. cities) suburban. Nixon ran headlong into this division in December 1969, when he returned to the Waldorf for what was supposed to be an innocuous event: the annual Hall of Fame dinner for the National Football Foundation. An hour before his arrival, a small contingent of the estimated 1,500 people swarming the hotel—antiwar protesters with a sprinkling of Black Panthers and other activists—broke through police barricades and rushed. Their objective: the Waldorf's exterior flag-poles, where they tried to hoist a pro-Communist banner. Policemen beat them with sticks. They then hoisted the flag at a nearby bank building before hitting the streets, smashing windows at Saks Fifth Avenue as programmed Christmas music tinkled "Hark, the Herald Angels Sing." Meanwhile, back at the hotel, rocks were thrown, police suffered jaw injuries, clubs fell, and someone else waved a flag of the Viet Cong. Lost in the melee was a small group of Nixon supporters standing outside the Waldorf. Dubbing them-selves "the Silent Majority," in tribute to a phrase the president had recently coined, a singing trio dressed in astronaut suits with tiny American flags jut-ting from the helmets sang, "We can fly to the moon, there ain't nothing that we can't do."[20]

Writing in the *New Leader* in 1969, journalist Roger Kingsbury pinpointed Nixon's appeal as one rooted in "spouting . . . *Reader's Digest* verities" and "measuring himself against the image of an Omaha Rotarian." Nixon, Kings-bury observed, "really is clutzy and cornball, enjoys Boy Scouts, Billy Graham and Montavani [*sic*] on the hi-fi." Others poked fun at the president's squareness: in an age of Aretha Franklin, Bob Dylan, and the Beatles, one of his favorite records was the music from *Victory at Sea*, a 1952 television documentary on the Second World War, scored by Broadway composer Richard Rodgers. In 1970, Nixon, though no fan of country music, invited superstar Johnny Cash to the White House for a highly publicized concert. Cash was an unconventional country performer who, despite his enormous following among the kinds of conservative audiences whose support Nixon sought to maintain, had often sung and spoken out against war, the U.S. prison system, and mistreatment of Native Americans. Despite this, Nixon, through advisers, advanced his guest a list of songs he hoped Cash would sing. Insultingly, one of them, "Okie from Muskogee," a critique of hippie culture, was associated with a competing artist, Merle Haggard. Another of the suggested songs—again, one popularized by someone else—caused even more of a stir, with the *New York Times* reporting Cash as "loath" to sing it. "Welfare Cadillac" was an out-of-left-field country hit whose lyrics, deliv-ered in a southern-drawl recitation, made fun of those on public relief:

Vice President Alben Barkley, center, tells a joke at the Waldorf, the morning after his "spreading adder" speech for the Democratic National Committee (Bettman).

> I know the place ain't much
> But I sure don't pay no rent
> I get a check the first of every month
> From this here Federal Government
> Every Wednesday I get commodities
> Sometimes four or five sacks
> Pick 'em up down at the Welfare Office
> Driving that new Cadillac[21]

"Welfare Cadillac" traded on the image of welfare recipients as lazy people who took advantage of government handouts. Its choice by Nixon baffled social leaders and activists, one of whom confessed to the *New York Times*, "I thought there must have been some mistake. . . . I couldn't believe that the President of the United States would request such a performance" (ultimately, Cash declined to sing it at the White House). The song choice was especially puzzling in light of Nixon's own policies on welfare. As recently as October 1968, in a radio address prior to the election, he had made the expected diatribe against "30 years of expensive federal efforts to eliminate dependency," which only, he argued, "succeeded in institutionalizing it." However, in 1969 Nixon (who himself grew up poor, the son of a lemon grower and merchant) had put forth what the *Los Angeles Times* hailed as "the most far-ranging, ground-breaking daring social-welfare reform since the early years of the New Deal." The Family Assistance Plan (FAP) was the brainchild of Nixon's new adviser on urban affairs, Daniel Patrick Moynihan, a Harvard professor and Democrat. Through FAP, the Aid to Dependent Children program would be taken apart and replaced with an income floor—a minimum financial amount guaranteed to the poorest Americans. FAP drew criticism from the left for its low benefits, about $1,600 per month for a family of four, as well as for several features designed to appeal to conservatives—most notably, enrollment in work programs as a condition of aid. Still, the plan was more than almost anyone expected from Nixon. Over the next three years, getting it passed became a key objective of his promoted domestic agenda.[22]

FAP's main liability, and the reason it would face so much pushback from Congress, was its price tag. Adding close to 12 million people to the country's welfare system was expected to cost around $4 billion a year. In August 1969, when Nixon unveiled FAP, the rate of inflation was at 7.2 percent—up from 2.2 percent when he had taken office. At the same time, national unemployment was on a small but significant rise, moving in the month of October from 3.5 to 4 percent. Economists were divided on the factors behind the increase, but most pointed to the enormous cost of the Vietnam War: in 1965, President Johnson had escalated troop levels while, on the domestic side, unveiling his expansive War on Poverty program. In what he later characterized as a mistake, Johnson allowed a plan for tax reform (one that would have eliminated certain loopholes for wealthy Americans) to be nixed. The only option, then, for funding American domestic and military programs was to borrow money—an initiative that weakened the American dollar and spurred inflation. When Nixon came to office, he attempted to slow the economy by raising interest rates, but this only led to higher prices (which businesses were forced to implement in order to cover loans) and consequent demands from workers for more money. By the start of 1971, the cost of living had increased, unemployment was up to 6 percent, and the United States faced a situation it had seldom known, one that puzzled economists: recession on top of inflation, "stagflation." This was the background for welfare's next phase, one that edged the system and its recipients to the point of crisis.

By the mid-1960s, New York's hotel industry was having problems of its own. For thirty years after the opening of the Waldorf-Astoria in 1931, no new hotels of large size were built in Manhattan. The old ones, constructed at a rapid pace during the boom years of the 1920s, were sufficient to meet the city's needs; supply had not yet thinned to the point where additions were warranted. This all changed with the announcement, in the summer of 1959, of plans for the 1964 World's Fair, estimated to bring 70 million visitors to the city. By 1962, Manhattan's classic hotels, among them the Waldorf, Astor, and Plaza, faced competition not just from the giant Americana but from Hilton's new flagship, the New York Hilton, then rising at Fifty-Third Street and Avenue of the Americas (in the latter case, the Hilton Corporation, by now the sole Waldorf shareholder, would compete against itself). In response, older establishments launched a program of renovations both cosmetic and structural: one hotel, for instance, dropped its lobby ceiling to add a new floor of exhibition rooms. The Waldorf's changes were less drastic but nonetheless significant: Oliver Smith, set designer for *My Fair Lady* and other Broadway shows, redecorated the Grand Ballroom in what was cited as a "modern baroque" style, with gilt surfaces and mirrors. Meanwhile, the Park Avenue lobby's Art Deco brightness was muffled with red velvet curtains,

wall coverings, red-and-gold chairs, and other fixtures meant to bring
the hotel back to what one Hilton executive described as its "Victorian
heritage."[23] (Tellingly, the renovations were designed to evoke the *original*
Waldorf-Astoria of the 1890s; they de-emphasized the Art Deco features
that made the 1931 building so noteworthy. In the late 1950s, many Americans
still had acute memories of the Depression and did not tend to look back on
the 1930s with nostalgia.)

Unfortunately, the World's Fair, its business softer than expected, had
little economic impact once the summer tourists went home, and New York
hotels stumbled into the fall of 1964 with the twin burdens of high costs and
lowered occupancy. It appeared the industry was undergoing another shift,
this time from a state of profitability back toward the shakiness of earlier
years: by 1963, hotel occupancy had dropped from the near capacity of wartime to just 70 percent—a good 5 percent less than ideal. The same influence
of technology that had forced a curtailment of job options for agricultural
laborers, driving them to cities, was now affecting the hospitality trade. Chief
factor was the rise in airline travel, which allowed for shorter business stays.
At the same time, fewer Americans were coming to New York by rail. One
executive recalled how the Hotel Commodore, built in 1918 as part of the
Grand Central area's development, once received "two hundred people a
day," coming from the train station, "without a reservation." By 1964, he
explained, the Commodore was only getting a dozen such daily walk-ins.
Growth of the highways played a similar role, with greater numbers of motor-
ists choosing to stay on the city's outskirts, in avoidance of midtown congestion. Aware of incipient change, a forward-thinking group of investors
financed the development, in 1959, of something many insiders had long
thought impossible due to real estate costs: Manhattan's first motel, the Skyline Motor Inn, built on an entire block of Tenth Avenue at Forty-Ninth
Street. Strictly a bare-bones operation allowing for maximum revenue (no
elevator operators, valets, or concierges), the Skyline offered self-service
parking, automatic registration, and other conveniences touted in newspaper ads: "Be modern . . . check in from your car."[24]

The Skyline Motor Inn ran at 90 percent capacity during its first year and inspired the construction of other motels along Manhattan's western edge. These further cut into the business of older establishments, weakening what had been a chief selling point: the appeal of luxury. It was the difference between Oscar's five-course meals and a TV dinner: to younger travelers, white-gloved doormen and epauletted bellhops were tip-hungry relics. Unlike many businesses, hotels were limited in the operational adjustments they could make related to volume: costs such as heat, electricity, and most of all labor, were essentially fixed, varying little whether capacity was at 60 or 95 percent. Further, industry experts often claimed that any hotel, however "modern," had a maximum life span of about thirty-five years. After that, replacement of plumbing and other infrastructure became necessary to ensure both economic efficiency and comfort of patrons. The early 1960s presented an optimal time for owners of aging hotels to sell, given rising demand for office space in midtown Manhattan. Soon after the close of the second season of the World's Fair in 1965, veterans such as the New Weston, Park Lane, and Savoy-Plaza all disappeared. To many New Yorkers the most sobering loss was that of the Astor, the 1904 Beaux-Arts landmark on Times Square—once second only to the original Waldorf-Astoria in reputation. Like the Waldorf, the Astor had been built with such solidity that demolition became an ordeal. Often the wrecking ball, hammering its target for nearly all of 1967, could bring down little more than what one observer described as "chips of brick and dust."[25]

In retrospect, these hotels were wise to bow out when they did. The 1970 recession, felt in so many areas of American life, had a contradictory effect upon the hospitality field. Higher interest rates and operating costs led to an increase in Manhattan room prices of as much as 8 percent. Simultaneously, greater levels of unemployment, salary reductions, and loss of expense accounts meant that people had less money to spend. Prices were up, but patronage was down. At the Waldorf, the effects of stagflation revealed themselves most acutely at the Empire Room. By 1970, the Empire numbered, along with the Copacabana, the Plaza's Persian Room, and the Maisonette at the St. Regis, among the last of Manhattan's chic entertainment spots. It also had the highest talent budget in New York, paying top performers such as Peggy Lee a salary of as much as $30,000 per week. With its cover charge of $8 per person, multiplied by a capacity crowd of 400 for two shows a night, six nights a week, the Empire Room had been able to make back the high talent fees it paid out. From there it operated, in the financial sense, just like any of the Waldorf's other restaurants. But in the spring of 1970, the Empire suffered two losing engagements back-to-back, one of them with a proven moneymaker, the glitzy pianist and entertainer Liberace. In response, it cut back to one show on weeknights and renegotiated its talent fees—always a sensitive operation with stars who could make more in large theaters and on television. In this way the Empire stumbled along, but signs for its future were clear.[26]

From the spring of 1969 to that of 1970, unemployment in New York City jumped by 26 percent. The size of the city's welfare rolls, which so far had reflected little evidence of the recession, ballooned as well. Clearly, more New Yorkers were going on welfare as their unemployment benefits ran out. For those already on welfare, a challenging situation grew even more difficult because of rising prices. Making a broad survey of the recession's effects for the *New York Times Magazine*, the writer Peter Benchley explained how the Bureau of Labor Statistics set the minimum standard for a family of four in New York City at $7,000 per year. The same family on welfare would receive, each month, a total of $394, which had to cover rent and all other costs—groceries, clothes, supplies. Welfare recipients, concluded Benchley, lived "by their fingernails even in the very best of times." One mother of four in Harlem, who refused to give her name because she was "embarrassed," told the writer that one child had had to forgo new shoes for so long that he developed a toe fungus. Another child required a suit for his high school graduation. Money for these costs had to come out of the food budget. In response, the family ate less protein, bulking up on starches and carbohydrates to the point where, as Benchley told readers, "the younger children's bellies began to bloat."[27]

In the meantime, Mayor Lindsay had devised a plan for the federal and state governments to cover a larger percentage of New York City's welfare costs. Lindsay and members of his administration believed they were being discriminated against doubly: first by federal policies offering less aid to states like New York, with high per capita incomes, and second by the way welfare contributions were divided up within the state as a whole. Because of its population size, New York City was required to pay a disproportionate percentage of the total state welfare cost. At first, Lindsay's efforts looked promising. Early in 1969, the persuasive mayor met with five members of President Nixon's new cabinet and received "general assurances" of increased federal aid for a range of programs. Naively, Lindsay walked away from the meeting with a certainty that the president, whose political base resided in suburbia, would be receptive to a liberal Republican's expertise on the problem of cities. As time wore on, however, Nixon, in the words of historian Vincent Cannato, "increasingly saw [Lindsay] as a political enemy," one who was overly tolerant of those urban social ills the president most wished to emphasize in his fight for a second term: rioting, crime, pornography. Simultaneously, Lindsay's relationship with Governor Rockefeller was deteriorating to the point of acrimony. The governor had never gotten over an early snub in which Lindsay, wanting to be viewed as his own man, took a large donation from Rockefeller, then refused to let him speak on the mayoral campaign trail. Later, Lindsay complained bitterly after his older peer stepped in to resolve the city's sanitation strike, railing against the governor's negotiations as "a direct and dangerous threat to the principle of home rule."[28]

During his second mayoral term, which began in 1970, Lindsay came under attack from all sides: conservatives rebuked his tolerance of crime while liberals criticized him for not living up to his early promises of a more livable, humane New York. Journalist Pete Hamill struggled to understand the vast antipathy directed toward the mayor in a column for the *New York Post*: "Why, for God's sake, is [Lindsay] hated by so many ordinarily decent human beings? Ask the Lindsay haters to explain and they tell you that the city's going to the dogs. . . . He is too soft; he is too hard. . . . The cabdrivers cause traffic jams, and in the middle of the horn-blowing and the screaming and the reach for the edge of sanity they turn and say: 'That goddam Lindsay!'"[29]

On November 17, 1970, the mayor fired 500 municipal workers in what the *Times* described as "the first mass layoff of city workers since the Depression." The action, which only affected provisional employees (those who lacked Civil Service status), was an effort to ameliorate the city's financial crisis and partially close a budget gap estimated at between $200 and $300 million. All employees, including civil servants, were stripped of merit pay increases. Days later, Lindsay told a lunch gathering at the Waldorf that "survival" was the issue for 1970, because inflation had "transformed rising costs into runaway costs." The number of New Yorkers on welfare continued to grow, with some of the biggest increases occurring among non–Puerto Rican whites. For the first quarter of the fiscal year (starting in July), the city had projected 16,500 new welfare cases. The total wound up being 45,000. More than 1.1 million New Yorkers—one out of seven residents—were now on public relief. Desperate for housing, the city's welfare department put more and more people into hotels. However, since most establishments refused to accept welfare clients, families were forced into places like the once-stylish Broadway Central near Greenwich Village, where walls now gaped with holes and cockroaches skittered on floors. On December 7, a four-year-old living at the Broadway Central died after falling down a stairwell whose railing had come off. On January 2, another child was killed at a similar "welfare hotel," the Earle.[30]

Tensions came to a head on January 5, 1971, when some fifty welfare residents from the Hotel Hamilton, which the city had ordered shut because of life-threatening conditions (raw sewage, peeling lead paint, rat infestation), staged a "live-in" at the offices of Jule Sugarman, director of the city's Human Resources Administration (HRA). The group, which included many children, eventually barricaded itself behind office doors after police came to force it back to the Hamilton. Sugarman faced down the police and called Mayor Lindsay's office: "We still haven't found housing for 40 families; we have condemned their present living quarters [the Hamilton] and we can't send them back." At last the city convinced them to leave by promising them apartments in a former nurses' home on East Twentieth Street. But when they arrived, they found broken plumbing and more flaking paint. "I wouldn't put a pig in that nursing home," one woman cried. The city gave families a choice: either move to the nurses' home, go back to the Hamilton, or face arrest. On January 13, Sugarman admitted failure: he had been able to find decent apartments for only nine of the forty-seven families. The *Washington Post* described Sugarman as confessing that the chief lessons he learned from the Hotel Hamilton protest were "the shortage of large-size habitable apartments and the high level of hostility of landlords to rent to welfare tenants."[31]

It was within this climate that, on the 19th of January, an African American woman named Cleola Hainsworth showed up at the DeKalb Avenue welfare center in Brooklyn with her four children and demanded assistance.

The Hainsworths' odyssey had begun some three months earlier, when, as one family member explained to a reporter, the house they occupied in Brooklyn for eight years became unlivable: "Some construction workers were building a church next door and dug too deep and our foundation cracked." Thereupon, recounted Mrs. Hainsworth, who had been receiving assistance since 1964, the welfare department began "moving us around"—first to one Brooklyn hotel, the Granada, and then, before Christmas, to another named the Manhattan Beach. All the while, city welfare workers searched for a permanent apartment in which to house the family. In an example of what was later pointed to as the ungrateful attitude of Mrs. Hainsworth, and of welfare recipients in general—beggars shouldn't be choosers—she made a point of refusing placement in a housing project in Red Hook, a neighborhood considered dangerous at the time: "I don't like that place. My kids are good kids and I want to live in a place they like."[32]

As son Victor, then twelve, later recalled, "Mom's beauty made it hard for others to argue with her, especially when she advocated for her children." So, the Hainsworths remained at the Manhattan Beach. Then, on January 19, hotel management informed them they would have to move out to make room for a trade conference of phone operators. When Cleola and her children, ranging in age from ten to eighteen, arrived at the DeKalb welfare center, it was already late afternoon. Dorrance Henderson, the center's housing adviser, had little time to find them a place. Single-digit temperatures made the situation urgent. Mrs. Hainsworth explained she had a friend in Brooklyn who was willing to rent to the family for $100 a week. But when Henderson submitted the price to a supervisor for approval, it was turned down as too expensive. Because the welfare department classed hotels as "emergency" housing, it assigned them a rate ceiling higher than that of apartments or houses. This meant that Henderson and his coworkers had to persuade Cleola to accept something that she didn't want and that would also cost the city more money. As she later explained, "I told the welfare people that I would rather go to my girlfriend's. . . . They said a flat, 'No.'"[33]

All city welfare offices kept a list of approved hotels. Some were tidy establishments like the Manhattan Beach; many were run-down or worse. As Henderson later testified in a departmental hearing, he called every hotel on the approved list, but none had a vacancy. Then, as similar circumstances had forced him to do in the past, he pulled out the Brooklyn yellow pages, turned to "Hotels," and began dialing. Every place he tried was either full or would not accept welfare guests. Finally, he got to the *Ws*. To his relief, the Waldorf-Astoria, which had sponsored a Brooklyn listing, agreed to take the family. One welfare employee later recalled that Mrs. Hainsworth "didn't want" the Waldorf, saying it was "too far for the kids to go to school and that the hotel was full of homosexuals and not a good environment for her children." As further indication that Cleola was not aware of the hotel or its expensive reputation, the DeKalb center's supervisor, Salvatore Ciccolella, noted that he had had "to convince [her] that the Waldorf was not a fleabag." In the end, she relented and, holding a welfare department check in the amount of $143.45 (two rooms for two nights), made her way to the East Side of Manhattan. By early that evening, Cleola Hainsworth and family were residents of the Waldorf-Astoria.[34]

For one night and morning, all went smoothly. The youngest and oldest Hainsworth sons, Alton and Charles, stayed in one room while Victor took another (the fourth child, Barbara, was staying with a friend in Brooklyn).

From the standpoint of luxury, Mrs. Hainsworth liked the Waldorf but was not overly impressed: it was "nice enough," but she had "stayed in others just as nice before—without the kids." Indeed, she preferred the Manhattan Beach in Brooklyn, where the room had had a refrigerator and stove. Food in the Park Avenue neighborhood was expensive, and there was no way the family could eat in one of the Waldorf restaurants because the prices were "silly." The children, on the other hand, "liked the Waldorf more," she said. Believing the lobby was "filled with movie stars," they would, like many guests before them, sit there and "watch the people." Charles may have been thinking of the first Brooklyn hotel, the Granada (where a family of four would later be killed in a fire), when he offered his impressions of the Waldorf's atmosphere: "It's nice here . . . the walls are clean and the people are nice to you." Overall, though, Cleola explained she was "just tired of moving": "They just keep telling you to move without any reason. Sometimes I think they do it so you'll be too tired to even look for an apartment."[35]

Shortly after noon on January 20, Victor Hainsworth received a call in his room: "Seemed some reporter, snickering on the phone, wanted to know how I felt about being on welfare and in the Waldorf." Victor hung up without responding, from fear of "being exposed": "My heart was racing: 'I'm going to be in the news about being on welfare . . . my schoolmates are going to ridicule me to death.' From a child's perspective, we used to play the 'dozens,' joke on each other about being on welfare: 'Oh, your mom's on welfare, you eat government cheese. . . . Better not be late, that welfare line is LONG when they have cheese.' We would laugh when someone could not take it, though most of us were on welfare."[36]

The reporter was calling from one of New York's daily newspapers, which, along with every major television station, had been notified—through an anonymous phone tip—that a black family on relief was living at what was reputed to be the poshest hotel in town. From the press's point of view, the situation had all the makings of a well-orchestrated joke. Journalist Drew Fetherston hinted at this possibility in his article for *Newsday*: "The City of New York, while sinking in a bottomless pit of debt, paying $75 a night to lodge a welfare family in that gilded national institution, the Waldorf-Astoria on Park Avenue. It was almost as if someone had deliberately schemed for the maximum shock value."[37]

First to respond to the tip and arrive at the Waldorf was Bryna Taubman, a young reporter for the *New York Post*. Taubman brought along a staff photographer, who captured three members of the family watching television in a "pale green room with bright curtains on the 10th floor," where Mrs. Hainsworth complained about the hotel's maid service: "'It's after noon, and no one has been in here to make the beds.'" Taubman also spoke with a representative of the Waldorf, who said he could not "be sure" if the manager who took the reservation "knew [the Hainsworths] were welfare clients" but added that "it really wouldn't make any difference." The hotel was "open to any guest" who could "pay the bill" and was "well-behaved." Taubman filed her story in time for it to make the *Post*'s afternoon edition on January 20. Soon, Mayor Lindsay's chief administrative assistant, Sid Davidoff, was under siege. As he recalled, "The press calls [were] going crazy." Davidoff, who had made his reputation as head of "Lindsay's Raiders"—a group of streetwise young men who guarded the mayor-to-be during his 1965 walking tours—recalled thinking, "How are we gonna deal with this?"

> At that time, Jule Sugarman was the head of Human Resources Administration. Dick Aurelio was first deputy mayor. We bring Sugarman into the first deputy mayor's office. I'm saying to Sugarman—nice guy, no political sense whatsoever—"What were you thinking? You don't understand the politics. My *mother* has never stayed in the Waldorf-Astoria hotel. And this welfare family was complaining about the amount of room service! You will get them out immediately or don't show up tomorrow!"[38]

As Davidoff acknowledged, it wasn't about the money—indeed, the Hainsworths still had a second night's lodging at the Waldorf, prepaid in city funds, which the mayor's office was ready to forfeit. At issue was the awareness that, in Davidoff's words, "lower-middle-class" citizens were going to ask, "*We* can't afford the Waldorf, [so] how the hell can *this* family afford the Waldorf?" Politically, it was "devastating . . . the worst thing you could

Cleola Hainsworth and two of her sons, Alton (sitting) and Charles, watching television in their Waldorf room, January 20, 1971 (author's collection).

imagine." To avoid appearing "clinically insensitive," attested Davidoff, "we had to resolve the fallout."[39]

So, around six thirty on January 20, just twenty-four hours after the Hainsworths had arrived at the Waldorf, they were being escorted out by an African American representative of the welfare department. Newspapers were again on the scene, documenting Cleola Hainsworth, fashionably dressed in high leather boots, loading an armful of what looked to be clothes fresh from the cleaners—arranged on hangers and covered in wrapping—onto an elevator next to a sign advertising the hotel's Bull & Bear steakhouse. "From Riches . . . ," *Newsday* proclaimed sardonically on its next-morning cover, alongside an image of the family as it packed up, ". . . To Rags."

Recalled Victor, "Mom did not seem distressed, although she had a beautiful poker face which [was] hard to read": "My brothers seemed okay, too—no emotions about being where we were, and no comments about it either. I guess the three of us were desensitized about moving into the hotel, as we moved into so many before just to move out again with our mom."[40]

The Hainsworths' destination was the Brooklyn home of the friend with whom Cleola had wanted to stay in the first place. Reached by the *Post* ten days later, this woman made a point of stating she had worked all her life, beginning in cotton fields. As far as the woman knew, Mrs. Hainsworth had been "in some hotel but had to leave suddenly." She too had no knowledge of the Waldorf: "I was never there . . . don't even know what it means." The woman's tone suggested she had taken the Hainsworths in for the money and because of obligation, rather than out of any compassion for welfare recipients. She declined to give her name or address: "In all respect, please understand. I'm not on relief and I don't have to go through all this."[41]

As Davidoff anticipated, neither did the general public display much in the way of sympathy. A woman named Phyllis Ceravolo wrote to the *Post*, complaining how "not only are the taxpayers feeding and clothing the 'poor,' but now we shelter them in hotels that even we cannot afford!" Annette Kruger, a *Newsday* reader from Wantagh, Long Island, observed caustically how Mrs. Hainsworth, "fur-coated" and shown in photographs as "clutching . . . new apparel," must have been "deeply embarrassed at not having a full set of leather luggage to pack her wardrobe properly." Soon, papers outside of the city added to the chorus. In the view of an Ogdensburg, New York editorialist, Cleola's observation that "she preferred a former Brooklyn hotel because the maid came in the morning instead of the afternoon, as at the Waldorf," suggested "a frightening attitude on the part of welfare recipients." Meanwhile, the *Pittsburgh Post-Gazette* observed, "Welfare mother Cleola Hainsworth is a woman of simple tastes—the best is good enough for her. . . . It is regrettable that Mrs. Hainsworth's income does not match her aspirations. We hope that she and her children may one day return in triumph to the Waldorf and will be able to foot the bill themselves."[42]

As it had years earlier, in explaining its decision not to cancel the "Red" Peace Conference, the Waldorf-Astoria was called upon to defend itself publicly. On January 21, as part of the *New York Times*' coverage, the hotel clarified that, yes, it did in fact know from the beginning that the rooms were for a welfare family. Wanting to emphasize that it was the city's choice, not the Waldorf's, to evict the Hainsworths, a Waldorf representative pointed out that, "so far as the hotel is concerned," the rooms were "paid up until checkout time tomorrow," and the family could "remain until then." By now, Carl Teisberg, the manager on duty when the Hainsworths checked in, had been found and was able to discuss the situation with reporter Fetherston of *Newsday*. Noting without explanation that the hotel's reservation book had been "impounded" by its "public relations office," Teisberg reiterated how the Hainsworths' status as welfare recipients did not deprive them of their right to hospitality as paying guests. Building on the Hilton credo, voiced so frequently during the 1950s, Teisberg now added a new category, one as reflective of the nation in 1971 as segregation had been during the 1950s: "The Waldorf has not discriminated on the basis of race, creed, color or even economic situations—as long as they get paid." In portraying the Hainsworths as legitimate guests (through a quote that was reprinted, in large type, on *Newsday*'s "From Riches . . . To Rags" cover), he made it clear that their booking had been made as neither a mistake nor a prank.[43]

But the controversy was just beginning. Mayor Lindsay, not satisfied with removing the Hainsworths from the Waldorf, ordered the immediate suspension of three city welfare employees: Dorrance Henderson and his supervisor at the center, Salvatore Ciccolella, along with a third man, Alan Baer, who worked as part of a small "case consultation" unit out of lower Manhattan. In the chaos that was New York, the *Times* observed, political leaders saw "sinister plots" whenever anything went wrong, which was (during a week in which the city had just gotten over another strike, this time by Lindsay's nemeses, the police) "practically always." Through his press office, the mayor announced he was "deeply angered and outraged" by the Waldorf incident, which bore signs of "colossal bad judgement or worse." A beleaguered Lindsay further voiced suspicion that his own welfare department "may well have [acted with] malicious intent," orchestrating the scandal as part of a plot to embarrass him.[44]

As paranoid as this statement may have appeared to observers at the time, the mayor, from his perspective, had reasonable grounds for making it. For one thing, there was the possibility that city employees wanted revenge for the November layoffs and cancellation of merit increases. But more significant were the mayor's ongoing efforts to shift the city's welfare burden to the federal government. Indeed, one week prior to the Waldorf tempest Lindsay announced the filing of a suit designed, in the words of the *Times*, "to free New York from Federal and state laws mandating large portions of city tax revenues for welfare programs." If successful, the suit would have entailed a scaling back of the city's welfare administration and, without question, the loss of jobs. What better way to sabotage the mayor's efforts and defang his suit than to demonstrate, for all to witness, how New York City squandered its welfare budget on luxury hotels? The truth, though, was that the welfare department, in booking the Hainsworths at the Waldorf, had merely been doing its job. "I thought that the mayor handled the situation very, very poorly," recalled Alan Baer, one of the suspended employees. "Instead of getting the facts, he just said, 'Suspend them all.'"[45]

Stanley Hill, head of the local Social Services Employees Union (of which Baer and Henderson were members), pointed out that "no hard and fast rule" existed to prevent workers from booking the Waldorf for emergency housing: "A worker has . . . leverage to use what hotels have rooms available when he can't get a hotel from the [approved] list." Hill further called Lindsay's order of suspension "an act of stupidity [and] desperation." *Newsday*, in a mild push against the tide of public backlash, asked, "Why can't a welfare family stay at the best place in town?" But, the paper conceded, "answers are for more tranquil times." Which these were not: upon learning of the suspensions on January 21, the entire 200-member staff of the DeKalb welfare center stopped work and began marching to the lower Manhattan office of the HRA's Jule Sugarman, who (no doubt trying to preserve his job) had announced an official inquiry into the circumstances behind the Waldorf placement. One of the welfare workers, a long-haired young woman in wide-brimmed hat and heavy, dark coat, carried a makeshift sign whose slogan, written in what appeared to be Magic Marker ink, countered the public outcry by reminding New Yorkers that they had long treated the Park Avenue building as a city fixture, open to all: "The Waldorf Belongs to the People."[46]

On January 22, Sugarman lifted two of the three suspensions, claiming the HRA's inquiry board had discovered no evidence of malice. Sugarman further invalidated Lindsay's charge of conspiracy by revealing that the Hainsworths had not, after all, been the first welfare family to stay at the Waldorf. Some months prior, a woman had been placed there, along with her children, after a husband or boyfriend tried to attack them with a knife. Sugarman's admission reinforced the point union leader Hill had been making: the idea of first-class hotels as a temporary response to the housing shortage was not unusual. During previous years, in fact, the city had placed homeless families in both the Commodore and the New York Hilton. Still, those hotels weren't the *Waldorf.* Ciccolella, the suspended director, made this point when defending himself through an attorney's statement: "If this was a different hotel without a world-famous name but with the same price, nothing would have been done about this." Then Ciccolella spoke directly: "I deny that Mr. Sugarman or any of his aides ever instructed me not to use the Waldorf-Astoria. . . . I deny [the placing of the Hainsworths there] was a conspiracy."[47]

Years later, discussing the possibility of malicious intent, Sid Davidoff would admit, "I never felt that." Still, the fact remained: someone had leaked the Waldorf story to the press. If not a city welfare employee, then who? Manager Teisberg's admission about the impounded reservation book offered a hint that the Waldorf was conducting its own investigation. With this in mind, it becomes evident that the culprit was, in all likelihood, a member of the front desk staff who had seen (or at least heard about) the city check Cleola Hainsworth used to pay for the rooms. This explanation provides a window into the frustration of rank-and-file hotel employees who, despite union representation, still struggled to provide for themselves at a time of recession and rising prices. One room clerk for a major hotel, interviewed in 1970, confessed to a reporter that he cared little about the industry's dwindling profits, given that his own salary had been "squeezed for years." The clerk explained that he had started at a rate of thirty-five dollars a week about twenty years earlier and was now making just a small amount over union scale: "[The] management expects us to dress like a banker but doesn't pay us enough to do so." In this climate, it seemed the only people who didn't resent the Hainsworths were their fellow guests. A "tanned gentleman with a handlebar moustache," interviewed in the Waldorf's lobby, told the *Daily News* that, "as a taxpayer," the situation bothered him, but that otherwise he "really [had] no objection to living next to poor people."[48]

As more details of New York's welfare crisis were publicized, however, the tone of the public's reaction started to change. Union representative Hill fought back with the release of jarring details culled from his own members: the city was paying $75 a night to house a welfare family of five at the unglamorous Traveler's Motel in Queens. A thirteen-member family at the Bronx Whitestone Motel was costing the city $1,240 per week, or $177 a night. These establishments were typical "welfare hotels" that made money by taking guests most other proprietors would turn away. By comparison, the Waldorf-Astoria's two rooms for a total of $72 per night were, in the words of the *Times*, "practically a bargain." International columnist Joyce Egginton added to the furor by reminding readers of the horrors already written about the Broadway Central and other hotels: "Two children killed by falling down [an] unprotected lift shaft . . . the little girl who innocently opened her hotel bedroom door to have lye thrown in her face by an addict about to burgle for a 'fix.'" There were welfare mothers, Egginton reported, who remained on the subway for hours, "clutching their exhausted children," out of fear of staying in their hotel rooms. Despite all of this having already been reported, wrote Egginton, the "real shock" didn't come until "a homeless black mother and her . . . children" were temporarily lodged in a hotel "more used to putting up royalty and diplomats."[49]

Writing for the *Observer* of the United Kingdom, Egginton touched upon a note that most of her colleagues in the American press avoided: the significance of race, both in the lack of concern exhibited toward African American children killed at welfare hotels and in the subsequent outrage over a black family infiltrating what had usually been thought of as a white preserve. In an interview for the then-liberal *New York Post*, Harlem activist Ruth Pressley brought the argument back to housing. Insisting that she

would "not stand idly by while buildings deteriorate and the city does nothing," Pressley announced that her group, the Harlem Welfare Mothers, had
plans to take over vacant city-owned structures and rehabilitate them for
welfare recipients. She also claimed the city had placed white welfare families in the Waldorf and similar hotels before, but that no one made a "stink"
until a black family moved in. While the ethnicity of the previous welfare
family at the Waldorf was never cited, Pressley nonetheless brought up a
question that would seem to acquire greater relevance as the 1970s progressed: Would there have been the same degree of outcry had the Hainsworths not been African American?[50]

By the early 1970s, diatribes against welfare had shifted away from the
exploitation of fears surrounding Communism. Politicians now attacked not
just the system but the recipients themselves, who were depicted as a cause,
rather than casualty, of the nation's economic problems. Beginning his second term as California's governor on January 4, 1971, Ronald Reagan (whose
political career had launched in 1964, after he made a televised speech for
Goldwater) promised to trim the welfare rolls of those whose "greed" was
"greater than their need." Later in the year, following Vice President Spiro
Agnew's suggestion that women on welfare not be allowed to have "any more
children," congressmen in South Carolina, Illinois, and Tennessee all introduced state legislation requiring the sterilization of women who, in the
words of Larry Bates, sponsor of the Tennessee bill, produced children "as
their only commodity."[51]

In coming years, racial implications that were hinted at in 1971—when
South Carolina representative Lucius Porth attacked welfare mothers' "lust
for sex"—would become direct. Reagan, in his 1976 campaign for the Republican presidential nomination, riled a crowd in Florida by citing the outrage
of working people in the grocery line, who watched as a "strapping young
buck" in front of them purchased T-bone steaks with food stamps. Reagan
had been particularly dismayed by the Hainsworths, holding on to their
story as evidence of how those on welfare abused the system. As late as
December 1986, when his mental faculties were showing signs of decline,

several congressional leaders who were meeting with the president noted how he drew upon the story of "the New York City welfare family living in a plush hotel at extravagant cost" to answer a question about federal health insurance for catastrophic illnesses. When it was explained to the president that "catastrophic health insurance was not a welfare program," Reagan simply "reiterated his story about the welfare family."[52]

President Reagan's obsession with the Hainsworths stemmed from a visit his wife, Nancy, had made to the Waldorf in early February 1971, when the controversy had been simmering two weeks. Speaking to a *Times* reporter in her Waldorf Towers suite, Mrs. Reagan confessed to working out frustra- tions, privately, through "long conversations" with herself in the bathtub: "I'm not a yeller or a screamer." She was, the reporter noted, a "shy, sensitive woman" who looked "elegant in her yellow Galanos mididress" (Reagan had just been selected to the International Best Dressed List for the second time). However, when it came to the subject of the black welfare family who had recently stayed at the same hotel, Reagan was "shocked"—and felt "the peo- ple of New York" deserved to be "shocked too." Then, through a remark Joyce Egginton, the *Observer* writer, characterized as "worthy of Marie Antoi- nette," Nancy Reagan took in the Hainsworths, the Waldorf-Astoria, the American welfare system, and the general public's conception of all three: "'There must be somewhere else to put these people.'"[53]

The morning after the Hainsworths left the Waldorf, 12-year old Victor took the subway to school as usual, but, once there, decided to "play hooky"— something that he "never did." Instead of going to class, he went to the school library, where the librarian (who also worked as Victor's chess coach) let him in early: "It seemed like he was ready for me at 8 a.m. when the library [didn't open until] 10:30. He knew, and I love him for anticipating my next move. Just around 9:30 my home room teacher and my mom showed up. I burst into tears and hugged my mom. My home room teacher said that she was moving me to another class, 8-1, to get away from the ridicule of my classmates. All the smart kids were in 8-1. I guess they were told not to bother me as I went to class, took my seat and pondered."

Victor, who recalled how "mom gave us middle-class values, such as go to school and the best will follow from there," would continue with his studies and, in time, earn his PhD. Looking back on the experience of welfare, he remarked how "nothing in the 'system' encouraged anyone to stay in the system:" "At the welfare office, lines were very long to get service and very off-putting. The attitude of staff was condescending, putting mom on the defensive all the time. The office had kids all over the place, crying and doing whatever without parental supervision, other than, 'put that down, stop that, you hit him one more time and I'll break your fingers.'"[54]

By the early 1970s, it had become clear that the plan to reform welfare, in the guise of Nixon's Family Assistance Plan, was doomed. Speaking to the American Newspaper Publishers Association at the Waldorf in 1970, Daniel Patrick Moynihan had called FAP "the most important piece of social legislation since the Social Security Act of 1935." After passing in the House, though, it failed in the Senate—twice. In his memoirs, Nixon expressed regret for the Senate conservatives who "denounced the plan as a 'megadole' and a leftist scheme," but he directed larger blame toward the "liberals," who "turned on the plan and practically pummeled it to death." According to Nixon, the Democratic left "complained that the dollar amounts were not enough and the work requirements were repressive." As a result, by 1971 the "momentum for FAP had passed." He had "fought hard," but in the end the president concluded that FAP was "an idea ahead of its time." The truth, noted by Nixon biographer John A. Farrell, was that the president himself issued "Machiavellian instructions," soon after Moynihan's departure from the administration in late 1970. These were revealed in the diary of chief of staff H. R. Haldeman, who wrote that Nixon "wants to be sure [FAP is] killed by Democrats and that we make big play for it, but don't let it pass, can't afford it." As Farrell observed, with a political "shape-shifter" such as Nixon, "little was indelible."[55]

Eventually, Mayor Lindsay lost the suit he had filed in hopes of getting the federal government to assume New York City's welfare burden. In 1972

a U.S. judge ruled that while the complaint served as a "forceful, well-doc-
umented description of the plight of tax-paying citizens who are called upon
to support the ever-increasing number of citizens who pay no taxes," in the
end it did not "present a substantial Federal constitutional question." By the
time he left office at the end of 1973, Lindsay—no longer the young idealist—
had become adept at former Mayor Wagner's old practice of avoiding larger
problems in the service of a short-term fix. In 1971, for example, his control-
ler, Abe Beame (a former accountant and veteran civil servant) balanced the
city budget by changing the date on teachers' checks from June 30 to July 1,
thereby pushing $25 million to the next fiscal year. Such financial sleight of
hand only added to the city's troubles, forcing a pattern of borrowing to meet
payrolls and other expenses. By the middle of 1975, with Beame now installed
as mayor, the city was moving precariously close to default: its primary lend-
ers, the banks that had long underwritten city notes and bonds, were refusing to purchase more. Again, the Waldorf played a role as host to dramatic
city events: it was there, after a conference with the governor in August, that
Beame suffered the public embarrassment of ceding oversight of the city's
budget to a state-controlled board.[56]

Paradoxically, the worst days of New York's crisis—when its near bankruptcy was met with President Ford's refusal, in October 1975, to provide a
federal bailout—coincided with the beginning of a financial turnaround for
hotels. More people were coming to New York, which in 1976 hosted 834 official conferences, among them the Democratic National Convention—the
first such gathering, Republican or Democrat, hosted by the city since 1924.
A hit Broadway musical, *Annie*, lured families into the city with its rags-to-
riches story of the lovable comic strip orphan, singing her way through a
romanticized vision of Depression-era New York. Led by a cast of African
American performers, *The Wiz*, another Broadway reinterpretation of 1930s
cultural nostalgia (it was inspired by the 1939 movie version of *The Wizard
of Oz*), continued to do strong business. Throughout 1976 and 1977, Manhattan hotels were averaging a respectable 74 percent of capacity. As observed
with a touch of sardonicism by one hotel manager at the Americana, tourists no longer seemed as afraid of New York and its dangerous reputation:

"People have found out that it's no better anywhere else . . . the crime, the street people, the city problems—New York was just ahead of its time."[57]

In fact, New York hotels appeared to be suffering in just one realm: the entertainment showrooms, which had continued their decline into unprofitability. Several factors, among them the increasing 1970s popularity of discos such as Studio 54, were suggested as contributors to the failure of hotel nightclubs, but the most significant of these was the rise in performers' salaries, in an age of arena rock and Vegas casinos. As vocalist Mel Torme observed in a 1977 *Times* essay, industry "monsters" of "the Elton John stripe" could "now make more money in a one night concert setting" than "many big stars," not long earlier, had "made in an entire year." In the fall of 1969, the Waldorf had attempted a recovery by moving the Empire Room across the Park Avenue foyer, to what had formerly been the Sert Room (as part of the renovation, the ebullient Don Quixote paintings were taken down and sold to a Spanish bank). This allowed for a slightly higher capacity and also made the room more attractive to performers: unlike the original setup, where artists occupied a built-in riser on the long side of the space, the new Empire Room featured, at its short end, a bona fide stage that obviated the need to turn back and forth in an effort to play both sides of the audience. Hilton's talent bookers also pushed further into contemporary fields, by hiring Philadelphia soul groups such as the O'Jays. But what Torme referred to as the "era of classy hotel-cafes" had passed. In 1976, first the Maisonette at the St. Regis closed, then the Plaza's Persian Room, and, finally, in December, after an engagement with dancer and singer Chita Rivera, the Empire Room.[58]

Torme wrote of how, throughout his career, he had longed for a chance to play the Empire Room, which to him had "symbolized the very best in hotel-room entertainment: Sinatra and Peggy Lee and Ella [Fitzgerald] . . . superb performers encompassing the broadest spectrum of talents, enriching the lives of thousands of admirers in [a] splendid setting." To Torme, the space's reputation and history only deepened its potential for inspiring a sense of artistic fulfillment. When his opportunity finally came, though, in May 1976, he confessed to feeling a slight disappointment in the new Empire Room, where, "somehow, the anticipation exceeded the realization. The magic was gone. I had waited too long and during the course of time, the business of entertaining had changed radically."

All the same, Torme admitted, "Manhattan" was still "the most exciting and romantic city in the world, despite its recent problems . . . the world's greatest conglomerate of buildings and theaters and shops and people." And, he added, in satisfaction at having played even an "ersatz" Empire Room, "the Waldorf" was "still the Waldorf."[59]

CHAPTER 9

Becoming Visible

In March 1977, Hilton Hotels took the final step in realizing a dream of its founder, now close to ninety but still making it to his Beverly Hills office six days a week. The Waldorf-Astoria, whose photograph Conrad had preserved as a far-off goal throughout his straitened Texas years, was now set to become a Hilton property—one wholly owned by the corporation. Since 1949, when Conrad Hilton became majority shareholder in the Waldorf, his company had been renting the hotel's land from New York Central Railroad and its successor, Penn Central. A source of concern for Hilton Hotels had been the lease's scheduled expiration in 1977, at which point Penn Central would be allowed to exercise a contractual option to purchase the Waldorf building itself. This possibility, which could have put the Hilton Corporation in the unwelcome position of having to fight to keep its own hotel, began to appear less likely in the summer of 1970, when Penn Central's transportation subsidiary—reeling from a loss of $121 million the previous year—filed for bankruptcy. Growth of the interstate highway system in the 1960s, which enabled semitrailers to handle many of the goods formerly shipped by train, had cut into the railroad's once-sizable freight income. Eventually, Penn Central's 1976 absorption into Conrail, a federally financed enterprise combining seven troubled railroads, freed it, legally, to begin selling off its vast Manhattan real estate holdings—the legacy of engineer William Wilgus's air-rights plan for Park Avenue, devised so many years before.

Penn Central's bankruptcy spoke to larger changes in American life. By the late 1960s, commercial rail travel had diminished to the point where Grand Central Terminal—built as a testament to the industry's strength—was mostly being used for short-distance, commuter trains. The sleek Twentieth Century Limited, which had once welcomed passengers by means of a sprawling red carpet, laid alongside the train on its departure platform, ceased operating in 1967. It had been made obsolete by the speed of airplanes, which reduced the train's sixteen-hour journey to Chicago to a single afternoon. Declining with Grand Central and its west-side counterpart, Penn Station (leveled to much protest in the 1960s), were the Midtown hotels built largely to accommodate their travelers. Lucius Boomer's cavernous McAlpin was converted to apartments in the 1970s; the New Yorker, anchoring Herald Square between Penn Station and Macy's, became headquarters for Sun Myung Moon and his religious followers, known informally as the "Moonies." Meanwhile, the Commodore, a faded remnant of the Grand Central development from the early 1910s, was bought by a young real estate developer, Donald Trump, and, with the help of millions of dollars in tax abatements from the city, clad in shiny glass panels and reopened as the Grand Hyatt. In this uncertain climate the Waldorf, built on the northernmost portion of Grand Central's holdings, survived by keeping its facilities up to date and, in continuance of traditions established by Claude Philippe, maintaining the Grand Ballroom as New York's premier event space for banquets.

During the 1970s and early 1980s, the closest the Waldorf came to an emblematic figure—a mascot such as Oscar, Boomer, and Philippe—was in the person of a genial, 250-pound hotel veteran named Eugene Scanlan. Balding, with front teeth that protruded above a fleshy chin, Scanlan was atypical in more than appearance: in 1961, at age thirty-eight, he became the Waldorf's first American-bred executive chef, having risen in a field dominated by men born and trained in France. Soon he was a minor celebrity, endorsing La Choy soy sauce in newspaper ads and offering tips to columnists on how best to prepare chicken in wine for a dinner party of six. An only child of Irish American parents, Scanlan grew up with a heart condition that kept him largely indoors, where he cultivated a love of cooking through the influence of his mother. Chided as "kitchen canary" by his father and subject to teasing from classmates, who called him "sissy," Scanlan became the only boy in his high school home economics class. He started at the Waldorf in 1942, working under chef Gabriel Lugot as part of a select apprenticeship program—created as one of Boomer's educational initiatives. There he was hazed by his French coworkers, who named him "Le Stupide" and gave him humiliating tasks. One day, he recalled years later, they sent him to fetch a "bucket of steam": "I knew the request was a joke, but I took the bucket anyway and the pastry chef took pity on me. He put some dry ice in the bucket and poured some hot water over it, producing steam. I took the steaming bucket back to the kitchen [and] set it on a table to a round of applause."[1]

Innately good-humored, Scanlan took it upon himself to learn the language of his kitchen-mates. Within three years he had become fluent to the extent that French visitors would sometimes ask him to identify his native province. After working at Miami Beach's new Hotel Fontainebleau for seven years beginning in 1954, Scanlan returned to the Waldorf, where he invented a dish that became nearly as popular as Oscar's old Waldorf salad: "fried ice cream," wrapped in a crepe, infused with Grand Marnier, then covered in macaroon crumbs and put in a deep fryer. In another feat, Scanlan became the Waldorf's manager in 1973—the first time a former chef had succeeded in attaining a top leadership position at a major American hotel. Later he was promoted to vice president of the Waldorf-Astoria Corporation. A devout Roman Catholic who spoke with pride of having once personally served a meal to Pope Paul VI, Scanlan was married with two children— even though, in later years, after leaving the hotel, questions would emerge about his sexuality and the possibility that he may have been a closeted gay man. To future Waldorf general manager Joe Rantisi, who started working for Scanlan in 1973, his boss "wasn't the kind of a guy who would say, 'this is the way to do it, [so] do it.'" Instead, he would outline what needed to be done, then suggest, "'see if you can figure out a way to do it'": "That [approach] gave me opportunities to grow, a whole lot more than any other position

I worked at. Eugene Scanlan came from the ranks. He knew what it was like to be on the lower end, so he appreciated what those guys went through when he was up in his position. I wouldn't see him doing something nasty or hard on someone, or demeaning."[2]

In March 1983, Scanlan announced his resignation: not yet sixty, he would be leaving the Waldorf to start his own consulting firm for new hotel projects. The reason for his abrupt departure from a place that had been the core of his life for forty years was never clear, but Rantisi believed it had something to do with corporate reorganization: "A task force, comprised of a bunch of senior VPs of Hilton, came to the Waldorf and did a study about how the Waldorf was running . . . to see if it [was] good enough or if they thought they could do better with it." Soon after, both Scanlan and Frank Wangeman, another veteran then functioning as the corporation's senior vice president, left. What turned out to be one of their final initiatives was the launch of a sweeping renovation of the hotel's physical structure, timed to coincide with its fiftieth anniversary. In late 1981 they began stripping away the frilly, neo-Victorian decor the Hilton Corporation had added during the 1960s. By now, enough years had passed since the Great Depression that the era's prime architectural form—Art Deco—could be appreciated and even sought out by the general public. For much of the 1980s, a flimsy retro vision of Deco would fill the interiors of diners, bars, and apartment houses; the Waldorf, Scanlan and Wangeman knew, had the real thing.

According to Rantisi, executives spent "millions of dollars" in peeling back the layers of wallpaper and paint that had made the lobby of the 1970s a "dark, stuffy" place. Curtains were taken down, vinyl padding removed, carpets lifted—all for the sake of bringing out the Waldorf's true design, so long unappreciated. By surprise, Louis Rigal's *Wheel of Life* mosaic, nearly forgotten after years of hiding beneath an umber rug, revealed itself in a swirl of patterns and colors that harmonized with the classical murals lurking near the ceiling—also uncovered with what architecture critic Paul Goldberger described as "a recognition, long overdue, that what existed was of real quality, and that to cover it up was to destroy what made [the Waldorf] so special in the first place."[3]

For longtime employees, several of whom were old enough to have been present when President Hoover spoke at the opening, back in 1931, the fiftieth anniversary celebration—highlighted by a twenty-five-foot revolving cake with a miniature Waldorf on top—offered a moment to reflect on how far the hotel had come. From uncertain beginnings, launched at a time of national disaster, the Park Avenue Waldorf had withstood strikes, economic downturns, competition, and changes in public taste to remain a solid institution—still the choice of kings and diplomats, along with anyone who wanted to draw on its status as cynosure to make a political statement, through speeches, demonstrations, or (increasingly in the 1980s) acts of civil disobedience. Even more, with the recent Hilton purchase from Penn Central, the future now seemed secure. Rantisi recalled the venturesome spirit of the time: "We kept spending [money], but we were also making it. We spent close to $60 million in a few years, just upgrading the ballroom, every meeting room that we had—[the whole] infrastructure. It was exciting to be alive and standing on our own pilasters there, over the railroad tracks, after fifty years."[4]

True to precedents set by Claude Philippe, the Waldorf-Astoria continued to host dinners for groups representing social issues not yet fully understood or embraced by the larger public. According to Jim Blauvelt, who began working in the Waldorf's banquet department in 1983, the only time a proposed event gave rise to slight hesitation, on his part, was 1987's Night of a Thousand Gowns. Conceiving of the event as a benefit for five organizations promoting equality for gay and lesbian Americans, planners decided to have fun with the Waldorf's reputation as a site of debutante coming-out parties—only, in this instance, the fashionable young women from society's upper echelons would be replaced by men in ballgowns and their tuxedoed female counterparts. Touted as the first charity ball of its kind, Night of a Thousand Gowns delighted in skewering elite patterns: the printed program announced itself as "A Debutante's Guide" and offered tips on "The Art of Conversation" and correct procedures for "Your Formal Introduction" and the keeping of dance cards. Blauvelt remembered feeling how, this time, his employers' tolerance might be tested: "[The organizers] said, 'You know, it's going to be twelve hundred guys dressed up as women, very formal and controlled.' And I thought, 'Well, I've only been here a couple of years, so I'm going to bump this up the ladder a little bit, just to make sure that there aren't any issues.' And I sent it up to [Hilton] corporate, said, 'This is what we're booking, this is what they're going to do,' and there was an immediate and unhesitating response: 'Of course, why do you even need to ask?'"[5]

On the night of the ball, the "debutantes," arriving with their escorts and entourages, ascended the Park Avenue stairs, then glided into the main lobby. There they posed for the out-of-towners who, eighty years after the heyday of Peacock Alley in the original Fifth Avenue building, still gathered each night to take in what they could of high-toned Manhattan life:

> Our regular, transient guests who were staying in the hotel would come
> down into the lobby on their way to the theater or dinner, and then they
> would see the spectacle of the black ties arriving for the various functions
> in the hotel. It was a parade of society, and people would just sit down in
> the lobby and watch this. But the Night of a Thousand Gowns, when those
> guys started coming in, all dressed up, a lot of our transient hotel guests
> didn't really know what was going on. They just thought they were *very*
> glamorously dressed women.[6]

While a gay and lesbian presence at the Waldorf-Astoria was not exactly new, rarely had it been so visible as it was that night in 1987. Indeed, gay life and events at the hotel can be charted in sequence, moving from a place of secrecy to one in which the existence of men and women who did not identify solely as heterosexual was both acknowledged and celebrated. During the early years of the twentieth century, Joe Smith and his team of Waldorf house detectives spent so much energy rooting out clandestine male-female pairings, those between unwed and adulterous couples, that the possibility of same-sex erotic activity did not seem to enter the field of investigation. Ironically, a form of sexual behavior that would have been considered outré, by standards of the time, carried the least risk of exposure—provided it was engaged in privately, behind the doors of hotel rooms. As Smith explained to his biographer in the late 1920s, "With men it is different . . . a male guest can take another man to his room at any time without . . . making any explanations."[7]

That men *did* use hotel spaces for sexual activity was attested to by Shelton Dewey, a dance instructor who, using the name of Harry Otis, was active in the undercover gay world of 1910s and 1920s New York. In a 1970s letter to gay activist Jim Kepner, Dewey offered frank descriptions of the Sunset Club, which he believed to have been "the oldest gay club in America." Founded by the son of the president of New York Central Railroad, the Sunset Club was reserved for men of high social standing. It had started in 1893 at the old Metropolitan Opera on Thirty-Ninth Street (where, in a studio-residence administered by the Met, Dewey lived as a young man). Later, after the club "got so wild the [Met] management had to close it," the "Sunseters" moved to the Hotel Plaza's Oak Room, which they reserved "for cocktails each day after the market closed." In addition to sponsoring dinners, the Sunset Club held one drag party at the Plaza each season. An atmosphere of propriety obtained: "The men in gowns were ladies of easy elegance suggestive of good breeding and not queens trying to be regal. . . . Camping, limp wrists and bitchy remarks were strictly taboo." Dewey claimed to have seen New York City's fun-loving mayor Jimmy Walker, whom he understood as bisexual, in drag at the balls on several occasions in the 1920s. But the Sunset Club did not limit its Plaza affairs to the purely social: "A lavish suite overlooking Central Park was available for those who wanted sex, day or night throughout the year."[8]

For men with financial means, hotels offered a space in which to explore homosexual inclinations—however those inclinations may have been described or understood by the men themselves. Occasionally, however, the world outside—and its attendant dangers—would intrude. Such was the case in 1948, when the Waldorf-Astoria made headlines for an unwelcome reason: the murder of a fifty-six-year old Canadian textile executive named Colin MacKellar, who had come to New York on business. While visiting the Hotel Astor bar, cited by historian George Chauncey as "a gay meeting place since the 1910s," MacKellar encountered Ralph Edward Barrows, a handsome, well-spoken youth of nineteen with a history of assaulting and robbing older men. Together the pair visited a number of Times Square taverns before winding up at MacKellar's Waldorf suite. There, Barrows attacked his companion, fracturing his skull. A subsequent examination revealed that MacKellar had been kicked so violently that his intestines ruptured. According to the *Daily News* in its coverage of the trial, prosecutors sought to ensure that prospective jurors "would not be influenced by evidence concerning homosexuality." The defense, meanwhile, claimed that Barrows had merely been repelling MacKellar's "improper" and "unnatural" advances, and attempted to paint the Canadian as an aging deviant. In the end, Barrows was found guilty based on the testimony of Waldorf maids who saw the body: MacKellar's pockets had been turned out and emptied. While MacKellar may have made a "verbal allusion," the judge conceded, his killer's prime motive had not been self-defense but robbery. A newspaper photo depicted the young man as he was carried to prison, smiling.[9]

The 1948 Waldorf murder, widely discussed within gay circles, took place at a pivotal moment in the American understanding of sexuality. Earlier that year, Alfred Kinsey had published what would become his landmark study, *Sexual Behavior in the Human Male*, which, in the words of Jim Kepner, told "thousands of lonely and guilty homosexuals that they weren't alone." The book, in which Kinsey and his researchers presented findings that 37 percent of all men had experienced at least one homosexual encounter leading to orgasm, inspired a new level of clinical frankness in discussions of sex. At the same time, the "Kinsey report" led to rebuttal from psychoanalysts such as Edmund Bergler, who argued that homosexuality was an illness that could be cured. This became the dominant medical view in the 1950s, as hostility against gay men and lesbians mounted. In 1953, after a Senate committee determined that "sex perverts," due to a "weakness" in their "moral fiber," were "susceptible to the blandishments of foreign espionage agents," the Eisenhower administration barred homosexuals from federal employment. Similar initiatives enacted outside the governmental sphere—in 1959, for example, the University of Florida dismissed fourteen employees for alleged

Ralph Barrows smiles for photographers as he is taken to prison after being sentenced for the 1948 murder of Colin MacKellar, Canadian textile executive, inside the Waldorf (Anthony Camerano/Shutterstock).

acts of homosexuality—instilled a climate of fear that kept many gay Americans silent and closeted.[10]

For a few, however, the urge to combat prejudice inspired the first stirring of gay activism in the United States. Early organizations associated with what was then called the "homophile" movement, including the Mattachine Society, worked to promote a scientific understanding of homosexuality, drawing on testimony from psychiatrists who questioned the idea of a "cure." They also raised money: in 1961, Mattachine's San Francisco chapter set up a defense fund for 103 men and women arrested after a police raid on a local gay restaurant. A municipal court judge, deriding the city as a "Parisian Pansies' Paradise," had charged patrons with "lewd and dissolute conduct" for same-sex kissing and dancing. At a time when even Mattachine members used pseudonyms in their public statements and newsletters, TV camera crews had been allowed to film the defendants at their arraignment. Meanwhile, the situation in New York, generally thought of as the most tolerant American city for "deviates" (a term used even in sympathetic accounts), was not always better. In December 1963, the State Liquor Authority revoked the licenses of two bars described by the authority chairman as "notorious congregating points for homosexuals and degenerates." Police had obtained evidence by going undercover and thereby outfoxing a light-signal system, common in gay bars of the era, that served to warn partners of the same sex to stop dancing if a cop's presence was suspected. On average, journalist Robert Doty reported in a subsequent article on "the problem of homosexuality" for the *New York Times*, 120 men and women were arrested in the city each year for consensual sodomy between adults, a misdemeanor.[11]

Throughout this period the Waldorf maintained its policy, held since postwar years, of welcoming any group that did not appear on the Attorney General's List of Subversive Organizations. On February 16, 1961, C. E. Kimball, of the hotel's banquet department, wrote a gay New Yorker working under the name "Albert De Dion": "It was indeed a pleasure to have had the opportunity of discussing the possibility of the Waldorf-Astoria acting as headquarters for the Mattachine Society, Incorporated's 1961 convention in New York City." In Claude Philippe's ingratiating style, still a Waldorf trademark two years after Philippe's departure, Kimball assured De Dion that "excellent arrangements can be worked out to the satisfaction of all concerned." The New York convention, designed as a companion to Mattachine's larger gathering in San Francisco, wound up going to the Commodore, no doubt for reasons of cost. But the Waldorf's first gay-oriented event—one in which organizers did not attempt to hide their goals or orientation—was not long in coming. In October 1964 another homophile organization, ONE, Inc., hosted a cocktail party in the fourth-floor Louis XVI Suite. The evening, conceived as a send-off for fifteen ONE members leaving on a seven-country "Cruise of Europe," represented a significant moment in American travel history—the first of many international tours, organized by ONE and other groups, for gay men and women in the coming decades. Guests, not all of whom were traveling, were treated to the full Waldorf experience, as suggested by a report in ONE's newsletter: "At 6 p.m. the elegantly paneled dining-room doors were flung open to reveal a stunningly decorative buffet spread before [the guests] and served at small intimate tables by handsomely garbed waiters, some of whom were distinctly decorative in their own right."[12]

During the speeches that followed, members offered glimpses of a nascent personal awareness and self-affirmation that would reveal themselves, in later years, through initiatives such as National Coming Out Day. At the time of ONE's party, most public socializing between gay people took place in the back rooms of Mafia-owned bars, tucked into side streets far from commercial centers. For ONE's guests to show their faces in a setting as public as the Waldorf was, in itself, a sign of strength. One participant, in a "rousing call" that "made the crystal chandeliers fairly rattle," challenged those present to "shed all pussyfooting and mask-wearing, to stand up and be counted as self-respecting homosexual citizens." Nonetheless, for all the courage activists displayed (one of those present at the Waldorf lamented that "timidity" had "kept some people away"), organizations such as ONE, Inc. and Mattachine generally emphasized the fight for tolerance over acceptance. Americans, it was understood, would never *approve* of homosexuality, but hopefully they could be made to acknowledge gay people as deserving of basic constitutional rights. An excerpt from a 1957 book, titled *Judge Not* and reprinted in Mattachine's newsletter of September 1961, reflected the prevailing thought: "First, it would seem desirable to acknowledge frankly that deviation from the heterosexual ideal is neither a crime, nor an abnormality, but rather a misfortune, for which the individual is not responsible. Secondly that it is desirable to mitigate this unfortunate condition so far as this is possible by removing the [laws against homosexual behavior]."[13]

After the 1969 events at Greenwich Village's Stonewall Inn, where bar patrons and bystanders fought raiding police, the struggle for gay rights became more politicized. Groups such as Gay Liberation Front and Gay Activists Alliance, drawing upon strategies initiated by the Black Panthers and other leftist organizations, took a radical approach designed to force awareness in a direct and, at times, confrontational way—most notably, through the encouragement of "zaps," public acts of disruption conceived to put politicians and officials in uncomfortable positions. In the spring of

1977 the battle expanded nationally when Anita Bryant, an early-1960s pop singer and born-again Christian, led a much-publicized campaign to defeat a bill that would have provided housing and employment protection for gays and lesbians in Florida's Dade County, where she lived. In one "zap," Bryant, who had made headlines with her claims that homosexuals were out to "recruit" children, received a pie in the face during a press conference (with what even enemies had to acknowledge as a clever retort, Bryant quipped, "Well, at least it's a fruit pie"). Determined to fight Bryant using what he described as the "number one" location in the country, Miami activist Bob Kunst organized a "Disco for Democracy" in the Waldorf's Grand Ballroom, where, according to Kunst, he and his life partner, psychologist Alan Rockway, "raised a lot of money" in the effort to "get New Yorkers off their behinds." What happened in Florida, New Yorkers needed to realize, affected gay people across the country: "When we came up to New York, we had to literally go from bar to bar on Christopher Street, [trying] to explain to everybody what was going on."[14]

As Kunst's remarks suggested, gay New Yorkers were often, in the view of organizers, slow to respond to calls for action—perhaps because the city's size and anonymity permitted gay residents to live their lives in relative comfort, provided they didn't stir trouble by drawing attention to themselves (at a time when public hand-holding between lovers, even in Greenwich Village, took on the dimensions of a political act). For this and other reasons, the first dinner benefit of the Human Rights Campaign Fund (HRCF), held at the Waldorf on September 29, 1982, became a watershed in New York history. Founded by lobbyist Steve Endean in 1980, HRCF softened the radical edge of its predecessors by steering gay activism in a consciously mainstream direction. The Waldorf dinner, described by the New York Times as "unlike any other held in New York City before," was notable for the high price of admission—$150 per plate—and also for landing as keynote speaker a name politician, former vice president Walter Mondale. Proceeds for the dinner, which reportedly netted $50,000 (after an outlay of $75,000), went into a fund for the support of gay-friendly candidates in the coming congressional elections. Journalist Andy Humm pointed to the evening as a sign of how far the gay movement had come: "If we had known that that's all it takes to raise big bucks, we would have done it years ago."

"Or would we have?" Humm added. "Could we have?"[15]

As observed by Endean in his posthumously published memoir, Walter Mondale's participation grew out of the specific historical moment: in 1980, the Democratic Party had, for the first time, included sexual orientation in its equal rights platform. Mondale, who previously had evinced signs of queasiness on the subject of gay rights, now sought to promote himself as a liberal leader in tune with the issues of the day. He also wanted to stand favorably against his leading competitor for the 1984 Democratic presidential nomination, Senator Ted Kennedy, a vocal supporter of gay rights (indeed, Endean felt that Mondale would not have participated if the dinner had taken place after Kennedy, navigating a divorce, announced his decision not to run). Nonetheless, Endean and his fellow organizers knew they would have a hard time getting Mondale to use the word "gay" in his spoken address. Verbalization of a term that, within the previous decades, had come to replace old epithets with something positive (in ways that built on "gay's" original meaning) would, in Endean's view, be "critical." Unfortunately, Mondale, "clearly very nervous," botched what generally had been thought of as a foolproof plan. When it came time to speak, the "straitlaced" politician merely thanked his "good friend, Steve Endean," either forgetting or consciously omitting the introduction's second part, "executive director of the Gay Rights National Lobby."[16]

Guests arriving at the Waldorf were reminded of antigay bigotry when, outside the Park Avenue doors, they encountered a group of Orthodox Jewish men bearing signs that proclaimed, "HOMOSEXUALITY IS AN ABOMINATION!!!" Having been subject to these kinds of attacks for most of their lives—whether from schoolyard bullies or homophobic evangelists such as Jerry Falwell—dinner attendees were overjoyed to be the recipients of positive attention and, for a change, encouragement. Their constant standing ovations, journalist Humm observed, "betrayed their obsequiousness toward any straight person who would sit in the same room with known homos." It was a reaction that came to be seen, by critics, as emblematic of

HRCF's annual dinners at the Waldorf. The organization was known for an integrationist stance, one that reached across social and political boundaries to embrace new allies: on occasion, HRCF (later shortened to HRC after "Fund" was dropped from the name) endorsed Republican candidates if they were perceived as sympathetic to gay rights. Observed journalist Bob Nelson, writing for *Gay Community News* in 1982: "HRCF is the product of a movement that is becoming increasingly concerned with its own narrow self-interest . . . and less concerned with broader issues of social justice and feminism or the marginalized members of our own community."[17]

The same night of the first Waldorf benefit, while (in Nelson's account) "800 well-dressed men and women, most of them gay, had just finished their dinner of walnut pate, veal roast and wild rice in the Grand Ballroom," police were entering Blue's, a West Forty-Third Street bar popular with gay African American men and women. There, while "disco music continued to pound through the loudspeakers," officers began swinging batons and beating heads, shouting, "'We'll show you how to fuck with cops!'" Nelson's photos, reprinted in the paper, gave proof of the attack's brutality: blood covered the walls, streaming downward in what resembled the aftermath of a murder. The juxtaposition of concurrent events at two Manhattan sites—one populated by gays with money, the other by those with little financial recourse— emerged as a sign of turbulence to come. With the gay movement becoming "mainstream," Nelson charged, it was now "vulnerable to all the prejudice and narrowmindedness that plague our society." The Waldorf represented, as it had for organizations such as the NAACP in earlier years, legitimacy— proof that a minority group could rise politically through alignment with larger economic forces (indeed, the driving theme of Mondale's speech had been that discrimination was bad for business). Gays with money, HRCF's success at the Waldorf seemed to indicate, could withstand and even overcome cultural antipathy—but what about those who were less fortunate?[18]

In the summer of 1981, newspapers had carried accounts of a "rare and often rapidly fatal form of cancer," diagnosed among forty-one gay men in New York and California. "Gay Cancer? Or Mass Media Scare?" questioned a report in the *Gay News* of London, Ontario, that November. The writers, both doctors who would later succumb to AIDS, viewed early reports of the disease with ambivalence, pointing out the "long history" of the "threat of venereal disease" as a way to "discourage sexual activity." But by the start of 1985, the number of reported AIDS cases had risen to 8,000 in the United States alone; with each passing span of six to twelve months, it had doubled. Meanwhile, President Ronald Reagan, who still had not mentioned the word "AIDS" in a public setting, seemed disinterested in the epidemic that was spreading under his watch. For young gay men coming to New York, it would be hard to reconcile lovemaking's excitement with the idea that something life-affirming could also kill. Novelist David Leavitt confessed the disease frightened him "so much" that he "wanted to block it out" of his mind. Human Rights Campaign Fund dinners at the Waldorf were generally not occasions for the facing of hard reality. As with all banquets and galas, people went there to forget their fears momentarily, not to be reminded of them. But Leavitt recalled one Waldorf party, around 1985, when writer and activist Larry Kramer insisted on breaking through what he viewed as HRCF's passivity: "I watched [Kramer] shake his fist at his audience and declare, 'Half of you in this room could be dead in five years,' and when no one responded, say again, this time louder, 'Half of you in this room could be dead in five years,' and when again no one responded, scream, 'Half of you in this room could be dead in five years!' this time so loudly some left the room."[19]

While the AIDS crisis united forces within the gay movement, it also sharpened divisions. In March 1987, Kramer and other activists founded the AIDS Coalition to Unleash Power (ACT UP) at the Lesbian and Gay Community Center in Greenwich Village. Reactivating the zaps and other confrontational tactics of earlier gay organizations, ACT UP combined Martin Luther King's policy of nonviolence with bold displays of theatricality. More federal money for AIDS research, speedier trials for experimental drugs, wider promotion of condoms and needle exchange—these were the goals for which ACT UP fought. With its loose organizational structure (there were never any chairpersons or directors), ACT UP drew upon the efforts of numerous "affinity groups," each composed of between five and fifteen people united by a specific cause or interest. These affinity groups, limited in size and focus, were able to execute demonstrations with a speed and efficiency that would have been difficult in larger numbers. In the description of activist Ron Goldberg, an actor who joined ACT UP in 1987, "Affinity groups were responsible for everything: for creating the action, for support—who's going to be on the outside, who's going to monitor you if you get arrested—for props, poster design. The affinity group thing [was] kind of amorphous. One of the understood things was that if you're doing an affinity group action, you don't put the general group at risk. You break off, you do it separately."[20]

In a 1992 protest, members of ACT UP marched with the open coffin of Mark Lowe Fisher (a thirty-eight-year-old architect who had proclaimed, "I want my own funeral to be fierce and defiant") from Greenwich Village to Republican Party headquarters on Forty-Third Street. In another, they drove to Washington and poured the ashes of friends who had died of AIDS on the White House lawn. Most notoriously, in 1989 they interrupted mass at St. Patrick's Cathedral—an action that included one member's crumbling of a communion wafer, in an unplanned show of contempt for the Catholic Church. At the time mainstream media tended to ignore all but the most dramatic gay-themed events; "softer" gay coverage was consigned largely to public-access television and small papers such as *Big Apple Dyke News*. Only by raising AIDS awareness to the level of controversy, ACT UP believed, could it gain the exposure needed for the Reagan and Bush administrations to begin acknowledging the epidemic's toll on American life. In the process ACT UP often entered into conflict with other gay organizations, particularly the Human Rights Campaign Fund, whose accommodationist stance the younger group found overly polite and out of touch. In 1990 ACT UP disrupted the annual HRCF dinner at the Waldorf, as members handed out flyers criticizing the Fund's decision to honor the Gay Games and its late founder, onetime Olympian Tom Waddell: "Dr. Tom Waddell is dead! He died from a disease called AIDS. Most of you may have heard of it."[21]

ACT UP charged the Gay Games with "blatantly" excluding "people of color, women, the elderly, people with physical disabilities (even the ones who are HIV infected) and people from lower socioeconomic backgrounds." It reminded HRCF's guests that the conservative Waddell had been "adamant about NOT ALLOWING drag queens, dykes on bikes, and the leather crowd from [sic] participating in the Gay Games." But its biggest complaint was that Games organizers had chosen to hold the coming 1994 celebrations in New York City, at a time when the U.S. Immigration and Naturalization Service barred entry to all foreigners who were known to be HIV-positive. As with most of ACT UP's protests, the larger target was, in fact, the U.S. government—particularly its then commander in chief, President George Bush, who once characterized AIDS as "a disease where you can control its spread by your own personal behavior." ACT UP members, many of them well-connected professionals in the visual and performing arts, had all the tools for honoring their mission as printed, in bold letters, on the Gay Games flyer: "People with AIDS and HIV infection will not be made invisible . . . !" And, in the Waldorf—used, in the recollection of Ron Goldberg, "repeatedly," to demonstrate against "visiting presidents"—they had an ideal stage.[22]

———

Even by the stodgy standards of political dinners, the New York State Republican Party fundraiser, scheduled for the Waldorf's Grand Ballroom on July 24, 1990, held little promise of excitement. New York Republicans, still suffering the loss of Nelson Rockefeller (who had died in 1979) and former mayor John Lindsay, who was out of public life after defecting to the Democrats, were weakened to the point that not even the promise of a speech by President Bush could nudge ticket sales above 400—some 700 less than expected. Worse, the presumptive honoree, Canadian-born economist Pierre "Pete" Rinfret, running for governor against the Democratic incumbent, Mario Cuomo, was viewed as an awkwardly dull candidate, even, as *Newsday* reported, by those "within his own party." That evening, when it came time for Rinfret to step to the Waldorf's dais, he tripped. Bush, who flouted custom by not meeting with the candidate privately, flew in early to give a decidedly unenthusiastic endorsement: "[Rinfret] may not be a politician, but maybe New York doesn't need another politician." Indeed, the night was set to become controversial only for Bush's splenetic remarks about New York as "a showcase of liberal policies" that had been responsible for "bad schools, dangerous streets, big deficits," and a city that "lives in fear." That, and the fact that the Waldorf's crack banquet team somehow slipped: despite requests made by advance planners in three separate phone calls, Bush's famously detested vegetable—broccoli—had found its way to the dinner menu.[23]

All in all, it seemed the Waldorf's other event that evening—a business seminar, "Future Global Ventures," being held one flight above the Grand Ballroom in the fourth-floor Duke of Windsor Suite, boasted a more committed group of attendees. Young men in Armani suits, sporting hair inspired by the movie *Wall Street* (slicked back, like that of Michael Douglas's rapacious Gordon Gekko) and accompanied by women in heels and cocktail dresses, made their way past an easel with signage promoting a talk on American financial dominance. One attendee carried a copy of *Fortune* magazine, tucked under his arm. Perhaps the New York State Republicans had missed their target. Here, a young generation, inspired by Gekko's "Greed Is Good" mantra (so what if director Oliver Stone had conceived Gekko as a villain?), were appearing to mobilize themselves for quick, easy money. From their looks, these children of the Reagan era favored high-end designers over Brooks Brothers and had no interest in what they likely would have derided as a rubber-chicken dinner. Observed one Republican senator, in discussing the Bush event's poor showing, "Very, very honestly, what's happened is that the New York market has been saturated with fund-raisers . . . people are just really dried out."[24]

At an early spot in the evening, as Republicans milled about the ballroom's outer foyer (used for pre-meal receptions), nine "Future Global Ventures" attendees left the Duke of Windsor Suite upstairs. They crossed a hallway to an elevator but discovered it wasn't programmed to stop at the ballroom. So the men and women—no longer pretending to be Gekkos—moved farther, to a bank of stairs on the Waldorf's eastern end, walked down, and pushed through a door: "We realized we had succeeded in landing on the 'safe side' of the security screens, right down the hall from the reception." Lifting signs—"Bush: End Bigotry," "Open Borders to HIV Positive Lesbians and

Gays"—they walked and shouted until the "press and secret service sur-rounded" them. Then the nine—all members of "the Costas," an ACT UP affinity group named after artist Costa Pappas—moved to an open area close to the Republicans, sat down, and chanted: "Stop Bigotry, Open the Borders, Bush Has the Power." Their goal, as with the Gay Games action, was to draw attention to immigration policy and denial of entry to People with AIDS (PWAs). Finally, the Costas "were interviewed by TV press" for late-news cov-erage. When that was over, they "got up and left" of their "own volition."[25]

Meanwhile, those ACT UP members still inside the Duke of Windsor Suite grabbed the ends of a banner, stretched it to the room's far corners and let it fall from the windows. On the street below, a crowd of 600 cheered. White let-ters emerged from a dark background, mocking Bush's unlived-up-to cam-paign slogan on taxes: "READ OUR LIPS: AIDS ACTION NOW." Fellow activists who were gathered on the corner of Forty-Ninth Street and Park Avenue—the outdoor flank of what ACT UP had designated, internally, as its "Bushlips" demonstration—lifted hollow, six-sided boxes shaped like coffins and decorated with skulls in which the eyeballs, glaring and accusatory, had been left to hover in their sockets. Others hoisted signs with the same words imposed on an angry-looking mouth filled with teeth—"George: Deja de Hablar Mierda," urged the sign's Spanish-language version: "Stop Talking Shit." Simultaneously, pro-choice demonstrators from the National Organiza-tion of Women (NOW), having joined the protest, held a five-foot wire hanger covered in fake blood, as they chanted, "Keep your laws off my body!"[26]

Protesters had arrived at the Waldorf by way of a New Orleans–style funeral procession that launched—in ACT UP's extension of the "lips" metaphor—at the Forty-Second Street Public Library, temple of reading and knowledge. Mournful sax, high trumpets, bleating trombones—all of it was underpinned by a slow drumbeat as the line advanced through the humid blocks. Frustrated drivers pressed horns, spewing car exhaust and four-letter words. Sweating beneath their death masks, activists shouted, "Serial Killer," as indictment of the president who had skipped an interna-tional AIDS conference in order to appear at a fundraiser for Jesse Helms, the gay-baiting senator. One punk-styled protester made the most of his

ACT UP "Bushlips" demonstration, July 24, 1990 (Dona Ann McAdams).

mohawk by attaching a button—"Silence = Death," ACT UP's official slogan, beneath a pink triangle—to the tip of each angry spike. Those closest to the Waldorf gathered mock dollar bills, tossed from upper windows by another affinity group, the Marys, who had also gotten inside ("people had real jobs," recalled one ACT UP member, "and knew how to call up a hotel" to rent a room). The bills were printed with figures that reflected the expansion of AIDS from crisis to epidemic, with no cure in sight: "1.5 million HIV-positive Americans . . . and counting."[27]

By now, a group of ACT UP members, having completed their activity in the fourth-floor conference rooms, were heading downstairs to the hotel's ground level. Spilling from elevators and covered in fake blood, they collapsed outside the main lobby entrance in a "die-in," writhing on the heavy Waldorf carpet. In an Associated Press photo appearing the next day, a policeman's muscular forearm reached down to grab a young man who resembled the victim of an execution: bloodstains covered his white polo shirt and khakis as he lay in a contorted pose, hands behind his back. Journalists marveled at how ACT UP had managed to evade metal detectors, police, and Secret Service agents in their infiltration of the Waldorf. "We were a lot of white guys," explained Ron Goldberg, referring to an exemption from the surveillance that was often applied, throughout the city and elsewhere, to people of color—"professional, of a certain age": "I could walk into any building without getting stopped, if I had a tie on. The amount of access— to resources, whether it was money, whether it was who knew *who*—was mind-boggling. And the idea that you could then take advantage of this. AIDS was such a broad topic. It was a nexus of all these late twentieth-century issues and problems. You could access that network of resources and do something to deal with needle exchange, something in terms of housing and homelessness for PWAs."[28]

ACT UP's own Housing Committee—it would later evolve into the non-profit Housing Works—took on what became the night's most audacious stunt. After dropping the "READ OUR LIPS" banner from the Duke of Windsor Suite, twelve members—among them a handsome Baptist minister, Charles King, and his African American lover, Keith Cylar, along with ACT UP cofounder Eric Sawyer—took an elevator downstairs and invaded the rose-scented main lobby. There they set off a team of airhorns in a wail so deafening it could be heard by Republicans two floors up. Tossing scraps of lipstick-covered paper, the twelve began to gather around the 1893 Columbian Exposition clock, its width now extended by a cushiony blue sofa. Then they handcuffed themselves, arm to outstretched arm, in a circle with the shiny symbol of Americanism—almost every side depicting a U.S. president—at its center. As Goldberg noted, "We used [the theme of] time a lot" in protests. Here was an opportunity: with the clock emitting chimes on the quarter hour, ACT UP responded with a chant, "ONE AIDS DEATH EVERY 10 MINUTES." The Victorian Waldorf of George Boldt and its 1990 descendant were meeting up, after a century's span, and finding themselves out of sync—a waltz unable to keep pace with the frantic rhythm of electronic house music. The Waldorf's regular lobby-sitters looked on as hotel workers called security.[29]

ACT UP "die-in," entrance to Waldorf lobby, July 24, 1990 (AP Photo/
Malcolm Clarke).

"That's America!" exclaimed then managing director, Per Hellman. For the recently restored Waldorf, it had been another return to the 1930s, when Selden Rodman and his pro-union friends, dodging tableware, led the "Battle of the Empire Room"—only this time the battle was fought by larger numbers of troops, who operated on multiple fronts inside the hotel. Hellman, a Swedish immigrant who had gotten his first Waldorf job in 1961, followed the maxim set by Boomer and other Waldorf leaders: stay calm in the face of hysteria. He chuckled at the remembrance of ACT UP's boldness: "They handcuffed themselves around the clock! You don't get too upset about it. You had to have a pretty cool head to work at the Waldorf-Astoria."[30]

The success of "Bushlips" could be gauged through its next-day press coverage, which downplayed Bush's speech in favor of the brash and daring activists. One photo, taken outside the Waldorf, captured a stylish young woman who had jumped the police barricade, just as "a burly cop" prepared to throw her "over his shoulder" on the way to the patrol wagon. Her lips curved with the hint of a smile (for ACT UP this was nothing new: cofounder Eric Sawyer recalled being "arrested [at the Waldorf] at least three times"). The *Daily News* relegated what Republicans likely hoped would be a cute sidebar—the Waldorf's broccoli mishap—to the bottom of a page dominated by a shot of protesters facing off against officers on horseback. "It's Prez' Night on the Town," the headline announced playfully. At a time when Bush wanted to assure his public that everything in America was fine—his 1988 campaign song had been Bobby McFerrin's "Don't Worry, Be Happy"—ACT UP forced a reshaping of the narrative. It seized attention in ways that made Americans understand the magnitude of the AIDS epidemic. Speaking to National Public Radio in 2019, author David France discussed one of ACT UP's biggest successes: pressuring the government to accelerate research on the lifesaving drugs—antiretroviral therapy, made available in 1996—that marked the first tangible victory in the fight against AIDS: "ACT UP's ethos was that they had united in anger. The task of ACT UP was to take that anger and turn it into action. They were no longer invisible sufferers of a disease. . . . What they were able to revolutionize was really the very way that drugs are identified and tested."[31]

At times ACT UP fell subject to the same criticism it had leveled against the Human Rights Campaign—that it was elitist and dominated by white men. ACT UP's weekly meetings gained a reputation, within the gay community of the early 1990s, for the presence of handsome, gym-bodied youth who reinforced a certain idealized standard of erotic male desire. Not everyone felt included: one female member, speaking at the first meeting held after the "Bushlips" action, requested that "all committees be more sensitive to women's issues." Explained Charles King, who was arrested at the Waldorf along with Keith Cylar, "ACT UP never really understood the deep, intricate link between homophobia and social and economic injustice writ large." Still, King observed, "[ACT UP] really was in so many ways the culmination of gay liberation." For people "forced" out of the closet because of AIDS, it "gave them a vehicle [through which] to fight." A 1990 *New York Times* article quoted an ACT UP member who recalled going to his first demonstration "in sunglasses," so that coworkers wouldn't recognize him in photos: "There's always a tendency for gays and lesbians to be a little apologetic about ourselves. But the position we should be coming from is, 'This is who we are and we've got nothing to apologize for.'"[32]

ACT UP discovered its power through the remaking of public space. Like drugstore lunch counters in the 1950s South, where activists conducted "sit-ins" to protest segregation, the Waldorf-Astoria could instantly transform into a site of contest. When ACT UP seized the Waldorf, it gained an upper hand in the fight for visibility: reporters instinctively bypassed mild Pierre Rinfret in favor of blood-slathered young people, chanting and firing air-horns. In size and strategy "Bushlips" climaxed decades of Waldorf-Astoria protests. Earlier groups had largely been content to remain outside the hotel, carrying signs, jeering visitors, and demonstrating on the sidewalk. ACT UP, going a step further, used the hotel's core standards of hospitality to its benefit. Manager Per Hellman recalled something about the activists that would unite them with Golda Meir and Yasser Arafat, red-baiting Walter Winchell and Dmitri Shostakovich, Nancy Reagan and the Hainsworth welfare family—everyone, indeed, who ever passed through the Waldorf's doors and took a room or a meal: they had "come in as guests."[33]

In September 1991 the Waldorf-Astoria took the unusual step of cosponsoring a conference in the Astor Salon. Rarely if ever had the hotel allowed its name to be used in a way that would suggest any kind of endorsement. But "Invisible Diversity" was atypical in more than one sense. Subtitled "A Gay and Lesbian Corporate Agenda," the conference was the first to explore issues of discrimination and sexual orientation in the American workplace. Mayor David Dinkins, citing the "valuable contribution gay men and lesbians" had made to the "daily life and business of New York," kicked off a series of discussions led by representatives from companies including AT&T and Levi Strauss. In the spirit of Walter Mondale's 1982 address for the Human Rights Campaign Fund (also, as it happened, a sponsor of "Invisible Diversity"), a number of speeches emphasized the ways that antigay prejudice hampered productivity and was therefore detrimental to business. Others explored the methods through which gay workers banded to form support groups and to lobby for partner benefits. At a time when only four U.S. states protected sexual orientation in the private sector, the conference also drew attention to employee vulnerability: one panel featured Cheryl Summerville, a cook for the Cracker Barrel chain who had been fired that year because, in the words of a company statement, her "sexual preferences" failed "to demonstrate normal heterosexual values."[34]

AIDS brought new urgency to questions of health coverage and employment. On the job, gay people "had almost no protections," observed Ed Mickens, a writer and employment specialist who organized the Waldorf conference. Given the absence of legal support, workers had to face the challenge of appealing to their companies for benefits such as domestic partner insurance. One of "Invisible Diversity's" goals was to create a model they could use for the future. According to Mickens, the conference inspired a number of similar, follow-up events organized and led by the rank and file: "We were empowering employees to stand up and say, 'Look, this is what we need.' They had our materials to support them: this is what's going on at Levi Strauss, this is what's going on at Xerox."[35]

Long-term effects notwithstanding, there was no denying that "Invisible Diversity"—with sessions titled "Establishing Standards" and "What Companies Gain"—reflected a slant toward the goals and interests of management. Writing for the gay newsmagazine the *Advocate*, journalist Donna Minkowitz criticized the conference's organizers for appearing, in her view, "to speak for queer working stiffs in absentia, as though the anger of real live lesbian and gay employees in nonmanagerial positions would have been too much for corporate executives to deal with." Cracker Barrel cook Summerville, she felt, had represented the "garnish, not the main course," and "the conference was clearly not intended for [workers], even though all the speakers blathered on about diversity." To Mickens, this kind of response pointed to the divisions that still, nearly ten years after HRCF's first dinner at the Waldorf, manifested themselves within the gay community as it fought for acceptance: "[The conference] was such a formal event. Back in those days, we were still dealing with our rabble-rousing roots: the Stonewall-outsider kind of mentality. The fact that you had all of these button-down folks coming forward as activists, and that this was at the Waldorf-Astoria—and that major corporations paid money to come and hear it—really sent a shock wave through the community."[36]

Indeed, Mickens recalled how his greatest concern was not the threatening mail that arrived in response to a promotional flyer sent to companies— angry letters and death threats were the occasional accompaniment to his work as a journalist covering gay issues—but the possibility of a "disruptive action by ACT UP." A proposal, he heard, "had been discussed at an ACT UP New York meeting," with the goal of "sticking it to the corporations," but nothing official was passed—likely because ACT UP was occupied that month with multiple anti-Bush demonstrations, including a parade and mass die-in at the president's ancestral home of Kennebunkport, Maine. Still, Mickens feared an ACT UP affinity group might do "something rogue," and, as a result, "all of us organizers, as well as Waldorf security, were on high alert the whole day."[37]

According to Mickens, the conference was originally considered for the auditorium of the Lesbian and Gay Community Center. However, the center had not yet been renovated, and organizers "knew the setting had to be top-notch corporate." An attorney named Michael C. P. Ryan, associated with "one of New York's most prominent law firms," offered to lead the search for space. At a meeting soon after, "he came in and announced, 'We have the Waldorf-Astoria.'" The hotel was offering to donate the entire conference space, along with the Starlight Roof, where attendees would gather for an evening reception that was open to the general public. In exchange the Waldorf asked for program credit as a cosponsor. "All of us were stunned and delighted," Mickens recalled, adding that the "contact and arrangements" with the hotel were likely made "the old-fashioned way, through discreet personal connections. Gay men and lesbians had long used this approach with success. [Michael C. P. Ryan] had a connection to somebody who was comfortable enough with a high-ranking staffer to float the idea and get results. Somebody at the Waldorf took a courageous step."[38]

With its contributions to the "Invisible Diversity" conference, the Waldorf-Astoria reasserted itself, in a subtle way, as an influencer of American life. For nearly a century, it had been first among hotels, setting standards and even, at times, anticipating change. By the middle 1990s, the Conrad N. Hilton College of Hotel and Restaurant Management at the University of Houston had established the Hospitality Industry Diversity Institute, offering "research, education, and resolutions in diversity issues" as related to employment. Meanwhile, the hospitality field had moved toward a more conscious awareness of the spending power of lesbians and gay men. One tourism specialist noted, in 1997, that "most quality mainstream hotels" had become, since the start of the decade, "well-suited . . . to meet the needs of the gay traveler." Back at the Waldorf, journalist Henry Alford, writing for *New York* magazine in 1996, decided to test the waters by appearing in person to claim, with his partner, that he was "getting married" and wanted to have a "ceremony and reception at the hotel." Meeting a "clean-cut, polished corporate fellow in his early thirties named Jim" (likely, Jim Blauvelt of the banquet department), Alford asked if a same-sex wedding would be acceptable to the Waldorf: "On our ensuing tour of the hotel, this charming gentleman made every indication that it was."[39]

In 2007, four years before the legalization of same-sex marriage in New York State, playwright Terrence McNally's *Some Men* appeared at Manhattan's Second Stage Theater. Spanning 1920s Hamptons to the then present, the play uses a multitude of characters to reflect on the struggles that united gay men in New York as well as set them apart. In the first scene, Bernie, an older man attending a gay wedding at the Waldorf, observes how the hotel "used to be quite the place for very discreet assignations." As vows are exchanged, the action shifts back to 1968, when Bernie is a closeted husband and father meeting Zach (a Columbia student and part-time sex worker) at the hotel for a paid encounter. Bernie is nervous, afraid of noises he perceives at the guest room door: "I think hotels like the Waldorf-Astoria have house detectives." The scene ends with Zach asking Bernie, "What's it going to be?" Though directed toward the specifics of erotic preference, writer McNally makes clear that the question speaks to broader choices along the path to a life of honesty and fulfillment. In the play's closing scene, when different generations dance with one another at the wedding reception, it's evident that the Waldorf-Astoria, as a societal institution, has traveled with the characters, accompanying them as they've moved out of a place of fear, toward one of openness and visibility.

Epilogue

In 1999, journalist Terry Trucco, longing to explore the mystique of the "grand hotel"—associated with "crystal chandeliers suspended from an impossibly high ceiling and plenty of fat sofas for watching a parade of visitors from around the world"—checked into the Waldorf-Astoria. She found much of what she was hoping for (the "older man" in tuxedo who "snored contentedly" in a lobby chair), along with a bit of what she wasn't. Her bathroom was lit by nothing more than a "dim florescent sconce"; the teaspoon that came with her room service hadn't been washed. Not every "grande dame," she admitted, "is as grande as it once was." While the Waldorf in the first decade of the twenty-first century enjoyed its share of big moments—the 2002 World Economic Forum, normally held in Switzerland, brought celebrities along with antiglobalization demonstrators—it nonetheless became, in the eyes of many, a symbol of past glory more than of present vitality. The hotel's reputation took a hit beginning in 2010 with a series of lawsuits, filed by guests, alleging they had been bitten by bedbugs during their stay. *Crain's* reported how the "Waldorf's stature" had, without doubt, "played a role" in the decision, made by a personal injury lawyer representing a couple from Michigan, "to hold a press conference" announcing their complaint. The result was a "public relations nightmare" that threatened, for a time, to link one of New York's most prestigious hotels with the unsavory Pennsylvania—a locus of 1940s big-band music now given over to insects and crime.[1]

But if the Waldorf wasn't quite what it had been, the same could be said of New York. The political vivacity that, years before, spurred the hotel to greatness had weakened in the twenty-first-century city. For many people, the United Nations once symbolized hope—a feeling central, as Jan Morris has suggested, to the experience of cities—but in the 2010s New Yorkers were more likely to reflect upon the UN as a cause of traffic jams. On a local level, it had been some time since New York had had a "personality mayor" in the style of Jimmy Walker, La Guardia, or even Rudy Giuliani—who, whatever else could have been said about him, never softened in his determination to remain a visible fixture. No longer could New Yorkers observe the symbiosis that prevailed, during the twentieth century, between large Manhattan hotels, City Hall, and institutions such as the *New York Times* (it was once asserted that Mayor Lindsay made key decisions based on his daily reading of the *Times*' editorial page—decisions he would then defend, on occasion, through speeches or interviews given at the Waldorf). While hotels would always be part of the New York landscape, it was uncertain if the city would continue to *need* one as significant, politically, as the Waldorf-Astoria.[2]

In 2015, not long after the Waldorf's sale to Anbang Insurance Group, the U.S. government announced that President Obama would no longer be staying at the hotel during his visits to New York. Even under the best of circumstances, explained the *Times*, hotels had "long represented a weak link in security for traveling officials" (one former government aide spoke of how the president's typical security detail in a hotel resembled "something like a mini submarine"). For decades, the Waldorf had been trusted. Now, under the ownership of Anbang, a company with close connections to the Chinese government, it could no longer be counted on to provide a secure environment: Why else, remarked one State Department official, "would you not stay at the Waldorf?" With the exception of Jimmy Carter, who, manager Joe Rantisi recalled, felt the Waldorf "was too expensive" and "didn't reflect his values of being frugal in his government," every U.S. president since Hoover had made of the hotel a temporary home during his tenure (Carter eventually stayed in the Presidential Suite, 35A, but after he left office). The State Department's subsequent decision, later in 2015, not to renew its lease on the U.S. ambassador's residence, 42A, signaled that the Waldorf's long history as a center of American political life was officially over.[3]

That didn't mean, however, that it had nothing left to contribute to the life of the city. In her 2018 book, *Honeybee Hotel*, naturalist Leslie Day writes of how Waldorf chefs reached out, in the early 2010s, to their next-door neighbor on Park Avenue, St. Bartholomew's Episcopal Church. St. Bart's had recently expanded its community outreach program, and the Waldorf believed it could help. Soon the two organizations were coordinating a system in which leftover food would be used, each day, to feed the homeless of New York. By 2012 the initiative had grown to include events such as Fare Share Friday, an annual post–Thanksgiving Day dinner held in the nave of St. Bart's. In 2014 the Waldorf secured the involvement of chefs at another hotel, the Lotte New York Palace, and the food-sharing program grew again: attendees at Fare Share Friday would now be made up of both the homeless and paying guests. In 2016 Day and her husband, having volunteered as servers during earlier years, decided to purchase tickets for the dinner instead. Sitting among people from "every walk of life," they experienced a night of "compassion, understanding, and plenitude." A quote from Day's interview with David Garcelon, the Waldorf's then director of culinary, reinforces how goals promoted by Lucius Boomer still informed the way the hotel conceived of itself in the twenty-first century: "'We are lucky with our resources . . . we can do more than most, and we should . . . ; that's part of being a good citizen, a good member of the community.'"[4]

All along Anbang had made clear its intention to convert a portion of the Waldorf into luxury condos. Soon after the hotel's closing, in March 2017, the venerable architectural firm of Skidmore, Owings & Merrill (founded in 1936) released its first digital renderings of the new design, which promised to reclaim "the full potential of one of New York City's most legendary buildings." The project appeared to be moving swiftly. Soon, though, signs of trouble began to appear. In June, Anbang's suave chairman, Wu Xiaohui, who in little more than a decade had transformed his company from a relatively small auto insurer into a giant with assets of $253 billion in U.S. dollars, was detained by Chinese authorities as part of an investigation into fraud. The following February, as Wu faced prosecution for illegal activity, the Chinese government seized temporary control of Anbang—a sign, financial experts believed, that China was working to crack down on risky overseas investment. Wu was eventually sentenced to eighteen years in prison. Meanwhile, at the Waldorf, little had taken place aside from interior demolition and what was described in the press as "pre-construction." By June 2019, Anbang, under the direction of its Chinese regulators, was taking bids in an effort to unload some of its largest American hotel assets, among them the Essex House on Central Park South. The Waldorf, however, was kept out of the portfolio: clearly, Anbang still held hopes for it. In July the company announced that its Waldorf condos, now given a new name—the Towers of the Waldorf-Astoria—were at last ready to be placed on sale.[5]

By 2019, though, New York's luxury condo market, suffering from a glut of oversupply, was hardly what it had been two years earlier. In September the *Times* reported that one in four of the city's new condo units was lacking a buyer. Manhattan alone had an estimated 9,000 empty units that would take, at "the current pace," nine years to sell. The foreign investors who had once viewed New York's high-rise apartments as opportunities for what journalist Julie Satow characterized as "depositing money in the real estate version of a Swiss bank account" were staying away, deterred by a higher mansion tax (implemented to fund repair of the city's decaying subway system) and concerns over the potential for another economic downturn. A spokesperson for Douglas Elliman Development Marketing, the company overseeing condo sales for the Waldorf, expressed hope that the site's rich history would encourage buyers: "In times of uncertainty, people gravitate toward something that feels certain and constant." But by year's end the launch for the project's 375 condos had again been delayed. Days after the sales office finally opened, in March 2020, the real estate market, like everything else, froze.[6]

———

April 2020

Manhattanites have often been able to preserve the notion that death resides in some indefinite spot far from the island: due to limitations of space, they don't even see many graveyards. The Waldorf-Astoria, with its cultivation of ideals related to permanence and relevancy, fed into this illusion: it was the city at its most resolutely alive. Like the AIDS crisis in the worst days of the 1980s and 1990s, COVID has forced New Yorkers to face mortality to a degree that is terrifying and immediate. In the days after the attacks of September 11, 2001, as black smoke hovered above rooftops and signs for the missing filled the surfaces of walls and lampposts, we found comfort in being together. Public spaces—restaurants, bars, hotel lobbies—offered refuge for the stunned and grieving. Many of us took to the streets, crossing the West Side Highway and dropping off supplies at the relief station there. Through giving us sites for active engagement, the city itself became a tonic. In the spring of 2020, though, New Yorkers were struggling with something different, and the only response to the challenge lay in physical isolation. The loss of the Waldorf in 2017 robbed New York of one of its great spaces, at a time when it was becoming increasingly difficult to find enclosed areas in which to sit without spending money. But that loss is now overshadowed by one in which our very understanding of space—as fosterer of dialogue and engagement—is being questioned.

When the Waldorf eventually reopens, it, like so many institutions, won't be the place we knew. But there is one hopeful spot: just before the hotel closed, the New York City Landmarks Preservation Commission was allowed inside to make a quick assessment. Soon after, the commission voted unanimously to landmark most of the hotel's interior on the main floor and ballroom level, singling out the Park Avenue lobby, the Silver Gallery with its murals from the original Waldorf, the Basildon Room and Empire Room, along with balustrades, elevator doors, pillars, and ceiling reliefs. It can be said with reasonable assurance that the Waldorf-Astoria will remain a place of beauty. Its polished walnut and nickeled bronze will continue to inspire; the Columbian Exposition clock will remind us of time, just as the *Wheel of Life* mosaic will assert a potential for rebirth. But, in all likelihood, the Waldorf will cease being a place where strangers can walk in off the street and experience the joy of anonymity, of occupying a space for no reason other than the desire to observe and be part of something larger than themselves. With several hundred rooms, it will be a boutique hotel, not a grand one. None of us will think of it as a city within a city. But at the right moments—attending an event in the Grand Ballroom, perhaps, or else striding through the lobby on a guided tour—we'll be able to come to the Waldorf-Astoria and be reminded of our eventful, and hospitable, American past.

Acknowledgments

This project began at a time of personal challenge, with the loss of my father, and ended during one of national and global crisis. In between I gained an appreciation for the special role that hotels have played in our society. As hosts, they provide space in which we celebrate our successes, air differences, and find unity in struggle and defeat. Throughout this book, I've emphasized the ways in which the American hotel has reflected larger societal events. As I write this, New York City's hotels are being used to house emergency medical workers—a reminder that hotels are perhaps the only institutions established, by definition, to meet two of the three basic human needs. Right now, they are both reflecting current problems and contributing, in some way, to their amelioration.

My deepest thanks go to my agent, Jane Dystel, of Dystel, Goderich & Bourret LLC. Not only did Jane conceive of the idea for this book, but her persistence, thoughtfulness, and kind support carried it from the proposal stage to completion. Special thanks also go to Eric Myers, for first suggesting me and for his encouragement and friendship. I'd also like to thank Peter Mickulas, my editor at Rutgers University Press, for his helpful ideas and suggestions, perceptive comments, and sharp editorial insight—as well as for being such an enthusiastic supporter of this project from the beginning.

Louise Tobin, lead vocalist with Benny Goodman's band at the Waldorf in 1939, was one of the first people I interviewed. Friendly and gregarious, Tobin offered a living link to the Waldorf of the 1930s and a sign of how the hotel sought the best in musical talent. My thanks go not only to Tobin but also to her son, Harry James Jr., who offered valuable insight into the working experience of musicians during the big band era. Another early discussion was with Frank Lewin, who shared loving memories of his mother, Merriel Abbott. Claudia Philippe, with whom I also spoke in the beginning stage of research, provided valuable observations of her father, Claude. These people helped shape my understanding of the Waldorf as a place of creativity, and I'm indebted to them all.

Two former general managers, Joe Rantisi and Per Hellman, offered helpful insight into the operation of the Waldorf at an administrative level. Rantisi, in particular, sharpened my awareness of how the Waldorf viewed itself as a community institution. His sincerity and generosity were most appreciated. Enormous thanks also go to the late Tom Margittai, who started his long, remarkable career by working at the Waldorf under Claude Philippe and who offered a candid assessment of his former boss's personality. I'm extremely grateful to the late Diahann Carroll for going back in her memories to the summer of 1957 and her appearances at the Waldorf's Starlight Roof; to Dr. Mark Young, of the Hospitality Industry Archives at the University of Houston, for the welcome he and his staff gave me in October 2018, as well as his insight into the life and work of Conrad Hilton; to Ed Mickens, for sharing a behind-the-scenes perspective on the challenges and rewards of the 1991 "Invisible Diversity" conference; and to James Locker, for his recollections of working at the Waldorf in the years before it closed. Ron Goldberg offered indispensable documents related to the 1990 ACT UP "Bushlips" action at the Waldorf, as well as fascinating details of his own involvement with ACT UP. And to Dr. Victor Hainsworth, I extend much gratitude for his humor, trust, and willingness to share impressions of his and his family's experience at the Waldorf in 1971.

My thanks also go to all of the other people who shared firsthand impressions of events detailed in this book: Alan Baer, the Waldorf's Jim Blauvelt (whose cordiality, humor, and vast knowledge were a pleasure to experience), John Consigli, Sid Davidoff, Drew Fetherston, Norman Hill, Charles King, Bob Kunst, Eric Sawyer, and Karen Stockbridge.

I also owe great appreciation to those who assisted, in various ways, with the book's research and development: Jay Blotcher of ACT UP; John Calhoun and Steve Massa of the New York Public Library for the Performing Arts; Eleanor Gillers and Charina Castillo of the New-York Historical Society; Kenneth Cobb of the NYC Department of Records; Cara Dellatte and the staff at the Brooke Russell Astor Reading Room for Rare Books and Manuscripts, New York Public Library; Douglas Di Carlo of the La Guardia and Wagner Archives, CUNY; Hilary Dorsch Wong, Peter Corina, and the staff at the Division of Rare and Manuscript Collections, Cornell University; Robert Dunkelberger of the Andruss Library, Bloomsburg University; Isabella Folmar and Hendry Miller of the State Archives of Florida; Miriam Goderich of Dystel, Goderich & Bourret LLC; Paul Hogroian and Camille Worrell of the Library of Congress; Susan Krueger of the Wisconsin Historical Society; Michael Kubiak; Tom Lisanti of the New York Public Library; Howard Mandelbaum of Photofest; Dona Ann McAdams; William Megevick; Alex Michelini; Carolyn Mills and Richard Bleiler of the University of Connecticut Library, Storrs; Walter Naegle; Danielle Nista and the staff at the Tamiment Library and Robert F. Wagner Labor Archives, New York University; Brian Panella; Sarah Patton of the Hoover Institution Library and Archives; Lauren Robinson at the Museum of the City of New York; Michael Romei of the Waldorf; Sarah Schulman (who graciously allowed me to quote from the ACT UP Oral History Project); Sharon and the staff of Firestone Circulation Services, Princeton University Library; and Randall Taubman. A general thanks to the incredible staffs at the New-York Historical Society Library and the various research libraries of the New York Public Library.

For their diligence, knowledge, and skill in tracking down hard-to-find documents, I am greatly appreciative of the work of research assistants Debbie Martin, Kevin Morrow (whose adroitness in navigating the massive Department of State Central Files of the National Archives was invaluable), and Elga Zalite.

Much gratitude goes to the excellent staff members at Rutgers University Press (among them, Publicity Manager Courtney Brach; Karen Li; Jeremy Grainger, Brice Hammack; Savannah Porcelli and their colleagues in the marketing department; and Alissa Zarro and her production colleagues, for the wonderful cover and interior design); to Michelle Witkowski of Westchester Publishing Services, and to Susan Ecklund for her meticulous, perceptive work in copyediting the manuscript.

Thanks to the friends, neighbors, colleagues, and associates who shared personal stories of the Waldorf, sent books and press clippings, put me in touch with valuable contacts, shared family documents and travel folders, offered suggestions, help, and support, and otherwise listened as I outlined my plans for the book's theme, structure, and narrative: Bill Buell, George Calderaro, Irane De Costa, Andrew Dolkart, Leroy Donovan Dyer, Laurence Frommer, Alex Garvin, Vicki Gold Levi, Regina Guggenheim, Hilary Knight, Bettye LaVette, John Longshore, Anthony Luciano, Ron Mandelbaum, Michael McStraw, Peter Mintun, Eric Myers, Amber Paul, Manny Rodriguez and Eric Leach, Sheryl Moller, Rita Sandler, Jorge Sevillano, Bella Stander, Steve Traxler, Eric Washington, and Estha Weiner. Extra special thanks to Elizabeth Gilbert, for her generosity and early endorsement, and to James Gavin, for his endorsement and for helping arrange the interview with Diahann Carroll. As always, I am grateful to Steven Schnepp, Jenny Bates, and Kent McIngvale at Broadway Booking Office NYC for their support and friendship. Thanks to my sister, Elizabeth Beal, my brother-in-law, John Beal, my nieces Lauren, Catherine, and Emma, and to other members of my family in California and Virginia, for coming to stay with me when I couldn't always get to them. The kindness of my family in Newfoundland has also been a source of great support. Lastly, thanks to my partner, Rafael DiazCasas, who, more than anyone, offered perspective, understanding, and encouragement, and who believed in this book from the beginning.

Notes

A NOTE ON SOURCES

My research for *American Hotel* has drawn extensively on the following archives, libraries, databases, and special collections (* indicates a digital collection):

ACT-UP Oral History Project*

Archives of Sexuality and Gender, Gale (includes ACT UP, Gay Activists Alliance, Jim Kepner Papers, Lesbian Herstory Archives, Mattachine Society of New York Records, ONE National Gay and Lesbian Archives, and National Gay and Lesbian Taskforce Records)*

Arnold Beichman Papers, Hoover Institution Archives, Stanford University

Babbidge Library journals, University of Connecticut, Storrs

Church League of America Collection of the Research Files of *Counterattack*, the Wackenhut Corporation, and Karl Baarslag, Tamiment Library and Robert F. Wagner Labor Archive, New York University

Congress of Racial Equality (CORE) Records, Wisconsin Historical Society (Madison), Division of Library, Archives, and Museum Collections

Crime, Punishment, and Popular Culture 1790–1920, Gale*

Department of State Central Files (RG 59), National Archives, Washington, DC

FBI Records (in particular, files on Leonard Bernstein, W.E.B. Du Bois, Robert Lynd, and Walter Winchell)*

Firestone Library, Princeton University

Gay Cable Network Archives, Fales Library and Special Collections, New York University*

General Research Division, New York Public Library

Hollywood Democratic Committee Records, Wisconsin Historical Society

Hospitality Industry Archives, Conrad N. Hilton College of Hotel and Restaurant Management, University of Houston, Texas

Hotel Files, New-York Historical Society Museum and Library

King Library and Archives, Atlanta*

Koreshan Unity Papers, ca. 1829–2006, State Archives of Florida, Tallahassee

Koreshan Virtual Archives (http://mwweb.org/koreshan/virtual_exhibit/)*

La Guardia and Wagner Archives, La Guardia Community College/CUNY, Long Island City

NAACP Papers, Library of Congress/ProQuest History Vault*

New York Hotel and Motel Trades Council Records, Tamiment Library and Robert F. Wagner Labor Archives, New York University

New York Real Estate Brochure Collection, Avery Architectural and Fine Arts Library, Columbia University*

Oscar Michel Tschirky Papers, No. 3990, Division of Rare and Manuscript Collections, Cornell University Library, Ithaca

School of Hotel Administration Director's Records, 1922–1981, Cornell University Library, Ithaca

Science, Industry and Business Library (SIBL), New York Public Library

Waldorf-Astoria Hotel Records, 1893–1929, Manuscripts and Archives Division, New York Public Library

Walter Winchell Papers, Billy Rose Theatre Division, New York Public Library for the Performing Arts

OTHER SOURCES

Ancestry.com was a valuable source for census data, information on residences, and family background for Oscar, Boomer, Philippe, Boldt, and others who appear in the text, as well as for travel and immigration documents and death certificates. The range of historical newspapers available for full-text digital search continues to widen. Some of the best digital sources I consulted for newspapers include ProQuest Historical Newspapers and America's Historical Newspapers (both available through the New York Public Library), Newspapers.com, NYS Historic Newspapers (a free source), Tom Tryniski's fultonhistory.com (also free, and invaluable for the size of its still-growing collection of New York papers), Chronicling America (offered free by the Library of Congress), and the Brooklyn Public Library's Brooklyn Newsstand site. For scholarly journals, JSTOR was a valuable service. Google Books offered a wide collection of early twentieth-century specialty magazines and trade periodicals (among them, *Hotel Weekly*, *The Hotel World*, and *New York Hotel Record*), as well as summaries of court cases. Casetext.com, Archive.org, Questia.com, and Hathitrust.org were all useful supplementary sources. For those newspapers not yet, or only partially, digitized (among them, the *New York Daily Mirror*, *World-Telegram*, *Journal American*, and *Sun*), the Milstein Microform Reading Room of the New York Public Library, Schwartzman Building, was an excellent resource.

PROLOGUE

1. "in all New York": *New York Times*, December 3, 1981.

2. Conrad Hilton, *Be My Guest* (New York: Prentice Hall, 1957), 22.

3. For examples of Herford's "exclusiveness" citation, see Hilton, 227; Lloyd Morris, *Incredible New York* (New York: Random House, 1951), 235; and Karl Schriftgiesser, *Oscar of the Waldorf* (New York: Dutton, 1943), 81.

4. "never discouraged": Jim Blauvelt, in conversation with author, May 6, 2019.

5. "through your veins": *New York Times*, December 3, 1981.

INTRODUCTION

1. "a Waldorf guest": *Christian Science Monitor*, August 17, 1978; Lucius Boomer, *Hotel Management: Principles and Practice* (New York: Harper, 1925), 4. For attribution of "home away from home" to Boomer, see *Herald Tribune*, June 27, 1947.

2. Boomer, *Hotel Management*, 192. With the exception of the early sections of chapter 1, detailing the hotel's history prior to the construction of the Astoria, or unless otherwise noted, the names Waldorf and Waldorf-Astoria will be used interchangeably throughout the book.

3. A. K. Sandoval-Strausz, *Hotel: An American History* (New Haven, CT: Yale University Press, 2007), 6.

4. "Hell, no": *Los Angeles Times*, November 12, 1974.

5. Joe Rantisi, conversation with author, April 22, 2019.

6. Rantisi.

7. "luxury . . . ease of living": Karl Schriftgiesser, *Oscar of the Waldorf* (New York: Dutton, 1943), 65.

8. Edward L. Bernays *Biography of an Idea* (New York: Simon and Schuster, 1965), 278–279; Edward Hungerford, *The Story of the Waldorf-Astoria* (New York: Putnam's, 1925), 281–282.

9. "done away with": *New York Times*, December 22, 1928; "larger and more beautiful": *New York Times*, March 10, 1929.

10. For Hoover's full speech, see *Los Angeles Times*, October 1, 1931.

11. "42-A": *New York Times*, November 2, 1968. For a reference to Boomer's meeting with a representative of the UN, see Leonard Lyons's column in the *Miami News*, April 15, 1946. For accounts of the Howard Johnson's incident, see *Atlanta Constitution*, *Herald Tribune*, *New York Times*, *Newsday*, and *Washington Post* (October 9, 1957 for all citations).

12. See Employee Handbook, p. 6, in New York Hotel and Motel Trades Council Records, Tamiment Library and Robert F. Wagner Labor Archives, New York University, Waldorf-Astoria, box 32.

13. James Locker, conversation with author, April 9, 2020; Horace Sutton, *Confessions of a Grand Hotel* (New York: Henry Holt, 1953), 53.

14. Annabel Jane Wharton, *Building the Cold War* (Chicago: University of Chicago Press, 2001), 162–163; Sutton, *Confessions of a Grand Hotel*, 52; "A Westerner in the Waldorf," *Reedy's Mirror* 13 (1903): 8.

15. Theodore Dreiser, *Sister Carrie* (Philadelphia: University of Pennsylvania Press, 1981), 353.

16. Perry Bradford, *Born with the Blues* (New York: Oak Publications, 1965), 125; "sit joint" and "King": *Herald Tribune*, May 31, 1933; "congregating places": *Herald Tribune*, March 15, 1932.

17. "statues or something": *Herald Tribune*, March 15, 1932; "lobby hours": *Herald Tribune*, May 31, 1933.

18. When the second Waldorf-Astoria opened in 1931, the eighteenth-floor space was known merely as a "roof garden." The hotel did not begin using the name "Starlight Roof" until the summer of 1932.

19. "great American habit" and "let them know": *Herald Tribune*, October 2, 1931.

20. Since dollar values change rapidly, it is suggested that readers consult online sources, among them usinflationcalculator.com and westegg.com, for the most up-to-date figures.

21. Ward Morehouse III, *The Waldorf-Astoria* (New York: M. Evans, 1991), 9.

CHAPTER 1 — A HAVEN FOR THE WELL-TO-DO

1. "Among My Souvenirs," Oscar as guest columnist for Walter Winchell, *Greenville (SC) News*, August 5, 1941.

2. "exhorbitant rents": *Sterling (KS) Gazette*, November 17, 1881; "gilded cads": *Salt Lake Herald*, July 26, 1900.

3. "palace": *New York World*, March 15, 1893 and *Indianapolis News*, March 13, 1893. For an account of the coupon story, see the *Pittsburgh Press*, March 8, 1890.

4. For examples of gossip related to Astor rivalry, see *Philadelphia Inquirer*, February 14, 1892 and March 18, 1895.

5. See "Three Men of Gloom," *Daily American* (Nashville, TN), January 16, 1889.

6. "splendid mirrors": *New York Evening Post*, May 31, 1836. For a reference to "new" Astor House, see *Catholic Journal*, November 22, 1890.

7. "no wood": *Forum* 17 (August 1894): 22.

8. Albert Stevens Crockett, *Peacocks on Parade* (New York: Sears, 1931), 23–24; "quiet elegance": Moses King, *King's Handbook of New York City* (Boston: Moses King, 1893), 226; "monsters": *New York Tribune*, October 22, 1893. Two months after the Waldorf's opening, another William Astor–financed project, the New Netherland, came along to anchor the northeast corner of Fifth Avenue and Fifty-Ninth Street, joining additional luxury hotels, the Plaza and Savoy, nearby.

9. In the late nineteenth century, alleys were considered lowly places. It's no surprise that official hotel records and documents from the Waldorf-Astoria's early

years make no reference to Peacock Alley. In fact, it appears the hotel did not begin to consider the term for its marketing value until the 1920s.

10. "Faithful performance": letter dated February 9, 1907, Waldorf-Astoria Hotel Records, 1893–1929, Manuscripts and Archives Division, New York Public Library, box 15, folder 3–15.

11. "smoothness of clockwork" and "military discipline": *New York Times*, April 23, 1905; see also *New York Sun*, February 5, 1899. "hard battle": letter dated August 28, 1906, Waldorf-Astoria Hotel Records, box 15, folder 3–15. For waiter's dissatisfaction, see *Los Angeles Herald*, February 19, 1899 (copy in Oscar Michel Tschirky Papers, No. 3990, Division of Rare and Manuscript Collections, Cornell University Library, Ithaca, box 3, scrapbook).

12. Karl Schriftgiesser, *Oscar of the Waldorf* (New York: Dutton, 1943), 36–37.

13. "gallows bird": *Democrat and Chronicle* (Rochester, NY), December 7, 1885.

14. Schriftgiesser, *Oscar of the Waldorf*, 33; "over and above this," letter dated September 4, 1906, Waldorf-Astoria Hotel Records, box 15, folder 3–15; "out of the dealers": quoted in Ward Morehouse III, *The Waldorf-Astoria* (New York: M. Evans, 1991), 36. For speculation regarding Oscar's salary, see *New York Times*, April 23, 1905.

15. Theodore Dreiser, *Sister Carrie* (Philadelphia: University of Pennsylvania Press, 1981), 332–333.

16. Schriftgiesser, *Oscar of the Waldorf*, 36.

17. Schriftgiesser, 36–48.

18. Crockett, *Peacocks on Parade*, 48; *New York Times*, March 30, 1875.

19. Crockett, *Peacocks on Parade*, 48.

20. "Napoleonic": *New York Sun*, August 28, 1898; "moves on wheels": ca. 1899 (both from Tschirky Papers, box 3, scrapbook).

21. Horace Smith, *Crooks of the Waldorf* (New York: Macaulay, 1929), 72, 100–101.

22. Letter dated December 27, 1906, Waldorf-Astoria Hotel Records, box 8, folder 6. The complaints surfaced from guests who had been told they could not keep pets with them, in their rooms.

23. "universal" and "dog howling": *Broadway Weekly*, May 26, 1904; "'Son . . . ,'" *New York Sun*, December 6, 1916.

24. Edward Hungerford, *The Story of the Waldorf-Astoria* (New York: Putnam's, 1925), 35.

25. *Philadelphia Times*, March 14, 1886.

26. For a reference to Louise as proprietor of the Bellevue, see *Philadelphia Times*, April 18, 1886.

27. Crockett, *Peacocks on Parade*, 44–45. This account, of course, contradicts the other that suggests Boldt and Bartlett may have met earlier, at Cornwall Mountain House.

28. For Cox's account, see *Cincinnati Enquirer*, November 13, 1909; "skyward course": *Philadelphia Inquirer*, February 14, 1892.

29. Schriftgiesser, *Oscar of the Waldorf*, 64; "jimmy": *New York Sun*, April 21, 1893.

30. "bachelor": *New York Times*, February 27, 1941; "Five Decades of Music," in *The Unofficial Palace of New York*, ed. Frank Crowninshield (New York: Hotel Waldorf-Astoria Corporation, 1939), 97; Frieda Hempel, *My Golden Age of Singing* (Portland, OR: Amadeus Press, 1998), 112.

31. Hempel, *My Golden Age of Singing*, 112.

32. Lloyd Wendt and Herman Kogan, *Bet a Million! The Story of John W. Gates* (Indianapolis: Bobbs-Merrill, 1948), 46.

33. Wendt and Kogan, 232.

34. Crockett, *Peacocks on Parade*, 207–210.

35. Peacock Alley has often been described, incorrectly, as a connecting hallway between the Waldorf and Astoria. Its actual location shifted over the years, but by 1900, patrons and reporters generally agreed that Peacock Alley referred to a corridor running near the building's Thirty-Fourth Street side, to the right of the main entrance.

36. Crockett, *Peacocks on Parade*, 164; letter dated May 15, 1907, Waldorf-Astoria Hotel Records, box 10, folder 2.

CHAPTER 2 — WOMAN SPELLED WITH A BIG "W"

1. For more on Loomis and Woodward, see *New York Times*, March 10, 1900; *Social Register, New York, 1903* (New York: Social Register Association, 1902); *Burlington (VT) Free Press* of February 3, 1909, March 8, 1909, November 18, 1910, and April 19, 1911; *Middlebury (VT) Register*, April 21, 1911; and *Medical Record*, November 25, 1916, 940. Also, Waldorf-Astoria guest register, vol. 357, no. 3, Waldorf-Astoria Hotel Records, 1893–1929, Manuscripts and Archives Division, New York Public Library.

2. See Waldorf-Astoria Hotel Records, section V, Investigator's Log, 1902, p. 68. The survival of two of these logbooks (one is from 1902 and the other from 1904) is a story in itself. When the Waldorf-Astoria donated a portion of its records to the New York Public Library in 1929, it never intended for the detectives' books to be included. Someone found the first (later joined by its companion) among papers and rubbish during the original hotel's demolition and brought it to the library.

3. "fine terrapin": *Baltimore Sun*, March 12, 1901.

4. "four generals": *New York Press*, January 10, 1904.

5. Smith, *Crooks of the Waldorf* (New York: Macaulay, 1929), 136.

6. Smith, 134–135.

7. "stenographer": Waldorf-Astoria Hotel Records, Investigator's Log, 1902, p. 68; "locking door": Waldorf-Astoria Hotel Records, Investigator's Log, 1904, p. 107; "damned rules": Waldorf-Astoria Hotel Records, box 16, folder E-F.

8. Smith, *Crooks of the Waldorf*, 205.

9. "make and enforce": see Boyce v. Greeley Square Hotel Co., *New York Supplement*, vol. 168 (1918).

10. *New York Annotated Cases* 15 (1905): 18; *The Social Evil* (New York: Putnam's, 1902), 159; Catherine Cocks, *Doing the Town: The Rise of Urban Tourism in the United States* (Berkeley: University of California Press, 2001), 99–100.

11. "distasteful to us": *Binghamton Press and Sun*, December 7, 1910.

12. Waldorf-Astoria Hotel Records, Investigator's Log, 1902 ("massage," p. 3, "very loose," p. 42, "covertly soliciting," p. 59; and Investigator's Log, 1904 ("flirting," p. 32, "indecent language," p. 8); Smith, *Crooks of the Waldorf*, 126–128.

13. "I was the first": *Buffalo Commercial*, February 13, 1912; G. W. Bitzer, *Billy Bitzer: His Story* (New York: Farrar, Straus and Giroux, 1973), 25.

14. Karl Schriftgiesser, *Oscar of the Waldorf* (New York: Dutton, 1943), 66; Edward Hungerford, *The Story of the Waldorf-Astoria* (New York: Putnam's, 1925), 36–37; *Broadway Weekly*, June 9, 1904; see also *Philadelphia Times*, April 20, 1897.

15. For Louise's ownership of land, see *New York Supplement* for 1913, 531–533.

16. "capital W": *Hotel Monthly* 31, no. 361 (April 1923): 45–50.

17. "What do you mean?": *New York Times*, September 21, 1901.

18. "oddest people": *Boston Globe*, June 30, 1885; "variety of business": *Indianapolis News*, April 12, 1872.

19. "mortification": *New York Journal*, March 28, 1897; "restaurant fiends": *New York Press*, January 10, 1904.

20. Nancy Schrom Dye, "Feminism or Unionism?," *Feminist Studies* 3 (Autumn 1975): 111; Eleanor Gates, *The Cosmopolitan*, January 1907, 308–315.

21. "would soon clamor": *New York Sun*, 1902, n.d.; "present location": *New York Journal*, March 28, 1897.

22. "Middle Ages": *New York Journal*, March 28, 1897

23. "Them's his orders": *New York Press*, February 28, 1897. See also *New York Herald*, February 28, 1897.

24. "free advice": *New York Journal*, March 28, 1897.

25. "guilty of a misdemeanor," "betrousered," and "moral standard": *Albany Morning Express*, March 15, 1897; "medieval restaurant": *Cortland (NY) Evening Standard*, March 16, 1897. See also *Albany Law Journal*, March 13, 1897, 161.

26. "moth eaten": *New York Sun*, 1902, n.d.; "What would a hotel be . . . ?": *New York World*, September 25, 1901.

27. Cocks, *Doing the Town*, 101–102.

28. "Englishman Warns Against Our Hotels," *New York Times*, December 4, 1906.

29. "It never": *New York Times*, December 5, 1906; "are safer": *New York World*, December 9, 1906; "Prudes": *Washington Times*, December 16, 1906.

30. "manager's office": *New York World*, December 9, 1906. For examples of the Waldorf's applications to the New York City police department, see Waldorf-Astoria Hotel Records, box 16, folder N-P.

31. "less suspicious": *New York Times*, December 5, 1906.

32. "Ladies without escort": *New York Times*, January 12, 1907; *Pittsburgh Press*, January 14, 1907; *London Daily Mail*, January 14, 1907; *Wisconsin Weekly Advocate*, January 24, 1907.

33. "Yes, we will serve women": *Wisconsin Weekly Advocate*, January 24, 1907.

34. "busy as the men": *New York Times*, August 7, 1898; "soda cocktails": *Kansas City Times*, January 11, 1900; "bars are down now": *Wisconsin Weekly Advocate*, January 24, 1907.

35. "delicate subject": *New York Times*, January 12, 1907.

36. "feminine supremacy": *New York Times*, January 12, 1907.

37. "glow-worms": *Argonaut*, July 9, 1900.

38. "objectionable men": *Baltimore Sun*, August 7, 1907.

39. "may dine at the Waldorf": *Evening World*, August 12, 1907; woman must starve," "exceedingly crooked," and "women of the underworld": *Oakland (CA) Tribune*, August 25, 1907.

40. For reference to the bill, see *New York Times*, February 7, 1908.

41. See Boyce v. Greeley Square Hotel Co.

42. Albert Stevens Crockett, *Peacocks on Parade* (New York: Sears, 1931), 297.

43. "stern but kind": see *Hotel Bulletin and Nation's Chefs*, February 1932 (copy in Oscar Michel Tschirky Papers, No. 3990, Division of Rare and Manuscript Collections, Cornell University Library, Ithaca); "thunderstruck": *New York Sun*, December 6, 1916.

CHAPTER 3 — "BOOM CENTRE"

1. Karl Schriftgiesser, *Oscar of the Waldorf* (New York: Dutton, 1943), 65; memo dated March 9, 1906, Waldorf-Astoria Hotel Records, 1893–1929, Manuscripts and Archives Division, New York Public Library, box 15, folder 1.

2. Edward L. Bernays, *Biography of an Idea* (New York: Simon and Schuster, 1965), 238; Howard B. Meek oral history, #47\2\O.H.86. Division of Rare and Manuscript Collections, Cornell University Library, Ithaca, p. 60.

3. Letter dated December 7, 1926, School of Hotel Administration Director's Records, Boomer folder.

4. "monumental work": letter dated June 10, 1949, School of Hotel Administration Director's Records, Boomer folder.

5. Waldorf-Astoria Hotel Records, box 15, folder 1; Bernays, *Biography of an Idea*, 239.

6. Meek oral history; Lucius Boomer, *Hotel Management: Principles and Practice* (New York: Harper, 1925); "home away from home": *Herald Tribune*, June 27, 1947.

7. "unprogressive": *Daily Review*, April 2, 1881. For Boomer family history, see also *Manufacturer and Builder*, January 1869, 16; Lucius Sylvius Boomer entry in *Record of the Class of 1872, Yale, for Twenty Years after Graduation* (New Haven: Tuttle, Morehouse & Taylor, 1892); *Sunday News Tribune* (Jefferson City, MO), March 19, 2002; and Boomer family tree, Koreshan Virtual Archives (http://mwweb.org/koreshan/virtual_exhibit/).

8. Koreshan Unity Papers, ca. 1829–2006, State Archives of Florida, Tallahassee, Berthaldine Boomer member file, box 234, folder 16; "hollow globe": *Philadelphia Times*, April 12, 1896; Lyn Millner, *The Allure of Immortality* (Gainesville: University Press of Florida, 2015), 154. At times Lucius Boomer's writings, particularly in their emphasis on the need to reorganize older methods of hotelkeeping along scientific lines, appear notably similar to those of Teed. In his book of essays, *The Cellular Cosmogony*, first published in 1898, Teed had described Koreshanity as a "scientific religion which must embrace scientific social organization" (Cyrus ["Koresh"] Teed, *The Cellular Cosmogony* [Chicago: Guiding Star Publishing House, 1898], 38).

9. For accounts of the expedition, see letters reprinted in *American Eagle*, Koreshan Unity Papers, series 5.

10. See Morrow letters as reprinted in *American Eagle*, Koreshan Unity Papers, series 5; "hard-earned filthy": see Koreshan Unity Papers, Berthaldine Boomer correspondence, letter dated November 12, 1911, box 216, folder 2. The phrase "hard-earned filthy lucre" was used occasionally in the nineteenth century. The Koreshan Unity was a self-described "communistic and co-operative body." As such, its members disavowed the individual possession of money.

11. "fair bookkeeper": see Joseph Kaye column, *Indiana (PA) Weekly Messenger*, November 4, 1926. For a standard account of Boomer's rise, see *American Magazine* 97 (March 1924).

12. "right-hand": *New York Times*, July 2, 1908.

13. "A City in Itself": *Washington Herald*, July 4, 1915; "so high": *New York Times*, December 30, 1912; Boomer, *Hotel Management*, chap. 33.

14. "indirect way": Berthaldine Boomer correspondence; "we are not sorry": *New York Times*, October 31, 1918; Robert K. Murray, *The 103rd Ballot* (New York: HarperCollins, 1976), 322.

15. See *New Orleans Times-Picayune*, January 3, 1919.

16. "multitude of matters": *New York Sun*, February 4, 1918; "cruel and barbarous": *New York Times*, November 16, 1915; "on the wane": *National Hotel Reporter*, February 9, 1918. For appraisal of Boldt's estate, see *New Orleans Times-Picayune*, January 3, 1919, and *Cornell Alumni News*, January 9, 1919.

17. See "Characteristics That Determine Individual Success," *National Association of Corporation Schools Bulletin* 5 (December 1, 1918): 549–557.

18. "big man mentally": *National Hotel Reporter*, February 9, 1918.

19. "empty when it finished": *New York Sun*, July 1, 1919. See also *New York World*, July 1, 1919.

20. Michael A. Lerner, *Dry Manhattan* (Cambridge, MA: Harvard University Press, 2007), 42; "At midnight": *New York Tribune*, July 1, 1919.

21. Koreshan University prospectus, Koreshan Unity Papers; "hypocrisy": *New York Times*, October 7, 1923.

22. Daniel Okrent, *Last Call: The Rise and Fall of Prohibition* (New York: Scribner, 2010), 165–166.

23. "Everybody who gets" and "big hotels": *New York Herald*, January 28, 1922.

24. "Closing the bar": *Buffalo Commercial Appeal*, September 7, 1921. What this meant, in terms of loss, was outlined by a former employee of an unspecified large hotel, who explained that pre-Prohibition liquor sales during peak months for catered affairs and banquets (between winter and early spring) would often yield a net profit as high as 250 percent. "unequal enforcement": *New York Times*, June 25, 1922. See also *Hotel World*, July 1, 1922, 19.

25. "Candy Possibilities," *Hotel World* 89 (September 6, 1919), 12–13; "Candy for Dessert," *Hotel World* 89, p. 31.

26. "night life was dead" et al.: *New York Times*, July 26, 1925.

27. "piece by piece": *New York Herald*, January 27, 1920.

28. "still an institution": *New York Times*, July 26, 1925. In the eyes of the law, clubhouses were more like private homes and thus not subject to the same restrictions as commercial establishments.

29. "New York, U.S.A.": *New York World*, January 16, 1924.

30. "decrepit candidates": *New York World*, January 16, 1924. New York's $255,000 set a record in 1924: no city had ever paid that much—around $3.9 million in current dollars—to secure a political convention.

31. *New York World*, January 16, 1924; "Waldorf Convention": *Asbury Park (NJ) Evening Press*, July 8, 1924.

32. "I cannot speak too highly": *New York Times*, January 24, 1924.

33. "boom centre": *New York Times*, June 18, 1924; "homely man": *New York World*, June 27, 1924. For full text of Roosevelt's nominating speech, see *Boston Globe*, June 26, 1924.

34. Murray, *The 103rd Ballot*, 130; "nearly smothered": *New York Sun*, June 25, 1924; "rush was started": *New York World*, June 28, 1924.

35. "all Democrats": *New York World*, June 20, 1924; "if clothes" et al.: *New York Times*, June 26, 1924; "slender young man" and "pumpkin": *Times*, June 22, 1924; "battered pulp": *Times*, July 5, 1924.

36. "many-colored cloth": *Outlook*, July 2, 1924, 333; "harmony": *New York World*, July 6, 1924.

37. "Room 310": see also *Brooklyn Eagle, New York World*, and *New York Times*, July 6, 1924; "convention in miniature": *Chicago Tribune*, July 6, 1924; "assaults" and "I'm disgusted": *Brooklyn Eagle*, June 27, 1924.

38. *New York Times*, July 11, 1924.

39. Christopher M. Finan, *Alfred E. Smith: The Happy Warrior* (New York: Hill and Wang, 2002), 184. Davis was widely respected as a lawyer and diplomat, but few Americans had heard of him. In the coming presidential election, he would lose to the Republican incumbent, Calvin Coolidge, by one of the largest margins of the popular vote in history.

40. "centrally located": *New York Times*, September 13, 1924. For tax assessment, see *Times*, October 2, 1925.

41. "shrewd foresight": *New York Times*, May 7, 1936; "You will realize": *Times*, December 22, 1928.

42. "American life": *New York Times*, December 21, 1928.

43. "rich men, poor men": *New York Times*, May 2, 1929.

44. "did not go gladly": John Tauranac, *The Empire State Building* (New York: Scribner, 1995), 202. For scenes of workers and demolition, see *Philadelphia Inquirer Magazine*, December 15, 1929.

CHAPTER 4 — TEMPORARY STORMS AND STRESS

1. Robert A. Taft, letter to William H. Taft, dated July 13, 1922, in Clarence E. Wunderlin, *The Papers of Robert A. Taft*, vol. 1 (Kent, OH: Kent State University Press, 1997); Lucius Boomer, *Hotel Management: Principles and Practice* (New York: Harper, 1925), 9.

2. Robert A. Taft, letter to William H. Taft; "blazing timbers" and "no way of fighting": *Herald Tribune*, April 13, 1927.

3. "wholly enclosed elevator": *Herald Tribune*, April 14, 1927; Niven Busch Jr., *21 Americans* (New York: Doubleday, 1930).

4. "very heavy building": *New York Times*, January 20, 1927; "unwelcome prophets": *New York Times*, September 26, 1926.

5. "breaking all records," "country's prosperity," "so flourishing": *New York Times*, November 11, 1925; "scientific methods": *Christian Science Monitor*, June 18, 1927.

6. "world development": *Herald Tribune*, July 22, 1928.

7. "Palaces": *Herald Tribune*, July 20, 1929. The Waldorf's "tallest" record would not be surpassed until 1957, when the Hotel Ukraina opened in Moscow.

8. "new international hotel standards": *Herald Tribune*, July 20, 1929.

9. Donald L. Miller, *Supreme City* (New York: Simon and Schuster, 2014), 158.

10. Samuel C. Florman, *Good Guys, Wiseguys, and Putting Up Buildings* (New York: Thomas Dunne Books, 2012), 35; Horowitz and Boyden Sparkes, *The Towers of*

New York (New York: Simon and Schuster, 1937), 249–253; "we retain all rights": *New York Times*, December 21, 1928; "Oscar will be in it": *New York Times*, February 22, 1929. See also "New Waldorf Site Sought for Year," *New York Times*, March 10, 1929.

11. Horowitz and Sparkes, *The Towers of New York*, 249–251.

12. "intricate and difficult": *New York Times*, February 16, 1930.

13. "unprecedented experiment": *New York Times*, February 16, 1930. See also *Scientific American*, June 1930, 458–459; *Railway Age*, March 15, 1930, 632–634.

14. "fortresslike": *Herald Tribune*, November 5, 1929; see also *New York Times*, November 5, 1929.

15. John Kenneth Galbraith, *The Great Crash, 1929* (New York: Harcourt, 2009), 108. Robert K. Murray observed that Hoover, who had earned universal admiration for his humanitarian efforts in Europe after the First World War, "believed that capitalism could transcend mere materialism and become socially-oriented and even spiritual" (Robert K. Murray, *The 103rd Ballot* [New York: HarperCollins, 1976], 260).

16. Galbraith, *The Great Crash, 1929*, 126–127.

17. Horowitz and Sparkes, *The Towers of New York*, 252–253.

18. "Just think": *Los Angeles Times*, November 16, 1929.

19. "sound investments": *Jewish Advocate*, December 19, 1929. The Black Tuesday connection would become a staple of Waldorf lore. At one of the opening dinners in September 1931, an official of New York Central would assert, inaccurately, that the construction deal for the new edifice had closed on that "gloomy day of the 'debacle' of 1929."

20. "fundamental conditions": *Jewish Advocate*, December 19, 1929; Galbraith, *The Great Crash, 1929*, 138–140; "maintenance of prosperity": *Daily Northwestern* (Oshkosh, WI), December 5, 1929.

21. "dream is underway": *New York Times*, March 25, 1930; Miller, *Supreme City*, 238.

22. "Hamilton County": *Herald Tribune*, January 4, 1931. See also *Herald Tribune*, July 13, 1930, and *American Builder*, October 1, 1929.

23. "dull limestone": Robert Wojtowicz, ed., *Sidewalk Critic: Lewis Mumford's Writings on New York* (New York: Princeton Architectural Press, 1998), 70; *WPA Guide*, 235; "restraint": *The Spur*, September 1, 1931.

24. "squads of bellboys": *New York Times*, September 30, 1931.

25. "All of New York": *New York Times*, October 1, 1931; "Dowagers": *Chicago Tribune*, October 1, 1931.

26. "inseparable": *New York Times*, October 1, 1931; see also *Herald Tribune*, October 1, 1931; Edward L. Bernays, *Biography of an Idea* (New York: Simon and Schuster, 1965), 280.

27. For full speech, see *New York Times*, October 1, 1931.

28. *New York Times*, October 1, 1931.

29. "economic body": *Herald Tribune*, December 3, 1930.

30. For Boomer's speech, see *New York Times*, October 1, 1931.

31. "At 7 a.m.": *Herald Tribune*, October 2, 1931; "WARREN ROSS": *Herald Tribune*, September 30, 1931.

32. See *Herald Tribune*, October 2, 1931.

33. For an example, compare *Detroit Free Press*, October 2, 1931, 2, with *Baltimore Sun*, August 31, 1931, 9.

34. "volume of business": see INS story as printed in *Shamokin (PA) News-Dispatch*, October 22, 1932. For net loss, see *New York Times*, September 23, 1933. For a discussion of occupancy rates and profit in New York hotels, see Morris A. Horowitz, *The New York Hotel Industry* (Cambridge, MA: Harvard University Press, 1960), 3–13.

35. See Barrow Lyons, "The Hotel Debacle," *The Nation*, October 4, 1933.

36. For an example, see *Boston Globe*, October 9, 1929.

37. Lyons, "The Hotel Debacle"; "adverse conditions": *New York Times*, September 21, 1932.

38. Lyons, "The Hotel Debacle." For New York Central's advance to the Waldorf, see *New York Times*, June 20, 1932.

39. "scourge," "ready and fit," and "horse feathers": *Binghamton Press* (NY), December 5, 1933; "head-on": *Pittsburgh Press*, December 6, 1933; "law-abiding": *Herald Tribune*, December 6, 1933.

40. "foot on a rail": *Pittsburgh Press*, December 6, 1933; "cellar": *New York Times*, December 3, 1933; "run for miles": *Daily News*, November 11, 1933.

41. "I am confident": *New York Times*, December 6, 1933; "Prohibition is dead!": *Evening Sun* (Hanover, PA), December 6, 1933.

CHAPTER 5 — NO MORE JUNIOR PROMS!

1. "clear view": *New York Times*, November 10, 1933; "doomed": *Variety*, December 12, 1933. See also Beebe column in *Herald Tribune*, December 8, 1934; *Variety*, January 30, 1934.

2. *Variety*, December 12, 1933; "impecunious young men": *Brooklyn Eagle*, January 4, 1934; "How's that?": *Chicago Tribune*, December 9, 1933.

3. "increasing prosperity": *New York Times*, March 14, 1934; "out of the red": *Variety*, March 27, 1934.

4. "speed-up": *Daily Worker*, February 2, 1934; "Banquet Service" guide August 1935, Oscar Michel Tschirky Papers, No. 3990, Division of Rare and Manuscript Collections, Cornell University Library, Ithaca, Memos Concerning the Waldorf-Astoria.

5. Joseph G. Rayback, *A History of American Labor* (New York: Macmillan, 1959), 330; "not feasible": *New York Times*, July 30, 1933.

6. Edward L. Bernays, *Biography of an Idea* (New York: Simon and Schuster, 1965), 284.

7. Bernays, 284; "Employee Handbook," 1935, found in New York Hotel and Motel Trades Council Records, Tamiment Library and Robert F. Wagner Labor Archive, New York University, series 4, box 32.

8. "inconsistent": *New York Times*, December 25, 1933.

9. Rayback, *A History of American Labor*, 330; Karl Schriftgiesser, *Oscar of the Waldorf* (New York: Dutton, 1943), 106.

10. "Lusitania": *The Nation*, February 28, 1934; *The Militant*, January 27, 1934; "better than usual": *Herald Tribune*, January 25, 1934.

11. *Hartford Courant*, January 25, 1934.

12. "Employee Handbook"; *Herald Tribune*, January 24, 1934.

13. "individual merit": *New York Times*, September 26, 1933; "split-watch": *New York Post*, January 25, 1934; "labor charter": *The Nation*, February 28, 1934.

14. "ready to respond" and "some of them did": *New York Times*, January 27, 1934.

15. *New York Times*, ibid; "storm center": *Daily Worker*, February 3, 1934. See also *New York Post, Herald Tribune, The Militant*, and *Daily Worker*, all of January 27, 1934.

16. Letter dated May 5, 1906, Waldorf-Astoria Hotel Records, 1893–1929, Manuscripts and Archives Division, New York Public Library, box 15, folder 1.

17. "napkins" and "I object": *New York Times*, April 17, 1893; "declared off": *New York Herald*, April 16, 1893.

18. Morris A. Horowitz, *The New York Hotel Industry* (Cambridge, MA: Harvard University Press, 1960), 24–25; Matthew Josephson, *Union House, Union Bar* (New York: Random House, 1956), 139.

19. Horowitz, *The New York Hotel Industry*, 22; James P. Cannon, *The History of American Trotskyism* (New York: Pathfinder Press, 1944), 165. The New York Trotskyists believed that Joseph Stalin had betrayed genuine Marxist principles. They remained in contact with the exiled Trotsky, printing his directives in their newspaper, *The Militant*, until his assassination in Mexico in 1940.

20. Cannon, *The History of American Trotskyism*; "Why did you not": *New York Times*, February 6, 1934; Josephson, *Union House, Union Bar*, 218.

21. "not cooperating": *New York Times*, January 25, 1934. See also *Baltimore Sun*, February 6, 1934.

22. "strikers are right": *New York Times*, February 4, 1934.

23. "anti-union attitude": *Boston Globe*, February 7, 1934.

24. For Rodman's full speech, see *World-Telegram*, February 7, 1934. For further accounts of the Empire Room demonstration, see *Brooklyn Eagle, New York Post*, AP story, *New York Sun, Albany Morning News, Daily News, Hartford Courant, Boston Globe*, and *New York Times*, all of February 7, 1934. See also Mary McCarthy, *Intellectual Memoirs: New York 1936–1938* (New York: Harcourt, 1992), 34.

25. "chief enemy": *New York Post*, February 7, 1934. For photo, see *Daily News*, February 7, 1934.

26. Thomas Kessner, *Fiorello H. La Guardia and the Making of Modern New York* (New York: McGraw-Hill, 1989), 284; Lawrence Elliott, *Little Flower: The Life and Times of Fiorello La Guardia* (New York: Morrow, 1983), 176.

27. Kessner, *Fiorello H. La Guardia*, 284; "our indefatigable mayor": *New York Times*, February 24, 1934.

28. Bamford letter dated February 8, 1934, La Guardia and Wagner Archives, La Guardia Community College/CUNY, Long Island City, STRIKES-HOTEL 1934 folder, microfilm no. 230, starts at image 366.

29. Bamford letter.

30. "whatever steps": *New York Times*, February 11, 1934; "get together": *Herald Tribune*, February 11, 1934.

31. "abuses": *New York Times*, February 16, 1934.

32. "symbol of the strike": *Herald Tribune*, February 17, 1934; Cannon, *The History of American Trotskyism*, 130.

33. "long enough": *World-Telegram*, February 19, 1934 (see also *New York Sun*, February 19, 1934); committee reports dated February 19, 1934, La Guardia and Wagner Archives, STRIKES-HOTEL 1934 folder.

34. Committee reports dated February 19, 1934; "Mayor Fails": *Herald Tribune*, February 20, 1934; "Mayor will act": *New York Sun*, February 20, 1934, and *Herald Tribune*, February 21, 1934. See also *World-Telegram*, February 20, 1934.

35. "turned the place" and "All in a day's work": *World-Telegram*, February 21, 1934; see also *Brooklyn Eagle*, *New York Post*, and *New York Sun*, all of February 21, 1934.

36. "astounding": *Herald Tribune*, February 23, 1934; "informed persons": *New York Sun*, February 24, 1934. See also *World-Telegram*, February 22, 1934. At the time, New York City food workers were required to be examined by a physician at regular intervals, and further needed to have an up-to-date card, proving they had been checked for communicable diseases, on their persons during working hours.

37. Gillet telegram dated February 21, 1934, La Guardia and Wagner Archives, STRIKES-HOTEL 1934 folder. "political attack": *New York Sun*, February 24, 1934; "precisely the methods": *New York Times*, February 24, 1934; "legitimate organized labor": *Brooklyn Eagle*, February 21, 1934; "HANDS OFF": *Times*, February 27, 1934.

38. "wash his hands": *Daily Worker*, February 28, 1934; "could not stand" and "on the chin: *Brooklyn Citizen*, February 27, 1934.

39. "many hotels . . . promises": *Herald Tribune*, March 30, 1934; "complete defiance": *New York Times*, March 23, 1934.

40. "general improvement" and "prosperous year": *New York Times*, December 5, 1934; "Washington has done": *Times*, April 24, 1934.

41. "stumped": *Herald Tribune*, September 8, 1934; "full code compliance": *Washington Post*, September 8, 1934; "They are dead": *New York Times*, January 21, 1935.

42. *New York Times*, May 29, 1935.

43. "no tag": *Herald Tribune*, July 19, 1934. See also *Washington Evening Star*, July 1, 1934.

44. "first tangible result": *Wall Street Journal*, February 27, 1937.

45. Letter dated May 15, 1942, from New York Hotel Trades Council to "All Waldorf-Astoria Employees"; "impregnable": statement by Jay Rubin dated March 28, 1946; "CONTRACT BENEFITS," flyer dated (in pencil) May 10, 1939. See New York Hotel and Motel Trades Council Records, Waldorf-Astoria file, series 4, box 32, folders 12–19.

46. "insecurity of poor business": letter dated July 24, 1945 from Boomer to Louis Sobel; "Boomer Talks on Employee Training," *Hotel World-Review*, November 13, 1937; flyer "To the Men and Women Operating the Waldorf-Astoria," dated June 12, 1937. See New York Hotel and Motel Trades Council Records, Waldorf-Astoria file.

47. "greatest victories": statement by Jay Rubin dated March 28, 1946, New York Hotel and Motel Trades Council Records, Waldorf-Astoria file, series 4, box 32, folders 12–19. Since its days of Paul Coulcher and gangsterism in the 1930s, the local AFL had reorganized and thus legitimized itself.

48. "no one expected": Louise Tobin in discussion with author, April 6, 2017.

CHAPTER 6 — WEEKEND AT THE WALDORF

1. "weird experience": *New York Herald Tribune*, October 7, 1945; "publicity jackpot": *New York Times*, October 5, 1945. The only portions of *Week-end at the Waldorf* actually filmed onsite were a handful of exterior shots. Among movie studios, MGM, in particular, had become masterful at re-creating faraway locales on its own stages. Thanks to favorable labor contracts and other factors, this was actually easier for the studios than a location shoot would have been. For further discussion, see James Sanders, *Celluloid Skyline* (New York: Knopf, 2002), 78–80.

2. "Coney Island": C. B. Palmer, *New York Times Magazine*, October 1, 1944. For the New York City hotel occupancy rate in 1945, see *New York Times*, August 29, 1946.

3. "they'll get chicken": Palmer, October 1, 1944.

4. "not unaccompanied": *New Yorker*, February 19, 1955; Edward L. Bernays, *Biography of an Idea* (New York: Simon and Schuster, 1965), 280.

5. "fired and rehired": *New Yorker*, February 19, 1955; "the woman fainted": Ward Morehouse III, *The Waldorf-Astoria* (New York: M. Evans, 1991), 82. Oscar would stay on as a part-time figurehead until his death in 1950.

6. "new Oscar": *Austin Statesman*, June 21, 1951; "extra-Oscarian": *New Yorker*, February 19, 1955. On weekends Philippe retreated to a farm and house he owned

near Peekskill, New York, where celebrity guests would be put to work washing lettuce and serving wine.

7. "able to avert war" and other Byrnes comments: *New York Times*, March 1, 1946; "fundamental shift": Ralph B. Levering, "Toward Cold War Thinking," *Journal of Transatlantic Studies* 14 (2016): 346. Earlier in the month, the Chinese ambassador had informed Byrnes that the Russians wished to consider Japanese property as "war booty."

8. "withdraw or modify": *Herald Tribune*, March 16, 1946; Levering, "Toward Cold War Thinking," 347.

9. "war is not inevitable": *Herald Tribune*, June 27, 1945.

10. "critical": telegram dated October 24, 1946; "outright eviction": memo from the Department of State to each ambassador, dated October 25, 1946; "disappointment of your prospective guests": letter dated October 15, 1946 from Dean Acheson to Frank Ready of the Waldorf. See also letter dated October 17, 1946, from Warren Kelchner of the Division of International Conferences to Frank Ready. For all references, see Department of State Central Files (RG 43), National Archives, Washington, DC, entry 399, box 57.

11. "selfishness": *Christian Science Monitor*, October 30, 1946; "worse time": *Manchester (UK) Guardian*, November 5, 1946; "each other's nerves": *Philadelphia Inquirer*, November 5, 1946.

12. James F. Byrnes, *Speaking Frankly* (New York: Harper, 1947), 138–155; Patricia Dawson Ward, *The Threat of Peace* (Kent, OH: Kent State University Press, 1979), 161–163; *Life*, December 23, 1946. The Soviets, as represented by Molotov, had supported Yugoslavia's claim. Under the agreement made at the Waldorf, Trieste became an international territory. It remained that way until 1954, when it was officially returned to Italy.

13. "one would think": *Philadelphia Inquirer*, November 5, 1946. For quotes of Waldorf employees, see *World-Telegram*, November 5, 1946.

14. *Life*, December 23, 1946.

15. Thomas Doherty, *Show Trial* (New York: Columbia University Press, 2018), 38.

16. "Mickey Mouse": quoted in Doherty, 19; "foe of censorship": *Boston Globe*, June 3, 1947; "what kind of picture": *Herald Tribune*, October 28, 1947.

17. "attempted subjugation": *Christian Science Monitor*, March 12, 1947; "supreme effort": *New York Times*, October 19, 1947; "Commie menace": *Chicago Tribune*, November 18, 1947.

18. "emergency conference": *New York Times*, November 22, 1947; "basis of all movies": *Christian Science Monitor*, December 22, 1947; "American industrial fields": *Times*, November 26, 1947; "under oath . . . Communist": *Times*, November 26, 1947. While it may seem unusual that the conference took place in New York, rather than in Hollywood, it should be noted that much of the money and, to some extent,

administrative power behind the American motion picture industry was located on the East Coast (see Steve Neale, ed., *The Classical Hollywood Reader* [New York: Routledge, 2012], 168).

19. Dore Schary, *Heyday: An Autobiography* (Boston: Little, Brown, 1979); "knowingly employ": *New York Times*, November 22, 1947.

20. "We call on all Americans": see Policy and Program for 1948, Hollywood Democratic Committee Records, Wisconsin Historical Society, box 6, folder 9.

21. "opposing and stopping": Policy and Program for 1948.

22. Letter from Albert Einstein to Harlow Shapley dated April 1, 1948, Hollywood Democratic Committee Records, box 6, folder 17. In August 1939, Einstein had signed a letter (ghostwritten by physicist Leo Szilard) to FDR, urging "quick action on the part of the Administration" in order to "speed up the experimental work" on setting up chain reactions in uranium.

23. "technical surveillance": FBI Records, file on Bernstein no. 100-360261, p. 17; "propaganda campaign": FBI Records, file on Du Bois no. 100-99729, p. 54.

24. "reactionary writers" and "world domination": quoted in *Review of the Scientific and Cultural [sic] Conference for World Peace* (Washington, DC: Committee on Un-American Activities, U.S. House of Representatives, 1949), 3.

25. "of known reliability": FBI Records, file on Du Bois, p. 54; "overgrown nursery": *Daily Mirror*, March 14, 1949; "shield of protection": *Journal American*, March 11, 1949; "giant and evil watch": *Mirror*, March 27, 1949.

26. See minutes of the National Executive Committee meeting, Hollywood Democratic Committee Records, box 6, folder 9; "only source of income": *New York Times*, March 25, 1949. Minutes from the NCASP meeting held May 9, 1948, reference "the correspondence between Dr. Shapley and Dr. Einstein" as having "initiated the plans for the conference" (Hollywood Democratic Committee Records, box 6, folder 9).

27. The myth of the Waldorf conference as a Cominform-led effort would survive for decades. In 1999, it was revived by Frances Stonor Saunders in her book *The Cultural Cold War* (New York: New Press, 1999).

28. "no intentions of breaking": minutes of the National Executive Committee meeting; "no room": *Hotel Monthly*, March 1948, 27; "American Way of Life": as detailed *Hotel Monthly*, October 1950, 34.

29. "dry sack": *World-Telegram*, March 24, 1949; "Borscht": *New York Sun*, March 25, 1949; "can't be Communists": *Counterattack*, February 25, 1949.

30. "as a public institution": *New York Times*, March 25, 1949; "guests of the house": *World-Telegram*, March 24, 1949.

31. "anxiety-monger": Neil Gabler, *Winchell* (New York: Vintage, 1994), 378; "clean-out": see Winchell FBI file, pt. 3, p. 61; "70,000 members of the American Legion": see Walter Winchell Papers, Billy Rose Theatre Division, New York Public Library for the Performing Arts, reel 7.

32. As reported in *Sixth Report of the Senate Fact-Finding Committee on Un-American Activities* (California Legislature, 1951), 269–270.

33. "Week-end at the Waldorf!": *World-Telegram*, March 25, 1949. For events of Friday, see also accounts dated March 25 in *New York Sun, Chicago Tribune, Daily Mirror, Herald Tribune, New York Times*, and *Journal American*.

34. "good deal of fortitude": Daniel S. Gillmore, ed., *Speaking of Peace* (New York: NCASP, 1949), 3; Arthur Miller, *Timebends: A Life* (New York: Grove Press, 1987), 235; Nicolas Nabokov, *Bagázh: Memoirs of a Russian Cosmopolitan* (New York: Atheneum, 1975), 235.

35. "Joe McCarthy": Nabokov, *Bagázh*, 233; "buried in the press": Gillmor, *Speaking of Peace*, 3; "EXTERMINATE": *Daily Mirror*, March 27, 1949.

36. "emotionally charged": Henry A. Singer, "An Analysis of the New York Press Treatment of the Peace Conference at the Waldorf-Astoria," *Journal of Educational Sociology* 23 (January 1950): 263; Terry Klefstad, "Shostakovich and the Peace Conference," *Music and Politics* 6 (Summer 2012); Nabokov, *Bagázh*, 235. Final conference program, along with AIF press releases, can be found in Arnold Beichman Papers, Hoover Institution Archives, Stanford University.

37. *World-Telegram*, March 25, 1949.

38. "innocent embarrassment": *Daily Mirror*, March 25, 1949; "playing footsie": *Journal American*, March 25, 1949.

39. Miller, *Timebends*, 235; "FUMIGATING": *Daily Mirror*, March 28, 1949.

40. "Can you imagine": quoted in Ward Morehouse III, *The Waldorf-Astoria* (New York: M. Evans, 1991), 48. See also obituary in *Herald Tribune*, June 27, 1947.

41. Letter from Boomer to Meek dated April 7, 1947, School of Hotel Administration Director's Records, 1922–1981, Cornell University Library, Ithaca, box 1, folder 41.

42. *Counterattack*, letter no. 130, November 18, 1949, and letter no. 33, December 9, 1949.

CHAPTER 7 — LITTLE AMERICA

1. Conrad Hilton, *Be My Guest* (New York: Prentice Hall, 1957), 57. While no ghostwriter was credited for *Be My Guest*, it's evident that Hilton had assistance in smoothing out the text and heightening the lyricism of certain passages.

2. Hilton, 39.

3. Hilton, 107–108.

4. Hilton, 139–140.

5. Hilton, 160.

6. "to all races": *Chicago Defender*, July 19, 1958; "rub elbows": Conrad Hilton as interviewed on *Art Linkletter's House Party*, May 12, 1954 (Hospitality Industry Archives, Conrad N. Hilton College of Hotel and Restaurant Management, University of Houston, Texas); "The Battle for Peace," as appearing in *Life*, July 7, 1952. As an

indicator of the industry's denial when it came to the issue of racism, the *Hotel Monthly* wrote twenty-six representatives of state hotel associations in 1960, asking for their policies on discrimination. Only four replies were received, "each stating that there was no evidence of discrimination, and that, therefore, the thought of having such a policy had not arisen" (see Congress of Racial Equality [CORE] Records, Wisconsin Historical Society [Madison], Division of Library, Archives, and Museum Collections, box 67, folder 3).

7. "stench of decay": *Manchester (UK) Guardian*, August 26, 1948; "baseless rumors": *Atlanta Daily World*, April 26, 1944; "watching America": *New York Times*, April 6, 1946.

8. "international prestige": *New York Times*, April 6, 1946; "propaganda mills": Reuters blog by Aryeh Neier, May 14, 2014

9. Ian Fagelson, "President Truman's Justice Department and the Fight for Racial Justice in the Supreme Court," *Journal of Supreme Court History* 43 (March 2018): 69–70; "Blow to Communism," *New York Times*, May 18, 1954; Mary L. Dudziak, "*Brown* as a Cold War Case," *Journal of American History* 91 (June 2004): 36; *New York Times*, February 22, 1956. Bunche address found in NAACP Papers, Library of Congress/ProQuest History Vault, folder titled Supreme Court: May 17th Celebration, 1956.

10. Typed copy with handwritten edits found in King Library and Archives, Atlanta.

11. "a national figure": *Chicago Defender*, June 2, 1956; "financial emergency": letter dated October 22, 1957, NAACP Papers, folder titled Freedom Fund Dinner, 1957, correspondence O-R.

12. Tom Margittai, conversation with author, August 23, 2018; Hilton, *Be My Guest*, 265.

13. "three black men": *New Orleans Times Picayune* (reprinted from *New York World*), June 24, 1895; *Tribune*, June 18, 1895. The tests were inspired by the efforts of Charles W. Anderson, a New York State Treasurer's secretary who had lobbied for the Malby law. At one point, Anderson, who led tests of his own, tried to distance himself from fellow African Americans whom he felt were not "making the fight on dignified lines."

14. "improbable": *Tribune*, June 18, 1895.

15. "open the doors": *National Notes* (Kansas City), January 1928; "the colored help": *Afro-American*, January 19, 1929.

16. "Senior Hop": *Amsterdam News*, March 9, 1932; "out of things": *Afro-American*, March 3, 1934.

17. "hallowed halls": quoted in Horace Sutton, *Confessions of a Grand Hotel* (New York: Henry Holt, 1953), 124; "racial prejudice": *Pittsburgh Courier*, November 12, 1938.

18. "Negroes a break": *Billboard*, January 2, 1943; "blazed a new trail": *Pittsburgh Courier*, November 28, 1942; James Gavin, *Stormy Weather: The Life of Lena Horne* (New York: Atria, 2009), 128.

19. "In recent months": *Chicago Defender*, August 31, 1946.

20. For Lucius Boomer's discussions with the UN, see Introduction. Charles Abrams, ". . . Only the Very Best Christian Clientele." *Commentary* 20 (1955): 11–12.

21. "We do not discriminate": *Peoples Voice*, February 2, 1946.

22. "nuts on the cake": *Amsterdam News*, March 5, 1949; "Move Over White Folks, Here We Come!" *Los Angeles Sentinel*, October 26, 1950; Marybeth Gasman, *Envisioning Black Colleges* (Baltimore: Johns Hopkins University Press, 2007), 59–60.

23. Margittai, conversation with author; letter dated January 11, 1958 from C. C. Philippe to John Morsell, NAACP Papers, folder titled Freedom Fund Dinner, 1957, Waldorf-Astoria. For reference to the joke, see *New Pittsburgh Courier*, April 6, 1963.

24. Letter dated March 24, 1958 from C. C. Philippe to John Morsell, NAACP Papers.

25. "resell the date": letter dated April 22, 1959 from C. C. Philippe to Roy Wilkins, NAACP Papers.

26. Donald Bogle, *Dorothy Dandridge: A Biography* (New York: Boulevard Books, 1998), 307–308. See also *Pittsburgh Courier*, November 13, 1954.

27. "Democracy, grace": *Pittsburgh Courier*, April 23, 1955; "this great advance": *San Francisco Examiner*, April 15, 1955; "major league baseball": *Los Angeles Sentinel*, April 28, 1955; *Billboard*, April 28, 1955; "democratic note": *Pittsburgh Courier*, June 4, 1955.

28. "ahead of his time": Claudia Philippe in conversation with author, March 23, 2018; "not Joe Binns": Margittai, conversation with author.

29. "appeared as an equal": quoted in Ward Morehouse III, *The Waldorf-Astoria* (New York: M. Evans, 1991), 73; "cloudless summer sky" and "final tableau": *New York Times*, April 10, 1952.

30. "natural mink coat" et al.: *New York Times*, April 18, 1956.

31. "a Negro headliner": *Variety*, December 31, 1958; "prep school boys" and other Earl Wilson comments, *New York Post*, January 2, 1958.

32. "on his death bed": from "A Realistic Look at Race Relations," King Library and Archives; "a small group of whites" et al.: *Amsterdam News*, May 26, 1956.

33. "it has impact" et al: *Amsterdam News*, May 26, 1956.

34. Margittai, conversation with author.

35. Margittai, conversation with author.

36. "long before it was acquired" and "innocent": *New York Times*, October 3, 1958; "nothing worked out": Margittai; "resigned": *Herald Tribune*, June 9, 1959; "east of Seventh Avenue": Morehouse, *The Waldorf-Astoria*, 86.

37. "hustling and selling," letter dated December 4, 1962 from Frank Wangeman to Conrad Hilton; "will steal the whole hotel," letter dated November 27, 1962 from Conrad Hilton to Frank Wangeman: Hospitality Industry Archives, Conrad Nicholson Hilton Papers, box 1, Hotels Domestic: New York City, Waldorf Astoria.

38. "leverage" and "I am certain you will agree": NAACP Papers, 1963 Freedom Fund Dinner planning folder.

39. Quotes from the *Houston Press*, January 20, 1962, copy in Hospitality Industry Archives, box 138, Shamrock Hilton, file 3.

40. "EMBARRASSED," telegram dated January 25, 1962, from Rev. Charles Kelly to Conrad Hilton; "spread of Communism," letter dated January 23, 1962, from Lawrence Katz to Porter Parris: Hospitality Industry Archives, box 138; "at least one Negro" and "incidents": *New York Times*, April 10, 1962.

41. "sold out complete": see "Regret" notice sent from Hilton Inn Atlanta to Thomas Allen, NAACP Papers, Allen v. Hilton Hotels Corp folder; "allusion," "race or color," and "it's not right": see Affidavit in NAACP Papers, Allen v. Hilton Hotels Corp.

42. "take a stand" et al: letter dated August 3, 1962, from Eugene T. Reed to Rev. William Johnson; "withhold patronage": report dated November 13, 1962; "we do not absolve": letter dated August 22, 1962, from Eugene T. Reed to Hilton Hotels, Inc. (NAACP Papers, Allen v. Hilton Hotels Corp for all references); "Tom Mix": Hilton, *Be My Guest*, 199.

43. Wangeman comments in letter to Governor Rockefeller, NAACP Papers, Allen v. Hilton Hotels Corp (first page of letter is missing from file).

44. "too late, frankly": *New York Times*, August 26, 1962; "temporarily rescind": press release dated September 10, 1962, NAACP Papers, Discrimination Hotels—Hilton Hotels folder; "that simple": *Amsterdam News*, September 15, 1962.

45. Gertrude Wilson column, *Amsterdam News*, September 22, 1962.

46. "We cannot do this alone" et al.: letter dated November 1, 1962, from Robert J. Caverly of Hilton Hotels Corporation to George Fowler, New York State Commission for Human Rights, NAACP Papers, Discrimination Hotels—Hilton Hotels.

47. "KHRUSHCHEV" et al.: *Amsterdam News*, November 17, 1962.

48. Letter dated November 26, 1962, from Clyde J. Harris to Kivie Kaplan, NAACP Papers, Discrimination Hotels—Hilton Hotels.

49. Letter dated March 4, 1963, from John Morsell to John O'Reilly, NAACP Papers, Freedom Fund Dinner, Correspondence T-Z, 1963.

50. "refrain from holding": CORE Records, box 67, folder 3; "racial justice": *Amsterdam News*, March 30, 1963.

51. For the CORE boycott, see *Amsterdam News*, March 30, 1963; CORE Records, box 67, folder 3; "be complied with": NAACP Papers, Allen v. Hilton Hotels Corp; "utmost in courtesy": letter dated May 1, 1963 from Millicent Smith to Roy Wilkins, NAACP Papers, Discrimination Hotels—Hilton Hotels.

52. Press release dated May 25, 1963, NAACP Papers, Discrimination Hotels—Hilton Hotels; "leading hotels and motels": *Atlanta Constitution*, June 21, 1963. Full text of the 1964 Civil Rights Act can be found at www.ourdocuments.gov.

53. A. K. Sandoval-Strausz, *Hotel: An American History* (New Haven, CT: Yale University Press, 2007), 308; "local incidents thereof": *New York Times*, December 15, 1964.

54. "sheer increase": *New York Times*, December 15, 1964.

CHAPTER 8 — THE WALDORF BELONGS TO THE PEOPLE

1. *New York Times*, January 16, 1964; see also *Newsday, Chicago Tribune*, and *Baltimore Sun*, all of January 16, 1964.

2. "interrupted by applause": *New York Times*, January 16, 1964; J. William Middendorf III, *A Glorious Disaster* (New York: Basic Books, 2006), 72.

3. "dreamland of the past": *Times of India*, November 5, 1964; Barry M. Goldwater, *The Conscience of a Conservative* (Princeton, NJ: Princeton University Press, 2007), 69.

4. For the full text of Hull's address at the Waldorf, see *New York Times*, April 24, 1934.

5. For drawing see *St. Louis Dispatch*, July 28, 1935. The full text of the 1935 Social Security Act is available at www.ssa.gov.

6. "one of the foremost": *Wall Street Journal*, August 26, 1935; "third rail": *Boston Globe*, May 25, 1982. For an example of protest against the domestic worker exclusion, see *Afro-American* (Baltimore), February 9, 1935.

7. Premilla Nadasen, Jennifer Mittelstadt, and Marisa Chappell, *Welfare in the United States* (New York: Routledge, 2009), 20. During the late nineteenth century, impoverished Americans had generally been forced to search for economic relief through appeal to the kinds of charities George Boldt and his blueblood friends had long supported. New York City's 1897 charter, which annexed Manhattan and the Bronx with the independent city of Brooklyn, contained just one provision for cash relief, in the form of "expenditures" to the blind.

8. "welfare state": *Herald Tribune*, September 22, 1949.

9. "tree frog": *Herald Tribune*, December 3, 1949; "blackness of Socialism": *Herald Tribune*, April 25, 1952 (features full text of Byrd's Waldorf address).

10. "cradle to grave": *Herald Tribune*, April 24, 1953 (contains full text of Nixon's Waldorf address).

11. "permanent, organized basis": *Chicago Tribune*, March 19, 1953.

12. *Time*, February 8, 1971, 21. When used in the context of discussions on welfare, "rolls" signifies an official list of registered persons.

13. For the full text of Johnson's Waldorf speech, see *New York Times*, August 13, 1964.

14. "peace in this land": *New York Times*, August 13, 1964.

15. Barry Gottehrer, ed., *New York City in Crisis* (New York: McKay, 1965), 196.

16. *Time*, November 12, 1965.

17. "Some obstreperous people": *New York Times*, February 24, 1966; "KEEP NEW YORK CLEAN": *Newsday*, February 24, 1966.

18. Leonard Lurie, *The Running of Richard Nixon* (New York: Coward, McCann and Geoghegan, 1972), 113; "plead not guilty": *Boston Globe*, October 26, 1968.

19. "fairly flew": *Boston Globe*, November 4, 1968; "gap between the races" et al.: see the full text of Nixon's acceptance speech at the Waldorf, *New York Times*, November 7, 1968; Howard comments in *UK Observer*, November 10, 1968.

20. "surgically divided": *UK Observer*, November 10, 1968; "We can fly to the moon": *Atlanta Constitution*, December 10, 1969; see also *Newsday* and *New York Times*, December 10, 1969.

21. "clutzy and cornball": *New Leader*, September 1, 1969; "loath": *New York Times*, March 31, 1970.

22. "some mistake": *New York Times*, March 28, 1970; "30 years of expensive": *Christian Science Monitor*, October 28, 1968; "the most far-ranging": *Los Angeles Times*, August 16, 1969.

23. "Victorian heritage": *Christian Science Monitor*, December 24, 1962.

24. "without a reservation": *New York Times*, October 20, 1964; "Be modern": ad in *Chicago Tribune*, November 24, 1959. For more on the Skyline Motor Inn, see *Times* of October 25 and December 6, 1959.

25. "chips of brick": *New York Times*, February 24, 1968.

26. For a discussion of the Waldorf's entertainment budget, see *Variety*, March 25, 1970.

27. Peter Benchley, "Hard Times in Manhattan," *New York Times Magazine*, September 6, 1970.

28. "general assurances": *New York Times*, January 31, 1969; "political enemy": Vincent J. Cannato, *The Ungovernable City* (New York: Basic Books, 2001), 453; "home rule": *Boston Globe*, February 12, 1968.

29. *New York Post*, January 27, 1971.

30. "first mass layoff": *New York Times*, November 18, 1970; "survival": *New York Times*, November 20, 1970. Regarding increased welfare cases, see *New York Times*, November 29, 1970; for a timeline of tragedies at welfare hotels, see *Washington Post*, January 17, 1971.

31. "can't send them back" et al.: *Washington Post*, January 17, 1971. The Human Resources Administration was one of ten new "superagencies" created by the mayor in 1966. The superagencies consolidated more than fifty departments, with the goal of streamlining city operations.

32. "moving us around": *New York Post*, January 20, 1971; "foundation cracked" and "I don't like that place": *Newsday*, January 21, 1971.

33. "Mom's beauty": Victor Hainsworth, correspondence with author, July 13, 2019; "a flat, 'No'": *New York Times*, January 21, 1971.

34. "full of homosexuals" et al.: *New York Post*, February 10, 1971.

35. "nice enough," "silly," "it's nice here," and "without any reason": *New York Post*, January 20, 1971; "filled with movie stars": *New York Times*, January 21, 1971.

36. Hainsworth, correspondence with author.

37. *Newsday*, January 21, 1971. Fetherston recalled his feeling that "this was an utterly bogus story, planted to embarrass the Lindsay administration" (Drew Fetherston, correspondence with author, January 3, 2019).

38. "pale green room" et al.: *New York Post*, January 21, 1971; "don't show up tomorrow!": Sid Davidoff, conversation with author, January 17, 2019.

39. Davidoff, conversation with author.

40. Hainsworth, correspondence with author.

41. *New York Post*, February 1, 1971.

42. "not only are the taxpayers": *New York Post*, January 27, 1971; "deeply embarrassed": *Newsday*, February 4, 1971; "frightening attitude": *Ogdensburg (NY) Journal*, January 26, 1971; "best is good enough": *Pittsburgh Post-Gazette*, January 26, 1971.

43. *New York Times*, January 21, 1971; "The Waldorf has not discriminated": *Newsday*, January 21, 1971.

44. "sinister plots": *New York Times*, January 24, 1971; "deeply angered" and "colossal bad judgement": *Boston Globe*, January 21, 1971; "malicious intent": *Austin Statesman*, January 21, 1971.

45. "to free New York": *New York Times*, January 10, 1971; Alan Baer, conversation with author, February 3, 2019.

46. "no hard and fast rule" et al.: *New York Post*, January 22, 1971; "Why can't . . . ?": *Newsday*, January 22, 1971; "The Waldorf Belongs": *New York Times*, January 22, 1971. See also *New York Post*, January 21, 1971.

47. "If this was a different hotel": *New York Post*, 23 January 1971.

48. "I never felt that": Davidoff, conversation with author; "squeezed for years": *New York Times*, February 8, 1970; "next to poor people": *Daily News*, January 22, 1971.

49. "practically a bargain": *New York Times*, January 31, 1971; "real shock": *Jerusalem Post*, February 17, 1971. For details on rates paid by the city, see *New York Post*, January 23, 1971.

50. "not stand idly by": *New York Post*, February 3, 1971.

51. "greed": *New York Times*, January 5, 1971; "any more children": *Times*, January 15, 1971; "only commodity": *Hartford Courant*, March 30, 1971.

52. "lust for sex": *Hartford Courant*, April 23, 1971; "young buck": *New York Times*, February 5, 1976; "story about the welfare family": *New York Times*, January 14, 1987.

53. "shocked" et al.: *New York Times*, February 3, 1971.

54. Hainsworth, correspondence with author.

55. "most important piece": *Women's Wear Daily*, April 23, 1970; "megadole" and "turned on the plan": Richard Nixon, *The Memoirs of Richard Nixon* (New York: Grosset and Dunlap, 1978), 427; "Machiavellian instructions" and "little was indelible": John A. Farrell, *Richard Nixon: The Life* (New York: Doubleday, 2017), 381–382. The ADC program, eventually known as Aid to Families with Dependent Children (AFDC), would survive for two more decades. In 1996, President Bill Clinton replaced it with the Personal Responsibility and Work Opportunity Reconciliation Act (PRWORA). Representing a fulfillment of Clinton's campaign pledge to "end welfare as we have come to know it," PRWORA established work requirements and a five-year lifetime limit on benefits, along with marriage counseling and other initiatives designed to "encourage the formation and maintenance of two-parent families."

56. "Federal constitutional question": *New York Times*, June 1, 1972; for accounts of Beame at the Waldorf, see *New York Times*, August 27, 1975 and September 7, 1975. See also *New York Times Magazine*, August 17, 1975.

57. "ahead of its time": *Newsweek*, December 12, 1977.

58. "Elton John stripe": *New York Times*, June 30, 1977.

59. *New York Times*, June 30, 1977.

CHAPTER 9 — BECOMING VISIBLE

1. "kitchen canary": *Long Island Star-Journal*, November 10, 1961; "sissy": *Times Recorder* (Zanesville, OH), March 11, 1962; "Le Stupide": *Adirondack Daily Enterprise*, June 14, 1979; "bucket of steam": *Calgary (AB) Herald*, July 14, 1982. See also *Rockland Co. Journal-News*, October 22, 1981.

2. Joe Rantisi, conversation with author, April 22, 2019. In 1993 the seventy-year old Scanlan retired from his position as manager of the Union Club on Park Avenue, after a male employee charged him with sexual harassment. Evidence suggests the suit, unusual for its day, was settled out of court. See *Daily News*, December 28, 1993.

3. Rantisi, conversation with author; "real quality": *New York Times*, December 3, 1981.

4. Rantisi, conversation with author.

5. Night of a Thousand Gowns, program in Lesbian Herstory Archives, Drag folder, March 28, 1987–June 24, 1994; Jim Blauvelt, conversation with author, May 6, 2019.

6. Blauvelt, conversation with author.

7. Horace Smith, *Crooks of the Waldorf* (New York: Macaulay, 1929), 179–180.

8. For Shelton Dewey remembrances, see Jim Kepner Papers, box 50, folder 15 and Jim Kepner Papers, box 16, folder 20. While Dewey's account of drag events at the Plaza can be regarded with some skepticism, it should be noted that female impersonation remained, during the years prior to the 1930s (when Mayor La Guardia clamped down on burlesque shows and other forms of entertainment thought to be decadent), a common presence on New York stages. Dewey claimed the most frequent performer at Sunset Club parties was Julian Eltinge, a gender illusionist so popular that a theater on Forty-Second Street was named for him.

9. George Chauncey, *Gay New York* (New York: Basic Books, 1994), 350–351; "would not be influenced": *Daily News*, January 7, 1950; "improper advances": *Daily News*, January 23, 1950; "unnatural advances": *Windsor (ON) Star*, January 17, 1950; "verbal allusion"; *Daily News*, March 2, 1950.

10. For references to both the MacKellar murder and the Kinsey Report, see "things I never learned in school," *Out! The Gay Newspaper*, no. 48; "foreign espionage agents": *New York Times*, December 16, 1950.

11. "Parisian Pansies' Paradise": *Mattachine Review*, September 1961, 12–13; "notorious congregating points" and "problem of homosexuality": *New York Times*, December 17, 1963.

12. For a copy of the Waldorf-Astoria letter, see Mattachine Society of New York Records, box 3, folder 18. Descriptions of the ONE, Inc. Waldorf event can be found in *One Confidential*, issues of October and November 1964.

13. *Mattachine Review*, September 1961, 12–13.

14. Bob Kunst, conversation with author, March 19, 2019; "Disco for Democracy": *Tallahassee (FL) Democrat*, June 5, 1977.

15. "unlike any other": *New York Times*, September 4, 1982; "Could we have?": *NYC News*, October 13, 1982.

16. Steve Endean, *Bringing Lesbian and Gay Rights into the Mainstream*, ed. Vicki L. Eaklor (Binghamton: Harrington Park Press, 2006), 104–105. Based in Washington, DC, the Gay Rights National Lobby (GRNL) was a lobbying organization directed by Endean. It merged with HRCF in 1985.

17. "ABOMINATION" and "narrow self-interest": *Gay Community News*, October 16, 1982; "known homos": *NYC News*, October 13, 1982.

18. For an account of the attack at Blue's, see *Gay Community News*, October 16, 1982.

19. "threat of venereal disease": *Gay News*, November 12, 1981; Leavitt essay, *New York Times*, July 9, 1989.

20. Ron Goldberg, conversation with author, April 27, 2019.

21. Flyer distributed October 20, 1990, copy in Archives of Sexuality and Gender, ACT UP Los Angeles Records, box 13, folder 7.

22. Flyer distributed October 20, 1990; Goldberg, conversation with author; "control its spread": *Pittsburgh Post-Gazette*, September 3, 1991.

23. "within his own party" and "another politician": *Newsday*, July 25, 1990; "showcase of liberal policies" and "lives in fear": *Daily News* and *New York Times*, July 25, 1990.

24. "dried out": *Newsday*, July 25, 1990.

25. Details of Costas action from "Letter to the Mulberry Group," March 2, 1991, detailing "A COSTA HER/HISTORY" (courtesy of Ron Goldberg). See also *New York Post*, July 25, 1990; *New York Times*, July 25, 1990; *Gay Community News*, August 11, 1990; and Emily Nahmanson interview by Sarah Schulman, April 27, 2003, ACT UP Oral History Project (http://www.actuporalhistory.org/interviews/images/nahmanson.pdf).

26. "Keep your laws": *New York Post*, July 26, 1990. See also *Outweek*, August 8, 1990; *Gay Community News*, August 11, 1990.

27. See "Bushlips" demonstration press release and flyers, ACT UP Records, series 4, box 17, folder 2; "People had real jobs": Nahmanson interview.

28. Goldberg, conversation with author. Also see "die-in" photo in AP story, July 26, 1990.

29. Goldberg, conversation with author, with additional details shared by Eric Sawyer and Charles King, in author's correspondence with Jay Blotcher, April 24, 2019. See also *Gay Community News*, August 11, 1990.

30. Per Hellman, conversation with author, May 8, 2019.

31. David France, NPR broadcast, "How the Activism of Stonewall Transformed into the Fight against AIDS," June 28, 2019; "Prez' Night": *Daily News*, July 25, 1990; "burly cop": *New York Post*, July 25, 1990; "at least three times": Sawyer, in author's correspondence with Jay Blotcher.

32. "women's issues": see Archives of Sexuality and Gender, ACT UP Files, series 7, box 36, folder 1; "culmination of gay liberation": Charles King interview by Sarah Schulman, January 20, 2010, ACT UP Oral History Project (http://www.actuporalhistory.org/interviews/images/king.pdf); "nothing to apologize for": *New York Times*, January 3, 1990.

33. Hellman, conversation with author.

34. See "Invisible Diversity" program, Archives of Sexuality and Gender, Lesbian Herstory Archives, Job Discrimination folder. See also *HR Focus* newsletter, December 1991; *Gay Community News*, October 12, 1991; *Sappho's Isle*, November 1991; *Daily News*, September 19 and 21, 1991; *Newsday*, September 21, 1991; *Gay USA* (cable TV program), vol. 9, episodes 37 and 39, Gay Cable Network Archives, Fales Library and Special Collections, New York University.

35. Ed Mickens, conversation with author, April 14, 2019.

36. Mickens; Minkowitz's comments in *Advocate*, November 5, 1991.

37. Mickens, conversation with author.

38. Mickens.

39. "needs of the gay traveler": *USA Today*, January 22, 1997; "every indication that it was": *New York*, June 17, 1996.

EPILOGUE

1. "grand hotel": *New York Times*, May 16, 1999; "public relations nightmare": *Crain's*, November 15, 2010.

2. In her book on Trieste, Morris observes how "an element of hope is the essence of cityness" (Jan Morris, *Trieste and the Meaning of Nowhere* [New York: Da Capo Press, 2002], 23).

3. "weak link in security," "mini-submarine," and "not stay at the Waldorf": *New York Times*, September 11, 2015; Joe Rantisi, conversation with author, April 22, 2019.

4. Leslie Day, *Honeybee Hotel* (Baltimore: Johns Hopkins University Press, 2018), 72, 129.

5. "most legendary buildings": *Curbed*, March 29, 2017; "pre-construction": *Curbed*, August 21, 2018.

6. "the current pace": *New York Times*, September 13, 2019; "Swiss bank account": Julie Satow, *The Plaza* (New York: Twelve, 2019), 247; "certain and constant": *Wall Street Journal*, November 13, 2019.

Bibliography

For newspaper and magazine articles, please refer to Notes.

Abrams, Charles. "...Only the Very Best Christian Clientele." *Commentary* 20 (1955): 10–17.

Annotated Consolidated Laws of the State of New York. New York: Banks Publishing, 1909.

Badger, Anthony J. *FDR: The First Hundred Days*. New York: Hill and Wang, 2008.

Barrett, William. "Culture Conference at the Waldorf." *Commentary* 8 (1949): 487–493.

Belafonte, Harry, with Michael Shnayerson. *My Song*. New York: Knopf, 2011.

Bernays, Edward L. *Biography of an Idea*. New York: Simon and Schuster, 1965.

Bitzer, G. W. *Billy Bitzer: His Story*. New York: Farrar, Straus and Giroux, 1973.

Bogle, Donald. *Dorothy Dandridge: A Biography*. New York: Boulevard Books, 1998.

Boldt, George C. *The Waldorf-Astoria New York* (promotional book), 1903.

Boomer, Lucius. *Hotel Management: Principles and Practice*. New York: Harper, 1925.

Bradford, Perry. *Born with the Blues*. New York: Oak Publications, 1965.

Brown, Henry Collins. *In the Golden Nineties*. Hastings-on-Hudson: Valentine's Manual, 1928.

Busch, Niven, Jr. *21 Americans*. New York: Doubleday, 1930.

Byles, Jeff. *Rubble: Unearthing the History of Demolition*. New York: Harmony Books, 2005.

Byrnes, James F. *All in One Lifetime*. New York: Harper, 1958.

———. *Speaking Frankly*. New York: Harper, 1947.

Cannato, Vincent J. *The Ungovernable City*. New York: Basic Books, 2001.

Cannon, James P. *The History of American Trotskyism*. New York: Pathfinder Press, 1944.

Carson, Clayborne. *The Papers of Martin Luther King, Jr.* Vol. 3. Berkeley: University of California Press, 1997.

Chappell, Marisa. *The War on Welfare*. Philadelphia: University of Pennsylvania Press, 2009.

"Characteristics That Determine Individual Success." *National Association of Corporation Schools Bulletin* 5 (December 1, 1918): 549–557.

Chauncey, George. *Gay New York*. New York: Basic Books, 1994.

Cocks, Catherine. *Doing the Town: The Rise of Urban Tourism in the United States*. Berkeley: University of California Press, 2001.

Crockett, Albert Stevens. *Old Waldorf Bar Days*. New York: Aventine, 1931.

———. *Peacocks on Parade*. New York: Sears, 1931.

Crowninshield, Frank, ed. *The Unofficial Palace of New York*. New York: Hotel Waldorf-Astoria Corporation, 1939.

Da Costa Nunez, Ralph, and Ethan Sribnick. *The Poor Among Us*. New York: White Tiger Press, 2013.

Day, Leslie. *Honeybee Hotel*. Baltimore: Johns Hopkins University Press, 2018.

Doherty, Thomas. *Show Trial*. New York: Columbia University Press, 2018.

Dolkart, Andrew S. "Millionaires' Elysiums: The Luxury Apartment Hotels of Schultze and Weaver." *Journal of Decorative and Propaganda Arts* 25 (2005): 10–45.

Doyle, Mary. *Life Was Like That*. Boston: Houghton Mifflin, 1936.

Dreiser, Theodore. *Sister Carrie*. Philadelphia: University of Pennsylvania Press, 1981.

Dudziak, Mary L. "*Brown* as a Cold War Case." *Journal of American History* 91 (June 2004): 32–42.

Dye, Nancy Schrom. "Feminism or Unionism?" *Feminist Studies* 3 (Autumn 1975): 111–125.

Elliott, Lawrence. *Little Flower: The Life and Times of Fiorello La Guardia*. New York: Morrow, 1983.

Endean, Steve. *Bringing Lesbian and Gay Rights into the Mainstream*. Edited by Vicki L. Eaklor. Binghamton, NY: Harrington Park Press, 2006.

Fagelson, Ian. "President Truman's Justice Department and the Fight for Racial Justice in the Supreme Court." *Journal of Supreme Court History* 43 (March 2018): 69–82.

Farrell, John A. *Richard Nixon: The Life*. New York: Doubleday, 2017.

Federal Writers' Project. *The WPA Guide to New York City*. New York: Pantheon, 1982.

Fick, Annabella. "Conrad Hilton, *Be My Guest* and American Popular Culture." *European Journal of Life Writing* 2 (2013): 18–34.

Finan, Christopher M. *Alfred E. Smith: The Happy Warrior*. New York: Hill and Wang, 2002.

Florman, Samuel C. *Good Guys, Wiseguys, and Putting Up Buildings*. New York: Thomas Dunne Books, 2012.

Foreign Relations of the United States 1946. Vol. 2, *Council of Foreign Ministers*. Washington, DC: United States Government Printing Office, 1970.

France, David. *How to Survive a Plague*. New York: Knopf, 2016.

Freedman, Paul. "Women and Restaurants in the Nineteenth-Century United States." *Journal of Social History* 48 (2014): 1–19.

Gabler, Neil. *Winchell*. New York: Vintage, 1994.

Galbraith, John Kenneth. *The Great Crash, 1929*. New York: Harcourt, 2009.

Gasman, Marybeth. *Envisioning Black Colleges*. Baltimore: Johns Hopkins University Press, 2007.

Gavin, James. *Stormy Weather: The Life of Lena Horne*. New York: Atria, 2009.

Gillmor, Daniel S., ed. *Speaking of Peace*. New York: NCASP, 1949.

Goldstein, Robert Justin. *American Blacklist*. Lawrence: University Press of Kansas, 2008.

Goldwater, Barry M. *The Conscience of a Conservative*. Princeton, NJ: Princeton University Press, 2007.

Gordon, Linda. *Pitied but Not Entitled*. Cambridge, MA: Harvard University Press, 1994.

Gottehrer, Barry, ed. *New York City in Crisis*. New York: McKay, 1965.

Heffernan, Joseph. "Corporate Reorganization under the Bankruptcy Act." *Indiana Law Journal* 10 (1935): 386–402.

Hempel, Frieda. *My Golden Age of Singing*. Portland, OR: Amadeus Press, 1998.

Hilton, Conrad. *Be My Guest*. New York: Prentice Hall, 1957.

Horowitz, Louis J., and Boyden Sparkes. *The Towers of New York*. New York: Simon and Schuster, 1937.

Horowitz, Morris A. *The New York Hotel Industry*. Cambridge, MA: Harvard University Press, 1960.

Hughes, Langston. "Come to the Waldorf-Astoria!" *New Masses*, December 1931.

Humphreys, Sexon E. "The Nomination of the Democratic Candidate in 1924." *Indiana Magazine of History* 31 (March 1935): 1–9.

Hungerford, Edward. *The Story of the Waldorf-Astoria*. New York: Putnam's, 1925.

"Innkeeper's Right to Exclude or Reject Guests." *Fordham Law Review* 7 (1938): 417–435.

Josephson, Matthew. *Union House, Union Bar*. New York: Random House, 1956.

Kahn, Gordon. *Hollywood on Trial*. New York: Boni and Gaer, 1948.

Kaplan, Justin. *When the Astors Owned New York*. New York: Viking, 2006.

Kessner, Thomas. *Fiorello H. La Guardia and the Making of Modern New York*. New York: McGraw-Hill, 1989.

King, Moses. *King's Handbook of New York City*. Boston: Moses King, 1893.

Klefstad, Terry. "Shostakovich and the Peace Conference." *Music and Politics* 6 (Summer 2012).

Lamonaca, Marianne, and Jonathan Mogul, eds. *Grand Hotels of the Jazz Age*. New York: Princeton Architectural Press, 2005.

Leff, Mark H. "Consensus for Reform." *Social Service Review* 47 (September 1973): 397–417.

Lerner, Michael A. *Dry Manhattan*. Cambridge, MA: Harvard University Press, 2007.

Levering, Ralph B. "Toward Cold War Thinking." *Journal of Transatlantic Studies* 14 (2016): 340–349.

Lurie, Leonard. *The Running of Richard Nixon*. New York: Coward, McCann and Geoghegan, 1972.

MacDonald, Dwight. "The Waldorf Conference." *Horizon* 19 (May 1949): 313–326.

McCarthy, James Remington. *Peacock Alley: The Romance of the Waldorf-Astoria*. New York: Harper, 1931.

McCarthy, Mary. *Intellectual Memoirs: New York 1936–1938*. New York: Harcourt, 1992.

McNally, Terrence. *Some Men and Deuce*. New York: Grove Press, 2007.

Middendorf, J. William, II. *A Glorious Disaster*. New York: Basic Books, 2006.

Miller, Arthur. *Timebends: A Life*. New York: Grove Press, 1987.

Miller, Donald L. *Supreme City*. New York: Simon and Schuster, 2014.

Millner, Lyn. *The Allure of Immortality*. Gainesville: University Press of Florida, 2015.

Morehouse, Ward, III. *The Waldorf-Astoria*. New York: M. Evans, 1991.

Morris, Jan. *Manhattan '45*. New York: Oxford University Press, 1987.

———. *Trieste and the Meaning of Nowhere*. New York: Da Capo Press, 2002.

Morris, Lloyd. *Incredible New York*. New York: Random House, 1951.

Murray, Robert K. *The 103rd Ballot*. New York: HarperCollins, 1976.

Nabokov, Nicolas. *Bagázh: Memoirs of a Russian Cosmopolitan*. New York: Atheneum, 1975.

Nadasen, Premilla, Jennifer Mittelstadt, and Marisa Chappell. *Welfare in the United States*. New York: Routledge, 2009.

Neale, Steve, ed. *The Classical Hollywood Reader*. New York: Routledge, 2012.

Nixon, Richard. *The Memoirs of Richard Nixon*. New York: Grosset and Dunlap, 1978.

Norwood, Stephen H. *Strike-Breaking and Intimidation*. Chapel Hill: University of North Carolina Press, 2002.

Okrent, Daniel. *Last Call: The Rise and Fall of Prohibition*. New York: Scribner, 2010.

Penal Code of the State of New York. Albany, NY: Banks and Co., 1902.

Rayback, Joseph G. *A History of American Labor*. New York: Macmillan, 1959.

"Representations against Soviet Removal of Japanese Industrial Equipment from Manchuria as War Booty." *Foreign Relations* 10 (1946): 1099–1129.

Review of the Scientific and Cultural [sic] *Conference for World Peace*. Washington, DC: Committee on Un-American Activities, U.S. House of Representatives, 1949.

Rich, Lance. "Nightclub Nights and the Woman Who Discovered Stars" (Merriel Abbott). *Magicol* 195 (January 2020): 8–31.

Robins, Anthony W. *New York Art Deco*. Albany, NY: SUNY Press, 2017.

Rugh, Susan Sessions. *Are We There Yet?* Lawrence: University Press of Kansas, 2008.

Sanders, James. *Celluloid Skyline*. New York: Knopf, 2002.

Sandoval-Strausz, A. K. *Hotel: An American History*. New Haven, CT: Yale University Press, 2007.

Satow, Julie. *The Plaza*. New York: Twelve, 2019.

Saunders, Frances Stonor. *The Cultural Cold War*. New York: New Press, 1999.

Scanlan, Charles M. *Law of Hotels, Boarding Houses and Lodging Houses*. Milwaukee: Riverside Printing, 1890.

Schary, Dore. *Heyday: An Autobiography*. Boston: Little, Brown, 1979.

Schlichting, Kurt C. *Grand Central's Engineer*. Baltimore: Johns Hopkins University Press, 2012.

Schriftgiesser, Karl. *Oscar of the Waldorf*. New York: Dutton, 1943.

Sharpe, May Churchill. *Chicago May: Her Story*. New York: Macaulay, 1928.

Singer, Henry A. "An Analysis of the New York Press Treatment of the Peace Conference at the Waldorf-Astoria." *Journal of Educational Sociology* 23 (January 1950): 258–270.

Sixth Report of the Senate Fact-Finding Committee on Un-American Activities. California Legislature, 1951.

Smith, Horace. *Crooks of the Waldorf*. New York: Macaulay, 1929.

The Social Evil. New York: Putnam's, 1902.

Social Register, New York, 1903. New York: Social Register Association, 1902.

Spingarn, Arthur B. *Laws Relating to Sex Morality in New York City*. New York: The Century Co., 1916.

Straus, S. W. "Building Bonds as Investments." *Buildings and Building Management*, February 1915, 30–31.

Sutton, Horace. *Confessions of a Grand Hotel*. New York: Henry Holt, 1953.

Tauranac, John. *The Empire State Building*. New York: Scribner, 1995.

Teed, Cyrus ("Koresh"). *The Cellular Cosmogony*. Chicago: Guiding Star Publishing House, 1898.

Trattner, Walter I. *From Poor Law to Welfare State*. New York: Free Press, 1999.

Trittschuh, Travis. "Words and Phrases in American Politics: 'Boom.'" *American Speech* 31 (October 1956): 172–179.

Ward, Patricia Dawson. *The Threat of Peace*. Kent, OH: Kent State University Press, 1979.

Warner, Michael. "Origins of the Congress for Cultural Freedom, 1949–50." *Studies in Intelligence* 38 (1995): 89–98.

Weiner, Joseph L. "Corporate Reorganization." *Columbia Law Review* 34 (November 1934): 1173–1197.

Wendt, Lloyd, and Herman Kogan. *Bet a Million! The Story of John W. Gates*. Indianapolis: Bobbs-Merrill, 1948.

Wharton, Annabel Jane. *Building the Cold War*. Chicago: University of Chicago Press, 2001.

Wilson, Earl. *Look Who's Abroad Now*. Garden City, NY: Doubleday, 1953.

Wojtowicz, Robert, ed. *Sidewalk Critic: Lewis Mumford's Writings on New York*. New York: Princeton Architectural Press, 1998.

Wunderlin, Clarence E. *The Papers of Robert A. Taft*. Vol. 1. Kent, OH: Kent State University Press, 1997.

Index

Note: page numbers in italics refer to figures.

About the Author

David Freeland is the author of *Ladies of Soul* and *Automats, Taxi Dances, and Vaudeville: Excavating Manhattan's Lost Places of Leisure*, which was selected as a Choice Outstanding Academic Title and won the Metropolitan Chapter of the Victorian Society in America's Publication Award for Popular Culture and Entertainment. As a historian and journalist, he has written for the *Wall Street Journal, am New York, Time Out New York, New York History, American Songwriter*, and other publications. He appeared in episodes of NBC TV's *Who Do You Think You Are* and NYC Media's *Secrets of New York*. Freeland lives in New York, where he leads walking tours and gives lectures on the city's culture and history.